THE POEMS OF BASIL BUNTING

The Poems of

BASIL BUNTING

edited with an introduction and commentary by

DON SHARE

ff

FABER & FABER

First published in the UK in 2016
by Faber & Faber Ltd
Bloomsbury House
74–77 Great Russell Street
London WC1B 3DA

First published in the USA in 2021

This paperback edition first published in 2021

Typeset by Donald Sommerville
Printed in England by TJ Books Ltd, Padstow, Cornwall

A CIP record for this book
is available from the British Library

ISBN 978–0–571–23501–8

10 9 8 7 6 5 4 3 2 1

CONTENTS

ANNOTATIONS

TEXTUAL VARIANTS

APPENDICES

ACKNOWLEDGEMENTS

So many people have been kind to me during the preparation of this work; the extraordinary generosity and calibre of those listed below is an exceptional tribute to Basil Bunting.

First and literally foremost, Christopher Ricks is a superlative mentor, and I am deeply grateful to him in ways this page cannot contain. Similarly, Tom Pickard has kept me steadily inspired and in perspective as both a friend, a living link to Bunting and to the North, and as a terrific poet. I acknowledge also Archie Burnett of the Editorial Institute, Boston University, Rosanna Warren of the University of Chicago, and John Burt of Brandeis University for their steady guidance in the formative years of this work.

I also wish to thank: Basil Bunting's literary executor, John Halliday, for years of generosity to me and for his diligent care for the poet's legacy; Bunting's devoted scholars, above all the late Richard Caddel, who gave me his blessing and so much of his time; Richard Burton, Bunting's estimable and ingenious biographer; Neil Astley for making so many things possible, faithfully keeping Bunting's work in print; Peter Makin and Peter Quartermain for responding to my queries about their own work with the warmest generosity imaginable; Michael Hofmann for keeping me in perspective about many things along the way; Stephen Regan and Annabel Hayes of Durham University for their anchoring academic work with regard to everything Bunting; Dr Alex Niven for his work on the poet's correspondence; David Slavitt and Michael Hendry for solving a puzzle; the late Robert Bertholf, former Curator of the Poetry Collection, SUNY Buffalo; Dr Martin Maw, Oxford University Press Archives; Laura Blue of The Ubyssey, University of British Columbia; Dr Todd Hearon; Britt Bell of Moyer Bell Ltd; James Jayo, MA; Helen Hills of the Rare Books Department, Cambridge University Library; the late Hugh Amory of the Houghton Library, Harvard University; Carol and the late Leonard Share; and Bob and Carol Pope. I am grateful to the Harry Ransom Research Center, for awarding me a 2014–15 Research Fellowship in the Humanities, and the staff of the Palace Green Library Special Collections at Durham University, especially

Mike Harkness and Francis Gotto, who did everything possible to facilitate my research. I am grateful to the Lilly Library, Indiana University, Bloomington; to the Harry Ransom Centre, University of Texas at Austin; and to the Basil Bunting Poetry Archive, Durham University Library Special Collections, for the use of manuscript and unpublished material. Eliot Weinberger graciously offered expertise greater than mine regarding the attribution of sources for the epigraph to 'Briggflatts'. Two editors at Faber, Paul Keegan and then Matthew Hollis, were incredibly devoted to bringing Bunting's work to the list of that great press. Moreover, I owe particular gratitude to Donald Sommerville, whose sharp study and long toil with regard to matters of design, copyediting and proofreading strengthened the text of this book in every way. The superbly stewarded revision of this book in 2021 could not have taken place without the unparalleled diligence of Rali Chorbadzhiyska at Faber. This edition would have been unthinkable without these, but impossible without the intelligent and enduring support of Jacquelyn Pope and the enormous good cheer of our daughter, Madeleine Share, who was born as these pages were composed.

I dedicate this work to Richard Caddel and Robert Dearborn Pope, neither of whom lived to see its completion, but who both had complete faith in me.

NOTE ON THE EDITION

The poems of Basil Bunting (1900–85), admired by Ezra Pound and Louis Zukofsky among many others, are increasingly regarded with great interest, particularly his challenging long poem *Briggflatts*. Bunting's work was published haphazardly throughout most of his life, and in many cases he did not oversee publication. Editions issued by small and large presses alike were afflicted with printing errors and editorial interventions. A critical edition of Bunting's work is necessary to examine and rectify these, and to annotate his complex, allusive verse. This book presents such an edition, and therefore corrects and presents as accurately as possible:

1) poems Bunting published or intended to publish during his lifetime;
2) poems published by his posthumous editor;
3) some fragments, mostly published in works by others, that illuminate the published poetry.

It also annotates the poems with entries that provide background information; detailed publishing histories; quotations from Bunting's writings and interviews with him; excerpts from correspondence (particularly with Zukofsky and Victoria Forde); and illuminating material transcribed from recordings of Bunting's poetry readings. In addition, source material, including Persian literature and classical mythology, is examined; and the Northumbrian roots of Bunting's poetic vocabulary and use of dialect are explored. Finally, textual variants from all traceable printed sources are provided.

The goal of this work is to rectify anomalies in the printing of Basil Bunting's poems; to present annotations that indicate analogues and sources for the poems; and to demonstrate the textual and textural complexity of the poems in such a way as to enhance their appreciation.

ABBREVIATIONS AND SYMBOLS

The following abbreviations relate to works referred to multiple times in the Annotations and Textual Variants sections.

Act. Ant.	*Active Anthology*, ed. Ezra Pound (1933)
Alldritt	Keith Alldritt, *The Poet as Spy* (1998)
Anglia	*Anglia* was 'a quarterly magazine in the Russian language prepared for the [UK] Foreign Office by the Central Office of Information, for sale throughout the USSR'
BB	Basil Bunting
BBP	Basil Bunting, *Basil Bunting on Poetry* (1999)
Boz-West	*Bozart-Westminister* 1, no. 1 (Spring/Summer 1935), 10–11
Briggflatts	Basil Bunting, *Briggflatts* (1966)
Burton	Richard Burton, *A Strong Song Tows Us: The Life of Basil Bunting* (2013)
Caddel	'Sharp Study and Long Toil: Basil Bunting Special Issue', ed. Richard Caddel, *Durham University Journal* (Special supplement, 1995)
Caddel & Flowers	Richard Caddel and Anthony Flowers, *Basil Bunting: A Northern Life* (1997)
CE	Basil Bunting, *Caveat Emptor* (unpublished TS, 1935)
Conf. Cumm.	*Confucius to Cummings: An Anthology of Poetry* (1964), ed. Ezra Pound with Marcella Spann
CP1968	Basil Bunting, *Collected Poems* (1968)
CP1978	Basil Bunting, *Collected Poems* (1978)
CP1985	Basil Bunting, *Collected Poems* (1985)
CP1994	Basil Bunting, *Complete Poems* (1994), associate ed., Richard Caddel

CP2000	Basil Bunting, *Complete Poems* (2000), associate ed., Richard Caddel
Descant	Jonathan Williams, *Descant on Rawthey's Madrigal: Conversations with Basil Bunting* (1968)
EDD	*English Dialect Dictionary*, ed. Joseph Wright (1898–1905)
EP	Ezra Pound
FBO	Basil Bunting, *First Book of Odes* (1965)
Forde	Victoria Forde, *The Poetry of Basil Bunting* (1991)
Forde thesis	Victoria Forde, 'Music and meaning in the poetry of Basil Bunting', PhD thesis, University of Notre Dame (1973)
Georgia Straight	Peter Quartermain and Warren Tallman, *Georgia Straight, Writing Supplement* 6 (18–25 November 1970), n.pag.
Guedalla	Roger Guedalla, *Basil Bunting: A Bibliography of Works and Criticism* (1973)
HRC	Harry Ransom Humanities Research Center, University of Texas at Austin
JW	Jonathan Williams
Lesch	Barbara Lesch, 'Basil Bunting: A Major British Modernist', PhD thesis, University of Wisconsin (1979)
Loquitur	Basil Bunting, *Loquitur* (1965)
LZ	Louis Zukofsky
Makin	Peter Makin, *Bunting: The Shaping of his Verse* (1992)
McGonigal & Price	*The Star You Steer By: Basil Bunting and British Modernism*, ed. James McGonigal and Richard Price (2000)
Mottram	Eric Mottram, 'Conversation with Basil Bunting on the Occasion of his 75th Birthday', *Poetry Information* 19 (Autumn 1978), 3–10
NB	Basil Bunting, *A Note on Briggflatts*, ed. Richard Caddel (1989)
Obj. Ant.	*An 'Objectivists' Anthology*, ed. Louis Zukofsky (1932)
OED	*Oxford English Dictionary*

P1950	Basil Bunting, *Poems: 1950* (1950)
Poetry	*Poetry* (Chicago)
Profile	*Profile*, ed. Ezra Pound (1932)
Quartermain	Peter Quartermain, *Basil Bunting, Poet of the North* (1990)
Quartermain DP	Peter Quartermain, *Disjunctive Poetics* (1992)
Quartermain & Tallman	Peter Quartermain and Warren Tallman, 'Basil Bunting Talks about *Briggflatts*', *Agenda* 16, no. 1 (Spring 1978), 3–19, revision of *Georgia Straight* (which see above)
Reagan	Dale Reagan, 'An Interview with Basil Bunting', *Montemora* 3 (Spring 1977), 66–80
RM	Basil Bunting, *Redimiculum Matellarum* (1930)
SBOO	'Second Book of Odes' section of *CP* from 1968
Spoils	Basil Bunting, *The Spoils* (1965)
Swigg	*The Recordings of Basil Bunting*, ed. Richard Swigg (n.d.)
Terrell	*Basil Bunting, Man and Poet*, ed. Carroll F. Terrell (1981)
UO	'Uncollected Odes' section of *CP1994/2000*
UP	Basil Bunting, *Uncollected Poems*, ed. Richard Caddel (1991)
Whips & Scorpions	*Whips & Scorpions: Specimens of Modern Satiric Verse 1914–1931*, ed. Sherard Vines (1932)
Zukofsky	Louis Zukofsky, *Bottom: On Shakespeare* (1963), vol. 1

Abbreviated titles are also used in the Textual Variants section for other works in which one (or a small number) of Bunting's poems have appeared. These works are fully detailed in the relevant poem's Annotations.

The King James Version is used when biblical passages are quoted; translations from Greek and Latin texts are from Loeb editions (which Bunting himself used), except where otherwise noted; and *The Arden Shakespeare Complete Works*, revised edition (2001), is used for quotations from Shakespeare.

Bunting's own notes are given in a separate section (Appendix III), as he wished; but they are also integrated into my notes, where they are designated with the device ▪ and keyed to line numbers, which are introduced for this edition.

A line break in quoted verse included in ordinary text is indicated by / and a stanza break by //. In the Poems section of the edition < or > at the foot of one of the line-numbering columns indicates a stanza break at this point in the poem concerned; << or >> indicates a larger than normal stanza space.

INTRODUCTION

I. The Poet

Basil Bunting has long been one of the legendary figures of twentieth-century English-language poetry. His work is much anthologized and revered among many kinds of readers, and his name appears in countless renditions of the history of modernist poetry. Yet, for many years, legend was almost all that we had; a proper biography did not appear until Richard Burton's *A Strong Song Tows Us*, published in 2013. The shilling facts, as Auden called them, are mostly known, but the poet himself made biography difficult. As Burton notes, an earlier biography, Keith Alldritt's *Basil Bunting: The Poet as Spy* (1998), was erratic, and contained some of the 'wilder speculations' in circulation at the time. It doesn't help that late in his life, Bunting himself composed a rueful autobiography that did him little justice; possibly wrong on both counts, it reads, in full: 'Minor poet, not conspicuously dishonest.'[1] When a young friend, the poet Tom Pickard, proposed a biography in 1979, Bunting wrote to him: 'As to writing my life, I can't stop you, but suggest you might preface it with the enclosed note. You can't possibly get it right . . .'[2] The note reads, in part: 'Take Heed. My biography appears in *Who's Who*, complete except for the date of my death which will not be delayed very long. Whatever else anybody writes must be looked on as fiction.' Even Burton said of his own biography that if it is 'fiction', it is at least 'based squarely on Bunting's own testimony'.

Arising from the murk of legend and the confusions of his biography are, of course, Bunting's poems; this is just how he wanted it to be. But the publication record of the poems constitutes its own multiplicitous narrative, and that is what this edition has set out to trace. As with Bunting's life, which took so many turns and twists, so it goes with the poems: there's no straightforward scheme by which to organize them, though rubrics emerge that are useful enough.

1 J. Vinson, ed., *Contemporary Poets* (London: St James Press, 1975), 213–14.

2 Richard Burton, *A Strong Song Tows Us: The Life of Basil Bunting* (Oxford: Infinite Ideas, 2013), 6.

This edition therefore has three aims. First, it presents and corrects poems Bunting published or intended to publish during his lifetime; poems published posthumously by Richard Caddel; and a selection of fragments, drafts or variant versions of poems published in works (including in facsimile) by others, or hitherto unpublished. Second, it annotates and provides a publishing history for each poem. Third, it provides textual variants from printed sources, which is important because of the limited input Bunting had until late in his life regarding the publication of his poetry.

The copy text used is the *Complete Poems* as published by Bloodaxe in 2000 and edited by Richard Caddel. Though Bunting did not see this edition into print, it is based on two volumes he did see into print: the Oxford University Press *Collected Poems* of 1978 – which is Bunting's revision of his 1968 Fulcrum Press *Collected Poems* – and the Moyer Bell *Collected Poems* of 1985. Caddel supplemented the work Bunting approved for inclusion in these volumes with a controversial 1991 edition from Oxford University Press, *Uncollected Poems*, which collected material Bunting had deliberately excluded from editions he oversaw. In 1994, Caddel combined the OUP *Collected Poems* and *Uncollected Poems* to produce a *Complete Poems*, also published by Oxford. That edition was reset and corrected for the 2000 Bloodaxe edition of *Complete Poems*, and reset again for American publication by New Directions in 2003. The text in both Oxford editions of the *Collected Poems* was modified by the publisher's considerations of house style and, in some cases, by preferences of Caddel's which I do not share. Differences between my text and presentation and Caddel's are indicated in the Textual Variants section.

Presentation of the poems

From his earliest book, the small 1930 pamphlet *Redimiculum Matellarum*, through the version of the *Collected Poems* that appeared in the year of his death, Bunting gathered his poems into thematic sections; these sections, as he last arranged them, are preserved, and therefore the poems are not presented in chronological order. And because Caddel's *Complete Poems* has become the most widely available edition of Bunting's work, I retain Caddel's unauthorized organization of the uncollected poems into sections of 'Uncollected Odes' and 'Uncollected Overdrafts', though I present different versions of certain works in cases where Caddel chose versions he preferred instead of Bunting's latest known revisions. In addition, an extended version of Bunting's version of Ferdowsī's 'Faridun's Sons' is included from my volume, *Bunting's Persia*, where it appeared in print for the first time; this sequence includes sections that were published separately elsewhere along with some that were unpublished until that book appeared, constituting a different text than had been in print before.

Specific questions of punctuation and format in the printing of Bunting's work are complex. Bunting characteristically – but not invariably – omitted apostrophes in contractions, and his publishers seem to have understood this. But otherwise, Bunting's punctuation was inconsistent, and so was his attention to its representation in his printed works. Moreover, every one of his publishers frequently yet inconsistently altered his punctuation to suit house style – and Bunting never objected. Inconsistencies particularly afflict quotation marks, end punctuation, dashes, turnovers and indents. Confusion about, or ignorance of, Bunting's intent naturally led to a number of gross errors. The resulting variants are recorded in this edition; Bunting's punctuation is explored in more detail below. For the *Collected Poems* of 1978 Bunting made a number of careful revisions, well documented in Oxford University Press's editorial file on the book, and the texts of his poems were generally stable from that volume on. Punctuation in this edition is therefore generally left as in the 1978 volume – and not necessarily as in the copy text, *Complete Poems* of 2000, which modified it again for house style, or as in *Collected Poems* of 1985, which Bunting did not live to correct. Emendations of punctuation are recorded in the Textual Variants section.

Annotations in this edition

Bunting provided notes to his poems in every collection of his work from the 1935 typescript titled *Caveat Emptor* on; but after *Poems: 1950* his sections of notes are introduced by the remark that notes 'are a confession of failure, not a palliation of it, still less a reproach to the reader, but may allay some small irritations'. My detailed annotations are not what he had in mind, but the editor's responsibility is to allay irritations both small and large. To that end I provide any factual material which can eliminate what William Empson called 'all trivial grounds for bafflement',[3] and also detailed information about matters which have or may have formed and informed the poems. This edition borrows a convention from John Haffenden's edition of

3 William Empson, *The Complete Poems of William Empson*, ed. John Haffenden (London: Allen Lane, 2000), xlix.

The Complete Poems of William Empson, and quotations of Bunting on his own work (from essays, letters, interviews and impromptu commentary taken from recordings of his poetry readings) are printed in bold. Bunting's own brief notes are given in a separate appendix, as in previous editions of his collected poems, to preserve his design and the implicit narrative they present; but they are also integrated into my notes, and variants for Bunting's notes are recorded. The annotations in this edition also provide publishing histories and pertinent definitions and citations from the *OED* and also, in order to illuminate the poet's lifelong preoccupation with Northumbrian dialect, Wright's *English Dialect Dictionary*.

Finally, there are two modest innovations I introduce. First, whenever possible, material in the annotations is correlated with specific volumes from Bunting's personal library, now held in the Basil Bunting Collection of the library at the University of Buffalo, State University of New York. Second, material is provided from numerous audio and video recordings of Bunting's readings: recordings of individual poems are collated with printed texts; and the poet's introductory remarks to poems in these recordings are quoted in annotations whenever useful.

Bunting's own view of such information was tersely articulated in a letter to Alan Neame, 1951: 'I do not see why people should want to "understand" everything in a poem.'[4] It is impossible to understand everything in a poem, but it is also impossible for a reader not to want to know things about a poem. And Bunting did, after all, provide some notes to his poems; his *Caveat Emptor* even contains, in an appendix, 'Further Notes', introduced by the sentence, 'Having devolved so much useless knowledge upon my reader, if any, I may as well go on unloading.'

Since my notes quote extensively from interviews Bunting gave about his work, a word about them is in order, too. In a written statement he sent to Dale Reagan to accompany the 1975 interview published in *Montemora*, Bunting commented:

> I am not much delighted with the recent habit of printing verbatim interviews; impromptu colloquial speech is too full of ambiguities, near misses and sheer confusions; answers too little considered and not hedged against easy misconceptions seem to wave the reader on in the wrong direction. It is as though the interviewer were scared of editing. He prefers a

4 Peter Quartermain, *Basil Bunting, Poet of the North* (Durham: Basil Bunting Poetry Centre, 1990), 11.

false 'authenticity' to the genuine authenticity his intelligence and sympathetic interpretation ought to provide (sympathetic to the reader as well as the person interviewed). So a new and wonderfully fertile crop of misunderstandings soon grows rank enough to hide whatever sense was meant.[5]

One takes his point, yet sampling, with appropriate caution and regard for dating and context, the wonderfully fertile crop of explanatory comments found in Bunting's interviews and letters does not interfere with 'whatever sense was meant' in the poems themselves, which in the beginning and end stand on their own.

It will be noticed that I rely heavily – and with great gratitude – upon the work of Makin, Forde, Lesch, and Burton, among others, for this material. While doing so is not in itself an original contribution to scholarship, I am sure that my bringing together and organizing this material from disparate sources as it bears upon individual poems is useful and unprecedented. Publication of Bunting's letters now seems possible; Alex Niven is, at the time of this writing, editing a selection. A volume of Bunting's collected prose would be very valuable, but at this time there seems to be no edition in preparation.

The annotations in this edition are supplemented with publishing histories which document appearances of poems in each of Bunting's books, as well as in periodicals and books printed during Bunting's lifetime; when there are citations in Guedalla's standard bibliography of Bunting I give these. I have verified all bibliographical information in my publication histories and section of textual variants, except in the case of one issue of a periodical which I was unable to find, *Grok* 2 (19 May 1967), 5 (cited by Guedalla as item D28), relating to 'Darling of Gods and Men, beneath the gliding stars', as noted in the section of Textual Variants.

As mentioned earlier, both the *OED* and *EDD* have been consulted. Bunting foresaw this kind of research, and tried to hedge against it in interviews and elsewhere, for example when writing to decline an invitation to write an introduction for a volume of Pound's early poems:

> No doubt it is fitting that maggots consume us in the end, or at least the rubbish we scatter as we go; but I'd rather leave the lid on my dustbin and the earth on my friend's graves. — Piety takes curious forms: the toenail clippings of Saint What's His

5 Dale Reagan, 'An Interview with Basil Bunting', *Montemora* 3 (Spring 1977), 67.

> Name are revered. I don't think religion is much advanced by that. It would be more profitable, more to his glory, to throw away some of the poems Pound printed than to print those he threw away himself. – I apologise for my lack of sympathy for the industrious compilers.[6]

The significance of this is not just that Bunting thought that book learning would interfere with transmission of the poem's sound-meaning. Bunting considered himself above all a Northumbrian, and believed that 'Northumbrian is only a spoken language.'[7] In his view, for instance, the reading of Northern poets in a 'southron' voice had led to misapprehensions such as regarding Wordsworth 'as a Romantic poet rather than an eighteenth-century poet . . . the music of the poetry has been lost simply because his southern readers can't hear it'.[8]

> Nobody had thought of standard English in Wordsworth's time. He spoke as a Northerner, in spite of the years spent in Cambridge, London and Somerset. In such a Northern way that Keats and Hazlitt found it hard to follow his conversation, and though he did not compose in dialect, he composed in his own voice aloud. His music is lost if his poems are read in Southern English, and no doubt that is why so many critics imagine he had none.[9]

But, as Quartermain observes, 'there are problems. Bunting is both outside and inside the culture / the koiné at the same time, using what he subverts, subverting what he uses. But it is not an ironic relationship, and his linguistic, syntactic and formal stance is not finally satiric. It is compositional.'[10] In order to illuminate this relationship, it is justifiable to explore the Northern roots of Bunting's poetic vocabulary. And while Bunting professed to eschew

6 In 1977, Faber's editorial director, R. B. Woodings, asked BB for an endorsement for the cover of EP's *Collected Early Poems*, and Bunting replied thus. Letter at the State University of New York, Special Collections; quoted by Tom Pickard in 'Sketches of My Voice Locked In: The Lives of Basil Bunting', *Chicago Review* 44, no. 3–4 (1998), 75.

7 Joseph Skipsey, *Selected Poems*, ed. Basil Bunting (Sunderland: Coelfrith Press, 1976), 7.

8 *Quartermain*, 12. This was egregious to Bunting, who told Lesch: 'All my life the most important English poet for me was Wordsworth, whom Pound despised' (Lesch interview, 24 April 1976).

9 Introduction to a radio broadcast of Bunting reading Wordsworth's 'The Brothers', quoted in *The Listener* (8 October 1970), 484.

10 *Quartermain*, 15.

the language of books, preferring 'any dialect of English or any other *spoken* language to the six-six-sixth generation of bastard Latin',[11] he was extremely well and widely read, as both his work and the contents of his personal library reveal. In fact, an additional purpose for consulting the *OED* and *EDD* is that their citations often coincide with works Bunting knew very well; these citations constantly elucidate his relationship with Northern literature: the *Lindisfarne Gospels*, Ælfred, the sermons and homilies of Ælfric (said by S. A. J. Bradley to 'manifest a . . . poetic structure'[12]), Bede, Mandeville, Burns, Scott and others recur. So do the names of such great 'southrons' as Spenser, Milton, Dryden and Tennyson. The tension – and symbiosis – between North and South figures throughout Bunting's work, and so it does in my annotations.

Textual variants

Bunting destroyed, on principle, many and perhaps most of his early drafts and fragments. Working versions of poems can, however, be found among the many letters he wrote to Louis Zukofsky held by the Harry Ransom Humanities Research Center, University of Texas at Austin; and surviving manuscript materials are preserved in the Basil Bunting Poetry Archive at Durham University and in a handful of other places. It is unfortunate that hardly any proof material can be located for consultation. As Curator of Poetry, I acquired for the Woodberry Poetry Room at Harvard University proof material Bunting apparently saw for his contribution to the *Active Anthology*, but he never received any for *Poems: 1950*. He seems to have marked up a typescript of *The Spoils* for publication, and this supplies a dropped line from the poem whose loss seems not to have bothered Bunting, because he never restored it; variants are relatively minor. The Fulcrum Press archive has not been located as of this writing, and Oxford University Press does not preserve proof material, though they hold an editorial file on the *Collected Poems* of 1978 which has been valuable. Although he issued specific instructions to the publisher of the 1985 *Collected Poems*, Bunting did not live to read proofs for that edition.

The principle at work in this edition is to represent all versions published in Bunting's book collections; those disseminated in any other form which involved Bunting's direct involvement; and first

11 BB to LZ, 27 April 1934, quoted but apparently misdated in *Quartermain*, 13; letter not found at HRC.

12 Peter Makin, *Bunting: The Shaping of His Verse* (Oxford: Clarendon Press, 1992), 244.

published appearances of poems. Variants from editions of Bunting's work as printed are therefore presented, and so are variants from a number of other sources: work in the typescript *Caveat Emptor*, which was intended for publication but which did not see print; first appearances of poems in periodicals (though it should be noted that some poems were simultaneously printed in different magazines) or monographic anthologies; versions printed in anthologies edited by Ezra Pound and Louis Zukofsky, whom Bunting habitually consulted during the work of revision; and versions represented in audio and video recordings of poetry readings given by Bunting. In addition, variant draft material published by Forde with Bunting's cooperation in *The Poetry of Basil Bunting* (1991) is accounted for, as are variants for this material discussed by Quartermain in his books and essays. A full variant version of 'The Well of Lycopolis' (sent in a letter to Zukofsky in 1935) is included in the Fragments and False Starts section, because it is so different from the published version and is among the few extant complete draft texts; similarly, I present a slightly longer version there of 'On the Fly-Leaf of Pound's Cantos'. Finally, this edition features, as Appendix I, a reproduction of a typescript draft of the first three movements of what Bunting called 'The Fifth Sonata', which eventually became *The Spoils*, to provide a rare illustration of Bunting's working methods.

It may be argued that presenting variants from poems published in literary magazines is not useful, since rather than true variants they may be mistakes introduced through editorial negligence or by the poet's having been unable to see and approve his work before publication. I do include these as variants, for two reasons. First, it is impossible in many cases to determine whether variants represent changes or editorial mishaps because Bunting destroyed as much draft material as he could, and because marked-up proof material is apparently non-existent. Second, including these variants tells an important story. It is a significant aspect of the poet's life that until the end of his life, his work was issued from small presses whose well-intentioned but inexperienced publishers did not always print the texts accurately; moreover, he seldom had the luxury or opportunity (or, arguably, the inclination) to correct each error in the printing of his work. That Bunting's work has so often been published defectively is a poignant and crucial fact about the circumstances of his life and the fate of his work; it is also a reflection upon twentieth-century small-press publishing and Anglo-American literary culture.

The formula I use to present textual variants is as follows: I] 1 *Briggflatts*. indicates that the Roman numeral I is given as the Arabic numeral 1 in the Fulcrum Press edition of *Briggflatts*. (Note that variants in punctuation of section numbers are given.)

II. The Work

The beginning of Basil Bunting's adult career as a poet is marked by the publication of 'Villon' in the October 1930 issue of *Poetry*; his work appeared thereafter in a variety of literary magazines, but substantial book publication did not ensue for some time. The first published collection of his poems was the small 1930 pamphlet *Redimiculum Matellarum*, privately published in Milan and subsidized by Margaret de Silver, widow of a wealthy American businessman; the title is intended to mean 'A Necklace of Chamberpots'. This pamphlet received just one review, from Louis Zukofsky (though Ezra Pound mentioned it, getting the title as *Redimiculum Metellorum*, in the *Cantos*, LXXXIV). The number of copies printed is unknown, but very few exist. The Beinecke Library at Yale University owns the copy that belonged to William Carlos Williams, and another is held by the Humanities Research Center, University of Texas at Austin; Bunting himself only had two copies in the end, one of which would be sold to a collector by Fulcrum Press publisher Stuart Montgomery in 1976 when Bunting needed money. This first and necessarily modest gathering contains the germ of an organizational scheme Bunting would use in all subsequent collections: 'Villon' appears in its own section, followed by poems in a group named 'Carmina' (in homage to Horace), followed in turn by a group headed 'Etcetera'. In the book's preface, Bunting wrote, 'These poems are byproducts of an interrupted and harassed apprenticeship. I thank Margaret de Silver for bailing me out of Fleet Street: after two years convalescence from an attack of journalism, I am beginning to recover my honesty.'

Bunting's work fared better in anthologies during the early 1930s. 'To a POET who Advised me to PRESERVE my Fragments and False Starts', 'Crackt Records' numbers one and two, and 'Reading X's "Collected Works"' were included in Sherard Vines's *Whips & Scorpions: Specimens of Modern Satiric Verse*, published by Wishart in 1932. More significantly, that same year a collection of poems by the contributors to Louis Zukofsky's 'Objectivists' issue of *Poetry* for February 1931 appeared: *An 'Objectivists' Anthology*, edited by Zukofsky and published by To Publishers in Paris and New York; the volume contained Bunting's 'Attis: Or, Something Missing'.

During this period Bunting's friend Ezra Pound featured Bunting's work in two anthologies. *Profile*, published in 1932 in Milan, presented excerpts from 'Villon', and *Active Anthology*, published by Faber & Faber in October 1933, included a generous selection: excerpts from 'Villon' as well as eleven other poems. Unfortunately, *Profile* was limited to 250 copies, and 750 of the 1,516 sets of sheets for *Active Anthology* were lost in a bombing during World War II, making it, in the end, a rather rare book.

While in Tenerife in 1935, Bunting prepared a 120-page typescript collection titled *Caveat Emptor*; it features 'Villon' along with 'Aus Dem Zweiten Reich', 'How Duke Valentine Contrived', 'Jenghis', 'Gin the Goodwife Stint' and 'The Complaint of the Morpethshire Farmer' as separate poems, followed by a 'First Book of Odes', which generally combines the sections previously titled 'Etcetera' and 'Carmina', rounded out with 'Chomei at Toyama' and 'Attis: or, Something Missing' as separate poems. In a five-part appendix, Bunting provides notes for the first time; they supplement his translations (of Machiavelli, Hafiz and Kamo-no-Chomei) and the poems 'Villon', 'Jenghis', 'Attis: Or, Something Missing', as well as three of the Odes. A mock 'bibliography' is provided, consisting solely of an entry for *Redimiculum Matellarum*, and an annotation: 'Out of print a month after publication. The contents have been absorbed into this volume, with the exception of a preface and two epigraphs.' Moreover, there is a revealing list of acknowledgments:

> T. Lucretius Carus, Muhammad Shamsuddin Shirazi Hafiz, Maslahuddin Shirazi Sadi, Q. Horatius Flaccus, Charles Baudelaire, François Villon, Niccolo Machiavelli, Kamo-no-Chomei, Jenghis Khan, G. Valerius Catullus, Clément Marot, Jesus Christ, Dante Alighieri and anonymous peasants for loans; as well as to Jonathan Swift, François de Malherbe, Ernest Fenellosa, Louis Zukofsky and Ezra Pound for advice and guidance; besides all the poets who ever were before me, particularly those I have read: but the editors who bought some of these poems at inadequate prices or printed others without paying anything I need not thank. On the contrary, they should thank me.

Despite trying for two years, he was unable to find a publisher for *Caveat Emptor*. As a result, Bunting's first comprehensive book publication would not come until the Cleaners' Press edition of *Poems: 1950*. The book is particularly significant because, as Caddel observes, 'Here we find for the first time the basic arrangement (Sonatas: Odes:

Overdrafts), and to a great extent the sequence of poems which was to be worked on and added to over the next 35 years.'[13] The book also includes a reconfigured section of Bunting's notes to the poems, which he retained with few alterations thereafter.

Poems: 1950 was compiled by Dallam Simpson, also known as Dallam Flynn, a disciple of Ezra Pound who had begun publication of a magazine, *Four Pages*, in Galveston, Texas, for the purpose of spreading Pound's views; Simpson published Bunting's work on Pound's suggestion. The text of the poems in the book is unreliable because Bunting was in Persia while it was in preparation; almost completely uninvolved with the project, he could not see or correct proofs. On 12 November 1950, Bunting wrote in understatement to Zukofsky, 'There are a number of misprints: Few vexing.' Perhaps worse, the book's preface consisted of Simpson's peculiar attempt to sound off in Poundian style on the state of British poetry; for example, in answering John Berryman's negative assessment of young British poets, Simpson wonders which poets are referred to: 'Perhaps he means Mr. Eliot? But no, one recalls now and then, that Eliot was American, is British only now, by virtue of documents of citizenship, an *affiliation* with anglo-catholicism, and a rapport with an assortment of notables, persons of peerage, etcetera.'[14] Bunting later described this preface to Forde as 'florid, effusive as John Barrymore', and said he saw the book only after someone else had corrected the proofs and cut out parts with a penknife.[15] According to Guedalla the book was printed in an edition of 1,000, not all of which were bound; there was a later issue, published by John Kaspar and David Horton, who acquired unbound copies from the Cleaners' Press and reissued them in their Square Dollar series with their own paper covers pasted down on the end pages. Since the back cover includes excerpts from reviews by Hugh Kenner and Thomas Cole, which appeared in *Poetry* for September 1951, these copies were issued after that date. Kaspar and Horton were among those who befriended Ezra Pound at St Elizabeths Hospital. Guedalla also claims that Eliot considered a Faber & Faber edition of the book, but wanted the preface removed – however, Bunting 'felt that, as Simpson had taken the trouble to compile and edit the book, the

---

13 Basil Bunting, *Complete Poems*, assoc. ed. Richard Caddel (Newcastle upon Tyne: Bloodaxe, 2000), 13.

14 Basil Bunting, *Poems: 1950* (Galveston: Cleaners' Press, 1950), iv.

15 Victoria Forde, *The Poetry of Basil Bunting* (Newcastle upon Tyne: Bloodaxe Books, 1991), 51. This copy has not been recovered.

preface should remain'.[16] According to Garth Clucas, however, the rejection was because Eliot found Bunting's work 'too Poundian'.[17] Whatever the case, such publication never ensued, and fifteen years later in the preface to *Loquitur*, Bunting still wanted 'to record my gratitude to Dallam Flynn for the edition he undertook in a more difficult time than this . . .'

That time was difficult because Bunting laboured in obscurity and penury; the story is told in detail in accounts of Bunting's life by Forde, Alldritt, and especially Burton. But this unhappy period ended in 1964 when the young poet Tom Pickard – who ran the Morden Tower Bookroom at which Bunting had recently given a reading – published, at his own expense, Bunting's long poem *The Spoils*, which had first appeared in *Poetry* 79, no. 2 (November 1951); the book was printed in 1965 by the Newcastle University printing department under the supervision of the well-known pop artist Richard Hamilton.[18] Migrant Press, formed in Worcestershire by the poets Gael Turnbull, Michael Shayer and Roy Fisher, agreed to distribute the book. The first shipment of printed books was apparently lost in the postal sorting room at Birmingham en route from Newcastle to the Midlands, so a second printing, number of copies unknown (perhaps 100), was hastily completed, and sent in its place. A limited edition may also have been produced, since a copy described in a book dealer's catalogue features a limitation statement in ink holograph on the inside rear cover: 'This is the only signed / limited edition / 26 copies numbered A–Z / Thomas Pickard.'

By November 1965 Fulcrum Press, operated by Stuart Montgomery, a young Rhodesian, together with his wife, Deirdre, had published a collection of Bunting's short poems, *First Book of Odes*. A limitation statement on the verso of the book's penultimate leaf states that the edition was 'limited to 175 numbered copies and 26 copies lettered A–Z and signed by the author'. But according to Guedalla, 'the colophon is misleading. It implied 175 copies of the ordinary edition whereas these copies are divided between 125 in the ordinary edition and 50 in the special edition.'[19] In addition, 26 special lettered and signed copies were produced. This selection of Bunting's 'Odes' is the same as that which appears in *Poems: 1950*, except for the

16 Roger Guedalla, *Basil Bunting: A Bibliography of Works and Criticism* (Norwood, PA: Norwood Editions, 1973), 17.
17 Garth Clucas, 'Basil Bunting: A Chronology', *Poetry Information* 19 (Autumn 1978), 71.
18 Tom Pickard, email of 14 March 2008.
19 Guedalla, 24.

addition of 'On highest summits dawn comes soonest . . .' and 'On the Fly-Leaf of Pound's Cantos'. There are no notes to the poems. Fulcrum ended the year with a Christmas keepsake, which printed 'Three Michaelmas daisies' (which would become the second poem in the 'Second Book of Odes' – not a separate book, but a section Bunting added to collections of his poems from 1968 on).

In December 1965 Fulcrum published *Loquitur*, a comprehensive collection of Bunting's poems which presented Bunting's selection from his earlier work including the contents of *First Book of Odes*. As Bunting pointed out in the preface, 'The edition of my poems which Dallam Flynn printed in Texas in 1950 is all sold, and Stuart Montgomery thinks there are still people curious to read them who cannot find a copy.' In addition to recording his appreciation for his earlier publisher, he acknowledged his 'continual debt to the two greatest poets of our age, Ezra Pound and Louis Zukofsky'. According to the book's colophon, 'None of these poems have previously appeared in a book by the author in Great Britain. This edition was limited to 1,000 copies, 200 bound in cloth and 26 specially bound, lettered A–Z, signed by Bunting. The design of the book and of the cover was by Richard Hamilton.' Actually, 224 ordinary copies, 200 special copies in black cloth boards, and 26 special signed copies in black leather boards were produced.[20]

Loquitur retained the structure initiated in *Poems: 1950* and, as Caddel remarks, 'extended the range and tinkered the sequence' of Bunting's poems 'towards its final form'.[21] Bunting explained in the preface:

> I have taken my chance to add two or three and take one away; to read the proofs more carefully than I could when I was in Teheran and my publisher in Texas; to insert a couplet in the Odes and promote The Orotava Road from limbo to its chronological place amongst them, which has obliged me to renumber many; and to give the book a title to replace the

20 The book's title, the Latin for 'Speaks', has a number of sources: 'loquatur' in Catullus LXVIII, 46 and perhaps 'loquaces' in Horace, *Carmina* 3. 14, 14; Swinburne's poem, 'Poeta Loquitur'; and 'Vir sapit qui pauca loquitur' ('It is a wise man who speaks little'), quoted in Shakespeare's *Love's Labour's Lost*, IV, ii. 43. Cp. Proverbs 17: 28, 'Even a fool, when he holdeth his peace, is counted wise; and he that shutteth his lips, a man of understanding.' Strangely, a typescript version of Pound's poem 'Cino', which figures in Bunting's own 'Attis: Or, Something Missing', includes the insertion of the word, *loquitur*. The word turns up in EP's *Cantos* (e.g. XXVIII and XXXIX).

21 Bunting, *Complete Poems* (2000), 13.

off-hand label by which it has been known or unknown for fifteen years.

In 1965 Bunting composed a long poem, *Briggflatts*; in June, Bunting sent the poem to *Poetry*, where it was accepted for publication. It was read before the public for the first time at Tom and Connie Pickard's Morden Tower Bookroom in Newcastle in December 1965, and appeared in the January 1966 issue of *Poetry*. The poem was published in book form in February 1966 by Fulcrum Press, correcting a few errors in the *Poetry* version. The book, designed by Stuart Montgomery and handset and printed at the Goliard Press in London, featured two illustrations, printed in red dots, in a design crudely resembling illuminations in the Lindisfarne codex. The edition included 224 ordinary copies, 100 special copies in black cloth boards, and 26 in red leather boards, lettered A–Z, and signed by Bunting. Fulcrum then produced 3,000 copies of a second edition in paperback in December 1966, featuring a photograph of Bunting by Richard Hamilton on the front cover and a commendatory comment by Sir Herbert Read on the back; a second impression hardback in 500 copies followed in November 1967, along with a second impression paperback edition. The poem appeared in all subsequent editions of Bunting's collected poems.

After *Briggflatts*, Bunting mostly wrote short poems, many of which would figure in what he came to call the 'Second Book of Odes'. In 1967, a hand-sewn pamphlet, *Two Poems*, was published in an edition of 250 copies, of which 30 were numbered and signed by the poet on the occasion of his poetry reading on 27 May 1967 at the Unicorn Book Shop in Santa Barbara, California; it was printed by Jeffrey Sorenson and Alan Brilliant at Unicorn Press, and featured 'Birthday Greeting' and 'All you Spanish ladies' ('Carmencita's tawny paps'). The same year, another pamphlet, containing 'What the Chairman Told Tom', was published by William Ferguson for the Pym-Randall Press in Cambridge, Massachusetts, in an edition of 200 numbered and 26 lettered copies. According to Guedalla, the signed, lettered copies indicate that six were printed for James Randall, five for William Ferguson, and fifteen for Bunting himself.

In 1968, Bunting compiled recent work in a new section 'Second Book of Odes', which was combined with the contents of *Loquitur*, *The Spoils*, and *Briggflatts* for the Fulcrum Press *Collected Poems*, published with a dust jacket designed by the well-known painter Barnett Newman. In the book's preface, Bunting remarked, 'A man who collects his poems screws together the boards of his coffin. Those outside will have all the fun, but he is entitled to his last confession.

These verses were written here and there now and then over forty years and four continents. Heaped together they make a book.' He again acknowledged a range of poets, saying of his poetry:

> If I ever learned the trick of it, it was mostly from poets long dead whose names are obvious: Wordsworth and Dante, Horace, Wyat and Malherbe, Manuchehri and Ferdosi, Villon, Whitman, Edmund Spenser; but two living men also taught me much: Ezra Pound and in his sterner, stonier way, Louis Zukofsky. It would not be fitting to collect my poems without mentioning them. With sleights learned from others and an ear open to melodic analogies I have set down words as a musician pricks his score, not to be read in silence, but to trace in the air a pattern of sound that may sometimes, I hope, be pleasing. Unabashed boys and girls may enjoy them. This book is theirs.

He also specifically thanked the staff of *Poetry*, 'whose editors have been kind to me one after another'.

The book was published in two editions of 1,000 copies, along with 150 signed copies that featured a silk-screen print of the Newman cover design tipped in; a second edition of 2,000 followed in 1970 (this included an errata slip), along with a paperback printing of 2,000 copies. An unknown number of copies were eventually distributed in the USA by Horizon Press.

The increasing interest in Bunting's work at this time is evidenced by the publishing history of the 1969 poem 'Version of Horace', a translation of Horace, Odes, II. 14. It was published in *Make* 9 (n.d. [?1969]); and in the *Sunday Times* (14 December 1969), which reproduced it from an autograph manuscript under the heading, 'A new poem by Basil Bunting'; and appeared once again in *Agenda* (Autumn–Winter 1970), now under the title, 'Eheu fugaces, Postume, Postume'. The poem was published as a pamphlet ('limited to three hundred numbered copies of which two hundred and fifty are for sale') in November 1972 by 'Guido Londinensis, former Master of The Latin Press, at the dynastic Officina Mauritiana at present established in Holborn, London'. This was actually Guido Morris, who had run the Latin Press in St Ives between 1946 and 1953. The poem was also printed as a broadside in an edition of 100 signed copies by Mark Bernhardt at the Sterling Memorial Library's Bibliographical Press in New Haven, Connecticut, in 1976.

In 1978, the Fulcrum Press *Collected Poems* served as the basis for a corrected and expanded *Collected Poems* published by Oxford

University Press. Bunting augmented the preface with a succinct new comment, dated 1977, that, 'A new edition of this book has given me a chance to put right a few words and stops the compositor got wrong, and to add four short new poems. A fifth seemed better lost.'[22] Either Bunting or OUP destroyed any marked-up sheets; while OUP does not preserve proof material, their archive does hold an editorial file on the book[23] that reveals much about Bunting's approach to preparing new editions of his work.[24] In a letter of 8 October 1976, he noted that he had doctored a Fulcrum edition to prepare 'a correct copy of my collected poems' into which he 'gummed 4 new ones at the proper place (one of them had to be folded in because there was no convenient place to gum it)'. As Bunting described in the preface, textual changes were minimal; '"Literals" etc. occur on pages 21, 26, 31, 44, 61, 71, 83, 96, 110, 140 and in the table of contents.' He added that 'a total of 11 lines needing resetting is not, I think, much, if you decide to use offset, plus the 4 new poems, all short, which will, of course, entail changes in the table of contents and the supplementary preface, and consider whether the new poems require new Notes probably not.' According to OUP archivist Dr Martin Maw, beyond ensuring that the poems appeared in the proper order Bunting apparently did not give additional instructions for the book.[25] OUP produced 1,750 ordinary paperback copies, along with 2,250 hardback copies. The book was reprinted several times, including an American issue.

In 1985, the last year of Bunting's life, a so-called 'first American edition' of the *Collected Poems* was prepared for publication by Moyer Bell Limited of Mount Kisco, New York; 1,000 copies were printed. The verso of the title page states that it was published 'by arrangement with O.U.P. and Basil Bunting'. The book reproduced the wording of Bunting's prefaces to the 1968 and 1978 editions, and added one more brief comment: 'There is one solitary short poem that I have added to the collected volume.' That poem, 'Perche no spero', was now poem 12 in the 'Second Book of Odes'. An introduction supplied

---

22 A letter to OUP poetry editor Jon Stallworthy, dated 10 November 1966, is revealing: 'I have just read some fool's preface to Carlos Williams, and am more determined than ever to have no preface but my own to anything I write.' Despite this, an introduction by Bunting's friend Jonathan Williams appeared in the 1985 Moyer Bell edition of the *Collected Poems*, the last such collection to be prepared during his lifetime.

23 File reference OP1420/10603.

24 I owe many thanks to OUP archivist Dr Martin Maw, who provided me with a detailed account of the contents of this file.

25 Email to Share, 5 June 2002.

by Bunting's friend Jonathan Williams explained that 'Jennifer Moyer and Britt Bell, the publishers, spent an afternoon with BB at Whitley Chapel only ten days before his death, and they have heeded his wishes: just the *one* extra poem.'[26] Bunting's editorial involvement with the printing was necessarily minimal. An uncorrected proof copy has surfaced for sale; and scrutiny of the text reveals some printed variants from earlier editions that are almost certainly errors, not revisions.

Bunting had excluded from his collections a poem called 'The Pious Cat', credited by him to 'Obaid-e Zakani (and Basil Bunting)'. According to Caddel, Bunting 'intended this fable to be published as an illustrated book for children'.[27] Work on the poem began in 1937 – the year his wife Marian left him, taking with her their two children. The poem was not published, however, until the year after Bunting's death, by Bertram Rota in London. The edition consisted of 200 numbered copies and ten presentation copies, each accompanied by a copy of the original Persian poem in a pocket. The book presents two versions: one set from Bunting's typescript, which includes a note dating the poem '1939–77' – the earlier date is a transcription error – and a facsimile autograph manuscript version which includes a note dating the poem '1937–77'. (Another, slightly variant, manuscript is held in the Basil Bunting Poetry Archive, Durham University Library, hereafter known as Durham.) This poem was later included, in slightly modified form, in my volume *Bunting's Persia*.

From *Loquitur* through the 1985 *Collected Poems*, Bunting also consistently excluded a number of poems and translations he had published in periodicals. In 1991 Caddel collected this work, along with two poems which are juvenilia, and two limericks, in the Oxford University Press volume, *Uncollected Poems*. The *Collected Poems* and *Uncollected Poems* were combined in the 1994 Oxford University Press *Complete Poems* with the intent of bringing all of Bunting's poetry together in a single volume. The book was reset for publication in 2000 by Bloodaxe Books, and was accompanied by a two-cassette selection of Bunting's readings of his work. An American edition, entirely reset but not corrected, was published in paperback by New Directions in 2003. The Bloodaxe and New Directions volumes of Bunting's poetry were the last comprehensive editions of his work until the present volume.

---

26 Basil Bunting, *Collected Poems* (Mt Kisco, NY: Moyer Bell, 1985), 7.

27 Basil Bunting, *Uncollected Poems* (London: Oxford University Press, 1991), 64.

It is important to note that the posthumous publication of work Bunting did not himself collect was at first controversial, given the poet's strict editing of his own oeuvre. However, as Tony Baker wrote in 2000, fifteen years after Bunting's death:

> Caddel presents convincing arguments for the inclusion of material that Bunting, at the time of his death, had *not* included in the complete poems. Bunting, who famously pruned chunks from Shakespeare's sonnets, was the severest of editors. If he preserved work it was not because he was casual about his manuscripts; everything printed here Bunting *chose* to publish or circulate at one time or another. Caddel has respected Bunting's own arrangement of the poems and has presented the uncollected work separately. If all this makes Bunting turn in his grave then I think we can only placate his crusty ghost by offering it a glass of rum and relishing the reading of the poems. For ultimately it's what Bunting wanted – that we should relish the *reading* of the poems.[28]

Baker's point is underwritten by a remark Bunting himself made shortly before his death to his friend Colin Simms. Asked about collecting his work in one volume, 'And not a very big volume,' Bunting commented, 'I think there are one or two other things which might be added, say a few more pages, but after I am no longer in the way.'[29]

I hope that this edition both respects and embodies this sentiment. Above all, I hope to have rectified anomalies in the printing of Basil Bunting's poems; to have presented annotations that indicate analogues and sources for the poems; and to have demonstrated the textual and textural complexity of the poems in a way which will enhance their appreciation.

III. The Editing

Punctuation

Bunting's use of punctuation was inconsistent, and so was his attention to its representation in his printed works. Beyond retaining Bunting's characteristic and clearly intentional omission of apostrophes in

28 'Tony Baker on Basil Bunting', *Jacket* 12 (July 2000), online at: http://jacketmagazine.com/12/bunt-bak.html.

29 Colin Simms, 'From "The Bunting Tapes"', *Chicago Review* 44, no. 3/4 (1998), 100.

contractions, publishers frequently and inconsistently altered his punctuation to suit house styles; at the same time, confusion sometimes resulted in gross error. It is difficult to ascertain Bunting's intention in every case. For example, he commonly, but not invariably, used double quotes in both manuscript and typescript drafts; he also commonly, but not invariably, avoided apostrophes in contractions, for example dont, wont, wouldnt, couldnt, hadnt, wasnt, doesnt, havent, oughtnt, its. Yet 'don't' is used in all versions of 'On the Fly-Leaf of Pound's Cantos'; it also appears in two of the 'Uncollected Overdrafts', as printed by Caddel, as do instances of 'didn't' and 'aren't'. An authorized 'aren't' appears in 'What the Chairman Told Tom', and 'can't' in 'You can't grip years, Postume'.

Much inconsistency can be found in the printing of quotation marks. In manuscript, he usually preferred double quotes. *Redimiculum Matellarum*'s only use of quotation marks – in 'Villon' – employs double quotes. In the *Caveat Emptor* typescript, which Bunting apparently typed himself and which he corrected by hand, single quotes are used throughout; in this collection, when Bunting supplies missing quotation marks by hand they, too, are single quotes. Yet double quotes are used throughout the *Caveat Emptor* versions of 'Aus Dem Zweiten Reich', 'Light of my eyes . . .', and 'The day being Whitsun . . .' *Poems: 1950* is not a reliable text, but double quotes are used throughout, while quotes within quotes are indicated by single quotes (for example 'The Well of Lycopolis') – presumably an Americanization of style in this case (though the word 'beautiful' appears in single quotes in the 'Fearful symmetry' ode). The 1965 Fulcrum Press *Loquitur*, which unlike *Poems: 1950* was published in Britain and under Bunting's supervision, is identical in this respect. However, with the 1968 *Collected Poems*, also published by Fulcrum under Bunting's supervision, all quotation marks are single quotes with the odd exception of the final couplet in section II of 'Attis: or, Something Missing'. It is not possible to document whether this indicates a change in Fulcrum's house style or a change Bunting himself effected. Yet the use of single quotes – with that single exception – is retained in every following edition, including the 1985 American *Collected Poems*, until Caddel's two editions of the *Complete Poems*, which silently eliminate the exception! Meanwhile, Rota's edition of 'The Pious Cat' presents an autograph MS of that poem in facsimile, dated after 1977, as well as a typeset variant which follows a TS version of the poem from the same year; both employ double quotes.

Related inconsistencies ensue with the placement of end punctuation within or outside of quotation marks (and parentheses).

Caveat Emptor is completely inconsistent in both. (Bunting's use of the typewriter spacebar is also inconsistent, as on leaf 24, where semi-colons at the end of consecutive lines are preceded by a single space in one line, and not on the next; also, he usually, but not always, follows an initial single quote by a space, but not the closing quote, and so on.) *Poems: 1950* generally deploys end punctuation within quotation marks and within parentheses, though single exceptions to the latter can be found in 'Chomei at Toyama' and 'They Say Etna'. *Loquitur* also generally deploys end punctuation within quotation marks and within parentheses, though the third-to-last stanza of 'Chomei at Toyama' contains a full stop outside a quotation mark. The 1968 *Collected Poems* encloses end punctuation within quotation marks and within parentheses except following the words 'fabelhaft' and 'America' in 'Aus Dem Zweiten Reich'. Despite Bunting's corrections for the 1978 Oxford *Collected Poems*, these inconsistencies remain in that volume, which simply redeployed the type from the earlier book, using paste-ins for the corrections. Caddel silently regularised – 'corrected' is his word – these for both editions of the *Complete Poems*.

Bunting (like Pound, though to a much lesser extent), adopted a style in both his poetry and prose in which he characteristically omitted apostrophes in contractions and indulged a tolerance for inconsistencies, as in his wavering between single and double quotation marks. These have been retained in the poems in the present edition, of course, but also in quotations from correspondence and other prose when they occur.

Other inconsistencies exist. In the *Collected Poems* of 1968, 1978 and 1985, and in the two editions of the *Complete Poems*, 'Mr' appears in Bunting's late poem 'What the Chairman Told Tom', alongside the use of 'Mr.' in 'How Duke Valentine Contrived'. The earliest appearance of the latter poem in *Caveat Emptor* does not employ the full stop, yet it turns up first in *Poems: 1950* and lingers through *Loquitur* and the ensuing volumes: Bunting never corrected or changed it in editions of his work prepared under his supervision. It appears possible that this is a holdover from *Poems: 1950* – but there is too little evidence to justify an alteration.

For the 1978 *Collected Poems*, as noted, Bunting made a number of careful revisions, and texts of his poems were generally stable from this volume forward. I therefore generally follow punctuation as it appears in this volume – and not as in the copy text *Complete Poems* of 2000 which modifies it – except for obvious errors, which I correct. This leaves the question of punctuation in previously published poems

Bunting excluded from the 1978 *Collected Poems* but which Caddel collected after Bunting's death. For these Caddel usually retains punctuation from published sources, and I follow this practice. I have examined the punctuation in each original publication of these poems and corrected obvious errors or changes for house style. For poems first published in *Uncollected Poems* and the 2000 *Complete Poems*, I follow Caddel entirely. In the case of 'The Pious Cat', I follow the later TS version as presented in Rota. In my edition, variants are not given for dashes, and in the presentation of the texts, em-dashes with surrounding spaces are used for consistency's sake. All corrections and emendations of punctuation are noted.

Turnovers and indents

Because Bunting sometimes used an occasional long line within stanzas that featured otherwise short lines, compositors have sometimes run into problems setting these lines. Corrections could be long in coming, as with 'The Well of Lycopolis'. *Poems: 1950* prints the long line '"What have you come for? Why have you brought the Goddess? You who' as two separate lines, with a break between 'the' and 'Goddess'. The lines are printed this same way in *Loquitur* – an edition in which Bunting specifically aimed to correct problems in *Poems: 1950* – and in the 1968 *Collected Poems*. But documentation in the archives of Oxford University Press shows that Bunting requested a correction of this for the 1978 *Collected Poems*, where the words, 'Goddess? You who' are at last printed as a turnover, which is how they appear in all subsequent editions including this one. As late as the 1985 *Collected Poems*, the compositor of 'Attis: Or, Something Missing' mistakenly ran on the first instance of the poem's refrain, 'to Dindyma', though the other two were printed properly.

In one case, Bunting actually changed a turnover line to an indented line. In Ode I. 13, as first published in *Poetry* and as typed in *Caveat Emptor* (where it is Ode XVIII), the words 'Kuala Lumpur' are indented deeply towards the right margin, clearly run over from the previous line. But in *Poems: 1950* the two words migrated flush left to become a separate line, and there they have remained in every subsequent publication of the poem, apparently with Bunting's blessing. Of course, Bunting himself sometimes introduced indents in the process of revision, as in the case of the *Caveat Emptor* version of 'Aus Dem Zweiten Reich', which contained no indents. The greatest case of confusion about turnovers can be found in the *Whips & Scorpions* version of 'Yes, it's slow, docked of amours', where almost all the lines of the poem snarl together, as if the compositor despaired of ever understanding where and why lines were intended to break. Fortunately, subsequent printers and printings of this poem did not suffer so.

In the textual variants for this edition, unambiguous turnovers are not indicated but problems like those mentioned here are noted.

Layout

The text of the poems is followed by a section containing annotations to the poems, and then a section of textual variants. The annotations for each poem include a publication history, and then a headnote and detailed line notes as appropriate. There are appendices that provide the following: details concerning Bunting's long interest in Persian poetry; full texts of Bunting's own notes for some of the poems; the tables of contents for each book of Bunting's poems; prefaces Bunting composed for his books; a list of my emendations to the copy text; and variants for several poems that Bunting copied out for Basilio Fernández. A full bibliography and index of titles and first lines are also provided.

THE POEMS

SONATAS

Villon

I

He whom we anatomized
'whose words we gathered as pleasant flowers
and thought on his wit and how neatly he described things'
speaks
to us, hatching marrow,
broody all night over the bones of a deadman.

My tongue is a curve in the ear. Vision is lies.
We saw it so and it was not so,
the Emperor with the Golden Hands, the Virgin in blue.
(— A blazing parchment,
Matthew Paris his kings in blue and gold.)

It was not so,
scratched on black by God knows who,
by God, by God knows who.

In the dark in fetters
on bended elbows I supported my weak back
hulloing to muffled walls blank again
unresonant. It was gone, is silent, is always silent.
My soundbox lacks sonority. All but inaudible
I stammer to my ear:
Naked speech! Naked beggar both blind and cold!
Wrap it for my sake in Paisley shawls and bright soft fabric,
wrap it in curves and cover it with sleek lank hair.

What trumpets? What bright hands? Fetters, it was the Emperor
with magic in darkness, I unforewarned.
The golden hands are not in Averrhoes,
eyes lie and this swine's fare bread and water
makes my head wuzz. Have pity, have pity on me!

To the right was darkness and to the left hardness
below hardness darkness above
at the feet darkness at the head partial hardness
with equal intervals without
to the left moaning and beyond a scurry.
In those days rode the good Lorraine

whom English burned at Rouen,
the day's bones whitening in centuries' dust.

Then he saw his ghosts glitter with golden hands,
the Emperor sliding up and up from his tomb
alongside Charles. These things are not obliterate.
White gobs spitten for mockery;
and I too shall have CY GIST written over me.

Remember, imbeciles and wits,
sots and ascetics, fair and foul,
young girls with tender little tits,
that DEATH is written over all.

Worn hides that scarcely clothe the soul
they are so rotten, old and thin,
or firm and soft and warm and full –
fellmonger Death gets every skin.

All that is piteous, all that's fair,
all that is fat and scant of breath,
Elisha's baldness, Helen's hair,
is Death's collateral:

Three score and ten years after sight
of this pay me your pulse and breath
value received. And who dare cite,
as we forgive our debtors, Death?

Abelard and Eloise,
Henry the Fowler, Charlemagne,
Genée, Lopokova, all these
die, die in pain.

And General Grant and General Lee,
Patti and Florence Nightingale,
like Tyro and Antiope
drift among ghosts in Hell,

know nothing, are nothing, save a fume
driving across a mind
preoccupied with this: our doom
is, to be sifted by the wind,

heaped up, smoothed down like silly sands.
We are less permanent than thought.
The Emperor with the Golden Hands

is still a word, a tint, a tone,
insubstantial-glorious,
when we ourselves are dead and gone
and the green grass growing over us.

II

Let his days be few and let
his bishoprick pass to another,
for he fed me on carrion and on a dry crust,
mouldy bread that his dogs had vomited,
I lying on my back in the dark place, in the grave,
fettered to a post in the damp cellarage.
            Whereinall we differ not. But they have swept the floor,
there are no dancers, no somersaulters now,
only bricks and bleak black cement and bricks,
only the military tread and the snap of the locks.
            Mine was a threeplank bed whereon
I lay and cursed the weary sun.
They took away the prison clothes
and on the frosty nights I froze.
I had a Bible where I read
that Jesus came to raise the dead –
I kept myself from going mad
by singing an old bawdy ballad
and birds sang on my windowsill
and tortured me till I was ill,
but Archipiada came to me
and comforted my cold body
and Circe excellent utterer of her mind
lay with me in that dungeon for a year
making a silk purse from an old sow's ear
till Ronsard put a thimble on her tongue.
            Whereinall we differ not. But they have named all the stars,
trodden down the scrub of the desert, run the white moon to a
        schedule,
Joshua's serf whose beauty drove men mad.
They have melted the snows from Erebus, weighed the clouds,

hunted down the white bear, hunted the whale the seal the kangaroo,
they have set private enquiry agents onto Archipiada:
What is your name? Your maiden name?
Go in there to be searched. I suspect it is not your true name.
Distinguishing marks if any? (O anthropometrics!)
Now the thumbprints for filing.
Colour of hair? of eyes? of hands? O Bertillon!
How many golden prints on the smudgy page?
Homer? Adest. Dante? Adest.
Adsunt omnes, omnes et
Villon.
Villon?
Blacked by the sun, washed by the rain,
hither and thither scurrying as the wind varies.

III

Under the olive trees
walking alone
on the green terraces
very seldom
over the sea seldom
where it ravelled and spun
blue tapestries white and green
gravecloths of men
Romans and modern men
and the men of the sea
who have neither nation nor time
on the mountains seldom
the white mountains beyond
or the brown mountains between
and their drifting echoes
in the clouds and over the sea
in shrines on their ridges
the goddess of the country
silverplated in silk and embroidery
with offerings of pictures
little ships and arms
below me the ports
with naked breasts
shipless spoiled sacked
because of the beauty of Helen

precision clarifying vagueness;
boundary to a wilderness
of detail; chisel voice
smoothing the flanks of noise;
catalytic making whisper and whisper
run together like two drops of quicksilver;
factor that resolves
                    unnoted harmonies;
name of the nameless;
                    stuff that clings
to frigid limbs
                    more marble hard
than girls imagined by Mantegna . . .

The sea has no renewal, no forgetting,
no variety of death,
is silent with the silence of a single note.

How can I sing with my love in my bosom?
Unclean, immature and unseasonable salmon.

1925

Attis: Or, Something Missing

SONATINA

Dea magna, dea Cybele, dea domina Dindymi,
procul a mea tuus sit furor omnis, era, domo:
alios age incitatos, alios age rabidos.

I

Out of puff
noonhot in tweeds and gray felt,
tired of appearance and
disappearance;
warm obese frame limp with satiety;
slavishly circumspect at sixty;
he spreads over the ottoman
scanning the pictures and table trinkets.

(That hand's dismissed shadow
moves through fastidiously selective consciousness,
rearranges pain.)

There are no colours, words only,
and measured shaking of strings,
and flutes and oboes
enough for dancers.
.... reluctant ebb:
salt from all beaches:
disrupt Atlantis, days forgotten,
extinct peoples, silted harbours.
He regrets that brackish
train of the huntress
driven into slackening fresh,
expelled when the
estuary resumes
colourless potability;
wreckage that drifted
in drifts out.

'Longranked larches succeed larches, spokes of a
stroll; hounds trooping around hooves; and the stolid horn's

sweet breath. *Voice*: Have you seen the
fox? Which way did he go, he go?
There was soft rain.
I recollect deep mud and leafmould somewhere: and
in the distance Cheviot's
heatherbrown flanks and white cap.

Landscape salvaged from
evinced notice of
superabundance, of
since parsimonious
soil . . . . .
Mother of Gods.'

Mother of eunuchs.

Praise the green earth. Chance has appointed her
home, workshop, larder, middenpit.
Her lousy skin scabbed here and there by
cities provides us with name and nation.

From her brooks sweat. Hers corn and fruit.
Earthquakes are hers too. Ravenous animals
are sent by her. Praise her and call her
Mother and Mother of Gods and Eunuchs.

II

(Variations on a theme by Milton)

I thought I saw my late wife (a very respectable woman)
coming from Bywell churchyard with a handful of raisins.
I was not pleased, it is shocking to meet a ghost, so I cut her
and went and sat amongst the rank watergrasses by the Tyne.

Centrifugal tutus! Sarabands!
music clear enough to
pluck stately dances from
madness before the frenzy.
Andante . . . . *Prestissimo!*
turbulent my Orfeo!
A tumult softly hissed
as by muted violins,
Tesiphone's, Alecto's

capillary orchestra.
Long phrases falling like
intermittent private voices
suddenly in the midst of talk,
falling aslant like last light:
VENGA MEDUSA
VENGA
MEDUSA SÌ L'FAREM DI SMALTO
Send for Medusa: we'll enamel him!

Long loved and
too long loved, stale habit, such decay of ardour,
love never dead, love never hoping, never gay.
Ageslow venom selfsecreted. Such shame!

The gorgon's method:
                    In the morning
clean streets welcomed light's renewal,
patient, passive to the weight of buses
thundering like cabinet ministers
over a lethargic populace.
Streets buffeted thin soles at midday,
streets full of beggars.
Battered, filthily unfortunate streets
perish, their ghosts are wretched
in the mockery of lamps.

And O Purveyor
of geraniums and pianos to the Kaiserin!
the hot smell of the street
conversing with the bleat
of rancid air streaming up tenement stairways!

Gods awake and fierce
stalk across the night
grasping favour of men,
power to hurt or endow,
          leave to inhabit
figure and name; or skulk
from impotence in light's
          opacity.
Day hides them, opaque day
hides their promenades; night

reveals them stalking
(VENGA MEDUSA)
passionately.

Polymnia
keeps a cafe in Reno.
Well, (eh, Cino?)
I dare no longer raise my eyes
on any lass
seeing what one of them has done to me.
So singlehearted, so steady
never lover, none so humble.
She made a new youth lord of her.
I lower my eyes. I say:
'I will not look on any,
maybe all are jilts.'

III

Pastorale arioso
(falsetto)

What mournful stave, what bellow shakes the grove?
O, it is Attis grieving for his testicles!
Attis stiffening amid the snows
and the wind whining through his hair and fingers!

'Pines, my sisters, I, your sister,
chaffered for lambs in the marketplace.
I also won the 14 carat halfhunter goldwatch
at the annual sports and flowershow.
The young girls simpered when I passed.
Now I am out of a job. I would like to be lady's-maid
to Dindyma.

Pines, my sisters, I, your sister,
tended the bull and the entire horse.
Pensive geldings gape stale adolescence religiously,
yearning for procreative energy;
call it God. I sat amongst the atheists,
I was bankrupted by affiliation orders
who now bow my chaste vegetable forehead
to Dindyma. <

Pines, my sisters, I, your sister,
parch in calm weather, swelter in Scirocco, sway in northwind,
I am passive to the heave of spring.
In the season I will pay my phallic harvest
to Dindyma.

Dindyma! Dindyma!
The wraith of my manhood,
the cruel ghost of my manhood,
limp in hell,
leapt sleeplessly in strange beds.
I have forgotten most of the details,
most of the names,
and the responses to
the ithyphallic hymns:
forgotten the syntax,
and the paradigms
grate scrappily against reluctant nerves.

(Oh Sis!
I've been 'ad!
I've been 'ad proper!)

Shall we be whole in Elysium?
I am rooted in you,
Dindyma!
assure me
the roses and myrtles,
the lavish roses,
the naively
portentous myrtles,
corroborate the peacock.

(I've been 'ad!)'

To whom Cybele:
'The peacock's knavery
keeps you in slavery.
The roses cheat
you, butcher's meat.
The myrtles' pretence
offends commonsense.
Yet a muse defrauds

the Mother of the Gods.
Ponder this allegorical
oracle.'

Attis his embleme:
Nonnulla deest.

1931

Aus Dem Zweiten Reich

I

Women swarm in Tauentsienstrasse.
Clients of Nollendorferplatz cafés,
shadows on sweaty glass,
hum, drum on the table
        to the negerband's faint jazz.
Humdrum at the table.

Hour and hour
meeting against me,
efficiently whipped cream,
efficiently metropolitan chatter and snap,
transparent glistening wrapper
        for a candy pack.

Automatic, somewhat too clean,
body and soul similarly scented,
on time,
rapid, dogmatic, automatic and efficient,
ganz modern.

'Sturm über Asien' is off, some other flicker ...
Kiss me in the taxi, twist fingers in the dark.
A box of chocolates is necessary.
I am preoccupied with Sie and Du.
        The person on the screen,
divorced and twenty-five, must pass for fourteen
for the story's sake, an insipidity
contrived to dress her in shorts
and a widenecked shirt with nothing underneath
so that you see her small breasts when she
often bends towards the camera.
Audience mainly male stirs,
        I am teased too,
I like this public blonde better than my brunette,
        but that will never do.
— Let's go,

arm in arm on foot over gleaming snow
past the Gedächtnis Kirche
to the loud crowded cafés near the Bahnhof Zoo.

Better hugged together ('to keep warm')
under street trees whimpering to the keen wind
over snow whispering to many feet,
find out a consolingly mediocre
neighbourhood without music, varnished faces
bright and sagacious against varnished walls,
youngsters red from skating,
businessmen reading the papers:
no need to talk – much:
what indolence supplies.
'If, smoothing this silk skirt, you pinch my thighs,
that will be fabelhaft.'

II

Herr Lignitz knows Old Berlin. It is near the Post Office
with several rather disorderly public houses.
'You have no naked pictures in your English magazines.
It is shocking. Berlin is very shocking to the English. Are you shocked?
Would you like to see the naked cabarets
in Jaegerstrasse? I think there is
nothing like that in Paris.
Or a department store? They are said to be
almost equal to Macy's in America.'

III

The renowned author of
more plays than Shakespeare
stopped and did his hair
with a pocket glass
before entering the village,
afraid they wouldnt recognize
caricature and picturepostcard,
that windswept chevelure. <

Who talked about poetry,
and he said nothing at all;
plays,
and he said nothing at all;
politics,
and he stirred as if a flea
bit him
but wouldnt let on in company;
and the frost in Berlin,
muttered: Schrecklich

Viennese bow from the hips,
notorieties
contorted laudatory lips,
wreaths and bouquets surround
the mindless menopause.
Stillborn fecundities,
frostbound applause.

1931

The Well of Lycopolis

cujus potu signa
virginitatis eripiuntur

I

Advis m'est que j'oy regretter

Slinking by the jug-and-bottle
swingdoor I fell in with
Mother Venus, ageing, bedraggled, a
half-quartern of gin under her shawl,
wishing she was a young girl again:
'It's cruel hard to be getting old so soon.
I wonder I dont kill myself and have done with it.

I had them all on a string at one time,
lawyers, doctors, business-men:
there wasnt a man alive but would have given
all he possessed
for what they wont take now free for nothing.
I turned them down,
I must have had no sense,
for the sake of a shifty young fellow:
whatever I may have done at other times
on the sly
I was in love then and no mistake;
and him always knocking me about
and only cared for my money.
However much he shook me or kicked me I
loved him just the same.
If he'd made me take in washing he'd
only have had to say: 'Give us a kiss'
and I'd have forgotten my troubles.
The selfish pig, never up to any good!
He used to cuddle me. Fat lot of good it's done me!
What did I get out of it besides a bad conscience?
But he's been dead longer than thirty years
and I'm still here, old and skinny.
When I think about the old days,
what I was like and what I'm like now,
it fair drives me crazy to

look at myself with nothing on.
What a change!
Miserable dried up skin and bone.

But none of their Bacchic impertinence,
medicinal stout nor portwine-cum-beef.
A dram of anaesthetic, brother.
I'm a British subject if I *am* a colonial,
distilled liquor's clean.
It's the times have changed. I remember during the War
kids carrying the clap to school under their pinnies,
studying Belgian atrocities in the Sunday papers
or the men pissing in the backstreets; and grown women
sweating their shifts sticky at the smell of khaki
every little while.
Love's an encumberance to them who
rinse carefully before using, better
keep yourself to yourself.
What it is to be in the movement!
'Follow the instructions on page fortyone'
unlovely labour of love,
'or work it off in a day's walk,
a cold douche and brisk rub down,
there's nothing like it.'
Aye, tether me among the maniacs,
it's nicer to rave than reason.'

Took her round to Polymnia's, Polymnia
glowering stedfastly at the lukewarm
undusted grate grim with cinders
never properly kindled, the brass head of the
tongs creaking as she twitched them:
'Time is, was, has been.'
A gassy fizzling spun from among the cinders.
The air, an emulsion of some unnameable oil,
greased our napes. We rhymed our breath
to the mumble of coke distilling.

'What have you come for? Why have you brought the
        Goddess? You who
finger the goods you cannot purchase,
snuffle the skirt you dare not clutch.
There was never love between us, never less

than when you reckoned much. A tool
not worth the negligible price. A fool
not to be esteemed for barren honesty.
Leave me alone. A long time ago
there were men in the world, dances, guitars, ah!
Tell me, Love's mother, have I wrinkles? grey hair?
teats, or dugs? calves, or shanks?
Do I wear unbecoming garments?'

'Blotched belly, slack buttock and breast,
there's little to strip for now.
A few years makes a lot of difference.
Would you have known me?
Poor old fools,
gabbing about our young days,
squatted round a bit of fire
just lit and flickering out already:
and we used to be so pretty!'

II

May my libation of flat beer stood overnight
sour on your stomach, my devoutly worshipped ladies,
may you retch cold bile.
Windy water slurred the glint of Canopus,
am I answerable? Left, the vane
screwing perpetually ungainlywards.
What reply will a
June hailstorm countenance?

'Let's be cosy,
sit it out hand in hand.
Dreaming of you, that's all I do.'
Eiderdown air, any
girl or none, it's the same thing,
coats the tongue the morning after.
Answer?
If words were stone, if the sun's lilt
could be fixed in the stone's convexity.
Open your eyes, Polymnia,
at the sleek, slick lads treading gingerly between the bedpots,
stripped buff-naked all but their hats to raise,

and nothing rises but the hats;
smooth, with soft steps, *ambiguoque voltu.*

Daphnis investigated
bubless Chloe
behind a boulder.
Still, they say,
in another climate
virgin with virgin
coupled taste
wine without headache
and the songs are simple.
We have laid on Lycopolis water.
The nights are not fresh
between High Holborn and the Euston Road,
nor the days bright even in summer
nor the grass of the squares green.

Neither *(aequora pontis)*
on the sea's bulge
would the 'proud, full sail'
avail
us, stubborn against the trades,
closehauled,
stiff, flat canvas;
our fingers bleed
under the nail
when we reef.

III

Infamous poetry, abject love,
Aeolus' hand under her frock
this morning. This afternoon
Ocean licking her privities.
Every thrust of the autumn sun
cuckolding
in the green grin of late-flowering trees.
I shall never have anything to myself

but stare in the tank, see
Hell's constellations,

a dogstar for the Dogstar:
women's faces
blank or trivial,
still or rippled water,
a fool's image.

At my time of life it is easier not to see,
much easier to tra-la-la
a widowed tune in poor circumstances —
                    tweet, tweet, twaddle,
                    tweet, tweet, twat.
Squalid acquiescence in the cast-offs
of reputed poetry. Here, Bellerophon,
is a livery hack, a gelding,
easy pace, easy to hire,
all mansuetude and indifference.

Abject poetry, infamous love,
howling like a damp dog in November.
Scamped spring, squandered summer,
grain, husk, stem and stubble
mildewed; mawkish dough and sour bread.
                    Tweet, tweet, twaddle. Endure
detail by detail the cunnilingual law.
'Clap a clout on your jowl for
Jesus sake! Fy for shame!
After hours, is it? or under age?
Hack off his pendants!
Can a moment of madness make up for
an age of consent?'

— with their snouts in the trough,
kecking at gummy guts,
slobbering offal, gobbling potato parings,
yellow cabbage leaves, choking on onion skin,
herring bones, slops of porridge.
Way-O! Bully boys blow!
The Gadarene swihine have got us in tow.

IV

Ed anche vo' che tu per certo credi
che sotto l'acqua ha gente che sospira.

Stuck in the mud they are saying: 'We were sad
in the air, the sweet air the sun makes merry,
we were glum of ourselves, without a reason;
now we are stuck in the mud and therefore sad.'
That's what they mean, but the words die in their throat;
they cannot speak out because they are stuck in the mud.
Stuck, stick, Styx. Styx, eternal, a dwelling.
But the rivers of Paradise,
the sweep of the mountains they rise in?
Drunk or daft hear
a chuckle of spring water:
drowsy suddenly wake,
but the bright peaks have faded.
Who had love for love
whose love was strong or fastidious?
Shadow and shadow noon shrinks, night shelters,
the college of Muses reconstructs
in flimsy drizzle of starlight:
bandy, hunchback, dot-and-carry-one,
praised-for-a-guinea.

Join the Royal Air Force
and See the World. The Navy will
Make a Man of You. Tour India with the Flag.
One of the ragtime army,
involuntary volunteer,
queued up for the pox in Rouen. What a blighty!

Surrendered in March. Or maybe
ulcers of mustard gas, a rivet in the lung
from scrappy shrapnel,
frostbite, trench-fever, shell-shock,
self-inflicted wound,
tetanus, malaria, influenza.
Swapped your spare boots for a packet of gaspers.
Overstayed leave.
Debauched the neighbor's little girl
to save two shillings . . .

muttering inaudibly beneath the quagmire,
irresolute, barren, dependent, this page
ripped from Love's ledger, and Poetry's:
and besides I want you to know for certain
there are people under the water. They are sighing.
The surface bubbles and boils with their sighs.
Look where you will you see it.
The surface sparkles and dances with their sighs
as though Styx were silvered by a wind from Heaven.

1935

The Spoils

الانفال لله

These are the sons of Shem, after
their families, after their tongues,
in their lands, after their nations.

Man's life so little worth,
do we fear to take or lose it?
No ill companion on a journey, Death
lays his purse on the table and opens the wine.

ASSHUR:
As I sat at my counting frame to assess the people,
from a farmer a tithe, a merchant a fifth of his gain,
marking the register, listening to their lies,
a bushel of dried apricots, marking the register,
three rolls of Egyptian cloth, astute in their avarice;
with Abdoel squatting before piled pence,
counting and calling the sum,
ringing and weighing coin,
casting one out, four or five of a score,
calling the deficit;
one stood in the door
scorning our occupation,
silent: so in his greaves I saw
in polished bronze
a man like me reckoning pence,
never having tasted bread
where there is ice in his flask,
storks' stilts cleaving sun-disk,
sun like driven sand.
Camels raise their necks from the ground,
cooks scour kettles, soldiers oil their arms,
snow lights up high over the north,
yellow spreads in the desert, driving blue westward
among banks, surrounding patches of blue,
advancing in enemy land.
Kettles flash, bread is eaten,
scarabs are scurrying rolling dung.
Thirty gorged vultures on an ass's carcass

jostle, stumble, flop aside, drunk with flesh,
too heavy to fly, wings deep with inner gloss.
Lean watches, then debauch:
after long alert, stupidity:
waking, soar. If here you find me
intrusive and dangerous, seven years was I bonded
for Leah, seven toiled for Rachel:
now in a brothel outside under the wall
have paused to bait on my journey.
Another shall pay the bill if I can evade it.

LUD:
When Tigris floods snakes swarm in the city,
coral, jade, jet, between jet and jade, yellow,
enamelled toys. Toads
crouch on doorsteps. Jerboas
weary, unwary, may be taught to feed
from a fingertip. Dead camels, dead Kurds,
unmanageable rafts of logs
hinder the ferryman, a pull and a grunt,
a stiff tow upshore against the current.
Naked boys among water-buffaloes,
daughters without smile
treading clothes by the verge,
harsh smouldering dung:
a woman taking bread from her oven
spreads dates, an onion, cheese.
Silence under the high sun. When the ewes go out
along the towpath striped with palm-trunk shadows
a herdsman pipes, a girl shrills
under her load of greens. There is no clamour
in our market, no eagerness for gain;
even whores surly, God frugal,
keeping tales of prayers.

ARPACHSHAD:
Bound to beasts' udders, rags no dishonour,
not by much intercourse ennobled,
multitude of books, bought deference:
meagre flesh tingling to a mouthful of water,
apt to no servitude, commerce or special dexterity,
at night after prayers recite the sacred

enscrolled poems, beating with a leaping measure
like blood in a new wound:
These were the embers ... Halt, both, lament ... :
moon-silver on sand-pale gold,
plash against parched Arabia.
What's to dismay us?

ARAM:
By the dategroves of Babylon
there we sat down and sulked
while they were seeking to hire us
to a repugnant trade.
Are there no plows in Judah, seed or a sickle,
no ewe to the pail, press to the vineyard?
Sickly our Hebrew voices far from the Hebrew hills!

ASSHUR:
We bear witness against the merchants of Babylon
that they have planted ink and reaped figures.

LUD:
Against the princes of Babylon, that they have tithed of the best
leaving sterile ram, weakly hogg to the flock.

ARPACHSHAD:
Fullers, tailors, hairdressers, jewellers, perfumers.

ARAM:
David dancing before the Ark, they toss him pennies.
A farthing a note for songs as of the thrush.

ASSHUR:
Golden skin scoured in sandblast
a vulture's wing. 'Soldier,
O soldier! Hard muscles, nipples like spikes.
Undo the neck-string. Let my blue gown fall.'
Very much like going to bed with a bronze.
The child cradled beside her sister silent and brown.
Thighs in a sunshaft, uncontrollable smile,
she tossed the pence aside in a brothel under the wall.

LUD:
My bride is borne behind the pipers,
kettles and featherbed,

on her forehead jet, jade, coral under the veil;
to bring ewes to the pail, bread from the oven.
Breasts scarcely hump her smock,
thighs meagre, eyes
alert without smile
mock the beribboned dancing boys.

ARPACHSHAD:
Drunk with her flesh when, polished leather,
still as moon she fades into the sand,
spurts a flame in the abandoned embers,
gold on silver. Warmth of absent thighs
dies on the loins: she who has yet no breasts
and no patience to await tomorrow.

ARAM:
Chattering in the vineyard,
breasts swelled, halt and beweep
captives, sickly, closing repugnant thighs.
Who lent her warmth to dying David, let her seed
sleep on the Hebrew hills, wake under Zion.

What's begotten on a journey but souvenirs?
Life we give and take, pence in a market,
without noting beggar, dealer, changer;
pence we drop in the sawdust with spilt wine.

II

They filled the eyes of the vaulting
with alabaster panes,
each pencil of arches spouting
from a short pier,
and whitewashed the whole, using
a thread of blue to restore
lines nowhere broken,
for they considered capital
and base irrelevant.
The light is sufficient
to perceive the motions of prayer
and the place cool.
Tiles for domes and aivans

they baked in a corner,
older, where Avicenna may have worshipped.
The south dome, Nezam-ol-Molk's,
grows without violence from the walls
of a square chamber. Taj-ol-Molk
set a less perfect dome
over a forest of pillars.
At Veramin
Malekshah cut his pride in plaster
which hardens by age, the same
who found Khayyam a better reckoner
than the Author of the Qor'an.
Their passion's body was bricks and its soul algebra.
Poetry
they remembered
too much, too well.
'Lately a professor in this university'
said Khayyam of a recalcitrant ass,
'therefore would not enter, dare not face me.'
But their determination to banish fools foundered
ultimately in the installation of absolute idiots.
Fear of being imputed
naive impeded thought.
Eddies both ways in time:
the builders of La Giralda
repeated
heavily, languidly,
some of their patterns in brick.
I wonder what Khayyam thought
of all the construction and organisation afoot,
foreigners, resolute Seljuks, not so bloodthirsty
as some benefactors of mankind; recalling
perhaps Abu Ali's horror of munificent patrons;
books unheard of or lost elsewhere
in the library at Bokhara,
and four hours writing a day
before the duties of prime minister.

For all that, the Seljuks avoided
Roman exaggeration and the leaden mind of Egypt
and withered precariously on the bough

with patience and public spirit.
O public spirit!

Prayers to band cities and brigade men
lest there be more wills than one:
but God is the dividing sword.

A hard pyramid or lasting law
against fear of death and
murder more durable than mortar.

Domination and engineers
to fudge a motive you can lay your hands on
lest a girl choose or refuse waywardly.

From Hajji Mosavvor's trembling wrist
grace of tree and beast
shines on ivory
in eloquent line.
Flute,
shade dimples under chenars
breath of Naystani chases and traces
as a pair of gods might dodge and tag between stars.
Taj is to sing, Taj,
when tar and drum
come to their silence, slow,
clear, rich, as though
he had cadence and phrase from Hafez.
Nothing that was is,
but Moluk-e-Zarrabi
draws her voice from a well
deeper than history.
Shir-e Khoda's note
on a dawn-cold radio
forestalls, outlasts the beat.
Friday, Sobhi's tales
keeping boys from their meat.

A fowler spreading his net
over the barley, calls,
calls on a rubber reed.
Grain nods in reply.
Poppies blue upon white

wake to the sun's frown.
Scut of gazelle dances and bounces
out of the afternoon.
Owl and wolf to the night.
On a terrace over a pool
vafur, vodka, tea,
resonant verse spilled
from Onsori, Sa'di,
till the girls' mutter is lost
in whisper of stream and leaf,
a final nightingale
under a fading sky
azan on their quiet.

They despise police work,
are not masters of filing:
always a task for foreigners
to make them unhappy,
unproductive and rich.

Have you seen a falcon stoop
accurate, unforseen
and absolute, between
wind-ripples over harvest? Dread
of what's to be, is and has been —
were we not better dead?

His wings churn air
to flight.
Feathers alight
with sun, he rises where
dazzle rebuts our stare,
wonder our fright.

III

All things only of earth and water,
to sit in the sun's warmth
breathing clean air.
A fancy took me to dig,
plant, prune, graft;
milk, skim, churn;

flay and tan.
A salt side of beef
for a knife chased and inscribed.
A cask of pressed grapes
for a seine-net.
For peace until harvest
a jig and a hymn.

How shall wheat sprout
through a shingle of Lydian pebbles
that turn the harrow's points?
Quarry and build, Solomon,
a bank for Lydian pebbles:
tribute of Lydian pebbles
levy and lay aside,
that twist underfoot
and blunt the plowshare,
countless, useless, hampering
pebbles that spawn.

Shot silk and damask white
spray spread from
artesian gush of our past.
Let no one drink unchlorinated
living water but taxed tap, sterile,
or seek his contraband mouthful
in bog, under thicket, by crag, a trickle,
or from embroidered pools
with newts and dytiscus beetles.

One cribbed in a madhouse
set about with diagnoses;
one unvisited; one uninvited;
one visited and invited too much;
one impotent, suffocated by adulation;
one unfed: flares on a foundering barque,
stars spattering still sea under iceblink.

Tinker tapping perched on a slagheap
and the man who can mend a magneto.
Flight-lieutenant Idema, half course run
that started from Grand Rapids, Michigan,
wouldnt fight for Roosevelt,

'that bastard Roosevelt', pale
at Malta's ruins, enduring
a jeep guarded like a tyrant.
In British uniform and pay
for fun of fighting and pride,
for Churchill on foot alone,
clowning with a cigar, was lost
in best blues and his third plane that day.

Broken booty but usable
along the littoral, frittering into the south.
We marvelled, careful of craters and minefields,
noting a new-painted recognisance
on a fragment of fuselage, sand drifting into dumps,
a tank's turret twisted skyward,
here and there a lorry unharmed
out of fuel or the crew scattered;
leaguered in lines numbered for enemy units,
gulped beer of their brewing,
mocked them marching unguarded to our rear;
discerned nothing indigenous, never a dwelling,
but on the shore sponges stranded and beyond the reef
unstayed masts staggering in the swell,
till we reached readymade villages clamped on cornland,
empty, Arabs feeding vines to goats;
at last orchards aligned, girls hawked by their mothers
from tent to tent, Tripoli dark
under a cone of tracers.
Old in that war after raising many crosses
rapped on a tomb at Leptis; no one opened.

Blind Bashshar bin Burd saw,
doubted, glanced back,
guessed whence, speculated whither.
Panegyrists, blinder and deaf,
prophets, exegesists, counsellors of patience
lie in wait for blood,
every man with a net.
Condole me with abundance of secret pleasure.
What we think in private
will be said in public
before the last gallon's teemed

into an unintelligible sea —
old men who toil in the bilge to open a link,
bruised by the fling of the ship and sodden
sleep at the handpump. Staithes, filthy harbour water,
a drowned Finn, a drowned Chinee;
hard-lying money wrung from protesting paymasters.

Rosyth guns sang. Sang tide through cable
for Glasgow burning:
                'Bright west,
                pale east,
                catfish on the sprool.'
Sun leaped up and passed,
bolted towards green creek
of quiet Chesapeake,
bight of a warp no strong tide strains. Yet
as tea's drawing, breeze backing and freshening,
who'd rather
make fast Fortune with a slippery hitch?
Tide sang. Guns sang:
                'Vigilant,
                pull off fluffed woollens, strip
                to buff and beyond.'
In watch below
meditative heard elsewhere
surf shout, pound shores seldom silent
from which heart naked swam
out to the dear unintelligible ocean.

From Largo Law look down,
moon and dry weather, look down
on convoy marshalled, filing between mines.
Cold northern clear sea-gardens
between Lofoten and Spitzbergen,
as good a grave as any, earth or water.
What else do we live for and take part,
we who would share the spoils?

1951

BRIGGFLATTS

An Autobiography

For Peggy

Son los pasariellos del mal pelo exidos

The spuggies are fledged

I

Brag, sweet tenor bull,
descant on Rawthey's madrigal,
each pebble its part
for the fells' late spring.
Dance tiptoe, bull,
black against may.
Ridiculous and lovely
chase hurdling shadows
morning into noon.
May on the bull's hide
and through the dale
furrows fill with may,
paving the slowworm's way.

A mason times his mallet
to a lark's twitter,
listening while the marble rests,
lays his rule
at a letter's edge,
fingertips checking,
till the stone spells a name
naming none,
a man abolished.
Painful lark, labouring to rise!
The solemn mallet says:
In the grave's slot
he lies. We rot.

Decay thrusts the blade,
wheat stands in excrement
trembling. Rawthey trembles.
Tongue stumbles, ears err
for fear of spring.
Rub the stone with sand,
wet sandstone rending
roughness away. Fingers
ache on the rubbing stone.
The mason says: Rocks
happen by chance.
No one here bolts the door,
love is so sore.

<

Stone smooth as skin,
cold as the dead they load
on a low lorry by night.
The moon sits on the fell
but it will rain.
Under sacks on the stone
two children lie,
hear the horse stale,
the mason whistle,
harness mutter to shaft,
felloe to axle squeak,
rut thud the rim,
crushed grit.

Stocking to stocking, jersey to jersey,
head to a hard arm,
they kiss under the rain,
bruised by their marble bed.
In Garsdale, dawn;
at Hawes, tea from the can.
Rain stops, sacks
steam in the sun, they sit up.
Copper-wire moustache,
sea-reflecting eyes
and Baltic plainsong speech
declare: By such rocks
men killed Bloodaxe.

Fierce blood throbs in his tongue,
lean words.
Skulls cropped for steel caps
huddle round Stainmore.
Their becks ring on limestone,
whisper to peat.
The clogged cart pushes the horse downhill.
In such soft air
they trudge and sing,
laying the tune frankly on the air.
All sounds fall still,
fellside bleat,
hide-and-seek peewit.

Her pulse their pace,
palm countering palm,
till a trench is filled,
stone white as cheese
jeers at the dale.
Knotty wood, hard to rive,
smoulders to ash;
smell of October apples.
The road again,
at a trot.
Wetter, warmed, they watch
the mason meditate
on name and date.

Rain rinses the road,
the bull streams and laments.
Sour rye porridge from the hob
with cream and black tea,
meat, crust and crumb.
Her parents in bed
the children dry their clothes.
He has untied the tape
of her striped flannel drawers
before the range. Naked
on the pricked rag mat
his fingers comb
thatch of his manhood's home.

Gentle generous voices weave
over bare night
words to confirm and delight
till bird dawn.
Rainwater from the butt
she fetches and flannel
to wash him inch by inch,
kissing the pebbles.
Shining slowworm part of the marvel.
The mason stirs:
Words!
Pens are too light.
Take a chisel to write.

<

Every birth a crime,
every sentence life.
Wiped of mould and mites
would the ball run true?
No hope of going back.
Hounds falter and stray,
shame deflects the pen.
Love murdered neither bleeds nor stifles
but jogs the draftsman's elbow.
What can he, changed, tell
her, changed, perhaps dead?
Delight dwindles. Blame
stays the same.

Brief words are hard to find,
shapes to carve and discard:
Bloodaxe, king of York,
king of Dublin, king of Orkney.
Take no notice of tears;
letter the stone to stand
over love laid aside lest
insufferable happiness impede
flight to Stainmore,
to trace
lark, mallet,
becks, flocks
and axe knocks.

Dung will not soil the slowworm's
mosaic. Breathless lark
drops to nest in sodden trash;
Rawthey truculent, dingy.
Drudge at the mallet, the may is down,
fog on fells. Guilty of spring
and spring's ending
amputated years ache after
the bull is beef, love a convenience.
It is easier to die than to remember.
Name and date
split in soft slate
a few months obliterate.

II

Poet appointed dare not decline
to walk among the bogus, nothing to authenticate
the mission imposed, despised
by toadies, confidence men, kept boys,
shopped and jailed, cleaned out by whores,
touching acquaintance for food and tobacco.
Secret, solitary, a spy, he gauges
lines of a Flemish horse
hauling beer, the angle, obtuse,
a slut's blouse draws on her chest,
counts beat against beat, bus conductor
against engine against wheels against
the pedal, Tottenham Court Road, decodes
thunder, scans
porridge bubbling, pipes clanking, feels
Buddha's basalt cheek
but cannot name the ratio of its curves
to the half-pint
left breast of a girl who bared it in Kleinfeldt's.
He lies with one to long for another,
sick, self-maimed, self-hating,
obstinate, mating
beauty with squalor to beget lines still-born.

You who can calculate the course
of a biased bowl,
shall I come near the jack?
What twist can counter the force
that holds back
woods I roll?

You who elucidate the disk
hubbed by the sun,
shall I see autumn out
or the fifty years at risk
be lost, doubt
end what's begun?

Under his right oxter the loom of his sweep
the pilot turns from the wake.

Thole-pins shred where the oar leans,
grommets renewed, tallowed;
halliards frapped to the shrouds.
Crew grunt and gasp. Nothing he sees
they see, but hate and serve. Unscarred ocean,
day's swerve, swell's poise, pursuit,
he blends, balances, drawing leagues under the keel
to raise cold cliffs where tides
knot fringes of weed.
No tilled acre, gold scarce,
walrus tusk, whalebone, white bear's liver.
Scurvy gnaws, steading smell, hearth's crackle.
Crabs, shingle, seracs on the icefall.
Summer is bergs and fogs, lichen on rocks.
Who cares to remember a name cut in ice
or be remembered?
Wind writes in foam on the sea:

Who sang, sea takes,
brawn brine, bone grit.
Keener the kittiwake.
Fells forget him.
Fathoms dull the dale,
gulfweed voices . . .

About ship! Sweat in the south. Go bare
because the soil is adorned,
sunset the colour of a boiled louse.
Steep sluice or level,
parts of the sewer ferment faster.
Days jerk, dawdle, fidget
towards the cesspit.
Love is a vapour, we're soon through it.

Flying fish follow the boat,
delicate wings blue, grace
on flick of a tissue tail,
the water's surface between
appetite and attainment.
Flexible, unrepetitive line
to sing, not paint; sing, sing,
laying the tune on the air,
nimble and easy as a lizard,

still and sudden as a gecko,
to humiliate love, remember
nothing.

It tastes good, garlic and salt in it,
with the half-sweet white wine of Orvieto
on scanty grass under great trees
where the ramparts cuddle Lucca.

It sounds right, spoken on the ridge
between marine olives and hillside
blue figs, under the breeze fresh
with pollen of Apennine sage.

It feels soft, weed thick in the cave
and the smooth wet riddance of Antonietta's
bathing suit, mouth ajar for
submarine Amalfitan kisses.

It looks well on the page, but never
well enough. Something is lost
when wind, sun, sea upbraid
justly an unconvinced deserter.

White marble stained like a urinal
cleft in Apuan Alps,
always trickling, apt to the saw. Ice and wedge
split it or well-measured cordite shots,
while paraffin pistons rap, saws rip
and clamour is clad in stillness:
clouds echo marble middens, sugar-white,
that cumber the road stones travel
to list the names of the dead.
There is a lot of Italy in churchyards,
sea on the left, the Garfagnana
over the wall, la Cisa flaking
to hillside fiddlers above Parma,
melancholy, swift,
with light bow blanching the dance.
Grease mingles with sweat
on the threshing floor. Frogs, grasshoppers
drape the rice in sound.
Tortoise deep in dust or

muzzled bear capering
punctuate a text whose initial,
lost in Lindisfarne plaited lines,
stands for discarded love.

Win from rock
  flame and ore.
Crucibles pour
  sanded ingots.

Heat and hammer
  draw out a bar.
Wheel and water
  grind an edge.

No worn tool
  whittles stone;
but a reproached
  uneasy mason

shaping evasive
  ornament
litters his yard
  with flawed fragments.

Loaded with mail of linked lies,
what weapon can the king lift to fight
when chance-met enemies employ sly
sword and shoulder-piercing pike,
pressed into the mire,
trampled and hewn till a knife
— in whose hand? — severs tight
neck cords? Axe rusts. Spine
picked bare by ravens, agile
maggots devour the slack side
and inert brain, never wise.
What witnesses he had life,
ravelled and worn past splice,
yarns falling to staple? Rime
on the bent, the beck ice,
there will be nothing on Stainmore to hide
void, no sable to disguise
what he wore under the lies,

king of Orkney, king of Dublin, twice
king of York, where the tide
stopped till long flight
from who knows what smile,
scowl, disgust or delight
ended in bale on the fellside.

Starfish, poinsettia on a half-tide crag,
a galliard by Byrd.
Anemones spite cullers of ornament
but design the pool
to their grouping. The hermit crab
is no grotesque in such company.

Asian vultures riding on a spiral
column of dust
or swift desert ass startled by the
camels' dogged saunter
figures sudden flight of the descant
on a madrigal by Monteverdi.

But who will entune a bogged orchard,
its blossom gone,
fruit unformed, where hunger and
damp hush the hive?
A disappointed July full of codling
moth and ragged lettuces?

Yet roe are there, rise to the fence, insolent;
a scared vixen cringes
red against privet stems as a mazurka;
and rat, grey, rummaging
behind the compost heap has daring
to thread, lithe and alert, Schoenberg's maze.

Riding silk, adrift on noon,
a spider gleams like a berry
less black than cannibal slug
but no less pat under elders
where shadows themselves are a web.
So is summer held to its contract
and the year solvent; but men
driven by storm fret,

reminded of sweltering Crete
and Pasiphae's pungent sweat,
who heard the god-bull's feet
scattering sand,
breathed byre stink, yet stood
with expectant hand
to guide his seed to its soil;
nor did flesh flinch
distended by the brute
nor loaded spirit sink
till it had glories in unlike creation.

III

Down into dust and reeds
at the patrolled bounds
where captives thicken to gaze
slither companions, wary, armed,
whose torches straggle
seeking charred hearths
to define a road.
Day, dim, laps at the shore
in petulant ripples
soon smoothed in night
on pebbles worn by tabulation till
only the shell of figures is left
as fragile honeycomb breeze.
Tides of day strew the shingle
tides of night sweep, snoring;
and some turned back, taught
by dreams the year would capsize
where the bank quivers, paved
with gulls stunned on a cliff
not hard to climb, muffled
in flutter, scored by beaks,
pestered by scavengers
whose palms scoop droppings to mould
cakes for hungry towns. One
plucked warm fruit from the arse
of his companion, who
making to beat him, he screamed:
Hastor! Hastor! but Hastor
raised dung thickened lashes to stare
disdaining those who cry:
Sweet shit! Buy!
for he swears in the market:
By God with whom I lunched!
There is no trash in the wheat
my loaf is kneaded from.
Nor will unprofitable motion
stir the stink that settles round him.
Leave given
we would have slaughtered the turd-bakers

but neither whip nor knife
can welt their hide.
Guides at the top claim fees
though the way is random
past hovels hags lean from
rolling lizard eyes
at boys gnawed by the wolf,
past bevelled downs, grey marshes
where some souse in brine
long rotted corpses, others,
needier, sneak through saltings
to snatch toe, forearm, ear,
and on gladly to hills
briar and bramble vest
where beggars advertise
rash, chancre, fistula,
to hug glib shoulders, mingle herpetic
limbs with stumps and cosset the mad.
Some the Laughing Stone disables
whom giggle and snicker waste
till fun suffocates them. Beyond
we heard the teeming falls of the dead,
saw kelts fall back long-jawed, without flesh,
cruel by appetite beyond its term,
straining to bright gravel spawning pools.
Eddies batter them, borne down to the sea,
archipelago of galaxies,
zero suspending the world.
Banners purple and green flash from its walls,
pennants of red, orange blotched pale on blue,
glimmer of ancient arms
to pen and protect mankind.
But we desired Macedonia,
the rocky meadows, horses, barley pancakes,
incest and familiar games,
to end in our place by our own wars,
and deemed the peak unscaleable; but he
reached to a crack in the rock
with some scorn, resolute though in doubt,
traversed limestone to gabbro,
file sharp, skinning his fingers,
and granite numb with ice, in air

too thin to bear up a gnat,
scrutinising holds while day lasted,
groping for holds in the dark
till the morning star reflected
in the glazed crag
and other light not of the sun
dawning from above
lit feathers sweeping snow
and the limbs of Israfel,
trumpet in hand, intent on the east,
cheeks swollen to blow,
whose sigh is cirrus: Yet delay!
When will the signal come
to summon man to his clay?

Heart slow, nerves numb and memory, he lay
on a glistening moss by a spring;
as a woodman dazed by an adder's sting
barely within recall
tests the rebate tossed to him, so he
ascertained moss and bracken,
a cold squirm snaking his flank
and breath leaked to his ear:
I am neither snake nor lizard,
I am the slowworm.

Ripe wheat is my lodging. I polish
my side on pillars of its transept,
gleam in its occasional light.
Its swaying
copies my gait.

Vaults stored with slugs to relish,
my quilt a litter of husks, I prosper
lying low, little concerned.
My eyes sharpen
when I blink.

Good luck to reaper and miller!
Grubs adhere even to stubble.
Come plowtime
the ditch is near. <

Sycamore seed twirling,
O, writhe to its measure!
Dust swirling trims pleasure.
Thorns prance in a gale.
In air snow flickers,
twigs tap,
elms drip.

Swaggering, shimmering fall,
drench and towel us all!

So he rose and led home silently through clean woodland
where every bough repeated the slowworm's song.

IV

Grass caught in willow tells the flood's height that has subsided;
overfalls sketch a ledge to be bared tomorrow.
No angler homes with empty creel though mist dims day.
I hear Aneurin number the dead, his nipped voice.
Slight moon limps after the sun. A closing door
stirs smoke's flow above the grate. Jangle
to skald, battle, journey; to priest Latin is bland.
Rats have left no potatoes fit to roast, the gamey tang
recalls ibex guts steaming under a cold ridge,
tomcat stink of a leopard dying while I stood
easing the bolt to dwell on a round's shining rim.
I hear Aneurin number the dead and rejoice,
being adult male of a merciless species.
Today's posts are piles to drive into the quaggy past
on which impermanent palaces balance.
I see Aneurin's pectoral muscle swell under his shirt,
pacing between the game Ida left to rat and raven,
young men, tall yesterday, with cabled thighs.
Red deer move less warily since their bows dropped.
Girls in Teesdale and Wensleydale wake discontent.
Clear Cymric voices carry well this autumn night,
Aneurin and Taliesin, cruel owls
for whom it is never altogether dark, crying
before the rules made poetry a pedant's game.
Columba, Columbanus, as the soil shifts its vest,
Aidan and Cuthbert put on daylight,
wires of sharp western metal entangled in its soft
web, many shuttles as midges darting;
not for bodily welfare nor pauper theorems
but splendour to splendour, excepting nothing that is.
Let the fox have his fill, patient leech and weevil,
cattle refer the rising of Sirius to their hedge horizon,
runts murder the sacred calves of the sea by rule
heedless of herring gull, surf and the text carved by waves
on the skerry. Can you trace shuttles thrown
like drops from a fountain, spray, mist of spiderlines
bearing the rainbow, quoits round the draped moon;
shuttles like random dust desert whirlwinds hoy at their
        tormenting sun?

Follow the clue patiently and you will understand nothing.
Lice in its seams despise the jacket shrunk to the world's core,
crawl with toil to glimpse
from its shoulder walls of flame which could they reach
they'd crackle like popcorn in a skillet.

As the player's breath warms the fipple the tone clears.
It is time to consider how Domenico Scarlatti
condensed so much music into so few bars
with never a crabbed turn or congested cadence,
never a boast or a see-here; and stars and lakes
echo him and the copse drums out his measure,
snow peaks are lifted up in moonlight and twilight
and the sun rises on an acknowledged land.

My love is young but wise. Oak, applewood,
her fire is banked with ashes till day.
The fells reek of her hearth's scent,
her girdle is greased with lard;
hunger is stayed on her settle, lust in her bed.
Light as spider floss her hair on my cheek which a puff scatters,
light as a moth her fingers on my thigh.
We have eaten and loved and the sun is up,
we have only to sing before parting:
Goodbye, dear love.

Her scones are greased with fat of fried bacon,
her blanket comforts my belly like the south.
We have eaten and loved and the sun is up.
Goodbye.

Applewood, hard to rive,
its knots smoulder all day.
Cobweb hair on the morning,
a puff would blow it away.
Rime is crisp on the bent,
ruts stone-hard, frost spangles fleece.
What breeze will fill that sleeve limp on the line?
A boy's jet steams from the wall, time from the year,
care from deed and undoing.
Shamble, cold, content with beer and pickles,
towards a taciturn lodging amongst strangers.

>

Where rats go go I,
accustomed to penury,
filth, disgust and fury;
evasive to persist,
reject the bait
yet gnaw the best.
My bony feet
sully shelf and dresser,
keeping a beat in the dark,
rap on lath
till dogs bark
and sleep, shed,
slides from the bed.
O valiant when hunters
with stick and terrier bar escape
or wavy ferret leaps,
encroach and cede again,
rat, roommate, unreconciled.

Stars disperse. We too,
further from neighbours
now the year ages.

V

Drip — icicle's gone.
Slur, ratio, tone,
chime dilute what's done
as a flute clarifies song,
trembling phrase fading to pause
then glow. Solstice past,
years end crescendo.

Winter wrings pigment
from petal and slough
but thin light lays
white next red on sea-crow wing,
gruff sole cormorant
whose grief turns carnival.
Even a bangle of birds
to bind sleeve to wrist
as west wind waves to east
a just perceptible greeting —
sinews ripple the weave,
threads flex, slew, hues meeting,
parting in whey-blue haze.

Mist sets lace of frost
on rock for the tide to mangle.
Day is wreathed in what summer lost.

Conger skimped at the ebb, lobster,
neither will I take, nor troll
roe of its like for salmon.
Let bass sleep, gentles
brisk, skim-grey,
group a nosegay
jostling on cast flesh,
frisk and compose decay
to side shot with flame,
unresting bluebottle wing. Sing,
strewing the notes on the air
as ripples skip in a shallow. Go
bare, the shore is adorned
with pungent weed loudly

filtering sand and sea.
Silver blades of surf
fall crisp on rustling grit,
shaping the shore as a mason
fondles and shapes his stone.

Shepherds follow the links,
sweet turf studded with thrift;
fell-born men of precise instep
leading demure dogs
from Tweed and Till and Teviotdale,
with hair combed back from the muzzle,
dogs from Redesdale and Coquetdale
taught by Wilson or Telfer.
Their teeth are white as birch,
slow under black fringe
of silent, accurate lips.
The ewes are heavy with lamb.
Snow lies bright on Hedgehope
and tacky mud about Till
where the fells have stepped aside
and the river praises itself,
silence by silence sits
and Then is diffused in Now.

Light lifts from the water.
Frost has put rowan down,
a russet blotch of bracken
tousled about the trunk.
Bleached sky. Cirrus
reflects sun that has left
nothing to badger eyes.

Young flutes, harps touched by a breeze,
drums and horns escort
Aldebaran, low in the clear east,
beckoning boats to the fishing.
Capella floats from the north
with shields hung on his gunwale.
That is no dinghy's lantern
occulted by the swell — Betelgeuse,

calling behind him to Rigel.
Starlight is almost flesh.

Great strings next the post of the harp
clang, the horn has majesty,
flutes flicker in the draft and flare.
Orion strides over Farne.
Seals shuffle and bark,
terns shift on their ledges,
watching Capella steer for the zenith,
and Procyon starts his climb.

Furthest, fairest things, stars, free of our humbug,
each his own, the longer known the more alone,
wrapt in emphatic fire roaring out to a black flue.
Each spark trills on a tone beyond chronological compass,
yet in a sextant's bubble present and firm
places a surveyor's stone or steadies a tiller.
Then is Now. The star you steer by is gone,
its tremulous thread spun in the hurricane
spider floss on my cheek; light from the zenith
spun when the slowworm lay in her lap
fifty years ago.

The sheets are gathered and bound,
the volume indexed and shelved,
dust on its marbled leaves.
Lofty, an empty combe,
silent but for bees.
Finger tips touched and were still
fifty years ago.
Sirius is too young to remember.

Sirius glows in the wind. Sparks on ripples
mark his line, lures for spent fish.

Fifty years a letter unanswered;
a visit postponed for fifty years.

She has been with me fifty years.

Starlight quivers. I had day enough.
For love uninterrupted night.

CODA

A strong song tows
us, long earsick.
Blind, we follow
rain slant, spray flick
to fields we do not know.

Night, float us.
Offshore wind, shout,
ask the sea
what's lost, what's left,
what horn sunk,
what crown adrift.

Where we are who knows
of kings who sup
while day fails? Who,
swinging his axe
to fell kings, guesses
where we go?

1965

CHOMEI AT TOYAMA

Chomei at Toyama

(Kamo-no-Chomei, born at Kamo 1154, died at Toyama on Mount Hino, 24th June 1216)

Swirl sleeping in the waterfall!
On motionless pools scum appearing
                disappearing!

Eaves formal on the zenith,
lofty city Kyoto,
wealthy, without antiquities!

Housebreakers clamber about,
builders raising floor upon floor
at the corner sites, replacing
gardens by bungalows.

In the town where I was known
the young men stare at me.
A few faces I know remain.

Whence comes man at his birth? or where
does death lead him? Whom do you mourn?
Whose steps wake your delight?
Dewy hibiscus dries: though dew
outlast the petals.

I have been noting events forty years.

On the twentyseventh May eleven hundred
and seventyseven, eight p.m., fire broke out
at the corner of Tomi and Higuchi streets.
In a night
palace, ministries, university, parliament
were destroyed. As the wind veered
flames spread out in the shape of an open fan.
Tongues torn by gusts stretched and leapt.
In the sky clouds of cinders lit red with the blaze.

Some choked, some burned, some barely escaped.
Sixteen great officials lost houses and
very many poor. A third of the city burned;

several thousands died; and of beasts,
limitless numbers.

Men are fools to invest in real estate.

Three years less three days later a wind
starting near the outer boulevard
broke a path a quarter mile across
to Sixth Avenue.
Not a house stood. Some were felled whole,
some in splinters; some had left
great beams upright in the ground
and round about
lay rooves scattered where the wind flung them.
Flocks of furniture in the air,
everything flat fluttered like dead leaves.
A dust like fog or smoke,
you could hear nothing for the roar,
bufera infernal!
Lamed some, wounded some.
This cyclone turned southwest.

Massacre without cause.

Portent?

The same year thunderbolted change of capital,
fixed here, Kyoto, for ages.
Nothing compelled the change nor was it an easy matter
but the grumbling was disproportionate.
We moved, those with jobs
or wanting jobs or hangers on of the rest,
in haste haste fretting to be the first.
Rooftrees overhanging empty rooms;
dismounted: floating down the river.
The soil returned to heath.

I visited the new site: narrow and too uneven,
cliffs and marshes, deafening shores, perpetual strong winds;
the palace a logcabin dumped amongst the hills
(yet not altogether inelegant).
There was no flat place for houses, many vacant lots,
the former capital wrecked, the new a camp,

and thoughts like clouds changing, frayed by a breath:
peasants bewailing lost land, newcomers aghast at prices.
No one in uniform: the crowds
resembled demobilized conscripts.

There were murmurs. Time defined them.
In the winter the decree was rescinded,
we returned to Kyoto;
but the houses were gone and none
could afford to rebuild them.

I have heard of a time when kings beneath bark rooves
watched chimneys.
When smoke was scarce, taxes were remitted.

To appreciate present conditions
collate them with those of antiquity.

Drought, floods, and a dearth. Two fruitless autumns.
Empty markets, swarms of beggars. Jewels
sold for a handful of rice. Dead stank
on the curb, lay so thick on
Riverside Drive a car couldnt pass.
The pest bred.
That winter my fuel was the walls of my own house.

Fathers fed their children and died,
babies died sucking the dead.
The priest Hoshi went about marking their foreheads
A, Amida, their requiem;
he counted them in the East End in the last two months,
fortythree thousand A's.

Crack, rush, ye mountains, bury your rills!
Spread your green glass, ocean, over the meadows!
Scream, avalanche, boulders amok, strangle the dale!
O ships in the sea's power, O horses
on shifting roads, in the earth's power, without hoofhold!
This is the earthquake, this was
the great earthquake of Genryaku!

The chapel fell, the abbey, the minster and the small shrines
fell, their dust rose and a thunder of houses falling.

O to be birds and fly or dragons and ride on a cloud!
The earthquake, the great earthquake of Genryaku!

A child building a mud house against a high wall:
I saw him crushed suddenly, his eyes hung
from their orbits like two tassels.
His father howled shamelessly — an officer.
I was not abashed at his crying.

Such shocks continued three weeks; then lessening,
but still a score daily as big as an average earthquake;
then fewer, alternate days, a tertian ague of tremors.
There is no record of any greater.
It caused a religious revival.
Months . . .
Years . . .
. . . .
Nobody mentions it now.

This is the unstable world and
we in it unstable and our houses.

A poor man living amongst the rich
gives no rowdy parties, doesnt sing.
Dare he keep his child at home, keep a dog?
He dare not pity himself above a whimper.

But he visits, he flatters, he is put in his place,
he remembers the patch on his trousers.
His wife and sons despise him for being poor.
He has no peace.

If he lives in an alley of rotting frame houses
he dreads a fire.
If he commutes he loses his time
and leaves his house daily to be plundered by gunmen.

The bureaucrats are avaricious.
He who has no relatives in the Inland Revenue,
poor devil!

Whoever helps him enslaves him
and follows him crying out: *Gratitude!*

If he wants success he is wretched.
If he doesnt he passes for mad.

Where shall I settle, what trade choose
that the mind may practise, the body rest?

My grandmother left me a house
but I was always away
for my health and because I was alone there.
When I was thirty I couldnt stand it any longer,
I built a house to suit myself:
one bamboo room, you would have thought it a cartshed,
poor shelter from snow or wind.
It stood on the flood plain. And that quarter
is also flooded with gangsters.

One generation
I saddened myself with idealistic philosophies,
but before I was fifty
I perceived there was no time to lose,
left home and conversation.
Among the cloudy mountains of Ohara
spring and autumn, spring and autumn, spring and autumn,
emptier than ever.

The dew evaporates from my sixty years,
I have built my last house, or hovel,
a hunter's bivouac, an old
silkworm's cocoon:
ten feet by ten, seven high: and I,
reckoning it a lodging not a dwelling,
omitted the usual foundation ceremony.

I have filled the frames with clay,
set hinges at the corners;
easy to take it down and carry it away
when I get bored with this place.
Two barrowloads of junk
and the cost of a man to shove the barrow,
no trouble at all.

Since I have trodden Hino mountain
noon has beaten through the awning

over my bamboo balcony, evening
shone on Amida.
I have shelved my books above the window,
lute and mandolin near at hand,
piled bracken and a little straw for bedding,
a smooth desk where the light falls, stove for bramblewood.
I have gathered stones, fitted
stones for a cistern, laid bamboo
pipes. No woodstack,
wood enough in the thicket.

Toyama, snug in the creepers!
Toyama, deep in the dense gully, open
westward whence the dead ride out of Eden
squatting on blue clouds of wistaria.
(Its scent drifts west to Amida.)

Summer? Cuckoo's *Follow, follow* — to
harvest Purgatory hill!
Fall! The nightgrasshopper will
shrill *Fickle life!*
Snow will thicken on the doorstep,
melt like a drift of sins.
No friend to break silence,
no one will be shocked if I neglect the rite.
There's a Lent of commandments kept
where there's no way to break them.

A ripple of white water after a boat,
shining water after the boats Mansami saw
rowing at daybreak
at Okinoya.
Between the maple leaf and the caneflower
murmurs the afternoon — Po Lo-tien
saying goodbye on the verge of Jinyo river.
(I am playing scales on my mandolin.)

Be limber, my fingers, I am going to play *Autumn Wind*
to the pines, I am going to play *Hastening Brook*
to the water. I am no player
but there's nobody listening,
I do it for my own amusement.

Sixteen and sixty, I and the gamekeeper's boy,
one zest and equal, chewing tsubana buds,
one zest and equal, persimmon, pricklypear,
ears of sweetcorn pilfered from Valley Farm.

The view from the summit: sky bent over Kyoto,
picnic villages, Fushimi and Toba:
a very economical way of enjoying yourself.
Thought runs along the crest, climbs Sumiyama;
beyond Kasatori it visits the great church,
goes on pilgrimage to Ishiyama (no need to foot it!)
or the graves of poets, of Semimaru who said:
Somehow or other
we scuttle through a lifetime.
Somehow or other
neither palace nor straw-hut
is quite satisfactory.

Not emptyhanded, with cherryblossom, with red maple
as the season gives it to decorate my Buddha
or offer a sprig at a time to chancecomers, home!

A fine moonlit night,
I sit at the window with a headful of old verses.

Whenever a monkey howls there are tears on my cuff.

Those are fireflies that seem
the fishermen's lights
off Maki island.

A shower at dawn
sings
like the hillbreeze in the leaves.

At the pheasant's chirr I recall
my father and mother uncertainly.

I rake my ashes.

Chattering fire,
soon kindled, soon burned out,
fit wife for an old man!

<

Neither closed in one landscape
nor in one season
the mind moving in illimitable
recollection.

I came here for a month
five years ago.
There's moss on the roof.

And I hear Soanso's dead
back in Kyoto.
I have as much room as I need.

I know myself and mankind.
. . . .
I dont want to be bothered.

(You will make me editor
of the Imperial Anthology?
I dont want to be bothered.)

You build for your wife, children,
cousins and cousins' cousins.
You want a house to entertain in.

A man like me can have neither servants nor friends
in the present state of society.
If I did not build for myself
for whom should I build?

Friends fancy a rich man's riches,
friends suck up to a man in high office.
If you keep straight you will have no friends
but catgut and blossom in season.

Servants weigh out their devotion
in proportion to the perquisites.
What do they care for peace and quiet?
There are more pickings in town.

I sweep my own floor
— less fuss.
I walk; I get tired
but do not have to worry about a horse.

My hands and feet will not loiter
when I am not looking.
I will not overwork them.
Besides, it's good for my health.

My jacket's wistaria flax,
my blanket hemp,
berries and young greens
my food.

(Let it be quite understood,
all this is merely personal.
I am not preaching the simple life
to those who enjoy being rich.)

I am shifting rivermist, not to be trusted.
I do not ask anything extraordinary of myself.
I like a nap after dinner
and to see the seasons come round in good order.

Hankering, vexation and apathy,
that's the run of the world.
Hankering, vexation and apathy,
keeping a carriage wont cure it.

Keeping a man in livery
wont cure it. Keeping a private fortress
wont cure it. These things satisfy no craving.
Hankering, vexation and apathy ...

I am out of place in the capital,
people take me for a beggar,
as you would be out of place in this sort of life,
you are so — I regret it — so welded to your vulgarity.

The moonshadow merges with darkness
on the cliffpath,
a tricky turn near ahead.

Oh! There's nothing to complain about.
Buddha says: 'None of the world is good.'
I am fond of my hut ... <

I have renounced the world;
have a saintly
appearance.

I do not enjoy being poor,
I've a passionate nature.
My tongue
clacked a few prayers.

1932

FIRST BOOK OF ODES

1

Weeping oaks grieve, chestnuts raise
mournful candles. Sad is spring
to perpetuate, sad to trace
immortalities never changing.

Weary on the sea
for sight of land
gazing past the coming wave we
see the same wave;

drift on merciless reiteration of years;
descry no death; but spring
is everlasting
resurrection.

1924

2

Farewell ye sequent graces
voided faces still evasive!
Silent leavetaking and mournful
as nightwanderings
in unlit rooms or where the glow
of wall-reflected streetlamp light
or hasty matches shadowed large
and crowded out by imps of night
glimmer on cascades of
fantom dancers.
Airlapped, silent muses of light,
cease to administer
poisons to dying memories to stir
pangs of old rapture, cease to conspire
reunions of inevitable seed
long blown barren sown gathered
haphazard to wither.

1924

3

To Peggy Mullett

I am agog for foam. Tumultuous come
with teeming sweetness to the bitter shore
tidelong unrinsed and midday parched and numb
with expectation. If the bright sky bore
with endless utterance of a single blue
unphrased, its restless immobility
infects the soul, which must decline into
an anguished and exact sterility
and waste away: then how much more the sea
trembling with alteration must perfect
our loneliness by its hostility.
The dear companionship of its elect
deepens our envy. Its indifference
haunts us to suicide. Strong memories
of sprayblown days exasperate impatience
to brief rebellion and emphasise
the casual impotence we sicken of.
But when mad waves spring, braceletted with foam,
towards us in the angriness of love
crying a strange name, tossing as they come
repeated invitations in the gay
exuberance of unexplained desire,
we can forget the sad splendour and play
at wilfulness until the gods require
renewed inevitable hopeless calm
and the foam dies and we again subside
into our catalepsy, dreaming foam,
while the dry shore awaits another tide.

1926

4

After the grimaces of capitulation
the universal face resumes its cunning, quick
to abandon the nocturnal elevation.
In repose majestic,
vile wakening, cowering under its tyrant
eager in stratagems to circumvent the harsh
performer of unveilings, revealer of gaunt
lurking anatomy, grin of diurnal farce;
yet when the fellow with the red-hot poker comes
truculently to torment our blisters, we vie
with one another to present scarified bums
to the iron, clutching sausages greedily.
O Sun! Should I invoke this scorn, participate
in the inconsequence of this defeat, or hide
in noctambulistic exile to penetrate
secrets that moon and stars and empty death deride?

1926

5

To Helen Egli

Empty vast days built in the waste memory seem a jail for
thoughts grown stale in the mind, tardy of birth, rank and inflexible:
love and slow selfpraise, even grief's cogency, all emotions
timetamed whimper and shame changes the past brought to no
utterance.

Ten or ten thousand, does it much signify, Helen, how we
date fantasmal events, London or Troy? Let Polyhymnia
strong with cadence multiply song, voices enmeshed by music
respond bringing the savour of our sadness or delight again.

1927

6

Personal Column

. . . As to my heart, that may as well be forgotten
or labelled: Owner will dispose of same
to a good home, refs. exchgd., h.&c.,
previous experience desired but not essential
or let on a short lease to suit convenience.

1927

7

The day being Whitsun we had pigeon for dinner;
but Richmond in the pitted river saw
mudmirrored mackintosh, a wet southwest
wiped and smeared dampness over Twickenham.

Pools on the bustop's buttoned tarpaulin.
Wimbledon, Wandsworth, Clapham, the Oval. 'Lo,
Westminster Palace where the asses jaw!'

Endless disappointed buckshee-hunt!
Suburb and city giftless garden and street,
and the sky alight of an evening stubborn
and mute by date and never *rei novae*
inter rudes artium homines.
                    never a spark of sedition
amongst the uneducated workingmen.

1928

8

Each fettered ghost slips to his several grave.

Loud intolerant bells (the shrinking nightflower closes
tenderly round its stars to baulk their hectoring)
orate to deaf hills where the olive stirs and dozes
in easeless age, dim to farce of man's fashioning.

Shepherds away! They toll throngs to your solitude
and their inquisitive harangue will disembody
shames and delights, all private features of your mood,
flay out your latencies, sieve your hopes, fray your shoddy.

The distant gods enorbed in bright indifference
whom we confess creatures or abstracts of our spirit,
unadored, absorbed into the incoherence,
leave desiccated names: rabbits sucked by a ferret.

1928

9

Dear be still! Time's start of us lengthens slowly.
Bright round plentiful nights ripen and fall for us.
Those impatient thighs will be bruised soon enough.

Sniff the sweet narcotic distilled by coupled
skins; moist bodies relaxed, mild, unemotional.
Thrifty fools spoil love with their headlong desires.

Dally! Waste! Mock! Loll! till the chosen sloth fails,
huge gasps empty the loins shuddering chilly in
long accumulated delight's thunderstorm.

Rinsed in cool sleep day will renew the summer
lightnings. Leave it to me. Only a savage's
lusts explode slapbang at the first touch like bombs.

1929

10 Chorus of Furies

Guarda, mi disse, le feroce Erine

Let us come upon him first as if in a dream,
anonymous triple presence,
memory made substance and tally of heart's rot:
then in the waking Now be demonstrable, seem
sole aspect of being's essence,
coffin to the living touch, self's Iscariot.
Then he will loath the year's recurrent long caress
without hope of divorce,
envying idiocy's apathy or the stress
of definite remorse.
He will lapse into a halflife lest the taut force
of the mind's eagerness
recall those fiends or new apparitions endorse
his excessive distress.
He will shrink, his manhood leave him, slough selfaware
the last skin of the flayed: despair.
He will nurse his terror carefully, uncertain
even of death's solace,
impotent to outpace
dispersion of the soul, disruption of the brain.

1929

11

To a Poet who advised me to preserve
my fragments and false starts

Narciss, my numerous cancellations prefer
slow limpness in the damp dustbins amongst the peel
tobacco-ash and ends spittoon licking litter
of labels dry corks breakages and a great deal

of miscellaneous garbage picked over by
covetous dustmen and Salvation Army sneaks
to one review-rid month's printed ignominy,
the public detection of your decay, that reeks.

1929

12

An arles, an arles for my hiring,
O master of singers, an arlespenny!

— Well sung singer, said Apollo,
but in this trade we pay no wages.

I too was once a millionaire
(in Germany during the inflation:
when the train steamed into Holland
I had not enough for a bun.)

The Lady asked the Poet:
Why do you wear your raincoat in the drawing-room?
He answered: Not to show
my arse sticking out of my trousers.

His muse left him for a steady man.
Quaeret in trivio vocationem.

(he is cadging for drinks at the streetcorners.)

1929

13

Fearful symmetry

Muzzle and jowl and beastly brow,
bilious glaring eyes, tufted ears,
recidivous criminality in the slouch,
— This is not the latest absconding bankrupt
but a 'beautiful' tiger imported at great expense from
Kuala Lumpur.

7 photographers, 4 black-and-white artists and an R.A.
are taking his profitable likeness;
28 reporters and an essayist
are writing him up.
Sundry ladies think he is a darling
especially at mealtimes, observing
that a firm near the docks advertises replicas
fullgrown on approval for easy cash payments.

♂Felis Tigris (Straits Settlements) (Bobo) takes exercise
up and down his cage before feeding
in a stench of excrements of great cats
indifferent to beauty or brutality.
He is said to have eaten several persons
but of course you can never be quite sure of these things.

1929

14 Gin the Goodwife Stint

The ploughland has gone to bent
and the pasture to heather;
gin the goodwife stint,
she'll keep the house together.

Gin the goodwife stint
and the bairns hunger
the Duke can get his rent
one year longer.

The Duke can get his rent
and we can get our ticket
twa pund emigrant
on a C.P.R. packet.

1930

15

Nothing
substance utters or time
stills and restrains
joins design and

supple measure deftly
as thought's intricate polyphonic
score dovetails with the tread
sensuous things
keep in our consciousness.

Celebrate man's craft
and the word spoken in shapeless night, the
sharp tool paring away
waste and the forms
cut out of mystery!

When taut string's note
passes ears' reach or red rays or violet
fade, strong over unseen
forces the word
ranks and enumerates . . .

mimes clouds condensed
and hewn hills and bristling forests,
steadfast corn in its season
and the seasons
in their due array,

life of man's own body
and death . . .
                    The sound thins into melody,
discourse narrowing, craft
failing, design
petering out.

Ears heavy to breeze of speech and
thud of the ictus.

1930

16

Molten pool, incandescent spilth of
deep cauldrons — and brighter nothing is —
cast and cold, your blazes extinct and
no turmoil nor peril left you,
rusty ingot, bleak paralysed blob!

1930

17

To Mina Loy

Now that sea's over that island
so that barely on a calm day sun sleeks
a patchwork hatching of combed weed
over stubble and fallow alike
I resent drowned blackthorn hedge, choked ditch,
gates breaking from rusty hinges,
the submerged copse,
Trespassers will be prosecuted.

Sea's over that island,
weed over furrow and dungheap:
but how should I recognise the place
under the weeds and sand
who was never in it on land I dont know:
some trick of refraction,
a film of light in the water crumpled and spread
like a luminous frock on a woman walking
along in her garden.

Oval face, thin eyebrows wide of the eyes,
a premonition in the gait
of this subaqueous persistence
of a particular year —
for you had prepared it for preservation
not vindictively, urged
by the economy of passions.

Nobody said: She is organising
these knicknacks her dislike collects
into a pattern nature will adopt and perpetuate.

Weed over meadowgrass, sea over weed,
no step on the gravel.
Very likely I shall never meet her again
or if I do, fear the latch as before.

1930

18 The Complaint of the Morpethshire Farmer

On the up-platform at Morpeth station
in the market-day throng
I overheard a Morpethshire farmer
muttering this song:

Must ye bide, my good stone house,
to keep a townsman dry?
To hear the flurry of the grouse
but not the lowing of the kye?

To see the bracken choke the clod
the coulter will na turn?
The bit level neebody
will drain soak up the burn?

Where are ye, my seven score sheep?
Feeding on other braes!
My brand has faded from your fleece,
another has its place.

The fold beneath the rowan
where ye were dipt before,
its cowpit walls are overgrown,
ye would na heed them more.

And thou! Thou's idled all the spring,
I doubt thou's spoiled, my Meg!
But a sheepdog's faith is aye something.
We'll hire together in Winnipeg.

Canada's a cold land.
Thou and I must share
a straw bed and a hind's wages
and the bitter air.

Canada's a bare land
for the north wind and the snow.
Northumberland's a bare land
for men have made it so.

>

Sheep and cattle are poor men's food,
grouse is sport for the rich;
heather grows where the sweet grass might grow
for the cost of cleaning the ditch.

A liner lying in the Clyde
will take me to Quebec.
My sons'll see the land I am leaving
as barren as her deck.

1930

19

Fruits breaking the branches,
sunlight stagnates in the rift;
here the curl of a comma,
parenthesis,

(Put the verb out of mind, lurking
to jar all to a period!)
discourse interminably
uncontradicted

level under the orchards'
livid-drowsy green:
this that Elysium
they speak of.

Where shall I hide?

1930

20 Vestiges

I

Salt grass silent of hooves, the lake stinks,
we take a few small fish from the streams,
our children are scabby, chivvied by flies,
we cannot read the tombs in the eastern prairie,
        who slew the Franks, who
        swam the Yellow River.

The lice have left Temuchin's tent. His ghost
cries under north wind, having spent
strength in life: life lost, lacks means of death,
voice-tost; the horde indistinguishable;
worn name weak in fool's jaws.

We built no temples. Our cities' woven hair
mildewed and frayed. Records of Islam and Chin,
battles, swift riders, ambush,
tale of the slain, and the name Jengiz.

Wild geese of Yen, peacocks of the Windy Shore.

Tall Chutsai sat under the phoenix tree.
— That Baghdad banker contracts to
double the revenue, him collecting.
Four times might be exacted, but
such taxation impoverishes the people.

No litigation. The laws were simple.

II

Jengiz to Chang Chun: China
is fat, but I am lean
eating soldier's food,
lacking learning.
In seven years
I brought most of the world under one law.
The Lords of Cathay
hesitate and fall.

Amidst these disorders
I distrust my talents.
To cross a river
boats and rudders,
to keep the empire in order
poets and sages,
but I have not found nine for a cabinet,
not three.
I have fasted and washed. Come

Chang: I am old
not wise nor virtuous,
nor likely to be much use.
My appearance is parched, my body weak.
I set out at once.

And to Liu Chung Lu, Jengiz:
Get an escort and a good cart,
and the girls can be sent on
separately if he insists.

1931

21 Two Photographs

It's true then that you still overeat, fat friend,
and swell, and never take folk's advice. They laugh,
you just giggle and pay no attention. Damn!
    you dont care, not you!

But once — that was before time had blunted your
desire for pretty frocks — slender girl — or is
the print cunningly faked? — arm in arm with your
    fiancé you stood

and glared into the lens (slightly out of focus)
while that public eye scrutinised your shape,
afraid, the attitude shows, you might somehow
    excite its dislike.

1932

22

Mesh cast for mackerel
by guess and the sheen's tremor,
imperceptible if you havent the knack —
a difficult job,

hazardous and seasonal:
many shoals all of a sudden,
it would tax the Apostles to take the lot;
then drowse for months,

nets on the shingle,
a pint in the tap.
Likewise the pilchards come unexpectedly,
startle the man on the cliff.

Remember us to the teashop girls.
Say we have seen no legs better than theirs,
we have the sea to stare at,
its treason, copiousness, tedium.

1932

23 The Passport Officer

This impartial dog's nose
scrutinizes the lamppost. All in good order.
He sets his seal on it and
moves on to the next.

(The drippings of his forerunners
convey no information,
barely a precedent.
His actions are reflex.)

1932

24

Vessels thrown awry by strong gusts
broach to, the seas capsize them.
Sundry cargoes have
strewn the gulf with flotsam
in parcels too small to be salvaged.

(In the purlieus? or the precincts?
Lord Shaw had it argued
a week in the Lords:
a guinea a minute
more or less.)

Some attribute the series of wrecks hereabouts to
faulty stowage, an illfound ship,
careless navigation or the notorious reefs,
just awash at low tide.
The place has a bad name.

(Stern in the purlieus, bow in the precincts,
the mate in the purlieus,
the chief engineer
together with the donkeyman
at that moment in the precincts.)

Nevertheless we have heard
voices speech eludes allude to
gales not measured by the anemometer
nor predicted in Kingsway.
They defy Epicurus.

(Lord Shaw quoted Solomon,
advised a compromise.
Lord Carson muttered
'Purlieus or precincts
the place has a bad name.')

Here was glass-clear architecture,
gardens sacred to Tethys.

Ocean spare the new twinscrew dieselengined tanker,
spare the owners and underwriters
litigation.

1933

25

As appleblossom to crocus
typist to cottage lass,
perishable alike, unlike
the middleclass rose.

Each sour noon
squeezed into teashops
displays one at least
delicate ignorant face

untroubled by
earth's spinning
preoccupied rather
by the set of her stocking.

Men are timid,
hotels expensive,
the police keep
a sharp eye on landladies.

— The cinema, Postume,
Postume, warm,
in the old days
before thirty.

1934

26

Two hundred and seven paces
        from the tram-stop
to the door,

a hundred and forty-six thousand
        four hundred
seconds ago,

two hundred and ninety-two thousand
        eight hundred
kisses or thereabouts; what else

let him say who saw and let
        him who is able
do like it for I'm

not fit for a commonplace world
        any longer, I'm
bound for the City,

cashregister, adding-machine,
        rotary stencil.
Give me another

double whiskey and fire-extinguisher,
        George. Here's
Girls! Girls!

1934

27

On highest summits dawn comes soonest.
(But that is not the time to give over loving.)

1935

28

You leave
nobody else
without a bed

you make
everybody else
thoroughly at home

I'm
the only one
hanged
in your
halter

you've driven
nobody else mad
but me.

1935

29

Southwind, tell her what
wont sadden her,
not how wretched
I am.

Do you sleep snug these
long nights or
know I am lying
alone?

1935

30 The Orotava Road

Four white heifers with sprawling hooves
trundle the waggon.
Its ill-roped crates heavy with fruit sway.
The chisel point of the goad, blue and white,
glitters ahead,
a flame to follow lance-high in a man's hand
who does not shave. His linen trousers
like him want washing.
You can see his baked skin through his shirt.
He has no shoes and his hat has a hole in it.
'Hu! vaca! Hu! vaca!'
he says staccato without raising his voice;
'Adios caballero' legato but
in the same tone.
Camelmen high on muzzled mounts
boots rattling against the panels
of an empty
packsaddle do not answer strangers.
Each with his train of seven or eight tied
head to tail they
pass silent but for the heavy bells
and plip of slobber dripping from
muzzle to dust;
save that on sand their soles squeak slightly.
Milkmaids, friendly girls between
fourteen and twenty
or younger, bolt upright on small
trotting donkeys that bray (they arch their
tails a few inches
from the root, stretch neck and jaw forward
to make the windpipe a trumpet)
chatter. Jolted
cans clatter. The girls' smiles repeat
the black silk curve of the wimple
under the chin.
Their hats are absurd doll's hats
or flat-crowned to take a load.
All have fine eyes.

You can guess their balanced nakedness
under the cotton gown and thin shift.
They sing and laugh.
They say 'Adios!' shyly but look back
more than once, knowing our thoughts
and sharing our
desires and lack of faith in desire.

1935

31

O ubi campi!

The soil sandy and the plow light, neither
virgin land nor near by the market town,
cropping one staple without forethought, steer
stedfastly ruinward year in year out,
grudging the labour and cost of manure,
drudging not for gain but fewer dollars loss
yet certain to make a bad bargain by
misjudging the run of prices. How glad
you will be when the state takes your farm for
arrears of taxes! No more cold daybreaks
saffron under the barbed wire the east wind
thrums, nor wet noons, nor starpinned nights! The choir
of gnats is near a full-close. The windward
copse stops muttering inwardly its prose
bucolics. You will find a city job
or relief — or doss-and-grub — resigned to
anything except your own numb toil, the
seasonal plod to spoil the land, alone.

1936

32

Let them remember Samangan, the bridge and tower
and rutted cobbles and the coppersmith's hammer,
where we looked out from the walls to the marble mountains,
ate and lay and were happy an hour and a night;

so that the heart never rests from love of the city
without lies or riches, whose old women
straight as girls at the well are beautiful,
its old men and its wineshops gay.

Let them remember Samangan against usurers,
cheats and cheapjacks, amongst boasters,
hideous children of cautious marriages,
those who drink in contempt of joy.

Let them remember Samangan, remember
they wept to remember the hour and go.

1937

33

To Anne de Silver

I

Not to thank dogwood nor
the wind that sifts
petals are these words,
nor for a record,

but, as notes sung and received
still the air,
these are controlled by
yesterday evening,

a peal after
the bells have rested.

II

Lest its meaning
escape the dogwood's
whiteness, these:

Days now
less bitter than
rind of wild gourd.
Cool breezes. Lips
moistened, there are words.

1938

34

To Violet, with prewar poems.

These tracings from a world that's dead
take for my dust-smothered pyramid.
Count the sharp study and long toil
as pavements laid for worms to soil.
You without knowing it might tread
the grass where my foundation's laid,
your, or another's, house be built
where my weathered stones lie spilt,
and this unread memento be
the only lasting part of me.

1941

35

Search under every veil
for the pale eyes, pale
lips of a sick child,
in each doorway glimpse
her reluctant limbs
for whom no kindness is,
to whom caress and kiss
come nightly more amiss,
whose hand no gentle hand
touches, whose eyes withstand
compassion. Say: Done, past
help, preordained waste.
Say: We know by the dead
they mourn, their bloodshed,
the maimed who are the free.
We willed it, we.
Say: Who am I to doubt?
But every vein cries out.

1947

36

See! Their verses are laid
as mosaic gold to gold
gold to lapis lazuli
white marble to porphyry
stone shouldering stone, the dice
polished alike, there is
no cement seen and no gap
between stones as the frieze strides
to the impending apse:
the rays of many glories
forced to its focus forming
a glory neither of stone
nor metal, neither of words
nor verses, but of the light
shining upon no substance;
a glory not made
for which all else was made.

1948

37 On the Fly-Leaf of Pound's Cantos

There are the Alps. What is there to say about them?
They don't make sense. Fatal glaciers, crags cranks climb,
jumbled boulder and weed, pasture and boulder, scree,
et l'on entend, maybe, *le refrain joyeux et leger*.
Who knows what the ice will have scraped on the rock it is
smoothing?

There they are, you will have to go a long way round
if you want to avoid them.
It takes some getting used to. There are the Alps,
fools! Sit down and wait for them to crumble!

1949

SECOND BOOK OF ODES

1

A thrush in the syringa sings.

'Hunger ruffles my wings, fear,
lust, familiar things.

Death thrusts hard. My sons
by hawk's beak, by stones,
trusting weak wings
by cat and weasel, die.

Thunder smothers the sky.
From a shaken bush I
list familiar things,
fear, hunger, lust.'

O gay thrush!

1964

2

Three Michaelmas daisies
on an ashtray;
one abets love;
one droops and woos;

one stiffens her petals
remembering
the root, the sap
and the bees' play.

1965

3 Birthday Greeting

Gone to hunt; and my brothers,
but the hut is clean, said the girl.
I have curds, besides whey.

Pomegranates, traveller;
butter, if you need it,
in a bundle of cress.

Soft, so soft, my bed.
Few come this road.
I am not married: —— yet

today I am fourteen years old.

1964

4

You idiot! What makes you think decay will
never stink from your skin? Your warts sicken
typists, girls in the tube avoid you. Must they
also stop their ears to your tomcat
wailing, a promise your body cannot keep?

A lame stag, limping after the hinds, with tines
shivered by impact and scarred neck — but
look! Spittle fills his mouth, overflows,
snuffing their sweet scent. His feet lift lightly
with mere memory of gentler seasons. Lungs
full of the drug, antlers rake back, he
halts the herd, his voice filled with
custom of combat and unslaked lust.

Did the girl shrink from David? Did she hug his
ribs, death shaking them, and milk dry
the slack teat from which Judah had sucked life?

1965

5

Under sand clay. Dig, wait.
Billy half full, none for the car.
Quartz, salt in well wall,
ice refract first ray.
Canvas udders sag, drip,
swell without splash the mirage
between islands. Knee-deep
camels, lean men, flap-dugged
matrons and surly children.

Aneiza, kin to the
unawed dynast haggling with God.
This brine slaked him as
this sun shrinks.

1965

6 What the Chairman Told Tom

Poetry? It's a hobby.
I run model trains.
Mr Shaw there breeds pigeons.

It's not work. You dont sweat.
Nobody pays for it.
You *could* advertise soap.

Art, that's opera; or repertory –
The Desert Song.
Nancy was in the chorus.

But to ask for twelve pounds a week –
married, aren't you? –
you've got a nerve.

How could I look a bus conductor
in the face
if I paid you twelve pounds?

Who says it's poetry, anyhow?
My ten year old
can do it *and* rhyme.

I get three thousand and expenses,
a car, vouchers,
but I'm an accountant.

They do what I tell them,
my company.
What do *you* do?

Nasty little words, nasty long words,
it's unhealthy.
I want to wash when I meet a poet.

They're Reds, addicts,
all delinquents.
What you write is rot.

>

Mr Hines says so, and he's a schoolteacher,
he ought to know.
Go and find *work*.

1965

7

Ille mi par esse deo videtur

O, it is godlike to sit selfpossessed
when her chin rises and she turns to smile;
but my tongue thickens, my ears ring,
what I see is hazy.

I tremble. Walls sink in night, voices
unmeaning as wind. She only
a clear note, dazzle of light, fills
furlongs and hours

so that my limbs stir without will, lame,
I a ghost, powerless,
treading air, drowning, sucked
back into dark

unless, rafted on light or music,
drawn into her radiance, I dissolve
when her chin rises and she turns to smile.
O, it is godlike!

1965

8

All you Spanish ladies

Carmencita's tawny paps
glow through a threadbare frock;
stance bold, and her look.
Filth guards her chastity,
Ay de mi chica!

Lips salty, her hair
matted, powdered with ash;
sweat sublimes from her armpit
when the young men go past

seeking silk and elaborate
manners and strange scent.
She turns to sigh,
lifting her hem to pick a louse from her thigh.
Ay de mi muchachita!

1965

9

All the cants they peddle
bellow entangled,
teeth for knots and
each other's ankles,
to become stipendiary
in any wallow;
crow or weasel
each to his fellow.

Yet even these,
even these might
listen as crags
listen to light
and pause, uncertain
of the next beat,
each dancer alone
with his foolhardy feet.

1969

10

Stones trip Coquet burn;
grass trails, tickles
till her glass thrills.

The breeze she wears
lifts and falls back.
Where beast cool

in midgy shimmer
she dares me chase
under a bridge,

giggles, ceramic
huddle of notes,
darts from gorse

and I follow, fooled.
She must rest, surely;
some steep pool

to plodge or dip
and silent taste
with all my skin.

1970

11 *At Briggflatts meetinghouse*

Boasts time mocks cumber Rome. Wren
set up his own monument.
Others watch fells dwindle, think
the sun's fires sink.

Stones indeed sift to sand, oak
blends with saints' bones.
Yet for a little longer here
stone and oak shelter

silence while we ask nothing
but silence. Look how clouds dance
under the wind's wing, and leaves
delight in transience.

1975

12

Perche no spero

Now we've no hope of going back,
cutter, to that grey quay
where we moored twice and twice unwillingly
cast off our cables to put out at the slack
when the sea's laugh was choked to a mutter
and the leach lifted hesitantly with a stutter
and sulky clack,

how desolate the swatchways look,
cutter, and the chart's stained,
stiff, old, wrinkled and uncertain,
seeming to contradict the pilot book.
On naked banks a few birds strut
to watch the ebb sluice through a narrowing gut
loud as a brook.

Soon, while that northwest squall wrings out its cloud,
cutter, we'll heave to
free of the sands and let the half moon do
as it pleases, hanging there in the port shrouds
like a riding light. We have no course to set,
only to drift too long, watch too glumly, and wait,
wait.

1980 [1977]

OVERDRAFTS

Darling of Gods and Men, beneath the gliding stars
you fill rich earth and buoyant sea with your presence
for every living thing achieves its life through you,
rises and sees the sun. For you the sky is clear,
the tempests still. Deft earth scatters her gentle flowers,
the level ocean laughs, the softened heavens glow
with generous light for you. In the first days of spring
when the untrammelled allrenewing southwind blows
the birds exult in you and herald your coming.
Then the shy cattle leap and swim the brooks for love.
Everywhere, through all seas mountains and waterfalls,
love caresses all hearts and kindles all creatures
to overmastering lust and ordained renewals.
Therefore, since you alone control the sum of things
and nothing without you comes forth into the light
and nothing beautiful or glorious can be
without you, Alma Venus! trim my poetry
with your grace; and give peace to write and read and think.

(Lucretius)

1927

Yes, it's slow, docked of amours,
        docked of the doubtless efficacious
bottled makeshift, gin; but who'd risk being bored stiff
every night listening to father's silly sarcasms?

If your workbox is mislaid
        blame Cythera's lad . . . Minerva
's not at all pleased that your seam's dropped for a fair sight
of that goodlooking athlete's glistening wet shoulders

when he's been swimming and stands
        towelling himself in full view
of the house. Ah! but you should see him on horseback!
or in track-shorts! He's a first-class middleweight pug.

He can shoot straight from the butts,
        straight from precarious cover, waistdeep
in the damp sedge, having stayed motionless daylong
when the driven tiger appears suddenly at arms'-length.

(Horace)

1931

Please stop gushing about his pink
neck smooth arms and so forth, Dulcie; it makes me sick,
badtempered, silly: makes me blush.
Dribbling sweat on my chops proves I'm on tenterhooks.
— White skin bruised in a boozing bout,
ungovernable cub certain to bite out a
permanent memorandum on
those lips. Take my advice, better not count on your
tough guy's mumbling your pretty mouth
always. Only the thrice blest are in love for life,
we others are divorced at heart
soon, soon torn apart by wretched bickerings.

(Horace)

1931

Verse and Version

In that this happening
        is not unkind
it put to
        shame every kindness

mind, mouths, their words,
        people, put sorrow
            on
        its body

before sorrow it came
        and before every kindness,
happening for every sorrow
        before every kindness

(Louis Zukofsky)

quia id quod accidit
        non est immitis
pudebat omnia
        mitiora.

mens, ora, dicta horum,
        hominesque, tristitiam
superimponunt
        eius membra.

prius quam tristitia accidit,
        omnisque prius quam mitiora;
accidit pro omnibus tristitiis
        prius quam omnia mitiora.

(Basil Bunting)

1932

Once, so they say, pinetrees seeded on Pelion's peak swam
over the clear sea waves to the surf on the beaches of Phasis
when the gamesome fleece-filchers, pith of Argos, picked for a foray,
bearded the surge in a nimble ship, deal sweeps swirling the waters.
The Lady of Citadels shaped them a light hull for darting to windward
and laid the cutaway keel with her own hands and wedded the timbers.
That ship first daunted untamed Amphitrite. When her forefoot
scattered the fickle calm and oarwrenched waves kindled with spindrift
the mermaids rose from the dazzling sluices of the sound to gaze at the marvel.
Then, ah then! mortal eyes, and by day, had sight of the sea-girls
and marked their naked bodies stretched breasthigh out of the tiderace.
Forthwith, thus the tale runs, love of Thetis flamed up in Peleus
and Thetis took Peleus spite of the briefness of man's lifetime;
even her father himself deemed Peleus worthy of Thetis.

Health to you, heroes, brood of the gods, born in the prime season,
thoroughbreds sprung of thoroughbred dams, health to you aye, and again health!
I will talk to you often in my songs, but first I speak to you, bridegroom
acclaimed with many pinebrands, pillar of Thessaly, fool for luck, Peleus,
to whom Jove the godbegetter, Jove himself yielded his mistress,
for the sea's own child clung to you

— and why Catullus bothered to write pages and pages of this drivel mystifies me.

1933

When the sword of sixty comes nigh his head
give a man no wine, for he is drunk with years.
Age claps a stick in my bridle-hand:
substance spent, health broken,
forgotten the skill to swerve aside from the joust
with the spearhead grazing my eyelashes.

The sentinel perched on the hill top
cannot see the countless army he used to see there:
the black summit's deep in snow
and its lord himself sinning against the army.

He was proud of his two swift couriers:
lo! sixty ruffians have put them in chains.
The singer is weary of his broken voice,
one drone for the bulbul alike and the lion's grousing.

Alas for flowery, musky, sappy thirty
and the sharp Persian sword!
The pheasant strutting about the briar,
pomegranate-blossom and cypress sprig!
Since I raised my glass to fifty-eight
I have toasted only the bier and the burial ground.

I ask the just Creator
so much refuge from Time
that a tale of mine may remain in the world
from this famous book of the ancients
and they who speak of such matters weighing their words
think of that only when they think of me.

(Firdosi)

1935

Abu'abdulla Ja'far bin Mahmud Rudaki of Samarkand says:

All the teeth ever I had are worn down and fallen out.
They were not rotten teeth, they shone like a lamp,
a row of silvery-white pearls set in coral;
they were as the morning star and as drops of rain.
There are none left now, all of them wore out and fell out.
Was it ill-luck, ill-luck, a malign conjunction?
It was no fault of stars, nor yet length of years.
I will tell you what it was: it was God's decree.

The world is always like a round, rolling eye,
round and rolling since it existed: a cure for pain
and then again a pain that supplants the cure.
In a certain time it makes new things old,
in a certain time makes new what was worn threadbare.
Many a broken desert has been gay garden,
many gay gardens grow where there used to be desert.

What can you know, my blackhaired beauty,
what I was like in the old days?
You tickle your lover with your curls
but never knew the time when he had curls.
The days are past when his face was good to look on,
the days are past when his hair was jet black.
Likewise, comeliness of guests and friends was dear,
but one dear guest will never return.
Many a beauty may you have marvelled at
but I was always marvelling at her beauty.
The days are past when she was glad and gay
and overflowing with mirth and I was afraid of losing her.
He paid, your lover, well and in counted coin
in any town where was a girl with round hard breasts,
and plenty of good girls had a fancy for him
and came by night but by day dare not
for dread of the husband and the jail.

Bright wine and the sight of a gracious face,
dear it might cost, but always cheap to me.
My purse was my heart, my heart bursting with words,
and the title-page of my book was Love and Poetry.
Happy was I, not understanding grief,

any more than a meadow.
Silk-soft has poetry made many a heart
stone before and heavy as an anvil.

Eyes turned always towards little nimble curls,
ears turned always towards men wise in words,
neither household, wife, child nor a patron —
at ease of these trials and at rest!
Oh! my dear, you look at Rudaki
but never saw him in the days when he was like that.

Never saw him when he used to go about
singing his songs as though he had a thousand.
The days are past when bold men sought his company,
the days are past when he managed affairs of princes,
the days are past when all wrote down his verses,
the days are past when he was the Poet of Khorassan.

Wherever there was a gentleman of renown
in his house had I silver and a mount.
From whomsoever some had greatness and gifts,
greatness and gifts had I from the house of Saman.
The Prince of Khorassan gave me forty thousand dirhems,
Prince Makan more by a fifth,
and eight thousand in all from his nobles
severally. That was the fine time!
When the Prince heard a fair phrase he gave, and his men,
each man of his nobles, as much as the Prince saw fit.
Times have changed. I have changed. Bring me my stick.
Now for the beggar's staff and wallet.

(Rudaki)

1948

Shall I sulk because my love has a double heart?
Happy is he whose she is singlehearted!
She has found me a new torment for every instant
and I am, whatever she does, content, content.
If she has bleached my cheek with her love, say: Bleach!
Is not pale saffron prized above poppy red?
If she has stooped my shoulders, say to them: Stoop!
Must not a harp be bent when they string it to sing?
If she has kindled fire in my heart, say: Kindle!
Only a kindled candle sends forth light.
If tears rain from my eyes, say: Let them rain!
Spring rains make fair gardens. And if then
she has cast me into the shadow of exile, say:
Those who seek fortune afar find it the first.

(from a qasida of Manuchehri)

1949

Came to me —
Who?
She.
When?
In the dawn, afraid.

What of?
Anger.
Whose?
Her father's.
Confide!

I kissed her twice.
Where?
On her moist mouth.
Mouth?

No.
What, then?
Cornelian.
How was it?
Sweet.

(Rudaki)

1949

This I write, mix ink with tears,
and have written of grief before, but never so grievously,
to tell Azra Vamiq's pain,
to tell Laila Majnun's plight,
to tell you my own
unfinished story.
Take it. Seek no excuse.
How sweetly you will sing what I so sadly write.

(attributed, probably wrongly, to Sa'di)

1949

Last night without sight of you my brain was ablaze.
My tears trickled and fell plip on the ground. That I with
sighing might bring my life to a close they would name
you and again and again speak your name till
with night's coming all eyes closed save mine whose every
hair pierced my scalp like a lancet. That was
not wine I drank far from your sight but my heart's
blood gushing into the cup. Wall and door wherever
I turned my eyes scored and decorated with shapes
of you. To dream of Laila Majnun prayed for
sleep. My senses came and went but neither your
face saw I nor would your fantom go from me.
Now like aloes my heart burned, now smoked as a censer.
Where was the morning gone that used on other nights
to breathe till the horizon paled? Sa'di!
Has then the chain of the Pleiades broken
tonight that every night is hung on the sky's neck?

(Sa'di)

1949

You can't grip years, Postume,
that ripple away nor hold back
wrinkles and, soon now, age,
nor can you tame death

not if you paid three hundred
bulls every day that goes by
to Pluto, who has no tears,
who has dyked up

giants where we'll go aboard,
we who feed on the soil,
to cross, kings some, some
penniless plowmen.

For nothing we keep out of war
or from screaming spindrift
or wrap ourselves against autumn,
for nothing, seeing

we must stare at that dark, slow
drift and watch the damned
toil, while all they build
tumbles back on them.

We must let earth go and home,
wives too, and your trim trees,
yours for a moment, save one
sprig of black cypress.

Better men will empty
bottles we locked away,
wine puddle our table,
fit wine for a pope.

(Horace)

1971 [1969]

How Duke Valentine Contrived

(the murder of Vitellozzo Vitelli, Oliverotto da Fermo, Mr Pagolo and the Duke of Gravina Orsini) according to Machiavelli:

Duke Valentine had been in Lombardy with the King
clearing up the slanders the Florentines had put about
concerning the rising at Arezzo and in Val di Chiana,
and lay in Imola scheming
how to keep his men occupied,
how to turn John Bentivoglia
out of Bologna, a
city he coveted
to make his capital there.
The Vitelli heard of it
and the Orsini and the rest of the gang
and it was more than they would put up with
for they supposed
it would be their turn next
one by one.
So they held a diet and asked the Cardinal,
Pagolo,
Gravina Orsini, Vitellozzo Vitelli, Oliverotto da Fermo,
John Paul Baglioni tyrant of Perugia,
and Mister Anthony of Venafro
representing Pandolfo Petruccio boss of Siena,
and discussed the Duke's intentions,
estimated his strength,
and said it was time to put a stop to it.
Resolved:
not to let Bentivoglia down
and to get the Florentines
on their side.
So they sent fellows
to hearten the one and persuade the other.

As soon as the news got about the malcontents took heart
throughout the Duke's territory. Some from Urbino
went out against a fortress held by the Duke's troops
who were busy hauling timber to mend their stockade
and certain beams were lying on the drawbridge
so they couldnt raise it

so the conspirators
hopped up onto the bridge and thence into the fortress:
upon which the whole province rebelled
and sent for their old duke,
trusting the lords of the diet to see them through,
and sent them word; and *they* thought
they oughtnt to let a chance like that slip,
collected an army
and marched at once
to reduce the strongholds.

Meanwhile they sent to Florence a second time,
'the game was won already and such a chance
not likely to happen again,' but the Florentines
loathed
both the Vitelli and the Orsini for various reasons
and sent Niccolo Machiavelli to the Duke instead
to offer help.
He found him in Imola, scared at the turn of events,
just what he hadnt expected
happening all of a sudden,
his soldiers disaffected,
disarmed, so to speak,
and a war on his hands. But he cheered up
and thought he might stave things off
with a few men and a lot of negotiations
until he could raise a reliable army.

He borrowed men from the King
and hired a few himself
men at arms or
anybody who knew how to manage a horse.
He even paid them.

All the same
his enemies came to Fossombrone
where some of his men were gathered and scattered them,
so he had to negotiate for all he was worth
(and he was a first rate humbug).
It seems 'they were taking by force
what they might have as a gift
for the title was all that he wanted,
let them do the ruling.'

Whereupon they suspended hostilities
          and sent Mr Pagolo
to draw up an armistice: but the Duke
          kept on recruiting
          men and remounts,
sending them into Romagna to be less conspicuous.

When five hundred French lancers arrived
          he was strong enough to fight
but thought it safer and more sensible, on the whole,
          to cozen his enemies,
and worked it so that they signed a treaty
getting back their former powers
with four thousand ducats indemnity,
and he promised to let Bentivoglia alone
and marry into the family: and they,
to hand over Urbino and other occupied places
          not to make war without his consent,
          not to take jobs in other armies.

Duke Guidobaldo had to clear out of Urbino
and go back to Venice, but first
he had all the forts pulled down
for as he judged
the people were on his side and how was another to rule them
without forts? Duke Valentine
sent the rest of his men into Romagna
and went to Cesena about the end of November
where he spent several days discussing what was next to be done
with envoys from the Vitelli and Orsini
who were with their armies in Urbino,
but nothing came of it till they sent Oliverotto
and 'they would deal with Tuscany if he liked,
or if that wouldnt do, should they go take Sinigaglia?'
He replied he was friends with the Florentines
          but Sinigaglia
          would suit him nicely.

          A few days later
they sent to him that the town had surrendered
          but the citadel
would not surrender unless to the Duke in person,
          would he please come?

It seemed a good opportunity
and there could be no offence
in going by invitation,
so to put them off their guard
he sent away the French troops,
back into Lombardy except a hundred lancers
under the Right Reverend Ciandeles, his brother-in-law,
and left Cesena about the middle of December
for Fano where, as craftily has he knew how,
he set about persuading the Vitelli and Orsini
to wait for him in Sinigaglia, pointing out
unneighbourliness did not make for a durable peace,
whereas he was a man who could and would appreciate
his allies' arms and advice. Vitellozzo
was uneasy, he had learned from his brother's death
not to trust a prince he had once offended,
but Orsini argued
and the Duke sent presents
and rotten promises
till he consented.
The night before (that was December the thirtieth
fifteen hundred and two) — the night before
he was leaving Fano the Duke explained his plan
to eight men he thought he could trust,
amongst them the Reverend Michael
and d'Euna, the Right Reverend,
afterwards Cardinal: and charged them,
when Vitellozzo, Pagolo Orsino,
the Duke of Gravina and Oliverotto
should come out to meet him,
a couple to each of them,
these two to this one,
those two to that one,
should ride beside them
and make conversation
right into Sinigaglia and not lose sight of them
until they should come to his lodging and be taken.
He ordered all the troops,
more than two thousand horse,
ten thousand foot,
to be ready at daybreak on the Metaurus' banks,
a river five miles from Fano,

and on the last of December
joined them there and sent five hundred horse ahead,
then all the infantry, and after them
he himself with the rest of the men-at-arms.

Fano and Sinigaglia are towns of the Marches
fifteen miles apart on the Adriatic.
Going to Sinigaglia you have the mountains on your right,
very close to the sea in some places,
nowhere two miles away.
Sinigaglia city
stands about a bow-shot from the foot of the mountains
less than a mile from the shore. A little stream runs by it
wetting the wall towards Fano. When the road
is nearing Sinigaglia it skirts the mountains,
turns left, follows the stream,
and crosses by a bridge nearly opposite the gate
which is at right angles to the wall. Between it and the bridge
there is a suburb with a square, and a bend of the stream
bounds it on two sides.

Since the Vitelli and Orsini
had made up their minds
to wait for the Duke
and do the handsome thing
they had sent their soldiers out of Sinigaglia
to a castle six miles away to make room for the Duke's troops.
There were none left in the town but Liverotto's lot,
a thousand infantry and a hundred and fifty horse,
who were billetted in the suburb. This was how things stood
while Duke Valentine was on his way to Sinigaglia.

When the advance guard came to the bridge
they did not cross
but formed up on either side of the road in two files
and the infantry went between and halted inside the town.
Vitellozzo, Pagolo, and the Duke of Gravina
took mules and went to meet the Duke
with a small mounted escort; and Vitellozzo,
unarmed, in a tunic with green facings,
as glum as though he knew what was going to happen,
was
(considering his courage and the luck he had had in the past)

rather admirable. They say when he quit his people
to come and meet the Duke at Sinigaglia
he took a sort of last farewell,
bid the captains look after his family,
and admonished his nephews not to rely on the clan's luck
but remember their father's and uncle's valour.

These three came to the Duke and greeted him politely.
He received them smiling; and immediately
those whose task it was were about them.
But Liverotto
was waiting in Sinigaglia with his men
on the square outside his billets by the river,
drilling them to keep them out of mischief.
The Duke noticed, and tipped a wink to the Rev. Michael
who was responsible for Liverotto. Michael rode ahead
and 'it was imprudent to keep his men out of their billets
since the Duke's troopers were sure to occupy them
if found empty. Let him dismiss the parade
and come with him to the Duke.'
When the Duke saw him he called out
and Liverotto saluted and joined the others.

They rode into Sinigaglia,
dismounted at the Duke's lodgings
and went with him into an inner room,
and there they were taken;
and the Duke got straight back on horseback and ordered his scallawags
to pillage Liverotto's men and the Orsini's.
Liverotto's were handy and were pillaged.
The Orsini's and Vitelli's
some distance away,
having had wind of the matter,
had time to prepare.
They got away
in close order
with the Vitelli's traditional courage and discipline
in spite of hostile inhabitants and armed enemies.
The Duke's soldiers
were not satisfied with plundering Liverotto's men
and began to sack Sinigaglia, and if he hadnt

checked their insolence by hanging a lot of them
they would have finished the job.

Night fell, the rioting abated,
and the Duke thought it opportune
to put an end to Vitellozzo and Liverotto,
and had them led out to a suitable place and strangled.
Neither said anything worthy of the occasion,
for Vitellozzo begged them to ask of the Pope
a plenary indulgence for his sins,
while Liverotto was blubbering
and putting all the blame for their treason on Vitellozzo.

Pagolo and the Duke of Gravina Orsini
were left alive until the Pope sent word
he had taken Cardinal Orsino, Archbishop of Florence,
together with Mr James da Santa Croce:
upon which, on the eighteenth of January, at Castel della Pieve,
they were strangled in the same manner.

1933

UNCOLLECTED POEMS

The Pious Cat

by Obaid-e Zakani (and Basil Bunting)

BY YOUR LEAVE!
Sagacious and circumspect persons, attend!
This is a story of cats and mice,
how constantly they quarrel and contend.
It is short, truthful and precise.
Listen sharply. Do not miss a minute,
there is so much meaning and deep wisdom in it,
and learned science and politic guile
and rime and rhetoric and style.

BY HEAVEN'S DECREE there was a cat
in Haltwhistle, rough, rich and fat.
His fur was like a coat of mail
with lion's claws and leopard's tail.
When he went out and wailed at night
he made policemen shake with fright.
When he crouched in a flowerbed
big game hunters turned pale with dread.
All creatures beside him seemed tame.
Tibbald was this hero's name.

One day he visited the cellar
to scout for mice. Behind a pillar
he lay in ambush like a bandit
and it fell out as he had planned it –
a mouse crept from a crack and squeaked,
then leapt on a cask of beer (that leaked)
to drink; and shortly drank again.
Beer made him truculent and vain.

He snapped his fingers. "Where's that cat?
I'll make his skin into a doormat.
I'll teach him. I'll give him what-for.
Cats! One good mouse can lick a score.
Tibbald? Who's he? Let him sneer and purr,
he'll cringe to me. The cat's a cur."

Tibbald kept mum, but in the pause
you could hear him sharpening his teeth and claws.
When they were keen he made one jump
and caught the drunken mouse by the rump.

Mouse said: "Please mister, let me off.
I did not mean to boast and scoff.
What I said was said in liquor,
and tipsy tongues talk ten times quicker
than sober sense. Dont bear a grudge."
But Tibbald only answered "Fudge!
Bring your remarks to a fullstop,"
then ate him, and lapped the gravy up.

Next Tibbald went to the wash basin
he used to scrub his hands and face in,
and brushed his tail and combed his hair
and went to church and said this prayer:

"Lord, I confess the awful vice
of breakfasting on little mice,
but, Father, I repent sincerely.
I'll pay for it — not a pittance merely
but more than ample compensation.
To every surviving relation
or legal representative
of my poor victim I will give . . .
some coffee beans and leaves of tea
(on proper proof of identity,
birth certificate and passport
and other documents of that sort);
and I will gobble no more mice
in stews or sausages or pies,
nor *table d'hôte* nor *à la carte*.
An humble and a contrite heart
thinks lettuces and things like that
as sweet as a tender farmyard rat."
Here his repentance went so deep
that Tibbald could not choose but weep.

A mouse had hidden behind the pulpit.
He heard Tib's sob and watched him gulp it,
then ran all the way home and blurted:

"Good news! The cat has been converted.
He has turned charitable and meek
and means to fast six days a week
and on the seventh he will eat
acorns and trash instead of mouse-meat."
So all the mice cried: "Halleluia!
You dont suppose he'll relapse though, do ye?"

To give their gratitude a vent
seven eminent mice were sent
to take St. Tibbald a testimonial.
They marched with dignified ceremonial
and every mouse of them had brought
gifts of the most expensive sort.
The first mouse brought a bottle of Schiedam.
The second brought a roast leg of lamb.
The third mouse brought a red currant tart;
the fourth, spaghetti by the yard;
the fifth, hot dogs, with Cocacola.
The sixth brought bread and gorgonzola.
The seventh mouse brought a home-made
plumcake and a jug of lemonade.
Their manners were courteous and wellbred.
They bowed respectfully and said:
"Long live the cat! May we enquire,
is your health all you can desire?
Deign to accept this trifling token
of compliments we will leave unspoken."

"Upon my word," said Tib, "here's dinner!
Since breakfast I have grown much thinner
by fasting. Service and self-denial
were evidently worth the trial
since Just and Merciful Providence
sends me the Reward of Abstinence.
It sees my worth (Who can deny it?)
and furnishes me a richer diet.
I am sure a good conscience always led
to a larger share of daily bread.
Dear friends! Kind comrades! Fellow creatures!
Come nearer. Let me see your features."

The mice were flustered and in a dither,
yet they stepped forward, all together,
until they came within arm's length.
Then Tibbald suddenly showed his strength
and skill, and in a little moment
they found out what fair words from a foe meant,
for two to left and two to right
and one between his jaws to bite
(that makes five) he caught in so cunning a way
that only two were saved by running away.

"Woe and disaster! Fellow mice,
can you stand by and watch your neighbours
chewed before your very eyes?
Quick, oil your rifles, whet your sabres.
This foul aggression must be fought out."
Then all the mice cried: "Shame and pity!
Refer the facts to a committee
and while they are getting a report out
we'll have our mourning made to order,
hem handkerchiefs with a black border
to wipe our turbulent tears away
with due and dignified delay
until they tell us the King of Mice is
ready to meet this urgent crisis."

The king was proud and still and prim.
They brought him the report to skim.
The gist and pith of it was that:
"O King! Consider the cruel cat.
Once on a time that ravenous ratter ate
his daily mouse at a steady flat rate,
but since he took to prayers and pieties
he bolts us down by whole societies."

On this His Majesty undertook
to bring the criminal cat to book
and signed a royal proclamation
to mobilise the mousey nation
with rifles, bayonets, pistols, shells,
bombs, gas-masks and whatever else
might come in handy on a campaign,
such as antidotes against rat-bane.
>

His general held a grand parade
where twenty regiments displayed
smart uniforms of every shade.
Their caps were stiff, their buttons bright,
belts and boots polished, blouses tight,
hair cut, trousers pressed, webbing white
and ribbons blazed on every bust.
The swaggering general staff discussed:
"What are our war aims? How shall we state 'em?
What must we put in our ultimatum?
Breach of treaty? Gross atrocity?"
But when they had whittled away their verbosity
the king's ambassador, grave and sly,
carried this message: "Submit or die."

Now stop your ears, maid, matron, bride!
Switch off your hearing aids and hide
your faces in your wraps and shawls,
for Tibbald answered roughly a word in cat language that
means "Oh dear me, *what* nonsense".
But when he had watched the messenger mount he
called all the cats he could find in the county
and drilled them daily on the fells
to scratch, bite and fire off rockets and shells,
till one cold dawn they saw the host
of mice advancing from Solway coast.

Grim was the onslaught. Dead and dying
lay close as chipped potatoes frying
with hiss, roar, groan and bubble.
Arms, legs, tails, whiskers strewed the moor
like muck spread thick on winter stubble.
A million dead? No, no! Far more.
When Tibbald charged with his best equipped
storm troops, near mouse HQ he slipped
and wallowed in the mud. In a trice
he was tied up by nearly five score mice.
"Victory!" the victors cried.
"Now this war criminal must be tried."

The warrant was drawn under the king's signet. He
called on the judges for speed with dignity,
so as they assembled to try the crime

they slapped on their black caps to save time,
and sentenced Tibbald with solemn squeals
to be hung by the neck and then by the heels.
Fast workmen got the gallows built
while the court established Tibbald's guilt.

But while the High Tribunal tried him
the cat was gnawing the thongs that tied him
till with a resolute wrench he bust his
bonds and swallowed the Lord Chief Justice.
King, heroes, hangman, all the hamper,
I wish you could have seen them scamper.

That's where this story comes to a stop.
Now, if you think I made it up
you're wrong. I never. It wasnt me,
it was Obaid-e Zakani.

They Say Etna [*Active Anthology*]

They say Etna
belches as much poison
as Duisburg's pudenda
a littering sow
helpless in the railroad ditch.

Gear and gear.

The Muses Ergot and Appiol,
Mr Reader.
Mr Reader,
the Muses Ergot and Appiol.
What violence or fraud
shall we record?

Popone or Kreuger?
A skipper of the Middle Passage
stinkproof and deaf
with a hundred and seventy slaves
damaged in transit
for Jamaica?

Gear and gear.

Shall we consider the evidence in Hatry's case?
Or take Lord Bunting — or
UKASE.
No one to be found outside his own village
without
PAPERS.

Also, to encourage more efficient tillage,
2/3 of the produce to be presented to the temporal lord,
1/5 of the produce to be presented to the parish pope.
Yours you may say lovingly
Boris Godunof.
Or Stalin.

*

<

Item, the Duke of Slumberwear can get more
by letting the shooting although there is nothing to shoot
but a dozen diseased grouse and a few thin leveret
than by cleaning the ditches to make the ground healthy for sheep.

Lord Cummingway, Lord Tommandjerry, gear and gear,
Lord St Thomas and the Duke of Oppenham
think coals too cheap and costs too dear.

* * * * *
* * * * *
*

Gear, then, and gear,
                    gritty-grinding.
The governor spins, raises its arms.
Two three-inch steel cables scream from the drum
seventy fathoms.
We carry lighted Davy lamps,
stoop along narrow track.
Trucks scold tunnel.
In a squat cavern a
naked man on his
knees with a
pickaxe rips a nugget from the coalface.

Four lads
            led the pownies
a mile and a half through rising water,
lampless because the stife
asphyxiates lamps,
by old galleries to the North Shaft.
The water rose.
                    The others
came five months later when it was pumped out
and were buried by public subscription.
(The widows were provided for.)

*

Sing, Ergot and Appiol, didactically:
"Toil! Accumulate Capital!"
Capital is land upon which

work has been done (*vide* textbooks).
Capital is everything except the desert,
sea, untunnelled rock, upper air.
Breathed air
is Capital, though not rented:
70 million tons of solid matter
suspended in the atmosphere,
November, in London,
not by an act of God.

"The sea is his and he
who made it" — Who
made Holland and whose is it?

**MAN IS NOT AN END-PRODUCT,
MAGGOT ASSERTS.**

Make? For the making? The system limps.
Everything in this category is deformed,
even the bookkeeping.
Waste accumulates at compound interest.

**MAN IS AN END-PRODUCT AFFIRMS
BLASPHEMOUS BOLSHEVIK.**

[They Say Etna] [*Caveat Emptor*]

They say Etna
belches as much poison
as Duisburg's pudenda
a littering sow
helpless in the railroad ditch.

Gear and Gear.

The Muses Ergot and Appiol,
Mr Reader.
Mr Reader,
the Muses Ergot and Appiol.
What violence or fraud
shall we record?

Mellon or Kreuger?
A skipper of the Middle Passage
stinkproof and deaf
with a hundred and seventy slaves
damaged in transit
for Jamaica?

Gear and gear.

Shall we consider the evidence in Hatry's case?
Or take Lord Reading? Or
UKASE.
No one to be found outside his own village
without
PAPERS.
Also, to encourage more efficient tillage,
2/3 of the produce to be presented to the temporal lord,
1/5 " " " " " " parish pope.
Yours you may say lovingly
Boris Godunof . . . ?
Or Stalin?

*

Item, the Duke of Northumberland can get more
by letting the shooting although there is nothing to shoot

but a dozen diseased grouse and a few thin leveret
than by cleaning the ditches to keep the ground healthy for sheep.

Lord Joicey, Lord Londonderry, gear and gear,
Lord St Oswald and the Duke of Hamilton
think coals too cheap and costs too dear.
Steel, steal: steal, steel, Lord Weir.
(An exercise in free association.)

*

Gear, then, and gear,
                                        gritty grinding.
The governor spins, raises its arms.
Two three inch steel cables scream from the drum
seventy fathoms.
We carry lighted Davy lamps,
stoop along narrow track.
Trucks scold tunnel.
In a squat cavern a
naked man on his
knees with a
pickaxe rips a nugget from the coalface.

Four lads
                        led the pownies
a mile and a half through rising water,
lampless because the stife
asphyxiates lamps,
by old galleries to the North Shaft.
The water rose.
                        The others
came five months later when it was pumped out
and were buried by public subscription.
(The widows were provided for.)

*

Sing, Ergot and Appiol, didactically:
'Toil! Accumulate Capital!'
Capital is land upon which
work has been done (*vide* textbooks).
Capital is everything except the desert,
sea, untunneled rock, upper air.

Breathed air
is Capital, though not rented:
70 million tons of solid matter
suspended in the atmosphere,
November in London,
not by an act of God.

'The sea is his and he
who made it' — Who
made Holland and whose is it?

MAN IS NOT AN END-PRODUCT,
MAGGOT ASSERTS.

Make? For the making? The system limps.
Everything in this category is deformed,
even the bookkeeping.
Waste accumulates at compound interest.

MAN IS AN END-PRODUCT AFFIRMS
BLASPHEMOUS BOLSHEVIK.

UNCOLLECTED ODES

1

Coryphée gravefooted precise, dance to the gracious music
Thoughts make moving about, dance to the mind's delicate
symphony.

2 Against the Tricks of Time

Why should I discipline myself to verse
blasting everyday occurrences
with a false flavour of longevity,
malignantly prolonging
two corsets in a shopwindow,
mumbling indiscreet apologies as now
for what is singularly my own affair,
or prophesying Death, the kind unmaker
in whom no man has faith? Utterly poet, therefore
adrift, perusing neglected streets, I
suppose I ought to be ashamed of myself.

Farewell, ye sequent graces,
voided faces, still evasive!
Silent be our leave-taking
and mournful

as your nightwanderings
in unlit rooms or where the glow
of wallreflected streetlamp-light
the so slow moon

or hasty matches shadowed large
and crowded out by imps of night
glimmer on cascades of
fantom dancers.

Airlapped and silent Muses of light!
Cease to administer
poisons to dying memories to stir
pangs of old rapture,

cease to conspire
reunions of the inevitable seed
long blown, barren, sown, gathered
haphazard to wither.

>>

The dragon rides the middle air like an irresistible wind
flowing from and to all quarters simultaneously.
His birth is cloudlike of the sea and sun,
dispersion his life, his death acclaiming voices.
He is the foe, the harbinger. The saints invoke
Michael PROPTER NOS HOMINES ET PROPTER
NOSTRAM SALUTEM but the silent dragon's
insinuated claw in wincing souls
answers their supplication. He abets
indifference with ceaseless splendour
smudging sketched tables valiantly renewed.
He unsays all words that have passed between men.

3 Reading X's 'Collected Poems'

I . . .
cemetery of other men's bastards let
wane and peter out
because I am jealous of the Muse's fornications
and over timid to be a cuckold!

Meanwhile you
have raised a sufficient family of versicles;
like you in the main.

4 Hymn to alias Thor

STRENGTH
inked with a light brush
in the copper kettledrum

Strength,
the edges turned down.

(Inverted scorpion)
Focus, strength,
focus of percussions.

Sky convenient in conversation, viz.,
for efficiency's sake,
blindness to the street

where a taxidriver
cocks his patentleather cappeak
perpendicularly over a squint at the weather
calculating chances
of reaching rank's head before lunch.

Or, the neatcreased laundryfresh handkerchief
might anticipate a sneeze
(if linen web trembles to thinking's tuning)

at any nose's tauttipped touch,
receive in convulsion of bloom
snot,

lap over and
cherish till desiccated.

Such charges, coupled lightning,
the rainbow signature on each scroll warrants
genuine, beware of imitations!

Secondly

The soil refuses the lightning!
Desolate air stagnates over that valley,
winds putrefy, silence, the offered storm

limp, dust hangs damp,
thin mud sags in the air,
a deathstink 's over the whole valley,

vinestakes' curtain of leaves droop
mottled blue with the wash,
hard peaches, bitter figs,
the stream niggard trickle of gall,

and flies drag sweat over the eyelids
and sour lips.

Thirdly

Oftener the soil accepts the lightning.

5

The flat land lies under water
hedge-chequer-grill above concealing
(not long) heliotrope monotony.

Cold water shin-embracing clacks
desolately, no overtones. Lukewarm
moist socks trickle sea-boot squeezed
black gutters muttering between the toes.
Moreover it rains, drizzles.

Utter-horizon-penetrating glances
spoil only paupers towing derelict home
the flat land hedge-grilled heliotrope under water.

6

Gertie Gitana's hymn to waltzing,
come to think of it, that's the goods.
You, thirdrate muse, Polymnia-alias-Echo
who'll foster our offspring
begotten in a Waterloo Road three-and-sixpenny bed-and-breakfast
between indifference and bad habit
established by Erasmus and other idiots
nuts on the classics?
No inclination,
inclination at the wrong time, soul
not at home to callers:
its possibly ultimate inhumation
made flesh under a neat strewing of granite chips
complete with kerb. (But no stone,
Sadi's right, dogs would piss on it.)
Without science, if you please, or psychology!
A mere prescription, as:
'Take one look at the truth about yourself,
you'll never want another.'

'An odds-on favourite's unexciting but
dont back outsiders, its a mugs game',
out of the *selva oscura*, oracle
without authority, 'give over swanking.'

Omar observed: 'Sobriety is unworthy
of anything that has life.' Supplemented
that proposition: 'Turf's pretty till
our grave's turf's pretty.'

Then Barbara
bribing the brain with dud cheques
for any figure on the Bank of Aeolus
(paid up capital twentyone consonants
and five vowels, debtor to
sundry windbags sundry bags of wind,
cent per cent cover in the vaults, vocables
on call or short notice to any amount)
made up so skilfully you wouldnt know her
works the same con-game on the same dupe twice.

Muleteers recite Firdusi, scots sing Burns.
Precedent allows
a moder-rate kettledr-rum r-r-roulade. In practice
keep an eye on the crocodiles, all power
to the congress of murdering crocodiles.
Or check up that syncopated
metre a rising sea never
conforms to?
Double-tongueing a corked flute
descant to the bass:
'Less three per cent deducted for
our compulsory Superannuation Fund.'

O, 'count upon it as a truth next to your creed
that no one person in office of which he is master for life
will ever hazard that office for the good of his country,'
no pedant with established circulation
take Polymnia's hand.
Gertie Gitana's hymn to waltzing
's the goods, you third-rate muse
with your head in the gas oven.

7 Envoi to the Reader

From above the moon
    to below the fishes
nobody knows
    my secret heart.
Do you suppose
    I'd publish it?
Spell out a fart
    and have it printed?

8 Trinacria

1

Child, I have counted
all the stones in this wall . . .

Even today
to find you alone at home
was impossible.

2

My prospective brother-in-law
sent me a gift, a fan.
It had three different colours,
rose, scarlet and gold.

Everybody asked me:
What did that fan of yours cost you?
I answered: Nothing. My
sister's sweetheart gave it me.

3

On highest summits dawn comes soonest
(But that is not the time to give over loving.)

4

I went to Hell: never before had I been there!
I did not want to see my sweetheart.

She said to me: Scoundrel and dog!
These pains I undergo on your account.

I said to her: You did not love me,
there are fairer women than you.

9 A Song for Rustam

Tears are for what can be mended,
not for a voyage ended
the day the schooner put out.
Short fear and sudden quiet
too deep for a diving thief.
Tears are for easy grief.

My soil is shorn,
forests and corn.
Winter will bare the rock.
What has he left of pride
whose son is dead?
My soil has shaved its head.

The sky withers and stinks.
Star after star sinks
into the west, by you.
Whirling, spokes of the wheel
hoist up a faded day,
its sky wrinkled and grey.

Words slung to the gale
stammer and fail:
'Unseen is not unknown,
unkissed is not unloved,
unheard is not unsung;'
Words late, lost, dumb.

Truth that shone is dim,
lies cripple every limb.
Where you were, you are not.
Silent, heavy air
stifles the heart's leap.
Truth is asleep.

10

To abate what swells
use ice for scalpel.
It melts in its wound
and no one can tell
what the surgeon used.
Clear lymph, no scar,
no swathe from a cheek's bloom.

11

Such syllables flicker out of grass:
'What beckons goes'; and no glide lasts
nor wings are ever in even beat long.
A male season with paeonies, birds bright under thorn.
Light pelts hard now my sun's low,
it carves my stone as hail mud
till day's net drapes the haugh,
glaze crackled by flung drops.
What use? Elegant hope, fever of tune,
new now, next, in the fall, to be dust.

Wind shakes a blotch of sun,
flatter and tattle willow and oak alike
sly as a trout's shadow on gravel.
Light stots from stone, sets ridge and kerf quick
as shot skims rust from steel. Men of the north
'subject to being beheaded and cannot avoid it
of a race that is naturally given that way'.
'Uber sophiae sugens' in hourless dark,
their midnight shimmers like noon.
They clasp that axle fast.

Those who lie with Loki's daughter,
jawbones laid to her stiff cheek,
hear rocks stir above the goaf;
but a land swaddled in light? Listen, make out
lightfall singing on a wall mottled grey
and the wall growls, tossing light,
prow in tide, boulder in a foss.
A man shrivels in many days, eyes thirst for night
to scour and shammy the sky
thick with dust and death.

12

Dentdale conversation

Yan tan tethera pethera pimp
nothing to waste but nothing to skimp.
Lambs and gimmers and wethers and ewes
what do you want with political views?
Keep the glass in your windows clear
where nothing whatever's bitter but beer.

UNCOLLECTED OVERDRAFTS

Night swallowed the sun as
the fish swallowed Jonas.

(Sa‘di)

Many well-known people have been packed away in cemeteries,
there is no longer any evidence that they ever existed.
That old corpse they shovelled under the dirt,
his dust's so devoured not a bone of him's left.

Naushervan's honourable name survives because he was open-
handed,
though a lot has happened since Naushervan died.
– Better be open-handed, What's-your-name, (write it off:
Depreciation)
before the gossip goes: 'What's-his-name's dead.'

(Sa'di)

Light of my eyes, there *is* something to be said.
Drink and give to drink while the bottle is full.
Old men speaking from experience, as I told you:
'Indeed, you will grow old.
Love has respectable people chained up for the torture.
You'd like to rumple his hair? Give up being good.
Rosary and veil have no such relish as drink.'

Put it in practice. Send for the wine-merchant.
Amongst the drinkers, one lifetime,
one purse cannot cramp you.
A hundred lives for your dear!
(In love's business the devil lacks not ideas,
but listen, listen with your heart to the angel's message.)

Maple leaves wither, gaiety's not everlasting.
Wail, O harp! Cry out, O drum!
May *your* glass never want wine!
Look gently behind you and drink.
When you step over the drunks in your gold-scattering gown
spare a kiss for *Hafiz* in his flannel shirt.

(Hafiz)

Desinas ineptire

O everlastingly self-deluded!
  If there's no love for you there's nothing for it
but to go crazy. Anyway, dont set up for
  a paragon of self-restraint.
Love's dizziness cant invade a head
  dizzy with alcohol?
You're jaundiced, misery-hideous!
  Anybody can read your symptoms.
Give respectability and pride the go-by, *Hafiz*,
cadge yourself a drop of booze and get
                    crapulously drunk.

(Hafiz)

Isnt it poetical, a chap's mind in the dumps?
Of course our cliché's true:
'Your lips the seal on my passport,
that's a hundred empires in hand.'
So, my heart, dont wince when they mock you,
mockeries rightly regarded are riches:
who doesnt take ghoulish sarcasms thus,
his marble was hacked out in haste.
Wine and tears in a cup — each offers it someone;
that's only polite, under Providence:
the routine of the perfumery business,
one rose crushed, one kept.
And it's false, the frenzy quitting *Hafiz*,
the durable frenzy warranted to
last ever so long.

(Hafiz)

I'm the worse for drink again, it's
got the better of me.
A thousand thanks to the red wine
put colour in my face.
I'll kiss the hand that gathered the grapes.
May he never trudge who trod them out!

You'd dock my drink for the fast, you!
God doesnt trifle.
Born with 'Rake' scrawled
on my forehead, dare you erase it?
Talk about wisdom! When it comes to dying
the soul may struggle – like a doomed hero.

Settle down, no nagging, placidity
's silk next your skin. If you
want eternity do so
they'll never use past tense of you.
Drink as *Hafiz*, you'll gather impetus
world without end.

(Hafiz)

The Beginning of the Stories

Country gentlemen such as there used to be, good talkers,
who is it they say set up the throne?
Who put on the crown? No one keeps track of the past,
or maybe a few
remember
word for word what their fathers told them—
who won a name, excelled ...

Let one who has learned the tales of the heroes
from books our ancestors wrote in the ancient language
tell you: throne and cap
Kayumart found out and was king.

When Sol entered Aries
Earth put on glory and order and honour:
the sun so shone in the Ram
the world came of age of a sudden.
Kayumart the husbandman
set up his home in the mountains
for his luck and power began there;
and he and his horde wrapped themselves in leopardskins
— civilization's start,
for clothes were a new thing and regular meals new.

Thirty years he was king,
and his throne sparkled, he a young cypress
on it, with the full moon at its tip.
All kinds of wild beasts made their dens in his neighborhood
and used to bow down to his crown's fresh splendour,
and took to worshipping it
and learned their religion there.

etc etc etc

(Firdosi)

From 'Faridun's Sons'

I

Afaridun cut the world in three,
Rome and the West, the Turks and
China, the desert and Iran.
First he thought over Salm,
chose him Rome and the West,
'Lead an army west in parade order,
take the throne and the title Lord of the West.'
He gave Tur Turan,
set him over the Turks and China.
Tur took troops the king picked out,
made sure of this throne, buckled his belt on,
began showing his bounty.
Wealthy men scattered jewels on him,
everybody acknowledged him King of Turan.
Iraj's turn. His father gave him
Iran city and all Iran,
the desert, its spearmen,
the crown paramount into the bargain
(seeing he thought him ablest)
and sword, seal, signet and kingly cap.
The shrewd dignified chiefs of the council
did him homage, Lord of Iran.
All three viceroys born in the purple
took their places in peace and all serene.

2

A long time, Fate keeping her face veiled.
Faridun grew old, dust drifted over the garden,
a changed conversation, strength turned weakness by age,
and the nobles huffed when any business was muffed.
Salm's heart slid away, his ways and ambitions altered,
greed swamped his mind, he brooded in public, chafed
at the settlement giving the youngest the Golden Throne.
Bitter, forever scowling,
he sent a messenger by fast camel
to open his heart to the King of China.

'Live forever in joy and gladness!
Consider, King of the kings of the Turks and China!
one who has snapped off prudence from his mind
has put a mean-spirited goodlooking bastard over us.
Think of it! Do they tell such tales of our forebears?
We were three sons fit for a throne, the least is preferred.
By rights the Seal's mine,
amnt I eldest, aye, and shrewdest?
But if I am passed over
isnt it right you should have it?
We would do well to give our father a piece of our mind,
giving Iran and the desert and Yaman to Iraj,
and me Rome and the West and you
the Steppes and China.
Our junior lords it in Iran.
What standing have we in such a settlement?
There is no sense in your father.'

The envoy sped to Turan, his piece by heart,
and filled Tur's skull with wind. Tur
heard him out then suddenly raged like a wild beast.

'Say to the king: Remember this, our father deceived us
when we were young.
With his own hand he planted the tree
whose fruit is blood and venom its foliage.
Now let us meet, talk, plan and gather an army.' <

The messenger gone he chose from among the nobility
a smoothspoken ambassador.
'Give the king this message from me:
No gentleman puts up with usurpation
or fraud. This business should be done out of hand.
What's long prepared is bungled.'

Fate was stripped stark. The brothers started
from Rome and China with honeyed poison,
met, discussed policy public and private.

3

They chose a sharpwitted, eloquent, prudent priest
with a good memory, cleared the room,
wrangled over rancorous phrases.
Salm who had shed all shame drafted the despatch.
He told the herald:
'Dont hang an arse,
dont let your own dust overtake you,
nor the wind either,
get to Faridun before the wind. Put
everything else but this journey out of your head.
Dont get down till you come to the castle,
greet Faridun from both sons, then say:

"There ought to be the fear of God in both worlds.
A young man might put his hope in old age
but hair once white will never grow black again.
Put off too late in this hard world,
world-without-end will be hard on you.
God gave you the world for your own from sun to soil
but you want to change law and custom to suit yourself.
You paid no heed to equity in your settlement.
Three sons, all cool and bold: an eldest, a youngest:
none abler than the rest, no excuse for preference.
You have made *one* Dragon of the Eclipse,
raised *one* to the clouds, crowned *one* on your cushions,
settled your gaze on *one*. His father our father,
our mother no less than his. You cut off our succession.
If this is the World-king's justice,
by no means blessings upon such justice.
Let the crown be lifted from that base head
and the world be rid of him
(give him a corner of ground
to sit there as we do, disgraced, out of sight)
or else I will bring an army with maces,
Turkish and Chinese horsemen, keen Roman soldiers,
to lay Iran waste and slay Iraj."'

The priest conned this surly message,
kissed the ground, showed his back,
rode till sparks flew in the wind.

Coming to Afaridun's court
he saw the ramparts far away,
towers lost in the clouds,
walls from mountain to mountain,
nobles about the gate,
only the greater nobles behind the curtain,
lions and leopards chained on the left,
huge war-elephants chained on the right,
and so many nobles and warriors talk
blended in one heartshaking roar
till he fancied the building another world,
the army afoot around it fairies.
Watchful sentinels told the Great King of his coming.
A dignified chamberlain bade lift the curtain.
The priest dismounted and went into the presence.
His glance lit on Faridun's form and was held:
cypress-tall, ruddy face, rosy cheek, hair like the vine,
smiling, modest, royally gentle voice.
He grovelled, beslavered the floor with kisses.
Instantly Faridun signalled Rise,
set him before him in honour.

'Are my dear sons happy and well?'

Next:
'The long road,
plains, hills, valleys, have tired you.'
'Noble king, may the court enjoy you forever.
Those you are asking about are as you wish them,
living stainless lives in the power of your name.
... ... I am a slave, unworthy of the King,
a man of no family, unclean to boot,
with a surly message from an angry sender.
No fault of mine. If your Majesty says so,
I will recite it.'
'Do.'
He did not leave out a word.

4

Afaridun listened intently.
The more he heard the angrier he grew.

'You neednt apologise, it is just as I supposed,
just what I expected of them. Say to those
two dirty stupid brainless Ahrimans:

"Good! You have shown what you are,
your message becomes you.
If you've bundled my teaching out of mind,
never heard tell of commonsense,
have no fear of God nor shame before God,
for sure there can be no flaw in your judgement!
Yes, my hair used to be black at one time,
my back straight, my cheeks plump.
But Time, that's bent my back, doesnt grow feeble,
Heaven's where it was.
You've an easy gait at your time of life,
it will last you barely a moment.
By God's holiest name! by the sun! by the soil that feeds us!
by my throne and crown! by Venus! by the moon!
I have never done you any wrong.
I got a committee together,
men of experience, astronomers and priests,
spent a long time contriving
a just division of the world with their help.
I wanted to do what was right and nothing else,
there was nothing crooked about it from first to last.
I was full of the fear of God.
I wanted to do what was right and nothing else.
The world came into my power prosperous:
I wanted not to dissipate its wealth,
I wanted to leave it to my dear sons as prosperous.
Now that Ahriman has enticed you away
from my guidance to dark and crooked paths
we shall see whether the Creator will approve of your doings.
Can you take in a proverb from the prophets?
'You shall reap as you sow: our eternal home is not here.'
You are putting passion in reason's room. Why
have you made a compact with devils?

When your soul leaves its mould those dragons will maul it.
Time I was quitting the world,
not a time for strife and bitterness.
This is the message an aged man
who used to have three noble sons once, sends you:
When the heart is drained of desire
the revenue's nothing but rubbish.
If a man will sell his brother for rubbish
they are right to deny whatever he claims by birth.
The world has seen many your like and will see many more,
will never be kindly to any. Henceforward
seek those things you think may procure your ransom
on the day of God's reckoning."'

Salm's man listened, kissed the ground,
turned away, went like a friend of the wind's.
Faridun sent for the dear prince and told him how things stood:

'These touchy brothers of yours are marching against us
from the West. Their stars have ordained
they shall take pleasure in doing wrong.
But the wellheads of the two continents
are not in *them*. Bitter fruit to those lands!
Brother as brother to brother
only in office: when your cheek yellows
no one to sit by the bed:
cherish a sword till your head's turned:
these are the profundities
your brothers have sent from the ends of the earth to teach me.
If you've a mind to war, get ready for war.
Open the treasury. Pack up your things.
If you dont reach out for your breakfast cup
others will drink it up for you, my boy!
But dont look for any ally
apart from uprightness and plaindealing.'

Iraj fixed his eyes on his dear father and said:

'See how unsteady life is,
for it passes over us like a wind
and why should a wise man repine
though poppy cheeks are continually fading,
clear minds growing dim?

As wealth it began, as poverty ends,
goes out like a pauper ejected from his lodging
with a clay mattress and a brick for pillow.
Then why should we plant a tree today
that however long it may stand
must be watered with blood to flower in vengeance?
There were kings before us,
lords of the throne and seal and sword,
and there will be others after us, but none before us
had blood-feud for a custom.
Let me take pattern by you,
I will not pass a lifetime wrangling.
There will be no need of royal trappings
nor any escort at all if I hurry to tell them:
"Dear noble brothers, very dear to me,
dont be angry, dont harbour revenge.
Do you think the domination of this world holds out such hopes?
Didnt it lure Jamshed? –
but took his crown from him and his life afterwards.
You too, I too, in the end
shall taste a fate like his."
So persuade away their vengeance.
Isnt that seemlier than taking vengeance?'

Faridun said:
'My son,
your brothers are going about looking for a fight
and you are for making it up, and I
have occasion to remember another proverb:
"If the moon shines, that's no wonder,"
which applies to your answer,
all for affection and mutual ties,
and applies to your fate,
since a man who peers down a dragon's throat,
the stench will stifle him however righteous.
Nevertheless,
if that's your intention get ready and go quickly
but take a few orderlies with you, and a letter
I am going to write with an aching heart
on the offchance it may bring you home safe and sound,
for I have no life but in you.'

5

This is the World-king's letter:

'Praise God who is and ever shall be!
A letter of good advice
to two rising suns, two august valiant powers,
King of the West and King of China,
from him who has seen every aspect of the world,
found out its secrets, swung sword and mace,
added lustre to a famous crown,
foretold night at daybreak, kept the keys of fear and hope,
eased all hardships, brought in enlightenment.
For my part I dont want the crown,
nor yet a crammed treasury nor royalty's trappings.
I want my three sons to be at peace and easy
when my long labour's done.
The brother you worry about (though he never
caused anyone worry) is hurrying to you
because of the fuss you are making
and because he is longing to see you.
He has spurned the kingdom and chosen you
as befits a magnanimous man,
swapped a throne for a saddle
to do you what service he can.
Remember he is your youngest brother
to love, pet and take care of.
Cherish his soul as I have cherished his body.
Send him back after a while
the better for his visit.'

They sealed the letter. Iraj
went out of the palace along the road and was gone
with a few indispensable servants, old men and boys.
All the way he had no idea what his brothers intended.
They brought the whole army to meet him.
Their scowls deepened seeing he was glad to see them.
The truculent pair made small talk against the grain,
two men full of malice,
conducting one serene one to their headquarters.
When the army saw how royally Iraj bore himself
they couldnt keep admiration out of their looks

till when Salm dismissed the parade they went off
in couples and threes
muttering Iraj's name
saying to each other:

'There's a king for you! There's nobody like him.
The man to be overlord without a doubt.'

Salm in low spirits watching them go's bitterness doubled,
he scowled worse than ever,
went and joined Tur and the privy council
discussing this and that,
high policy and provincial business.
During the talk Salm said to Tur on the quiet:

'The army scattered in little groups
when we got back from the march: did you notice?
All the way home they were gazing at Iraj.
It's not the army it was when we set out.
I dont like the look of affairs—trouble on trouble.
As far as I can see neither your troops nor mine
will stand any other king after this but Iraj.
You'll be thrown down for him to trample on
if you dont root him up—now!'

They adjourned the sitting
and spent the night plotting.

6

At early dawn the blackguards could wait no longer,
came out and went in state to the royal quarters.
Iraj saw them and ran to meet them affectionately,
received them in his tent, but their talk
was nothing but Why and Wherefore. Tur said:

'Why have *you* assumed the crown?
you, younger than us,
Lord Paramount of Iran, is that as it should be?
and we to put up with obscurity.
Your elder brother the irksome West,
you the splendour and the revenue?
The division that Potentate made
was all in your favour.'

Iraj gave him a gentle answer:

'Look to get all you ask for by peaceful means.
I dont want the crown any longer,
nor the title nor the troops,
nor Iran nor the West either nor yet China
nor to be a king, nor any parcel of ground.
Power that leads to dissension's a great misfortune.
Luck seems to have you in tow,
they lay your head on a brick at the last for all that.
I have laid down the crown, handed over the great seal,
dont bear me a grudge.
I have no quarrel with you, you neednt
guard against me.
I dont wish you bad luck behind your back.
My tastes are modest.
I dont pretend to be more than another man.'

No impression on Tur. Not gratified. Did not want peace.
He jumped up from his chair and stalked about storming:
passing the chair, seized it, heavy with gilt,
swung it, struck Iraj over the head.

'For God's sake, for our father's sake,
is this your meaning? Dont
be a murderer, you will pay for it in the end!

Dont kill me, let me go
where you will never hear of me again.
Will you take my life and I your guest?
Somewhere where I can work for a living,
at the ends of the earth.
Not even an ant! Dont injure even an ant,
it has life, life is sweet.
Why seek my life, your brother's life?
Bringing such grief
on your father in his old age?
You have all you wanted. Dont shed blood.
Dont pick a quarrel with Almighty God!'

Tur heard. Made no answer.
Pulled a dagger from his boot,
ripped up his belly
so that the blood covered him like a shroud
matching the red of his cheek and he died.
He severed the head with his knife and finished the job.

Why does God abandon his nurslings?
Who are his friends? What's his character?
He brings so many matters for tears to pass.

They stuffed Iraj's head with amber and musk
to send to his father with this message:

'Here is the spoiled child's head
that wore our ancestors' crown.
Now crown it, enthrone it as much as you like:
the trunk is felled.'

The ruffians parted and went home,
one to China one to Rome.

7

Faridun watched the road
and the army missed the young king.
When the time came for his homecoming
they were getting a welcome ready,
wine, music and dancers.
They had fetched the drums and led the elephants
out of the stable,
hung the whole land with garlands.
. . . A cloud of dust on the road,
presently a fast camel,
a rider in mourning, keening,
a gold box on his lap,
in the box a piece of brocade,
in the brocade . . . !
Came to Faridun
pale, crying, sighing woe,
they could not make out what he said,
prised the lid off the box,
snatched the cloth, there was Iraj's head.
Faridun fell from his horse like a dead man.
The army tore their clothes,
not for this the king
led them out, this return, torn flags,
drums reversed, drawn faces;
kettledrums, elephants foreheads, draped black,
the horses splashed with indigo,
a dismounted general, an army dismounted,
dust on their heads, officers gnawing their arms,
or calling out:
'Never fancy Fate favours you,
the heavens turning above us
ready to snatch whatever they smile on.
Defy them, they smile. Call them Friend,
they never return your devotion.'

To Iraj's garden,
merry at festival time,
Afaridun with unsteady steps,
clutching the young king's head,
his son's head.

He looked at the gorgeous throne—
tawdry without the king,
and the pool, the cypresses,
rosetrees, willows, quinces.
When they strewed dust on the throne
a wail from the army,
groaning, tearing their hair, shedding tears,
clawing their own cheeks.
Faridun put on the ritual crimson sash,
set the pleasure house alight,
dug up the flowerbeds, burned the cypresses,
all the eye's delight,
and hugging Iraj's head turned to heaven:

'God of justice, see how the innocent fare!
His head, the marks of the knife on the neck, I have it.
His body, devoured.
Scald those cruel hearts, let their days be black, all,
blister their hearts, let their hurts fester
till brute beasts pity them.
You who adjust all things, let me find refuge from Time
till I see one of Iraj's blood make ready for vengeance,
till I see those heads cut off like this innocent head.
Then of your mercy let the soil take my measure.'

He mourned so long on the bare ground
his beard grew down to his chest. Wept his sharp eyes blind,
behind closed doors in the great hall.
'You brave young man, no king ever died as you did,
no king beheaded by devils
wild beasts' maws his coffin.'

There was such crying and keening
even the animals could get no sleep.
Assemblies, every man and woman
throughout the country with tears in their eyes,
in black, past consolation,
many a day, as though all life were death.

(Firdosi)

Baudelaire in Cythera

Heart trapezing gaily about the ropes: hull
a-roll under a clear sky.
— That sombre beach?
— Songfamous Cythera.
— Indeed?
—Yes,
bachelor's paradise. Look at it ... wretched place!
Festivals of love, eh? ... whispers and all that?

The moist smell of amours clings to it, isle of blown
roses, still adored. Devout whimpers drift
above like pollen, like ringdove murmurs. A harsh
stony hungry land, harassed by shrill cries.
Nothing Baedeker stars: though I did see something ...

Not a temple shaded by ancient planes, nor yet
a young priestess of love slacking her tunic to
feel the breeze. We ranged very close in shore,
so close our sails set the birds fluttering over a
black gallows cut out of the sky.

They were perched on
carrion, their beaks driven precisely into
putrid sores. The eyes, rotted. Heavy bowels
dangling. Vultures had castrated him. Dogs
were howling.

Cytherean!
Child of sublime skies! Comic corpse, wretched
contemptible corpse!

Bright sky, shining sea, Venus' land; Baudelaire
bows to Baudelaire through the looking-glass.

(After Baudelaire)

Amru'l Qais and Labīd and Ahktal and blind A'sha and Qais
who keened over the bones of dead encampments and fallen tents,
as we mourn for the ruins of poetry and broken rhymes —
Bu Nuvās and Bu Haddād and Bu Malik bin al Bashar,
Bu Duvaid and Bu Duraid and Ibn Ahmad. Do you hear
him who sang 'She has warned us,' who sang 'The honest sword,'
who sang 'Love has exhausted' — ?
Bu'l Ata and Bu'l Abbās and Bu Salaik and Bu'l Mathil,
and the bard of Lavaih and the Harper of Herat.
Where are the wise Afghans, Shuhaid and Rudaki,
and Bu Shakūr of Balkh and Bu'l Fath of Bust likewise.
Bid them come and see our noble century
and read our poetry and despair —

(Manuchehri)

Night is hard by. I am vexed and bothered by sleep.
Dear my girl, bring me something to cure me of sleep.
Not quick and alert, as well be dead as asleep:
what argument have the dead? How shall the sleeping answer?

I for one strive not to die before my time.
Who shall hire the untimely dead? Have they compensation?
I snatch the sleep from my eyes with strong wine,
aye! with strong wine, foe of a young man's sleep.

Much do I wonder at him whom sleep bears away
where there is yet a bottle of wine in the house,
and yet more wonder at him who drinks without music,
without an air on the harp, guzzles his wine.
No horse will drink without you whistle to him:
is a man less than a horse, water more than wine?

Three things, and the more the better, nourish the free:
one is wine and one is music and one is meat.
No cash let there be among us, no book, no dice:
these are three things unfitting to our freedom.
Books to the school, cash to the marketplace,
dice to the taverns of the low.
We, men of wine are we, meat are we, music . . .
Well, then! wine have we, meat have we, music . . .

(Manuchehri)

You, with my enemy, strolling down my street,
you're a nice one! Arent you ashamed to meet me?
Didnt you call me 'malignant', and 'quarrelsome'?
Dont you complain of my 'impossible' character?

You looked round and found someone more to your liking.
You escaped neatly from my 'temper' and 'dullness'.
Plainly, your love is flooding his brook:
the day is gone when it trickled into mine.

Now that you've found someone such as you wanted
why do you blunder so far down my street?

(Manuchehri)

The thundercloud fills meadows with heavenly beauty,
gardens with plants, embroiders plants with petals,
distils from its own white pearls brilliant dyes,
makes a Tibet of hills where its shadow falls,
San'a of our fields when it passes on to the desert.
Wail of the morning nightingale, scent of the breeze,
frenzy a man's bewildered, drunken heart.
Now is the season lovers shall pant awhile,
now is the day sets hermits athirst for wine.

Shall I sulk because my love has a double heart?
Happy is he whose she is singlehearted!
She has found me a new torment for every instant
and I am, whatever she does, content, content.
If she has bleached my cheek with her love, say: Bleach!
Is not pale saffron prized about poppy red?
If she has stooped my shoulders, say to them: Stoop!
Must not a harp be bent when they string it to sing?
If she has kindled fire in my heart, say: Kindle!
Only the kindled candle sends forth light.
If tears rain from my eyes, say: Let them rain!
Spring rains make fair gardens. And if then
she has cast me into the shadow of exile, say:
Those who seek fortune afar find it the first.

(Manuchehri)

Hi, tent-boy, get that tent down.
The first are gone and one drum's growled,
loads on the camels, nearly prayer-time,
and tonight full moon, up as soon
as the sun drops behind Babyl.

O silver-white Sanubar! Could a day
fade without our noticing?
Leave me now, lovely girl.
There'll be no harvest of the love we sowed.

— Tears pelting as though pepper thrown
had blistered her eyes, stumbling and fluttering
she belted her arms around me,
hung as a sword hangs, crying:
'Is it to please all jealous Primnesses?
How can I tell whether you will come back?
Perfect I thought you in every art,
but in love you are not perfect.'
And I: 'I am no tyro.
Love's taste's sharpest at a hasty parting.'

Patience heavy on my heart, I looked
where the tents had been, and the camels,
saw neither mount nor rider
but my Najib, restless;
loosed the hobbles from her knees
like one releasing a bird from a fowler's net;
made the headstall fast at her ears' root,
slung the blanket loose to her shoulder,
mounted. She leapt to go,
I praying: 'God make it easy',
counting her steps for the stages
as surveyors measure the ground,
into a hard, cold desert.
Wind froze my blood, the pools frozen
like silver dishes on a gold tray.

Before morning night was blacker
for the white snow wasting away
and out of the hard ground rose a mud like fishglue.

One long watch of the night
was done when the Dogstar rose
bright over Mosul's mound
then the Great Bear, and I came close
behind the caravan like a boat nearing the beach.
The sound of their anklets reached me
with chatter and clatter of bells
and I saw the peacock litters
stilted on herony legs;
bells within bells, gilded,
hanging to the camels' knees,
and lances, making the valley a cornfield.

(After Manuchehri)

You've come! O how flustered and anxious I've been,
chill as a stone ever since you went away
but not forgetful; silent, yes, and confused,
longing, longing always to see you again.

Without you I've not slept, not once, in the garden
nor cared much whether I slept on holly or flock,
lonely to death between one breath and the next
only to meet you, hear you, only to touch;

waiting all night for the breeze to bring me your scent
till the cocks called up the sun from jail, and
poppy, peony, primula glowed yet I
shivered and sank, sick for consolation
sick day long for the pain of your going, saying
'You broke your word. I have stood fast by mine.'

You broke your word. I have stood fast by mine,
counting old kisses, tasting past praise again,
a heavy, cumbersome bundle not to set down;
but 'Keep' you said. I've let no dust of it drop.

Thorns in our tangled garden pock my cheeks
when I go down to the burn, eyes turned in
from day to night in my head, your night,
heavy for ever over the garden now.

At the heel of my door they'll ask what fruit life bore.
Tell them the night I talked with my darling was sweet.
Who has judged that the bond you gave them is null,
judged unjustly. I have performed my part.
Will you be glad one day to hear me greet you:
'You've come. O how flustered and anxious I've been.'

(After Sa'di)

Ginger, who are you going with?
Some slim kid? One who squeezes you
among the early meadowsweet?
You do your hair to please him,
or he thinks so, loose and smooth.

Change your mind and he'll cry.
He's not reckoned with storms
but fancies your glow is
all for him, always at hand,
always gentle; winds don't veer.

You'll shine on them all, poor brats,
till one of them gets you.
But as for me,
I've wrung my shirt out long since.

(Horace)

Like a fawn you dodge me, Molly,
a lost fawn.
A breath of wind scares her.
Leaves rustle, or a rabbit
stirs, and her heart flutters,
her knees quiver.
But it's me chasing you, Molly,
not a tiger, not to tear you.
Let mother go,
you're old enough for a man.

(Horace)

That filly couldnt carry a rider nor
pull her weight in a plow team. How
could she stand up under a stallion?
All she thinks about is fields or a
brook when it's warm to plodge in.
Prancing round with the colts is her fun. Why
bite green apples? Come October they'll redden.
Then she'll match you: Time will give her the years
it snatches from you. She'll toss her head soon
to challenge a man, the besom, cuter
than Jane who hides or Leslie who lets her blouse
slip from her shining shoulder or even Jimmy.
You cant tell him from a girl if he keeps his mouth shut
with his long, loose hair and unguessable face.

(Horace)

Dante: *Inferno* XXIX

Many people, unheard-of wounds,
had made my eyes so drunk with tears
that I'd have liked to stay and shed them,
but Vergil said: "What are you staring at?
Why is your gaze still hovering down there
over the sad, dismembered spirits?
You did not do this at the other *bolge*.
If you are thinking of counting them, consider,
this valley is two-and-twenty miles around.
By now the moon is underneath our feet,
the time allowed to us is getting short
and other things you have not seen to see."
"If you," I answered instantly, "had waited
to hear why I was watching
you might have let me stay there still;"
for he was moving off, and I behind him,
my leader, even while I was answering;
and I went on: "Down in that hollow
where I had forced my eyes to peer
I think a spirit of my kin is wailing
the guilt that costs so dear there."
To this the master said: "From now on
dont let your thought be scattered by such as him.
Pay heed to something else and let him bide there.
I noticed him, under the foot of the bridge,
point you out and threaten with his finger,
and heard the others call him Geri del Bello.
But you were so completely taken up
with the man who formerly held Altaforte
you never glanced towards him; so he walked on."
"Violent death not yet avenged," I said,
"made him contemptuous of anyone
who shares the shame, and so he went away
without speaking to me – or so I suppose so –
and that has made me pity him the more."

Snow's on the fellside, look! How deep,
our wood's staggering under its weight.
The burns will be tonguetied
while frost lasts.

But we'll thaw out. Logs, logs for the hearth!
And dont spare my good whisky. No water, please.
Forget the weather. Elm and ash
will stop signalling
when this gale drops.

Why reckon? Why forecast? Pocket
whatever today brings
and dont turn up your nose, it's childish,
at making love and dancing.
When you've my bare scalp, if you must, be glum.

Keep your date in the park while light's whispering.
Hunt her out, well wrapped up, hiding and giggling,
and get her bangle for a keepsake.
She wont make much fuss.

(*says Horace, more or less*)

Poor soul! Softy, whisperer,
hanger-on, pesterer, sponge!
Where are you off to now?
Pale and stiff and bare-bummed,
It's not much fun in the end.

(Hadrian)

SCHOOL POEMS

The Song of the Ackworth Clock

Clock beneath the Cupola,
Never near yet never far
        From the Green below!
You have seen a score of years
Full of schoolboy ink and tears,
Cricket's, football's hopes and fears.
        Tell me what you know!
Tick tock, tick tock, tick tock, slow.

When the Lamb goes twirling round
And the classroom windows sound
        With the winds that blow;
No one then upon the scene
Where the footer match has been;
All deserted is the Green.
        Is this what you know?
Tick tock, tick tock, tick tock, slow.

When the Flags are frozen white
With half a foot of sheer delight
        Crisp and even snow;
Sledges running all day long
All is right and nothing's wrong,
Bursts of happy schoolboy song,
        Is this what you know?
Tick tock, tick tock, tick tock, slow.

When the asphalt bubbles tar,
And lazy lads from near and far
        Wander to and fro,
Or seek the Elms' welcome shade
Where record cricket scores are made,
And Simpson's do a roaring trade.
        Is this what you know?
Tick tock, tick tock, tick tock, slow.

Or when at Easter's happy time
Old Scholars here from every clime
        Make a lordly show:
When Tommy B. meets Johnny A.,

When aged fogeys leap and play,
When all the world feels young and gay.
Is this what you know?
Aye, this is what I know;
Tick tock, tick tock, all of this I know,
Tick tock, tick tock, tick tock, slow.

Keep Troth

When Algebra is done, boys,
    And Latin is no more;
And when the war is won, boys, —
    When boyhood's past and o'er —
        What will you do for England,
            Who's done so much for you?
        Keep troth, speak true, for England,
            Be straight, keep troth, speak true.

And while we're still at school, boys,
    The principle's the same;
Stick to the golden rule, boys,
    Play up, and play the game.
        What do you do for England,
            Who does so much for you?
        Keep troth, speak true, for England,
            Be straight, keep troth, speak true.

And when you're growing old, boys,
    And sinking to your grave,
You'll find that it will nerve you,
    The rule the Captain gave, —
        What have you done for England?
            How will you answer, you?
        I've lived a Man for England,
            Kept troth, and spoken true.

LIMERICKS

What a pity that Bela Bartok
Cannot give his smug public a shock
By writing in parts
For the hiccups and farts
And conducting the piece with .

Yes, obviously.

That volatile poet called Jonathan
He never gets here till he's gone again.
He holds one night stands
In a great many lands
But folks think he's just making fun o'them.

An overfat guest at the Ritz
Tried a diet of casseroled tits.
But it can't be denied
It did no good. He died
Of a series of fits of the squits.

FRAGMENTS AND FALSE STARTS

Do not think that I am contented here
Although I am idle, wellfed and brown.
        There's nothing to see but the sun
        And nothing but the wind to hear.
The sea is always flashing messages
But I cant decode his conversation.
        Mountains give no occupation
        To the mind: dam'd sterile ridges.
As to the natives, they are gay but dull,
And that imbecile who tries to teach me
        Is the blockhead of Italy:
        Teacher! Pah! Gu'il me leche le cul!
Besides this, to say nothing of the flies
Or of the other visitors, the wine
        Is — Spanish toothwash (that's urine) —
        And the long and short of it is
I may turn up in London any day
And put up with the noise, to get blotto
        In some good pub with you, Otto,
        And listen to what you've to say.

Powder and lipstick and lace on their drawers
Are all very well for young women and whores
They look a bit more human in that sort of stuff;
But for a man, cock and balls are enough.

(Sa'di)

Sonnet II

Time and no inclination
inclination at the wrong time
painless stupidity
soul not at home to callers:

its possibly ultimate inhumation
made flesh under a neat strewing of granite chips
complete with kerb. (But no stone,
Saadi's right, dogs would piss on it.)

Without science, if you please, or psychology!
a mere prescription, as:
take one look at it, the truth about yourself,
you'll never want another.

And the rime? You have my permission.
Muse? Apply to the
Divorce Admiralty and Probate Division.

The Well of Lycopolis [variant]

cujus potu signa
virginitatis eripiuntur.

I

Advis m'est que j'oy regretter.

Slinking by the jug-and-bottle
swingdoor I fell in with
Mother Venus, aging, bedraggled, a
half-quartern of gin under her shawl,
wishing she was a young girl again:
"It's cruel hard to be getting old so soon.
I wonder I dont kill myself and have done with it.

I had them all on a string at one time,
lawyers, doctors, business-men:
there wasnt a man alive but would have given
all he possessed
for what they wont take now free for nothing.
I turned them down,
I must have had no sense,
for the sake of a ready young fellow:
whatever I may have done at other times
on the sly
I was in love then and no mistake;
and him always knocking me about
and only cared for my money.
However much he shook me or kicked me I
loved him just the same.
If he'd made me take in washing he'd
only have had to say: 'Give us a kiss'
and I'd have forgotten my troubles.
The selfish pig, never up to any good!
He used to cuddle me. Fat lot of good it's done me!
What did I get out of it besides a bad conscience?
But he's been dead longer than thirty years
and I'm still here, old and skinny.
When I think about the old days,
what I was like and what I'm like now,

it fair drives me crazy to
look at myself with nothing on.
What a change!
Miserable dried up skin and bone."

And tapping the bottle: "Swill!
But none of their Bacchic impertinence,
medicinal stout nor portwine-cum-beef;
a dram of anaesthetic, brother.
I'm a British subject if I *am* a colonial:
distilled liquor's *clean*.
It's the times have changed. I remember during the War
kids carrying the clap to school under their pinnies,
studying Belgian atrocities in the Sunday papers
or the men pissing in the backstreets; and grown women
sweating their shifts sticky at the smell of khaki
every little while.
Love's an encumbrance to them who
rinse carefully before using, better
keep yourself to yourself:
sedative gymnastics in stuffy bloomers.
Coppers to harry the whores, bankers
and taxcollectors to harry the married women,
but 'follow the instructions on page fortyone'
says the authoress of *The Labour of Love*,
unlovely labour of love.
(What it is to be in the movement!)
'Or work it off in a day's walk
followed by a cold douche
and brisk rub down at the Youth Hostel,
there's nothing like it
for eliminating the poisons generated by
body and mind.'
Aye, tether me among the maniacs,
it's nicer to rave than reason.
If it wasnt so far to my place
I'd ask you to step in and have a drink."

So I took her round to Polymnia's, Polymnia
glowering stedfastly at the lukewarm
undusted grate grim with cinders
never properly kindled, the brass head of the

tongs creaking as she twitched them:
'Time is, was, has been.'
A gassy fizzling spun from among the cinders.
The air, an emulsion of some unnameable oil,
greased our napes. We rhymed our breath
to the heavy mumble of coke distilling.

"What have you come for? Why have you brought the goddess
out of what unindexed file? You who
finger the goods you cannot purchase,
snuffle the skirt you dare not clutch.
There was never love between us, never less
than when you reckoned much. A tool
not worth the negligible price. A fool
not to be esteemed for barren honesty.
Leave me alone. A long time ago
there were men in the world, dances, guitars, ah!
then, then, love tore through the calyx,
every petal shed, the stigma
panting, then there was fruit.
Tell me, Love's mother, have I wrinkles? grey hair?
Teats, or dugs? Calves, or shanks?
Do I wear unbecoming garments?"

"Blotched belly, slack buttock and breast,
there's little to strip for now.
A few years makes a lot of difference.
Would you have known me?
Here are we poor old fools
gabbing about our young days,
squatted round a bit of fire
just lit and flicker out already:
and we used to be so pretty!"

2

Damn slow movement.

May my libation of flat beer stood overnight
sour on your stomach, my devoutly worshipped ladies,
may you retch cold bile!
Windy water slurred the glint of Canopus,
am I answerable? Left, the vane

screwing perpetually ungainlywards.
What reply will a
June hailstorm countenance?

Bear in mind
fig-tinctured nights, the sea
maundered: 'Let's be cosy,
sit it out hand in hand.
Dreaming of you, that's all I do.'
Eiderdown air, any
girl or none, it's the same thing,
coats the tongue the morning after,
Eurasian hag!

Dawn like a snack of cheese on the rim
sickens the sky,
churned between wind and water rockets
a sour cud into the throat.
There you are, Morning-star, paler than I,
caught without an answer
to indigestion in the bowels of memory.

Even if
there were words the don-begotten debauchees
hadnt sweated into Polymnia's sheets,
if words were stone, if the sun's lilt
could be fixed in the stone's convexity,
what we have seen and been and undergone
a poetico sermone plane abhorret.

Open your eyes, Polymnia!
at the sleek, slick lads trending gingerly between the bedpots,
stripped buff-naked all but their hats to raise,
("After you, Mr Hampstead." "Not at all, Mr 14th Street."
and nothing rises but the hats;
smooth, with soft steps, *ambiguoque voltu.*

Daphnis investigated
bubless Chloe
behind a boulder.
Still, they say,
in another climate
virgin with virgin

coupled taste
wine without headache
and the songs are simple
for canoes, fields, or dancing.
We have laid on Lycopolis water
and the nights are not fresh
between High Holborn and the Euston Road,
nor the days bright even in summer
nor the grass of the squares green.

Neither (*aequora pontis*)
or the sea's bulge
would the 'proud, full sail'
avail
us, stubborn against the trades,
closehauled,
stiff, flat canvas;
our fingers bleed
under the nail
when we reef;
seasick in your sea-foam Paphian.
"Pray accept this worthless offering."

3

Slump.

Infamous poetry, abject love.
Aeolus' hand under her frock
this morning. This afternoon
Ocean licking her privities.
Every thrust of the autumn sun
cuckolding, cuckolding,
in the green grin of late-flowering trees.
I shall never have anything to myself

but stare in the tank, see
Hell's constellations,
a dogstar for the dogstar:
women's face
blank or trivial,
still or rippled water,
a fool and his image.

At my time of life it easier not to see,
much easier to tra-lal-la
a widowed tune in poor circumstances —
                    tweet, tweet, twaddle,
                    tweet, tweet, twat.

'His squalid
acquiescence'
Hell triumphs,
'in the cast-offs
of reputed
poetry: tattered Shakespearean velvet,
plush out of Spencer with the nap gone,
fancy-good,
imported,
wrapped in stained
calico,
for Polymnia
to warm her twat.
An easy pace,
easy to hire,
all mansuetude and indifference.

Time (and again) tropical
randy red sun bounds above the treetops,
filches the sap,
wilted foliage soon lost in
blowsy proliferation.
(Time and) again
tundra under starry noon,
lichen, rock, grey lichen,
you may have the tundra to yourself
and welcome. Whereas
                    tweet, tweet, twaddle,
                    tweet, tweet, twat.
A window on Hell.

Abject poetry, infamous love,
howling like a damp dog in November.
Scamped spring, squandered summer,
grain, husk, stem and stubble
mildewed; mawkish dough and sour bread. <

Mazdak said we should have all things in common,
our wives in common:
sent for the king's and set up
in a house and garden not his own.
   Mani before Mazdak
reproved the tendency to live and flourish:
studied painting in China:
practised elimination and a glib surface.
   Before Mani
Zarathustra Spitama:
"Sow corn, sow holiness.
Digging is better than a hundred prayers.
He who has a wife is above him who has none,
he who has children above him who has none,
he who has riches above him who has none,
he who has health above him who has none.
Every sin can be ransomed and overpaid
by useful actions, except lying.
It is a lie to reject anything desirable
or not to strive to obtain it."

Neither syphilitic nor epileptic
nor rose from the dead nor took
a rear elevation of I-am, nor
visited paradise; knew nothing
of dialectic, there was no history,
his scientific education was deficient,
he lacked practical experience of
administration, did not even
amass a large fortune. Naturally
you, Venus, deny? Polymnia?
"The tinkle of paradox
insults our decorum."

Endure
detail by detail
the cunnilingual law!
"Clap a clout on your monniker for
Christ's sake! Fy for shame!
After hours, is it? or under age?
Hack off his pendants!
Can a moment of madness make up for

an age of consent?"
— with their snouts in the trough
kecking at gummy guts,
slobbering offal, gobbling potato parings,
yellow cabbage leaves, choking on onion-skin,
herring-bones, slops of porridge.
Way-o! Bully boys, blow!
The gadarene swihine have got us in tow.

"But a plate? Better company?"
Squall, Polymnia! Cry murder, Venus!
"Though their ways be foul
they shall be washed as
white as laundered
diapers.
Now altogether, dears, your little hymn:
tweet, tweet, twaddle,
tweet, tweet, twat."

4

Dead March and Polka.

Ed anche vo' che tu per certo credi
che sotto l'acqua ha gente che sospira.

1. *P–K4*
(resigns)

(Withdraw! Withdraw!)

(Resigns).

Stuck in the mud they are saying: "We were sad
in the air, the sweet air the sun makes merry,
we were glum of ourselves, without a reason;
now we are stuck in the mud and therefore sad."
That's what they mean, but the words die in their throat;
they cannot speak out because they are stuck in the mud.
Stuck, stick, sticks: Styx, eternal, a dwelling.
But the rivers of Paradise,
the sweep of the mountains they rise in?
Drunk or daft, hear

a chuckle of spring-water:
drowsy, suddenly wake
— but the bright peaks have faded
trivial ghosts.
Zamzam's brackish,
at least they say so,
and no man in his senses
drinks Helicon unchlorinated.
The blackeyed girls, the heavenly whores,
registered and licensed by competent authorities,
certified sound by Hippocrates in person, —
mistrust them! The saints were before you.

Who had love for love,
whose love was strong or fastidious?
Shadow and shadow noon shrinks, night shelters,
the college of Muses reconstructs
in flimsy drizzle of starlight:
bandy, hunchback, dot-and-carry-one,
praised-for-a-guinea.

Manly Mars for Coda!

"Evening Poly. You here, Venus?
Friend? In the blues? Join the Royal Air Force
and See the World. The Navy will
Make a Man of you. Tour India with the Flag.
Regeneration in the Tercio. O Africa!
Have you heard of the Senussi war?

Peace-maggot gnawing a barbarian.
Induced the tribes against nature
to cultivate oases in permanent truce,
trading safely Sudan to Cyrenaica:
that's Islam these days! — No damn nigger
follow those trade routes now!
Sand gaining on the melon-grounds
at Kufra. Graziani
got the Brethren, all of three or four thousand,
safe behind wires, civilized 'em, pacified 'em.
Teach 'em to hamper me, Mohammedan Quakers!
What did you do in the Great War?"

"Guess."

"One of the ragtime army,
involuntary volunteer.
In hutments, served out chatty blankets.
Three weeks squad drill, fortnight musketry,
five days bayonet-and-dummy;
'Beg pardon, mister, would you mind
standing to attention while
I skewer your tripes?'
Queued up for the pox in Rouen. What a blighty!
Surrendered in March. Or mayve
ulcers of mustard gas or a rivet in the lung
from scrappy shrapnel. Sweet and honorable!
Frostbite, trench fever, shell shock,
self-inflicted wound,
tetanus, malaria, influenza,
according to schedule.
Swapped your spare boots for a packet of gaspers.
Overstayed leave.
Debauched the neighbour's little girl
to save two shillings. War,
natural, necessary, glorious war,
ennobles and elevates man.
The national honour demands it
for the pocket of Lombard bankers
and to hide the deficit.
Maecenas, Wendel, Deterding, Mellon,
and to hide the deficit."

"Cells, exile, and therefore sad,
muttering inaudibly beneath the quagmire,
irresolute, barrent, dependant, my page
ripped from Love's ledger and Poetry's.
Dare I return King Apollo's decorations,
counter contempt with a sneer?
Dare I establish my peace where Cyrus
shares with Alexander? But,
and besides I want you to know for certain
there are people under the water. They are sighing,
the surface bubbles and boils with their sighs.
Look where you will you see it.
The surface sparkles and dances with their sighs
as though Styx were silvered by a wind from Heaven."

To Mr Lewis Alcock the Wonder of Greenwich Village

O.K.
Thursday
We
        will
see
        Bill.
Dont worry
        unduly.
Yours vurry
        truly,

Frog & Rosbif.

On the fly-leaf of Pound's 'Cantos' [variant]

There are the Alps. What is there to say about them?
They dont make sense. Fatal glaciers, crags cranks climb,
jumbled boulder and weed, pasture and boulder, skree,
et l'on entend, maybe, le refrain joyeux et leger.
Who knows what the ice will have scraped on the rock it is
        smoothing?

There they are, you will have to go a long way round
if you want to avoid them.

Ethical or aesthetic exaltations
are out of scale. Ridiculous
to praise a peak, take exception to a rift.
Sun on high snow snatches the heart, awe
the only appropriate emotion.
It takes some getting used to. There are the Alps,
fools! Sit down and wait for them to crumble!

DIALOGUE Non-Platonic

THE TRAVELLER: Sir, I would like you to see
This very fine perfume invented by me.
It penetrates more than the smell of a bug.
It's stronger than chloroform, attar of roses
Or lemons in blossom. Its virtue suffuses
Itself through the body — one drop on the skin
Will make your intestines smell pleasant within,
The sweat of your armpits will be such a liquor
As ladies delight in, and as for your feet,
Wherever you set them a footprint of sweet
Honeysuckle will be and inhere in the street
For a month. It will vanquish the stifling fug
Of the Tube or the odour of petrol and rubber
In Great Portland Street or convert the damp slubber
Of stale fish in Billingsgate into a chic-er
Aroma than Coty can furnish, and quicker
Than any explosion or Edison's brains
It will make a Kurot of the sewers and drains —
You can sell off your urine for Clicquot!
If you want to deodorize belches and farts
To a delicate flavour of Pekoe
Or conquer the stench of your sexual parts,
We have tried out the mixture on several tarts
And assure you it makes the vagina distill
An odour of oranges. Now Sir, I will
Take your order?

THE CUSTOMER: That's a poor stunt.
Can't you make oranges smell like a cunt?

Grandma's Complaint

Yesterday morning my old man Jack
Left off his waistcoat and got a stiff back;

And the day before that the doddering wreck
Left off his collar and got a stiff neck.

— I wish to the Lord that the bloody old crock
Would leave off his trousers and get a stiff cock.

The scholar ought to be like the poet,
an Ishmael, scanted and feared;
a magician, impious, to be
consulted in secrecy and shame.
Only men rejected by men can keep
either truth or beauty in view.
The moment advantage has a
part in his studies or his craft,
his work perishes.

[Verses for the Quartermain Children]

I

David and Ian
may not talk or giggle —
That rule is too me-an,
enough to make a pig ill.

She labours and slogs
yet misses the mark —
She trains them like dogs
but wont let them bark.

2

When Ian and David
Get a quarter they save it
Because at Frosterley
Coke is kind of Costerly

Drafts of 'Such syllables flicker out of grass'

I. [From *Caddel and Flowers*]

Such syllables flicker out of grass:
'What beckons goes;' and no glide lasts
nor wings are ever in even beat long.
A male season, with paeonies; birds bright under thorn.

Light pelts hard now the sun's low.
It carves my stone as hail mud.
Its net drapes the haugh, glaze crackled by drops flung.
Wind shakes a blotch of sun.
Flatter and tattle willow and oak alike,
sly as a trout's shadow on gravel.

Light stots from the stone, sets ridge and kerf quick
as shot skims rust from steel.

He twists his patter afresh? What use?
Elegant hope, fever of time,
new now, next, in the fall, to be dust.

II. [Transcribed by Peter Quartermain]

1

Such syllables flicker out of grass:
'What beckons goes'; and no glide lasts
nor wings are ever in beat long.
A male season, with paeonies; birds bright under thorn
Light pelts hard now the sun's low.
It carves my stone as hail mud.
It's net drapes the haugh, glaze crackled by drops flung.
What use? Elegant hope, fever of tune,
new now, next, in the fall, to be dust.
Wind shakes a blotch of sun.
Flatter and tattle willow and oak alike
sly as a trout's shadow on gravel.
Light stots from the stone, sets ridge and kerf quick
as shot skims rust from steel.
He twists his pattern afresh.

2

Light pelts hard now the sun's low.
It carves my stone as hail mud.
Lintel and ridge ease,
there is room to see and say
worm-casts pimple shale
or willowherb
feathers float athwart light.

Tub, tub counted they team,
rock shattered, sunk stone,
what riddles or eyes skim,
or forsaken fen. They reckon
by studded rods all outcast,
wrenched from dark
to overlay flags and rushes.

Level light fired before dusk
scrubs my stone bare
as shot trims steel. cleans skims

Crystals and colour show,
fish petal-white, a dance
with no end to its geometry.

3

Light pelts hard now the sun's low.
It carves my stone as hail mud.
Lintel and ridge ease,
there is room to see and say.

Tub, tub, counted they team.
Wormcasts pimple shale or willowherb
feathers float athwart light.
What riddles or eyes sort, team
till our fen saps. They reckon
by studded rods all outcast
to lay over rushed and flags. to overlay

Level light fired before dusk
scrubs my stone bare
as shot skims steel.
Crystals and colours show, fish
pluck a tune pause by pause,
petal-white, their pond a dance
with no end to its geometry.

Untitled poem, 1978: opening of 'A New Moon'?

Transcribed by Peter Quartermain

Now we've no hope of going back,
cutter, to that grey quay
where we moored twice and twice unwillingly
cast off our cables to put out at the slack
when the sea's laugh was choked to a mutter
and the lead lifted hesitantly, with a stutter
and sulky clack,

how desolate the swatchways look,
cutter with the chart stained,
stiff, old, wrinkled and uncertain
seeming to contradict the new pilot book.
On naked banks a few birds strut
walking the ebb sluice through a narrowing gut
loud as a brook.

Soon, while this northwest squall wrings out its cloud,
cutter, we'll heave to
free of the sands and let the half moon do
as it pleases, hanging there in the port shrouds
like a riding light. We have no course to set,
only to drift too long, watch too glumly, and wait,
while the buoy's bowed

by the current, asking:
what has new bracken to hang and hide,
or heather, a singed shawl,
or thorn, a tree at a time?
Our fields keep to themselves.
No asking, no offering; only
a braid of gorse about the hem,
sequins caught in the bent's nap.
Choir to choir of light
answers and echoes.
Sty banks, if you walk,
with gapers checking
impertinence of dead misgovernment
who see as bidden; rarely

a looking glass.
The whin's eaves drip to sopping mires
spread out to dry if they can, or loughs
that say no grace for drams,
sombre indeed; with gold,
more than a match for an emperor
who took no rest but mocked his soul,
on whom Rome gilded at last
the ugliest tomb bar Pharaoh's
a man might hope to avoid.

Waterspouts sway their hips,
cutter, have you seen? Curtsy, rise,
circle and sidestep in agreed disorder.
One sinks and is gone,
another is born in foam.
Have you heard, fast and as many
as graces draped on a stone
whales slap the Gulf's taut skin?
Dolphins too rejoice around them.
More than a match for an emperor
one whale alone, arrogant,
carving his wake between
reefs and eddies, heedless of the Vancouver ferry.
Islands look on and always clouds.
Sparks fall from the night sky
into a glow, dawn
filching hours from then dark   time
kindles the gorse again
more lasting than masonry.
Stitch by stitch the stole is lit,
few yarns, few dyes,
mating and matching tumbled lines

The North Sea's grey-green petticoat
is edged with lace, always torn.
Slattern, termagant, wakeful,
and can clamour. Seals fondle her,
she is tickled with wings, invites
intimacy of gannets, and scowls.
Borders, boundaries, terms, thresholds, partings,
all valves, no hope of going back;

not a day, not an hour,
not an emperor beating his bounds,
desolate marches,
no pause to fetch Antinous.
His trudge done games,
solitary, elegant, bar impatience.

Poor soul!, Softy, whisperer,
hanger-on, pesterer, sponge!
Where are you off to now?
Pale and stiff and bare-bummed,
It's not much fun in the end.

Better to part than bicker, you who
stumble between pen and paper;
and hoy my bones to the hoodies
among the gorse
that lines the rim of our world.

Here and there Autumn honey,
~~layer cake maybe~~

ANOMALIES

They Say Etna [*Poems: 1950*]

They say Etna
belches as much poison
as Duisburg's pudenda
a littering sow
helpless in the railroad ditch.
                    Gear and gear.
The Muses Ergot and Appiol,
                         Mr. Reader.
Mr. Reader,
      the Muses Ergot and Appiol.
What violence or fraud
shall we record?

Popone or Kreuger?
A skipper of the Middle Passage
stinkproof and deaf
with a hundred and seventy slaves
damaged in transit
for Jamaica?

                    Gear and gear.
Shall we consider the evidence in Hatry's case?
Or take Lord Bunting — or

UKASE.

No one to be found outside his own village
without

PAPERS.

Also, to encourage more efficient tillage,
2/3 of the produce to be presented to the temporal lord,
1/5 of the produce to be presented to the parish pope.
                    Yours you may say lovingly
                         Boris Godounoff.
Or Stalin.

*

Item, the Duke of S. can get more
by letting the shooting although there is nothing to shoot

but a dozen diseased grouse and a few thin leveret
than by cleaning the ditches to make the ground healthy for sheep.

Lord C., Lord T., gear and gear,
Lord A. and the Duke of H.
think coals too cheap and costs too dear.

* * * * *
* * * * *
*

Gear, then, and gear,
                    gritty-grinding.
The governor spins, raises its arms.
Two three-inch steel cables scream from the drum
seventy fathoms.
We carry lighted Davy lamps,

stoop along narrow track.
Trucks scold tunnel.
In a squat cavern a
naked man on his
knees with a
pickaxe rips a nugget from the coalface.

Four lads
                    led the pownies
a mile and a half through rising water,
lampless because the stife
asphyxiates lamps,
by old galleries to the North Shaft.
The water rose.
                    The others
came five months later when it was pumped out
and were buried by public subscription.
(The widows were provided for.)

*

Sing, Ergot and Appiol, didactically:
"Toil! Accumulate Capital!
Capital is land upon which
work has been done (*vide* textbooks).
Capital is everything except the desert,

sea, untunneled rock, upper air.
Breathed air
is Capital, though not rented:
70 million tons of solid matter
suspended in the atmosphere,
November, in London,
not by an act of God.

"The sea is his and he
who made it." — Who
made Holland and whose is it?

MAN IS NOT AN END-PRODUCT,
MAGGOT ASSERTS.

Make? For the making? The system limps.
Everything in this category is deformed,
even the bookkeeping.
Waste accumulates at compound interest

MAN IS AN END-PRODUCT AFFIRMS
BLASPHEMOUS BOLSHEVIK.

ANNOTATIONS

SONATAS

Richard Burton quotes speculation that BB learned from EP in 1922 that James Joyce 'had planned *Ulysses* as a sonata and Pound would have introduced Bunting to the work on the eighteenth-century sonata of the Paris Conservatory's professor of harmony, Albert Lavignac, whose "consummate manual," as Pound called it, *La Musique et les Musiciens*, had been published in 1895.' See *Burton* (123ff) for details of Lavignac's description of the sonata and how it can be applied to BB's work, 'Villon' in particular. BB reflected, late in his life, upon having used a sonata-like form: '**Music has suggested certain forms and certain details to me, but I have not tried to be consistent about it. Rather, I've felt the spirit of a form, or of a procedure, without trying to reproduce it in any way that could be demonstrated on a blackboard. (There's no one–one relationship between my movements and any of Scarlatti's). You could say the same about the detail of sound. Eliot – and Kipling – show prodigious skill in fitting words to a prearranged pattern, very admirable: yet they don't do it without losing some suppleness . . . Critical notions are in control from the outside so that the poem is constrained to fit them, as though it had never been conceived in the form it wears . . . My matter is born of the form – or the form of the matter, if you care to think that I just conceive things musically. There's no fitting, at least consciously. Whatever you think I am saying is something I could not have said in any other way**' (BB to Forde, 23 May 1972; quoted *Forde*, 149).

For more on BB and the sonata form, see note to *Briggflatts* IV. 45; also Anthony Suter, 'Musical Structure in the Poetry of Basil Bunting', *Agenda* 16, no. 1 (1978), 46–54; and D. M. Gordon, 'The Structure of Bunting's Sonatas', in *Terrell*, 107–23.

To compare BB's views on music and poetry to EP's and Hulme's, see EP, *ABC of Reading* (New York: New Directions, 1960), 61; Samuel Hynes, ed., *Further Speculations of T. E. Hulme* (Lincoln, NE: University of Nebraska Press, 1962), 73.

Villon

Cp. Villon, *Le Grand Testament* (1461, published 1489); BB owned a 1929 edition of the *Oeuvres complètes de François Villon*; and D. G. Rossetti's versions of Villon, 'The Ballad of Dead Ladies', 'To Death, of

His Lady', and 'His Mother's Service to Our Lady'; also Swinburne's 'A Ballad of Burdens', 'Translations from the French of Villon', 'A Ballad of François Villon', 'Ballad of the Fair Helmet-Maker', and 'The Ballad of Villon and Fat Madge'. *Guedalla* B11 suggests that parts of the poem contain 'borrowings from Hamlet, The Vulgate Bible, and Chapman's translations of Homer's Odyssey'.

BB describes a 1924 encounter with EP in Italy: **'I climbed a mountain, and on top of the mountain, to my astonishment, Ezra appeared. So I saw more of him. He was busy writing his first opera [*Villon*], and I was busy with poems'** (BB to James G. Leippert, 30 October 1932; quoted *Forde*, 25, and, in slightly different form, *Lesch*, 2. See also *Descant*, [10]). ('Heaulmiere' from EP's opera, *Villon*, accompanied by his essay, 'Villon and Comment', was published in 1938; both also appear in the 1952 rev. ed. of *Guide to Kulchur*, a book partly dedicated to BB).

In about 1924, BB was arrested for trying to batter his way into a hotel room in Paris which he thought was his, and assaulting a policeman who had been summoned. **'The next day I was herded into the Grande Salle along with a flock of petty thieves, pickpockets, prostitutes, pimps, and other assorted characters. I happened to have a copy of Villon in my pocket, so while waiting my turn, I sat on a bench reading him quite aware of the ironies. For Villon himself, centuries before, had sat in this same salon and waited his turn before the magistrate.'** BB appealed to EP for help: **'He was always interested in helping young writers in trouble; but I think it was seeing me reading Villon that really got him. After he had heard my story, he rushed away to get lawyers and money or whatever to get me off and see justice done'** (*Terrell*, 41–2; also *Alldritt*, 36–7). **'It was Ezra who discovered me, still half blank with something approaching D.T.s, and perjured himself in the courts to try to get me off'** (BB to James G. Leippert, 30 October 1932; quoted *Makin*, 26). EP mentions this in his essay 'Cavalcanti', in *Make It New* (London: Faber & Faber, 1934): 'I was once engaged in trying to get a Northumbrian intellectual out of jail *emprès Ponthoise* . . .' 'Villon' draws on this event, as well as BB's prison time in England for refusing military service during World War I. In 1926, BB wrote to EP describing his work on 'Villon', **'The only thing I have at present that seems of any value at all is a study, story, what-you-will, of a state of mind engendered by incipient D.T. plus influenza plus a clubbing from the French Police. Eliot has it at present, but I expect he will return it, he is so infernally cautious. Also I know it is immature'** (BB to EP, 2 December 1926; quoted *Makin*, 26–7).

In a letter written *ca.*1929 to Louise Theis, BB described being pleased that EP, reading the poem, **'recognised quotations of phrases that stand out like mountain peaks in the Grand Testament'** (undated letter quoted in bookseller's catalogue). Much later, BB explained that EP **'did for my "Villon" exactly what he'd done for Eliot and *The Waste Land*. He took a blue pencil and scratched out about half the poem, though it's true**

when he came to Part III of "Villon" he sighed and said, "I don't know what you young men are up to"' (Lesch interview, 24 April 1976; quoted *Lesch*, 151). In a later account, BB told Reagan that EP '**must have chopped out at least one fifth, perhaps one quarter of the first two parts, maybe more than that. He didn't touch the third part because he said, "I don't know what you young fellows are up to nowadays!"'** (*Reagan*, 72). EP remarked in a letter to LZ that he thought the third section [of *Villon*] was 'remarkable' but 'the ending possibly too universul' (*Pound/Zukofsky: Selected Letters of Ezra Pound and Louis Zukofsky*, ed. Barry Ahearn [New York: New Directions, 1987], 71). EP's selection of BB in *Conf. Cumm*, *Guedalla* B10, contains (316) the remark: 'There are unforgettable lines in his "Villon."'

Asked about the influence of EP's early poetry, BB told Reagan, **'I don't think I did organize my poems around personae, except, partly, "Villon" . . . Persona in the sense used by Pound and by Browning is almost foreign to me. I use very little of it. But if you mean by persona simply that the poet isn't always speaking in his own person, not everything he says is a personal confession, and so on, of course that is true. I don't go in for personal confessions. I like describing things I see, but if it goes beyond that, you can be fairly sure that it's not necessarily me that's supposed to be making these remarks'** (*Reagan*, 77). Yet BB introduced the poem at a reading by saying that Villon felt, as BB did at the time of this poem's composition, '**sorry for himself. All young men are sorry for themselves**' (Air Gallery, 1977, in *Swigg*), and wrote to Makin that '**"Villon" . . . is about my experiences, and Villon only supplies the decoration**' (BB to Makin, 1 April 1985; quoted *Makin*, 27). Cp. EP's 'Villonaud for This Yule' and 'A Villonaud: Ballad of the Gibbet' in *Personae*, as well as his chapter on Villon, 'Montcorbier, alias Villon', in *The Spirit of Romance*; EP quoted Villon in *Cantos*, e.g. LXXIV, LXXX, XCI, XCV, C.

See also note to I. 42–76, below.

Publication history

First published in *RM* and in *Poetry* 37, no. 1 (October 1930), 27–33, *Guedalla* D1. Last nine stanzas of section I published in *Poetry* 39, no. 2 (November 1931), 110–11, *Guedalla* D5; notice appeared on p. 101 that 'the Lyric Prize of fifty dollars . . . is awarded to Basil Bunting an English poet now living mostly in Rapallo, Italy, for his poem, *Villon* . . . especially the song in its first section'. Sections I and II published in EP's *Profile* (Milan, 1932) *Guedalla* B1 and *Act. Ant.*, *Guedalla* B4. Included in *CE*. Later published in *P1950*, *Loquitur*, all editions of *CP*; reprinted in *King Ida's Watch Chain* (Link One, n.d. [?1965]), n.pag., *Guedalla* D22. Last nine stanzas of section I, and all but last six lines of section II appeared in *The Penguin Book of Modern Verse Translation*, ed. George Steiner (London: Penguin, 1966), 154–6, *Guedalla* B11, under heading, 'Imitations of François Villon'; last eight sections of section I also published in *Georgia Straight*, n.pag., *Guedalla* D34; last nine stanzas of section I in *Shake the Kaleidoscope* (New York: Pocket Books, 1973), ed. Milton Klonsky, 4–5, later issued as *The Best of Modern Poetry* (1975). Variants of parts of I and II in letter to Basilio Fernández; see Appendix VI.

Notes

I. Lesch (159) suggests that this section 'may well have influenced Yeats's *Last Poems*'. Cp. 'Under Ben Bulben' and 'Lapis Lazuli'. Yeats knew BB in Rapallo during the 1930s; he called BB 'one of Pound's more savage disciples' (Charles Norman, *Ezra Pound*, rev. ed. [New York, 1969], 300).

I. 2–3. 'whose words we gathered as pleasant flowers / and thought on his wit and how neatly he described things'. BB's version of lines by the French poet, Clément Marot (1496?–1544), a contemporary of Ronsard; from Marot's preface to his 1533 edition of Villon's poems. Marot imitated the forms and themes of antiquity, and composed *chansons* as well as *blasons* – satiric verses describing some aspect of the female form; these probably drew BB's interest, as would have the fact that Marot translated Catullus, Virgil and Ovid, and also edited the works of Villon. Perhaps of note, too, is that Marot's French versions of the Psalms provided the basis for those by Philip and Mary Sidney. BB owned a 1900 edition of Marot's *Oeuvres complètes*. The phrase 'hatching marrow' (5) puns on Marot's name. *Burton* (127) remarks: 'Marrow (pronounced marra) has another submerged meaning that may be unfamiliar to those who don't know Bunting's northern English. In the north of England marra is a friend or companion, a peer or one of a pair, a match in a contest. The poet is incubating other poets, strengthening the link between Bunting and Villon as poets and as prisoners.'

I. 9. Emperor with the Golden Hands. Based on Villon's 'Voire, ou soit de Constantinobles / L'emperieres au poing dorez.' Makin: 'Bunting refers, with "the Emperor", to Villon's *Testament*, 391–400: "Indeed, whether it be the Emperor of Constantinople with the gilded hand, or the King of France . . . if he was honoured in his time, the wind carries off as much." Bunting thinks Villon's lines refer to manuscript illuminations [see note to I. 11, below]. Villon students have generally taken them to refer to the gilded tomb of Alphonse, count of Eu, at Saint-Denis, whose inscription stated that he was the son of the emperor of Constantinople. However, it has been pointed out that Villon is more likely to be speaking of the gilded orb in such a figure's hands, as commonly depicted in the *danse macabre* (Villon, *Testament*, vol. ii: *Commentaire*, ed. J. Rychner and A. Henry [Geneva, 1974], 60–1). Bunting's plural ("hands") is presumably a mistake, prompted by the morphology of Villon's French: "au poing dorez"' (*Makin*, 28, n. 28). *Burton*, however, notes (128–9) that the complex of buildings at the Byzantine court, which housed many Christian relics, included 'the Hagios Stephanos, the Church of St. Stephen of Daphne, the first martyr of the Christian church, which was built specifically to house St. Stephen's right arm. Within the Church of St. Stephen was a portico called "the Golden Hand".' Villon, and 'by extension Bunting, consciously evoke the holiest of holies . . . Bunting silently amends Villon by shifting the plural to "hands" and away from "l'emperieres". It is the emperors of the golden hand that Villon conjures rather than the emperor of the golden hands.'

I. 11. Matthew Paris. Succeeded Roger of Wendover as chronicler, compiling the *Chronica Majora*, and also the *Historia Minor*, a summary of English history 1200–50, among other works; d. 1259. **'Matthew Paris embellished his historical chronicle with lovely miniatures. The reference is to them'** (BB to Forde, 4 July 1973; quoted *Forde*, 153).

I. 26. Averrhoes. Twelfth-century Muslim physician and philosopher Averroës, famous for his commentary on Aristotle; he was known to Chaucer's Physician in *Canterbury Tales*, and was placed by Dante in the Limbo of the Philosophers. He is mentioned by Villon in *Le Grand Testament*. EP mentions him in a number of places including his essay 'Cavalcanti', in *Make It New* (London: Faber & Faber, 1934).

I. 28. wuzz. Not in *OED*; in *EDD* as meaning hoarseness or cold, e.g. Hardy, *Wessex Tales*, I. 5: 'Upon the whole they were less inconvenienced by "wuzzes and flames" (hoarses and phlegms) than when they had lived by the stream.'

Have pity, have pity on me! Translation of 'Ayez pitié, ayez pitié de moy', the first line of Villon's 'Epistre, en forme de ballade, à ses amis'.

I. 34–5. the good Lorraine / whom English burned at Rouen. Translation of Villon's lines (st. 3, 5–6) in 'Ballade des dames du temps jadis' about Joan, 'la bonne Lorraine, / Qu'Anglois bruslèrent à Rouen.'

I. 38–9. the Emperor . . . Charles. See note to I. 9.

I. 40. spitten. *OED* etymology for 'spit' has Northern OE, *spittan*.

I. 41. CY GIST. From first line of Villon's 'Epitaphe', 'Cy gist et dort en ce sollier . . .'

I. 42–76. These ballad-like stanzas resemble and perhaps parody Villon's 'Ballade des dames du temps jadis'. As Anthony Suter observes,

BB 'employs the same verse form as Villon, octosyllabic quatrains with a basic iambic rhythm, rhyming ABAB, with the only exception being that he arranges his lines in groups of four instead of in the groups of eight of Villon' (Suter, 'Time and the Literary Past in the Poetry of Basil Bunting', *Contemporary Literature* 12, no. 4 [Autumn 1971], 513–14).

I. 43. sots. A common word in British poetry, including six appearances in Samuel Butler's *Hudibras* and several in the works of George Crabbe, etc. Cp. notably Dryden, 'To Sir Godfrey Kneller', 160, 'Good heaven! that sots and knaves should be so vain', and 'Palamon and Arcite', I. 432–3: 'Like drunken sots about the street we roam / Well knows the sot he has a certain home'; also 'Pope, 'An Essay on Man', IV. 215: 'What can ennoble sots, or slaves, or cowards? / Alas! not all the blood of all the HOWARDS', and 'An Essay on Criticism', 271: 'Concluding all were desp'rate sots and fools.'

I. 49. fellmonger. OED: 'A dealer in skins or hides of animals, *esp.* sheep-skins.'

I. 51. fat and scant of breath. Cp. Siegfried Sassoon, 'Base Details', 1, 'If I were fierce, and bald, and short of breath'.

I. 52. Elisha's baldness, Helen's hair. 2 Kings 2: 23–4: 'And [Elisha] went up from thence unto Bethel: and as he was going up by the way, there came forth little children out of the city, and mocked him, and said unto him, Go up, thou bald head; go up, thou bald head. And he turned back, and looked on them, and cursed them in the name of the Lord.' In Greek myth, Helen of Troy was described with the epithet, 'fair-haired Helen', e.g. *The Iliad*, III. 329, Pindar, 'Olympia Ode' 3. 1 (Loeb), and 'rich-haired Helen' (Loeb), Hesiod, 'Works and Days', 165.

I. 57. as we forgive our debtors. Cp. 'The Lord's Prayer', Matthew 6: 12: 'And forgive us our debts, as we forgive our debtors'; and version in Luke 11: 4: 'we also forgive every one that is indebted to us'.

I. 58. Abelard and Eloise. Peter Abelard (1079–1142), a dialectician and popular teacher at Sainte-Geneviève and Notre-Dame in Paris; he fell in love with his pupil, Héloïse, daughter of the canon of Notre-Dame in whose house he was staying. Their love resulted in their separation and famous correspondence; when she died in 1163, she was buried in Abelard's tomb. They were the subject of Pope's poem 'Eloisa to Abelard'.

I. 59. Henry the Fowler. Henry I (876?–936), German king (919–36), first of the Saxon line and father of Otto I, the first of the Holy Roman Emperors.

Charlemagne. (742–814), King of the Franks and later Emperor of the West. He and his paladins were the subject of the *Chanson de Roland* and other *chansons de geste*. He established a tradition of learning at his court which was led by a Northumbrian scholar, Alcuin.

I. 60. Genée. Richard Genée (1823–95), German conductor, librettist and composer known, among other things, for having worked with Johann Strauss on *Die Fledermaus*, and for a satire, sung to nonsense words, on the older style of Italian operas.

Lopokova. Lydia (Vasilievna) Lopokova (1892–1981), Russian ballerina in Diaghilev's Ballets Russes. BB knew her in London, where she danced in Massine's *Les femmes de bonne humeur* (1916) and appeared as the Can Can Dancer in *La boutique fantasque* (1919); she married John Maynard Keynes, and together they founded the Arts Theatre, Cambridge.

I. 62. General Grant and General Lee. Generals in American Civil War, Grant on the Union side, Lee on the Confederate.

I. 63. Patti and Florence Nightingale. Perhaps Adelina Patti (1843–1919), celebrated opera singer; Florence Nightingale (1820–1910), English nurse and philanthropist, subject of one of Lytton Strachey's portraits in *Eminent Victorians*, which BB probably read.

I. 64. Tyro and Antiope. Cp. Homer, *Odyssey*, Book XI. During Odysseus' descent to the underworld, the ghosts of these legendary women (among others) appear.

I. 70. silly. OED: 'A.1.b. Of inanimate things. Now *Sc.*' E.g., Burton, *Anatomy of Melancholy* (1651), II. iii. III. 329: 'When as the lofty oke is blown down, the silly reed may stand.' Cp. Kipling, 'The Destroyers', 57: 'silly smoke'. *EDD* notes usage related to 'zelli' or conger eel, as in 'Scilly Islands'; perhaps here refers to eel-like shape in shifting sands.

I. 76. the green grass growing over us. BB sings this phrase while reading an extract of the poem in the 1973 television programme, *Basil Bunting, Poet of Northumberland* (Kent, CT: Creative Arts Television). Perhaps from a seventeenth-century Scottish border ballad, 'Jamie Douglas' (no. 87 in the 1910 ed., which BB owned, of Arthur Quiller-Couch's *Oxford Book of Ballads*), which tells of Lady Douglas's dismissal by her husband in 1681 on his hearing accusations of her adultery. A typical version of a stanza in this ballad is: 'Oh, oh! if my young babe were born, / And set upon the nurse's knee; / And I mysel' were dead and gane, / And the green grass growing over me!' However, this stanza also appears in a folk lyric – a forsaken girl's lament for her lover – first printed in

Tea-table Miscellany, ed. Allan Ramsay (Edinburgh, 1724), but variously known as 'The King's Daughter Jane' (*The English and Scottish Popular Ballads,* ed. Francis James Child, Ballad no. 52), 'Waly, Waly' (no. 388 in the 1919 ed. of Arthur Quiller-Couch's *Oxford Book of English Verse, 1250–1900*, which BB owned), and 'The Forsaken Bride' (no. 106 in Palgrave's 1875 ed. of *The Golden Treasury*). The music for the song is given in Rimbault's *Musical Illustrations of Percy's Reliques* (102) and Chamber's *Scottish Songs Prior to Burns* (280), among other places. The phrase, 'The long green grass growing over me', occurs in versions of the Celtic folk song known as 'The Butcher Boy' or 'Love is Teasing (Love is Pleasing)'.

II. 1–2. Let his days be few and let / his bishoprick pass to another. Based on Psalm 109, *l.* 8. The first six lines of this section adopt Villon's cursing of Thibault d'Aussigny, bishop of Orléans, who had sentenced him to a term in prison. According to Forde, the '"mouldy bread" and "dry crust" allude to lines in "Ballade pour laquelle Villon crye mercy à chascun", and the vanished dancers and somersaulters recall lines in the "Epistre, en forme de ballade, à ses amis"' (*Forde*, 154).

II. 21. Archipiada. **'Archipiada is a mysterious person mentioned in Villon's *Ballade des Dames*, etc. Guesses are no use – most editors tell you that St Thomas made some confusion and thought Alcibiades was a woman, but I think that is based on a misreading of St Thomas' text, and anyway that Villon, who was far from profound in his theological studies, probably never read St Thomas with sufficient attention to remember such a minute detail. So for me she is any product of the imagination'** (BB to Forde, 23 May 1972; quoted *Forde*, 155). Makin remarks that 'Villon's "Archïpiadés" (*Testament*, *l.* 331) is generally held to be an error, and one of Villon's most celebrated. Certain medieval commentators, we are told, read of Alcibiades, Socrates' friend, and took him for a woman; Villon followed them. Bunting disputed this explanation [as above], since he thought Villon did not read theological literature closely enough to pick up such a detail. (The text of St. Thomas he refers to is a commentary on Boethius wrongly attributed to St. Thomas). He concluded that Villon's "Archipiada" was an insoluble mystery' (*Makin* 30, n. 30).

II. 23. Circe. In Homer's *Odyssey*, the sorceress who changed Odysseus and his crew into swine; protected by the magical herb moly, Odysseus prevailed upon her to change them back to men. He stayed with Circe for a year before resuming his journey.

II. 26. till Ronsard put a thimble on her tongue. Cryptic. Pierre de

Ronsard (1524–85), major poet among the group of French Renaissance poets called La Pléiade. Cp. EP's 'Ode pour l'élection de son sépulchre', which mentions Circe and is partly based on Ronsard, Book IV, Ode IV.

ll. 27–8. But they have named all the stars . . . run the white moon to a schedule. In 'Philosophic Criticism', *The Outlook* 60 (6 August 1927), BB wrote that he scorned science because it pretends that **'its universe of exact measurement and strict logic'** exhausts **'all the subjects of thought and knowledge . . . There remain two realms at least that cannot be explored by scientific methods, that of Religion on the one hand, that of Art on the other; both wide regions in which the mind must wander without a chart, in which the dominant mode of thought is not logical but intuitive.'** In 'The Whole Man', *The Outlook* 61 (19 May 1928), BB wrote that science **'deals only with measurables or with facts submissive to the forms of logic . . . What these two instruments, mathematics and logic, cannot reach, it neglects and is inclined, in self-protection, to deny, lest the vastness of the universe should overwhelm it.'**

ll. 29. Joshua's serf whose beauty drove men mad. Untraced, but perhaps BB has in mind the harlot, Rahab, in Joshua 2 who sheltered Joshua's men and was therefore later spared in the destruction of Jericho.

ll. 30. Erebus. Son of Chaos, often used metaphorically for Hades itself. According to Hesiod's *Theogony*, Erebus was born with Night, and was the father of Aether (the bright upper atmosphere) and Day.

ll. 37. Bertillon. Alphonse Bertillon (1853–1914), Paris police chief known for inventing anthropometrics, a method of classifying criminals using measurements of their physical characteristics.

ll. 39–41. Homer? Adest. Dante? Adest. / Adsunt omnes, omnes et / Villon. Roughly, 'Homer? He is here. Dante? He is here. / Everyone is here, everyone and / Villon.' BB recalled his first meeting with T. S. Eliot and what Terrell called that poet's 'tendency to be oracular': **'he spent a long time urging upon me the necessity to read Dante. And being a modest young man and not wanting to put him off his stride, I never once mentioned that I had already read Dante and knew a good deal of the *Inferno* by heart'** (*Terrell*, 45). Cp. Kipling, 'Pan in Vermont', 12: '*Numen adest!*'

ll. 43–4. Blacked by the sun, washed by the rain, / hither and thither scurrying as the wind varies. From Villon, 'Frères humains qui après nous vivez', which describes corpses hanging from a gallows. Cp. Tennyson, 'St Simeon Stylites', 75: 'Blacked with thy branding thunder'.

III ▪ **The image of two drops of quicksilver running together is from the late E. Nesbit's *Story of the Amulet*. To her I am also indebted for much of the pleasantest reading of my childhood.** E. Nesbit (1858–1924), *The Story of the Amulet* (London, 1906), 352: 'And then, as one drop of water mingles with another on a rain-wrinkled window-pane, as one bead of quick-silver is drawn into another bead, Rekh-mara's Amulet slipped into the other one, and, behold! there was no more but the one Amulet!' 366: 'And then, as one drop of water mingles with another when the panes of the window are wrinkled with rain, as one bead of mercury is drawn into another bead, the half Amulet, that was the children's and was also Rekh-mara's, slipped into the whole Amulet, and, behold! there was only one – the perfect and ultimate Charm.' 371: 'And, as one drop of water mingles with another, when the window-glass is rain-wrinkled, as one quick-silver bead is drawn to another quick-silver bead.'

III. 24. shipless. Cp. Byron, *Ode to Venice*, I. 11: 'That drives the sailor shipless to his home.'

III. 25. Helen. Lesch (164) points out that Ronsard (see note to II. 26 above) celebrated Helen of Troy in his poems. **'Helene is the Attic form of the older Greek Selene, a goddess, goddess of the moon, Artemis, Diana, Latona – who presides over childbirth – and several other goddesses, all tying up with the moon, with each other, and with Helen . . . There is no end to the ramifications of image of which Helen, Eleanor, Artemis, and so on, are all facets'** (BB lecture on EP dated 1974; quoted *Terrell*, 258). Cp. Campion's 'When thou must home to shades of under ground', 4: 'blith Hellen'. BB read this poem in a lecture about music and poetry given at SUNY Buffalo in April 1976 (in *Swigg*) in which he discussed both Ronsard and Campion as poets who wrote verse to fit music.

III. 38. girls imagined by Mantegna. Andrea Mantegna, Italian painter, 1431–1506.

III. 43. salmon. Harriet Monroe queried BB here: 'Why salmon?' BB wrote back, **'It would be easy to answer why not? But though I am shy of giving partial explanations which often seem to mislead people, which is probably worse than leaving them in the dark, I will say that by line 180 odd I had been angling for a very long time for a very big fish and only landed something for which the Board of Fisheries formula seems an exact and fitting description'** (BB to Monroe, 30 November 1930; quoted *Forde*, 159, and *Lesch*, 166).

Attis: Or, Something Missing

Written in Rapallo, 1931, from where BB wrote to Harriet Monroe: **'Ezra says *Attis* is obscure, from which he deduces that he is getting old. It certainly wouldnt be easy to write a synopsis, but I think it's really fairly plain for all that, if the reader doesnt spend time and energy looking for a nice logical syllogistic development which isnt there. I dont like formal logic. There are better ways of connecting things up and anyway Wittgenstein reduced logic logically to the noble conclusion "*Woruber man nicht reden kann, daruber musz man schweigen*" some years ago and there seems nothing more to be done with that instrument after that'** (*Translation:* 'Whereof one cannot speak, thereof one must be silent'; 13 July 1931; quoted *Forde*, 159–60).

▪ **Parodies of Lucretius and Cino da Pistoia can do no damage and intend no disrespect.** BB relied extensively on Lucretius' *De rerum natura* in this poem, especially regarding its concern with the ecstatic rites of Cybele, who was known to Romans as Mater Deum Magna Idaea, 'Great Idean Mother of the Gods'. Anthony Suter finds that 'much of Bunting's argument depends on aspects of the Latin poet's thought; the atheism of Lucretius, his desire to banish superstitious fear from peoples' minds' (Suter, 'Time and the Literary Past in the Poetry of Basil Bunting', *Contemporary Literature* 12 [Autumn 1971], 514. Lucretius also informed *Briggflatts* (see especially note to III. 68–71); 'Darling of Gods and Men, beneath the gliding stars', in 'Overdrafts'; and *FBO* 34. Cp. Spenser's adaptations of *De rerum natura* in *Faerie Queene* IV, and Dryden's translations of Lucretius.

Publication history

In *CE*. First published complete in *P1950*; also in *Loquitur* and all editions of *CP*. Section III published in LZ's *An 'Objectivists' Anthology* (1932), *Guedalla* B3, 33–5, with sub-heading '3rd movement of a Sonatina. // *Pastorale arioso* / (for male soprano)'. Last two stanzas of section I reprinted in *Georgia Straight*, n.pag., *Guedalla* D34.

Notes

[Note] Cino da Pistoia. See note on Cino, below.

Epigraph] From Catullus LXIII, 91–3; Loeb: 'Goddess, great goddess, Cybele, goddess, lady of Dindymus, far from my house be all thy fury, O my queen; others drive thou in frenzy, others drive them to madness.' (Peter Whigham's later translation: 'Great Cybele, Mother Goddess, Berecynthian Queen, / avert your fury from Catullus' house / goad others to your actions, / others trap in the snarl of frenzy', about which BB remarked to Forde, **'Whigham's version tries**

to ornament Catullus. "Drive others frantic, drive others mad" is the real last line – no "snarl of frenzy" etc.' (BB to Forde, 4 July 1973; quoted *Forde*, 161). Cybele, sometimes known as the Mountain Mother, was associated with Mount Dindymus. In Catullus' poem, as Forde summarizes, 'Attis, a young Phrygian leader, sails away from the mainland with his friends, and at the foot of a mountain dedicated to Cybele, they emasculate themselves in a religious frenzy. But when the religious fervour wears off, Attis alternately mourns and rages at his unalterable deed. Cybele, hearing him, sends one of her lions to the shore where Attis is looking toward his fatherland, to drive him back among the mountain pines as her subservient eunuch' (*Forde*, 160). As a eunuch, moreover, Attis would now be unable to participate further in ordinary Greek life. Julia Haig Gaisser notes that the Catullus poem possibly attracted interest in English poetry first through the influence of Gibbon, who mentioned it in a footnote to a discussion of the Attis story in *Decline and Fall of the Roman Empire*, chap. 23, n. 18: 'The transition of Atys from the wildest enthusiasm to sober pathetic complaint for his irretrieveable loss, must inspire a man with pity, an eunuch with despair'; Gaisser also mentions Landor's interest in the poem (*Catullus in English* [London, 2001], xxxiv–xxxv). See discussion of BB and Gibbon in note, below, to 'Well of Lycopolis'. Cp. Landor's disciple, Swinburne, 'Dolores', esp. 345–52: 'Out of Dindymus heavily laden / Her lions draw bound and unfed / A mother, a mortal, a maiden, / A queen over death and the dead. / She is cold, and her habit is lowly, / Her temple of branches and sods; / Most fruitful and virginal, holy, / A mother of gods.'

'The fable of Atys is astronomical in its origin. Atys, deprived of his virility, is a symbol of the sun, shorn of its generative powers in the season of winter, and moving in the lower hemisphere . . . every year he returns to the upper world, and celebrates anew his union with Cybele. This return, this renewal of the productive powers and fecundity of nature, gave rise of all those demonstrations of savage joy which are so well described in the verses of Lucretius' (Charles Anthorn, *A Classical Dictionary* [New York, 1854], 235).

I. [stanzas 1–3]. Cp. generally T. S. Eliot, 'The Love Song of J. Alfred Prufrock', and parts of *The Waste Land* (see below), which also describe, in some measure, decay of sexual ardour. Makin observes that BB's poem 'appears to have been partly an attack on Eliot', quoting BB's letter to EP, (undated, ?1931; *Makin*, 88, n. 46): **'Atthis [*sic*], if ever penetrated . . . is unfair to Eliot. These Bodenh.s and other too-good-for-America s shd have been slain first, being more indubitably gelded.'** Also EP's 'Ιηέρρω' and 'Prayer for his Lady's Life'; EP wrote about these poems to H. L. Mencken that 'they lose a little force unless your audience know that Atys cut out his testicles in a fit of religious enthusiasm' (*The Letters of Ezra Pound: 1907–1941*, ed. D. D. Paige [New York: Harcourt Brace, 1950], 56); and *Cantos* V: 'Atthis, unfruitful', etc. (in which EP puns on the Atthis of Sappho 96, and Attis, the priest of Cybele in Catullus, 63) and CXIII. In his 'Notes on "The Waste Land"' Eliot acknowledges *The Golden Bough*, 'especially the two volumes *Adonis, Attis, Osiris*'.

I. 1. Out of puff. Out of breath, slang as *OED* n.1.e, and *EDD* 3.

I. 13–15. measured shaking of strings, / and flutes and oboes / enough for dancers. Lesch (174) observes that these lines contain 'echoes of the rites of Cybele'; cp. EP's 'Salutation the Second', e.g. 'Dance the dance of the phallus / and tell anecdotes of Cybele / Speak of the indecorous conduct of the Gods', etc. For more on Cybele, see notes to poem epigraph, above.

I. 18. Atlantis. A legendary Atlantic Ocean island said to have been swallowed up by the sea, supposedly located west of the Strait of Gibraltar. Cp. Shelley, *Hellas*, 70–1: 'From far Atlantis its young beams / Chased the shadows and the dreams', and 991–5: 'At length they wept aloud, and cried, "The Sea! the Sea!" / Through exile, persecution, and despair, / Rome was, and young Atlantis shall become / The wonder, or the terror, or the tomb / Of all whose step wakes Power lulled in her savage lair.'

I. 22. fresh. OED n.2.a: 'A rush of water or increase of the stream in a river; a freshet, flood. Also, a flood of fresh water flowing into the sea.'

I. 28. Longranked. Not in *OED* or *EDD*.

I. 33. leafmould. See note on Darwin for *FBO* 34; BB owned the 1882 ed. of Charles Darwin, *The Formation of Vegetable Mould*.

I. 34. Cheviot's. Cheviot is the highest peak in the Cheviot hills along the English–Scottish border. Cp. Wordsworth; among others, 'Peter Bell', 225: 'lofty Cheviot hills'; 'Yarrow Revisited', I. 50.

I. 35. heatherbrown. Not in *OED* or *EDD*.

I. 43–50. Praise the green earth . . . Mother of Gods and Eunuchs. A parody of *De rerum natura*, II. 592–660, e.g. 'Wherefore she is called great Mother of the gods, and Mother of the wild beasts, and maker of our bodies . . . They give her eunuchs, as wishing to indicate that those who have violated the majesty of the Mother . . . should be thought unworthy to bring living offspring into the regions of light' (Loeb). As the wife of Chronos, Cybele was, in effect, the 'Mother of Gods'. Cp. Swinburne, 'Dolores', 351–2: 'Most fruitful and virginal, holy, / A mother of gods.' When Forde suggested to BB that the rhythms in these lines were from the Psalms,

BB responded, **'You'll find this metre not in the psalms but in Horace'** (BB to Forde, 4 July 1973; quoted *Forde*, 163).

II. [epigraph]. a theme by Milton. Burlesque of Milton, 'Methought I saw my late espousèd saint'. This burlesque is somewhat similar to EP's 'Go, little naked and impudent songs,' etc. in 'Salutation the Second', which also contains the lines, 'Dance the dance of the phallus / and tell anecdotes of Cybele / Speak of the indecorous conduct of the Gods!'

II. 2. handful of raisins. Cp. T. S. Eliot, *The Waste Land*, 209–10: 'Mr. Eugenides, the Smyrna merchant / Unshaven, with a pocket full of currants'.

Bywell churchyard. 'Bywell is a strange place. There is no village, yet two churches right next to each other! It sits at the boundary of two Norman baronies. St. Peter's was actually the church of Bywell where the castle and Bywell Hall remain. St. Andrew's served the now non-existent community of Styford. Both churches pre-date the Conquest, but only St. Andrew's is substantially Saxon in date. The first church – from which only one carved stone remains – may have been founded by St. Wilfred in the 7th century, but its circular churchyard shows even more ancient origins. The base of the present tower, however, dates from shortly before AD 850; possibly from around the turn of the century when Danish raids forced members of the diocenal community on Lindisfarne to seek refuge here. Egbert was consecrated bishop in St. Andrew's in AD 803. The upper stages of the tower are 10th and 11th century, making it one of the finest Anglian structures in Northumbria' (http://www.britannia.com/history/northumberland/churches/bywellstand.html). BB mentions Bywell in discussing Northumbrian art and culture; see note to *Briggflatts* IV. 25–30.

II. 4. sat amongst the rank watergrasses by the Tyne. Cp. Psalm 137: 1: 'By the rivers of Babylon, there we sat down.' Cp. Shakespeare, *Merry Wives of Windsor* III. i. 23: 'Whenas I sat in Pabylon'. Also T. S. Eliot, *The Waste Land*, 182: 'By the waters of Leman I sat down and wept'. Cp. *The Spoils*, I. 77–8. In November 1771, the River Tyne flooded, and is said to have ripped coffins and bodies out of St. Andrew's churchyard; gravestones in the churchyard only go back to 1724. Cp. Swinburne, 'The Sea-Swallows', in which 'Tyne' provides the end-rhyme for the last line of each quatrain. Alex Niven suggests that BB's source for 'lyrical sections [of the poem and its draft material] written from Peggy's perspective was the popular Northumbrian folk song "Water of Tyne"':

I cannot get to my love if I would dee,
The water of Tyne runs between him and me;

And here I must stand with a tear in my e'e,
Both sighing and sickly my sweetheart to see.
Oh where is the boatman, my bonny hinny!
Oh where is the boatman? bring him to me;
To ferry me over the Tyne to my honey
And I will remember the boatman and thee.

(See Niven, 'The Formal Genesis of Basil Bunting's *Briggflatts*'.)

Niven notes that BB owned a copy of William Whitaker's *North Countrie Ballads, Songs and Pipe-tunes*, which contains a version of 'Water of Tyne'. BB played (on recorders) and sang material from this work all his life, according to *Caddel & Flowers*.

II. 10. Orfeo. Probably reference to *Orfeo*, 1607 opera by Monteverdi (though there is also one by Gluck, 1762); Eurydice dies, and her husband, Orpheus, descends into Hades, rescues her but loses her again. Cp. also *Sir Orfeo*, fourteenth-century English Breton lay, which represents Orpheus and Eurydice in Celtic guise. Ovid tells the story in *Metamorphoses* X (BB owned the 1724 ed. of *Ovid's Metamorphoses Made English by Several Hands*; as well as a Latin version with a French translation by Georges Lafaye). EP's epigraph to *Homage to Sextus Propertius*, *'Quia pauper amavi'*, from Ovid, *Ars Amatoria*, II. 165, is given with the heading, 'Orfeo'.

II. 13. Tesiphone's, Alecto's. In Greek and Roman religion and mythology, two of the three Furies (the other being Megaera) who were daughters of Mother Earth; Tesiphone is the blood avenger, and Alecto the unceasing in pursuit. The Furies personified conscience and punished crimes against kindred blood. In the myth of Orestes they serve as agents of Clytemnestra's revenge (*Columbia Encyclopedia*).

II. 19–21. VENGA MEDUSA / VENGA / MEDUSA SÌ L'FAREM DI SMALTO. Medusa, the only mortal among the Gorgons, snake-headed monsters of Greek mythology (appearing in the work of Homer and Hesiod), who could turn onlookers to stone. Here, a reference to Dante, *Inferno*, IX. Cp. *FBO* 10. The Furies, at the entrance to the sixth circle of Hell, threaten Dante with Medusa's head; Vergil protects Dante from the sight, which would have turned him to stone – the 'gorgon's method' as below. Makin: 'Scartazzini, one of Bunting's preferred commentators on Dante, says that the Erinyes in the *Comedy* figure "remorse of conscience", and Medusa represents doubt (Dante, *Divina commedia*, ed. G. A. Scartazzini [Milan, 1896], 79, 81). For Bunting, "**Medusa hardly does more than confirm the accidie**" – that is, the hopelessness of those who wallow in it [quoted from BB to Makin, 3 December 1985]. As for the figure who appears to quell the Erinyes and to let the poets into Dis, he is identified by Dante only with the words "I perceived clearly that he was a messenger of heaven" (*Inferno*, IX. 85), and modern commentators, dismissing various allegories, agree that he is an angel. Bunting, in *Reagan*, p. 79, simply calls him **"an angel"**. But in an earlier version of the poem now printed as "Farewell ye sequent graces", Bunting gives another figure clearly derived from this scene in Dante; and this "silent dragon" or "Michael" is another blaster (by his alien splendour) of the shrivelled psyche' (*Makin* 84, n. 38).

II. 22. *Send for Medusa: we'll enamel him.* BB's version of Dante's lines, above, about turning onlookers to stone. *OED*, 'enamel', 2a: 'To apply a vitreous glaze by fusion to (surfaces of any kind, *e.g.* pottery).' Citation for Mandeville. Makin: 'The commonest meaning of *smalto* [in Dante's original] is indeed "enamel", but the word can also mean "mortar"; and commentators generally agree that the meaning is "we'll turn him into stone", which would fit the source in Ovid (*Metamorphoses*, iv. 615ff). Bunting's remarks in *Reagan*, p. 79, make it quite clear that he understood the sense "turn him into stone"' (*Makin*, 84, n. 37). EP thought Bunting's reading of this passage more 'penetrating', to use Makin's word, than Binyon's: 'I don't know that it is necessary to assume that Dante's Medusa is the strictly classical female. Bunting has perhaps pierced deeper with his "Come, we'll enamel him." Enamel is both stone and fusing heat' (*Literary Essays*, ed. T. S. Eliot [London, 1960], 209). EP referred to Dante's 'elysian enamelled fields' in 'Psychology and Troubadours', originally published in *The Quest* (1912), and added to later editions of *The Spirit of Romance*. Cp. BB's use of 'enamelled' in *The Spoils*, I; and in BB to EP, ? April 1954, as below in Appendix II. C; and 'enamel' in 'Mr. Ezra Pound' (*Caddel*, 39, originally published in *New English Weekly*, 26 May 1932, *Guedalla* E45). Medusa also appears in Ronsard (e.g. *Le second livre des amours*, 79), who in turn figures in 'Villon' – see notes to that poem, above. Medusa also figures in BB's 'Chorus of Furies' and 'The Well of Lycopolis'; see notes to these poems. Cp. Marvell, 'Bermudas', 13–14: 'He gave us this eternal spring, / Which here enamels everything.'

II. 24. *such decay of ardour*. Cp. EP, Canto XXX, especially st. 1.

II. 26. *Ageslow*. Not in *OED* or *EDD*.

II. 27. *the gorgon's method*. From Dante, *Inferno* VII. See also notes to 'The Well of Lycopolis' IV, below.

II. 28–42. *In the morning . . . stairways*. The words, 'street', 'street-lamp', 'geraniums' and 'smells' constitute a pastiche of T. S. Eliot, respectively: 'Rhapsody on a Windy Night', 2: 'Along the reaches of the street'; 8, 14–16, 34: 'Every street-lamp that I pass', 'The street-lamp sputtered, / The street-lamp muttered, / The street-lamp said', etc.; 12: 'As a madman shakes a dead geranium'; 60, 68: 'With all the old nocturnal smells', 'cocktail smells in bars'. Also 'Preludes', I. 11: 'And at the corner of the street', II. 3: 'From the sawdust-trampled street', III. 10: 'You had such a vision of the street', IV. 8: 'The conscience of a blackened street'. Also I. 2: 'smell of steaks in passageways'.

Through Eliot there may also be an indirect debt to Jules Laforgue (1860–87), whom BB had read. Cp. also the quotation from Laforgue beginning '*O géraniums*' in Eliot's 1921 essay, 'The Metaphysical Poets'.

II. 39. Kaiserin! German, wife of a Kaiser.

II. 56–7. Polymnia . . . Reno. Polymnia, muse of sacred hymns and poetry; literally, 'she of the many hymns'. Sometimes considered mother of Orpheus or Eros. Also occurs in 'Well of Lycopolis' I, *FBO* 5, and *UO* 6. *Polyhymnia* was the title of a 1590 poem long attributed to George Peele, now thought to be by Sir Henry Lee; Thackeray quoted part of the song at its end, 'His Golden lockes, / Time hath to Silver turn'd', in *The Newcomes*, chap. 76. Hemingway's title, *A Farewell to Arms*, also comes from this poem. Reno, Nevada, was a famed destination for those seeking quick divorces.

II. 58. eh, Cino. Cino da Pistoia (*ca.*1270–1336/7) was one of Dante's best friends; in *De vulgari eloquentia* Dante called him the best Italian love poet, perhaps with some irony, since they were poetic rivals. Cino was also an influence on Petrarch. Forde calls this passage 'a parody of the *dolce stil nuovo* which Dante advocated and encouraged Cino to use'. She also compares 'Rossetti's criticism of Cino's "elaborate and mechanical tone of complaint which hardly reads like the expression of true love." (*The Collected Works of Dante Gabriel Rossetti*, ed. William M. Rossetti [London, 1888], vol. 2, 19)' (*Forde*, 164). BB told Peter Bell that his earliest reading included **'Rossetti's translations of the early Italian poets'** (interview 3 September 1981, in *Swigg*). He had been given Rossetti's poems at the age of fourteen, and **'got an enormous lot of them by heart'** (interview with Lawrence Pitkethly and James Laughlin, October 1982, in R. Swigg, 'Basil Bunting on Ezra Pound', *Paideuma* 38 [2011], 9). EP's *The Spirit of Romance* owes much to Rossetti as well, and Cino is discussed in Chap. VI, 'Lingua Toscana'. Dante, in his *De vulgari Eloquentia*, frequently compares himself to Cino, and refers to himself as 'Cino's friend'; (a work about which BB said, **'I think that a man who will read *De vulgari Eloquentia* will have got most of the literary criticism he's ever going to require.'** (*Mottram*, 8). [EP also commended this work, e.g. in a letter dated

8 July 1922 to Felix E. Schelling (*The Letters of Ezra Pound: 1907–1941*, 179); and in his essay, 'Cavalcanti', in *Make It New* [London: Faber & Faber, 1934]). Cp. EP's 'Cino': '"Cino?" "Oh, eh, Cino Polnesi / The singer is't you mean?"' TS2 of this EP poem includes the manuscript insertion, 'C. Polnesi not to be confounded with the better known "Cino da Pistoia".' EP had used the name 'Cino' as a pseudonym. TS1 of the poem includes the insertion of the Latin word, *loquitur* ('he speaks') – later used by BB for the title of his 1965 Fulcrum Press volume (*Collected Early Poems of Ezra Pound* [New York, 1976], ed. M. J. King, 293). BB's early mentor, Ford Madox Ford, cites Cino in *The Critical Attitude* (1911).

II. 67. jilts. Probably *OED* n.1: 'A woman who has lost her chastity; a harlot or strumpet; a kept mistress. *Obs.*' or 3, '*Sc.* A contemptuous term for a girl or young woman.' Cp. Scott, *Old Mortality*, st. viii: 'Though she's but a dirty jilt'.

III. Cp. generally Catullus' LXIII, the lament of Attis; and Lucretius, *De rerum natura*, II. 618–28.

[Subheading] Pastorale arioso / (falsetto). Opera with a pastoral theme in the style of an aria for a falsetto voice (*Lesch*, 178–9). *Forde* (164) explains this as part of BB's mockery: that this section of the poem is designated as 'a pastorale which is neither wholly song nor wholly recitative, but a combination, to be rendered here in a falsetto voice'. Cp. Kipling's 'The Masque of Plenty', which also employs mock musical directions.

III. 2. Attis. God of vegetation, and Cybele's counterpart, with whom she falls in love. Chosen to be a priest of Cybele, he undertook a vow of chastity, which he broke. Cybele punished him with an attack of delirium, during which he mutilated himself; on recovering, Cybele turned him into a fir tree (*Lesch*, 173); also a volume published five years after the composition of the poem indicating a continuing interest in Attis: William A. Brend, *Sacrifice to Attis: a Study of Sex and Civilization* (1936). Cp. generally Swinburne, 'Dolores', esp. 329–52; quoted in notes to poem epigraph and I. 43–50, above.

III. 5. Pines. If a noun, then the grove of pines in which the poem is apparently set is being addressed. (*OED* has citations for pines as a transitive verb, to cause pain or suffering, from King Ælfred, and *Lindisfarne Gospel* Matthew 8: 29). Cp. Tennyson, 'Lucretius', 86: 'whom all the pines of Ida shook to see', and 213: 'no larger feast than under plane or pine'. Ovid has Atys changed by Cybele into a pine tree in *Metamorphoses* X. 104. Also 'Œnone' – based on Ovid's 'Heroides', which EP wrote about in his essay, 'Notes on Elizabethan Classicists' – 4, 'creeps from pine to pine'; 48–9, 'aloft the mountain pine' (see Forde's summary above, where Attis is driven to the 'mountain pines'); 86, 'whispering tuft of oldest pine'; 91, 'lost his way between the piney sides'; 205, 'my tall dark pines', etc.

III. 6. chaffered. OED: Trafficked or dealt in, bartered. Cp. Wordsworth, 'chaffering', in *The Prelude* (1850), VIII. 22.

III. 7. halfhunter. OED 'hunter' 4, hunting watch, as in the citation, 'A hunter, engraved, enamel dial'. See note on *enamel*, at II. 22 above. Cp. perhaps Joyce, *Ulysses*, II: 'John Henry Menton . . . holding a fat gold hunter watch not looked at.'

III. 8. annual sports and flowershow. Cp. Catullus LXIII, 63–8; Loeb: 'I, to be a woman – I who was a stripling, I a youth, I a boy, I was the flower of the playground, I was once the glory of the palaestra: mine were the crowded doorways, mine the warm thresholds, mine the flowery garlands to deck my house when I was to leave my chamber at sunrise. I, shall I now be called – what? a handmaid of the gods, a ministress of Cybele?'

III. 17. affiliation orders. OED, 'affiliation', 4, citation for 1914: 'an order made under the Bastardy Laws Amendment Act, 1872 . . . adjudging a man to be the putative father of a bastard child and ordering him to pay a sum of money weekly or otherwise to the mother of the bastard child or to any other person who is named in the order.'

III. 18. chaste vegetable. Cp. Marvell, 'To his Coy Mistress', 11: 'vegetable Love'.

III. 19. Dindyma. See note to epigraph, above, concerning Mount Dindymus.

III. 21. Scirocco. Var. of sirocco, a hot, dust-filled wind that blows on the northern Mediterranean coast, especially in Italy, Sicily and Malta.

III. 29–30. sleeplessly in strange beds. / I have forgotten most of the details. Cp. again T. S. Eliot, 'The Love Song of J. Alfred Prufrock', generally, and also 104: 'It is impossible to say just what I mean!'

III. 33. ithyphallic. From Greek 'erect phallus'. *OED*: 'A. *adj.* a. Pertaining to or associated with the phallus carried in procession at the Bacchic festivals; *spec.* composed in the metre of the Bacchic hymns (the trochaic dimeter brachycatalectic). Also, B. *n.* A poem in ithyphallic metre; also, a poem of licentious or indecent character.' Cp. Byron, *Vision of Judgment*, Preface, 'I omit noticing some edifying Ithyphallics of Savagius.' Also D. H. Lawrence, 'Doors', 2–5: 'No, not the ithyphallic demons / not even the double Phallus of the devil himself / with his key to the two dark doors / is evil.'

III. 37–9. (Oh Sis! / I've been 'ad! / I've been 'ad proper!). Cp. Lil's complaint in *The Waste Land*, 158–9: 'I can't help it, she said, pulling a long face, / It's them pills I took, to bring it off, she said.'

III. 40. Elysium. Homeric Elysian fields, a land to which heroes pass without dying; or the lower world described by Latin poets where the good spirits of the dead reside. Cybele and Attis 'were protectors of the grave and her priests had one supposed consolation for their self-castration: the promise of greater happiness in Elysium' (*Lesch*, 191). Cp. *FBO* 19.

III. 44–8. roses and myrtles . . . peacock. The rose was an ancient symbol of purity; in Christian iconography, red roses denote martyrdom. The myrtle was an ancient symbol of love; in Christian iconography it denotes the Gentiles' conversion. In Greek mythology, the 'eyes' of the peacock's feathers represented the vigilant eyes of Argus as he watched Zeus. The peacock can denote human vanity; in early Christian symbolism, however, it was a sign of immortality because it was thought that the peacock's flesh did not decay after death. By the middle ages, the peacock had become an emblem of the resurrection of Christ.

III. 50. Cybele. Goddess of earth in its primitive state; worshipped on mountaintops, including Ida and Dindymus. See notes to poem epigraph, above.

III. 61. embleme. OED n.5: 'In *pl.* The evidences of sex. *Obs.*'

III. 62. Nonnulla deest. 'Something is missing.' Perhaps derives from Marlowe's famously unfinished 'Hero and Leander', II. 335: '*Desunt nonnulla*' ('Some sections are missing'). EP's *Guide to Kulchur* (New York, 1970) contains a chapter heading, 'Pergamena Deest'. The book is dedicated to LZ and BB.

Aus Dem Zweiten Reich

BB remarked in a letter that, after trying to earn a living in Britain, he **'took advice and went to Berlin and it was the worst thing I ever did'** (BB to Leippert, 30 October 1932; quoted *Forde*, 31). Years later he still felt the same way, telling JW, **'I found that I didn't like the Germans at all'** (*Descant*, [12]). Referring to Isherwood and others, he remarked, **'I got in before the novelists did'** (reading at Air Gallery, 1977, in *Swigg*).

'"Aus Dem Zweiten Reich" is very obviously a Scarlatti sonata in my mind. I don't think that anyone has said so, but *I* think it is!' (interview with Peter Bell, 3 September 1981, in *Swigg*).

In some readings of the poem (e.g. Air Gallery, 1977, in *Swigg*), BB read aloud the lines in quotation marks with a faux-German accent.

Publication history

Written in Rapallo, 1931. In *CE*. Published in *P1950*, *Loquitur*, and all editions of *CP*.

Notes

[Title] Aus Dem Zweiten Reich. 'From the Second Reich'. The title is anachronistic, since the Second Reich ended in 1918; the events described in the poem actually took place during the Weimar Republic.

I. 1–2; 35–6. Tauentsienstrasse . . . Nollendorferplatz; Gedächtnis Kirche . . . Bahnhof Zoo. 'The narrator and his date are taking a walk down Tauentsienstrasse, which runs from the Nollendorferplatz, with its cafés, past the Kaiser Wilhelm Memorial Church ('Gedächtnis Kirche') and the zoo railway station, into the middle-class neighborhood of Charlottenburg. The route itself can easily be traced on a map' (*Lesch*, 195).

I. 5. negerband. Jazz band of black musicians.

I. 17. ganz. Literally, 'quite'.

I. 18. 'Sturm über Asien. 'Storm over Asia', a 1928 film by V. I. Pudovkin.

flicker. Slang for motion picture; see *OED*, 'flick' n.1.e, and 'flicker', n.3.3.

I. 21. Sie and Du. Formal and familiar forms, respectively, of 'you'.

[Stanza 5]. Cp. T. S. Eliot, 'Preludes', I.

I. 48. fabelhaft. Literally, 'gorgeous'.

II. 1. Herr Lignitz. A common German surname. Lignitz (or Liegnitz; modern Legnica in Poland) was one of the principal cities of Silesia; the thirteenth-century Battle of Lignitz is discussed in Gibbon, *Decline and Fall of the Roman Empire*, chap. LXIV, Pt. III. , n. 27.

II. 9. Macy's. American department store.

III. ▪ **The great man need not be identified but will, I believe, be recognized by those who knew him.** German playwright, Gerhart Hauptmann (1862–1946), awarded the Nobel Prize for Literature in 1912; BB wrote to Forde: **'He and his entourage are perfectly recognizable [in this poem], but not of course, from acquaintance with his writings only'** (BB to Forde, 23 May 1972; quoted *Forde*, 168). BB's first wife, Marian, kept a clipping of part of a newspaper article dated 5 January 1932, headlined, 'Prominent Literati Arriving At Rapallo To Pass Winter Season', which mentions that 'Gerhardt

Hauptmann, venerable figure of the literary constellation, is shortly due from Switzerland.' The article also mentions EP, Yeats, Max Beerbohm, among others, and notes the birth of BB's daughter Bourtai (*Forde*, 34–5). The poem was written in Rapallo.

III. 8. chevelure. OED: '1. The hair of the head, a head of hair; a wig; 2. *transf.* The luminous appearance surrounding the nucleus of comets; also the diffused light round certain nebulous stars.'

III. 18. Schrecklich. Literally, 'dreadful'.

The Well of Lycopolis

Three draft versions were sent to LZ (including a longer version sent with a letter of 28 October 1935, reproduced above in full in 'Fragments and False Starts', with additional annotations in that section, below).

Lycopolis was a 'city noted for trade which is located at the head of the Nile' (*Lesch*, 207), from Gibbon, *Decline and Fall of the Roman Empire*, II. 40. See note below on *cujus potu signa / virginitatis eripiuntur*. ▪ **Gibbon mentions its effect in a footnote. The long quotations from Villon and Dante will of course be recognized. Americans may care to be informed that as a native of Paphos Venus was until recently entitled to a British passport. Her quotation from Sophie Tucker will not escape the attention of those who remember the first world war, and need not engage that of those who dont. The remarks of the brass head occur in the no longer sufficiently well-known story of Friar Bacon and Friar Bungay, of which I think Messrs Laurel and Hardy could make use. Some may remember that the only one of the rivers of Paradise to which we have access on earth, namely Zamzam, is reported to be brackish.**

Publication history

Published in *P1950*, *Loquitur*, and all editions of *CP*. Reprinted in *Georgia Straight*, n.pag., *Guedalla* D34, and section I in *Shake the Kaleidoscope*, 2–4, later issued as *The Best of Modern Poetry* (1975).

Notes

[Note] Paphos. In antiquity, the capital of Cyprus; Venus' birth from the foam of the sea and having been carried by waves to Paphos is recounted in Homeric Hymn 11 to Aphrodite and Hesiod's *Theogony*; the story was quoted by Ovid, Virgil and others. Ingres painted 'Venus at Paphos', *ca.*1852–3. BB owned a 1920 book, *The Handbook of Cyprus*. Cp. generally Swinburne's *Atalanta in Calydon*; also Byron, *Don Juan* V, st. 96, 1–4: 'The lady rising up with such an air / As Venus rose with from the wave, on them / Bent

like an antelope a Paphian pair / Of eyes', and XI, st. 30, 4–5: 'those pedestrian Paphians, who abound / In decent London when the daylight's o'er'; also EP, *Cantos* XXX. 19: 'In Paphos, on a day'; and 'Kipling, 'The Second Voyage', 21: 'any Port o' Paphos mutineer!'

Sophie Tucker. Vaudeville entertainer (1884–1966) known as 'the last of the red-hot mamas'.

Friar Bacon and Friar Bungay. *The Honorable Historie of Frier Bacon, and Frier Bongay*, a comedy (printed 1594) in verse and prose by Robert Greene (1558?–92). The title characters were based on the Franciscans Roger Bacon and Thomas Bungay. With the Devil's help, Bacon creates a brass head that can speak; Bacon falls asleep while waiting for the head to speak, and misses it talking three times. What the head says, before falling to the floor and shattering into pieces, is: 'Time is', 'Time was', and 'Time is past'.

rivers of Paradise . . . Zamzam. Zamzam is a sacred well in Mecca, Saudi Arabia.

BB made various comments about this poem over the years: **'I got very gloomy in the Canaries and wrote a poem called, "The Well of Lycopolis", which is about as gloomy a poem as anyone would want.'** (*Descant*, [16]). **'I have parodied part of the Belle Heaulmiere for a poem now in the making'** (BB to EP, 'Day after saint bloody John' [1935]; quoted *Makin*, 82). **'You are past being damaged by a draught of it'** (BB to LZ, 28 October 1935; quoted *Makin*, 82). **'NO ONE will publish the W of L. Perhaps as well, not sure I want it published'** (BB to EP, 14 March 1936; quoted *Makin*, 82). **'We need sensuality because without it we stumble into the ways of hollering he-man Hemingway sentimentality, or else the medical text-book school which forces itself unwillingly to admit, item by item, what is really half our life. (The last I expressed my dislike for in "Lycopolis")'** (BB to LZ, 13 March 1951; quoted *Forde*, 185–6). **'A very bitter poem'** (BB, deciding not to read it, Air Gallery, 1977, in *Swigg*). **'It's the most disgruntled of all my works . . . I used large passages, some from Villon, some from Dante, translated in my own manner of doing it, as a large part of the body of the poem, so that if you find something familiar there it's deliberate, it's not accident'** (reading at Riverside Studios, London, February 1982, in *Swigg*).

[Epigraph] cujus potu signa / virginitatis eripiuntur. Translation: 'By whose potion the seal / of virginity is broken.' **'The well of Lycopolis, is . . . I learned of it from Edward Gibbon, who has the most fascinating footnotes in his *Decline and Fall of the Roman Empire*, and he describes, at one place, the well of Lycopolis which is visited by the emperor Hadrian. "Cujus potu signa, virginitatis eripiuntur" – I leave the Latin, I think, it's intended to be left in Latin, as Gibbon left it in Latin, because, he said, for many of the notes he had to make he preferred the decent obscurity of a learned**

language' (reading at Riverside Studios, London, February 1982, in *Swigg*). According to Gibbon, chap. XXVII, Pt. V, n. 112, an inscription written on a well in an Egyptian city. (Gibbon's note reads: 'Lycopolis is the modern Siut, or Osiot, a town of Said, about the size of St. Denys, which derives a profitable trade with the kingdom of Senaar, and has a very convenient fountain, "cujus potu signa virginitatis eripiuntur". See D'Anville, *Description de l'Egypte*, p. 181, Abulfeda, *Descript. Egypt.*, p. 14, and the curious Annotations, p. 25, 92, of his editor Michaelis.')

I. [Epigraph to section] Advis m'est que j'oy regretter. 'It seems I can hear the complaint.' From first line of Villon, 'Les Regrets de la belle Heaulmière', in *Le Grand Testament*. On Forde's request, BB later translated this as **'Oh dear! where do these mournful sighs come from? I am reminded (or I notice) that I heard (the beauty) regretting'** (BB to Forde, 4 July 1973; quoted *Forde*, 172–3). In Anthony Bonner's translation: 'It seemed I heard the one they called the Belle Hëaulmiere complain, longing for the days when she was young.' **'I would like to say, in case there's anybody here who's been misled by half the commentators and so on, that Heaulmière was the wife or daughter of a helmet-maker. And in Villon's day, the 1400's, next to the goldsmiths, the helmet-makers were the most skilful, the most highly-paid, much the richest of the artisans. They were the foundation of what became the middle class. Many *heaulmières* became bankers, just as goldsmiths did. They were rich people. And so when you read the people discoursing on Villon who treat la belle Heaulmière as a prostitute it is absolutely wrong, she is nothing of the sort. She was a rich woman. And she'd no doubt spent her money and became poor, all the rest of it, [but] the man she's regretting and worried about, is not, as you'll find in half the French editions of Villon, a pimp. Nothing of the sort. He is her boyfriend that she no doubt is exploited by in every possible way, but he's the boyfriend of a rich woman, she was [a] rich woman, it's not in the least what you often find. I use her for the introduction of Venus, the first part being a dialogue between the goddess Venus and the goddess Polymnia, the muse of the more complicated kinds of song'** (reading at Riverside Studios, London, February 1982, in *Swigg*).

I. 1. jug-and-bottle. *OED*, 'jug' n.2.3, 'used *attrib*. of the bar of a public house at which alcoholic liquors are sold for consumption off the premises'.

I. 3. Mother Venus. Cp. generally Lucretius, *De rerum natura*; *OED* 'way', n.1., cites Marlowe and Nashe (1593), *Dido*, 221: 'Æneas is my name . . . / With twise twelue Phrigian ships I plowed the deepe, / And made that way my mother Venus led.'

I. 4. *half-quartern*. Half of a quarter of a pint. *OED* 'quartern', n.1. cites Ælfric; n.2.g cites Mandeville; cp. Marryat (1835) *Jac. Faithf.* xxii, 'There is my mother with a quartern of gin before her,' and Carlyle (1839) *Chartism*, iv. 132: 'Liquid Madness [Gin] sold at ten-pence the quartern.' *OED* 'sensation', 4, cites *Hotten's Slang Dict., Sensation* (1859), 'a quartern of gin'. (A very early use is given under 'upright', a. and n.5, in the citation of *Sporting Mag.* VII. 107 [1796]). Under 'mop', vol. 2, citation for Mayhew (1851–61), *Lond. Labour* III. 250: 'I have seen the youngest "mop up" his half-quartern as well as I did.' Cp. Keats, letter to J. H. Reynolds, 21 September 1819: 'O how I admire the middle siz'd delicate Devonshire girls of about 15. There was one at an Inn door holding a quartern of brandy – the very thought of her kept me warm a whole stage' (*Letters of John Keats*, ed. Robert Gittings [Oxford, 1970], 293).

I. 6ff. 'It's cruel hard . . .' At readings, BB read the sections within quotation marks in a voice made to sound like an old woman's, e.g. Riverside Studios, London, February 1982, in *Swigg*.

I. 37. Bacchic. Relating to Bacchus, Greek god of wine.

I. 43. pinnies. *OED*: 'Nursery and colloquial name for pinafore', citing R. D. Blackmore's *Tommy Upmore*, II. 240: 'All the children . . . with their pinnies full of sugar-plums'; *EDD* cites George Eliot, *Adam Bede* I. 329: 'Now then, Totty, hold our your pinny.'

I. 44. Belgian atrocities. Stories were circulated during World War I of atrocities committed by German soldiers in Belgium.

I. 48. encumberance. BB's spelling.

I. 54–5. work it off . . . rub down. Describes methods used for preventing conception or aborting pregnancy.

I. 59. Polymnia. Muse of sacred hymns and poetry; see note to 'Attis: Or, Something Missing', II. 56–7.

I. 62–64. brass head / of the tongs . . . 'Time is, was, has been.' See headnote re the 'brazen head' in Greene's *Friar Bacon and Friar Bungay*.

I. 69. the Goddess. Venus.

I. 82–5. Blotched belly . . . known me? Cp. Villon, 'Les regrets de la belle Heaulmière'.

II. In the longer draft sent to LZ, BB called this the **'Damn slow movement.'**

II. 4. Canopus. *OED*: 'The bright star α in the southern constellation Argo, situated in the rudder of the ship.' Cp. Tennyson, 'A Dream of

Fair Women,' 146: 'We drank the Libyan sun to sleep, and lit lamps which out-burn'd Canopus.' But also perhaps the British battleship HMS *Canopus*, which BB might have noted in the news in 1914–15, when it was involved in prominent battles

II. 11. Dreaming of you, that's all I do. At readings, BB sang this phrase, e.g. Riverside Studios, London, February 1982, in *Swigg*. From 'Meet Me Tonight in Dreamland', words by Beth Slater Whitson, music by Leo Friedman, 1909.

II. 18. Open your eyes, Polymnia. BB wrote to LZ that here Polymnia needs to open her eyes to the activities of '**"sleek, slick lads", pale, smooth and effeminate like [Samuel] Butler's "smockfaced boys"**' (28 October 1935; quoted *Forde*, 171, and *BBP*, 193, n. 2).

II. 19. bedpots. Not in *OED* or *EDD*.

II. 22. ambiguoque voltu. 'With ambiguous face.' Reference to Horace, *Odes*, II. 5, 24, which Loeb gives as 'girl-boy face'. *Ambiguus* can 'refer either to the uncertainty of somebody's sex or to sexual ambivalence itself' (R. G. M. Nisbet and M. Hubbard, *A Commentary on Horace* Odes, *Book II*, 92); quoted Gilonis, *McGonigal & Price*, 218, n). Cp. BB's version of this poem, 'That filly couldnt carry a rider nor', in 'Uncollected Overdrafts'. As in the letter to LZ quoted above, 'Butler's "smockfaced boys"' are those with *ambiguoque voltu*.

II. 23–4. Daphnis . . . Chloe. Alludes to 'the adolescent sexual explorations' (*Lesch*, 213) of the goatherd, Daphnis, and shepherdess, Chloe, in Longus' pastoral novel *Daphnis and Chloe*, *ca.* second century CE, supposedly set on the island of Lesbos. Daphnis is said to have invented bucolic poetry (*Lesch*, 214).

II. 34. between High Holborn and the Euston Road. '**[the] boundaries of Bloomsbury**' (BB to LZ, 28 October 1935; quoted *Lesch*, 214). In a letter to James G. Leippert, BB described EP's flat in Rapallo as evoking '**the ungenteel, lively side of Bloomsbury Bohemia (whatever he says about Bloomsbury)**' (30 October 1932; quoted *Makin*, 64). BB had spent time between 1919 and 1923 in Bloomsbury, where he got to know people associated with the 'Bloomsbury Group'. In a 1933 review written in Italian for *Il Mare*, BB described Bloomsbury as '**a dung heap believed to be a bed of lillies**', the source of '**the sweet, drippy, unbearable smell of decadence**' that pervaded English art and life; Bloomsbury was '**the stubborn rear-guard of a dying golden age in which the servants were servile and even the well-off tradesmen prudently bowed to Birth and Education**' (*Terrell*, 249). In a review of a book on Samuel Butler by Malcolm Muggeridge ('Butler', *New English Weekly* 9, no. 25 [1 October 1936], 411–12),

BB placed Muggeridge with Strachey and other Bloomsbury critics, whom he called **'the hard-boiled but half-baked race of perfunctory debunkers'**. In an interview much later, he said, **'What I resented about the Bloomsbury group in particular might be said to be two things: one, a certain cocksureness which in particular made me distrust Maynard Keynes. The other was that they were all of that well-to-do middle class, bordering on county gentry who felt that if you couldn't afford to live in Bloomsbury or Regent's Park or some similar, desirable, but very expensive part of the world, well, poor devil, there wasn't much to be expected from you. Then also, their patronage was something I didn't like the smell of. They took up a fellow like Lawrence, for instance, and Lawrence was, unfortunately, very willing to be taken up by the rich. I think they spoilt what chances he had of being a good writer. They were considerable at the time'** (*Reagan*, 75). *Forde* (26) reports the following exchange between BB and her about some of the Bloomsbury Group: 'Q. Roger Fry? A. **Fidgety**. Q. Clive Bell? A. (Dismissed with **'hmph'**). Q. Forster? A. **Nice enough chap, but the whole Bloomsbury Group didn't really like anyone not wealthy, with an inheritance, and educated.**'

II. 37. (aequora pontis). 'the level ocean'. From the opening invocation to Venus in *De rerum natura* (I. 8), 'aequora ponti' ('the wide stretches of ocean' [Loeb]). Cp. BB's 1927 translation of the introduction to *De rerum natura* in 'Overdrafts', 'Darling of Gods and Men'.

II. 39. 'proud, full sail'. Cp. Shakespeare, Sonnet 86, 1–2: 'Was it the proud full sail of his great verse, / Bound for the prize of all-too-precious you. . .' According to Caddel: 'The story goes that whilst he was at school Basil Bunting took the school copy of Shakespeare's sonnets and edited it: cutting out the inessential bits, straightening the syntax and so on to reveal the essence of the poems. That copy no longer exists – presumably laid to rest by teachers scandalised as much by the literary heresy as the schoolboy vandalism – but in the late 1920's Bunting repeated the exercise, apparently for the benefit of Dorothy Pound. That copy has survived in a private collection' (*Caddel*, 48, where eight 'edited' sonnets – not including 86 – from the later copy are reproduced). BB mentions in a letter to Harriet Monroe that he is **'engaged in rewriting Shakespeare's sonnets. They can do with it'** (13 July 1931, held by University of Chicago).

II. 42. closehauled. 'Close haul' is a sailing term; trimming the sails so as to sail close to the wind.

II. 46. reef. *OED* v.1, I.1.a.: 'To reduce the extent of (a sail) by taking in or rolling up a part and securing it.' Cp. Swift, *Gulliver's Travels* II. i, 'We reeft the Fore-sail and set him.'

III. In the longer draft sent to LZ, BB called this movement the **'Slump'**.

III. 2. Aeolus. Made keeper of the winds by Zeus.

III. 4. Ocean. In Greek mythology, a river, personified as a God, which came from the underworld and flowed around the earth in a circle. Odysseus crossed this body of water in his descent to the underworld. Cp. also perhaps Wordsworth *The Prelude* (1850), V 33: 'Old Ocean, in his bed', and Byron, *Don Juan* II st. 70, 2: 'And Ocean slumber'd like an unwean'd child'.

privities. OED 'privity,' 4. 'The private parts. Chiefly in *pl.*' Cp. Chaucer, *Monk's Tale, l.* 724: 'For no man sholde seen his priuetee.'

III. 8–15. I shall never have anything to myself . . . a fool's image. BB wrote about these lines to Forde: **'I am inescapably part of a detested generation. To see, and to have a mirror amongst what you see, is less than usual in satire. Hence the difficulty'** (BB to Forde, 4 July 1973; quoted *Forde*, 175).

III. 11. a dogstar for the Dogstar. OED 1: 'The star Sirius, in the constellation of the Greater Dog, the brightest of the fixed stars.' The star's appearance coincides with the heat of August. Cp. Horace, *Odes*, III. 13, 9: 'te flagrantis atrox hora Caniculae', etc., where the fountain wards off what Michael C. J. Putnam has called the Dog Star's 'heated advances'; Pliny (tr. Philemon Holland (1634), 1. 522–3: 'the rising of the Dog-starre'; Ronsard's ode, 'Ô Fontaine Bellerie', *l.* 22; also E. K.'s gloss of Spenser's *Shepheardes Calender*, July 21: 'The Dogge star, which is called Syrius, or Canicula reigneth' (for E. K., see http://shakespeareoxfordfellowship.org/who-was-spencers-ek); Marvell, 'Damon the Mower', 17–18: 'This head the sun could never raise, / Nor Dog Star so inflames the days'; and perhaps also Hopkins's translation of Horace, *Odes* III. i, 31: 'The dog-star with the fields abake.' The first reappearance of Sirius in the east was used by ancient Egyptians to signal the beginning of the new lunar year, shortly after which the Nile would produce its soil-enriching floods. The dog star turns up also in EP's *Cantos*, LXXXII. Sirius also appears in 'Hi, tent-boy, get that tent down' (in 'Uncollected Overdrafts'), and *Briggflatts* V. 104–5.

III. 19–20; 31. tweet, tweet, twaddle, / tweet, tweet, twat . . . Tweet, tweet, twaddle. At readings, BB sang these lines, e.g. Riverside Studios, London, February 1982, in *Swigg*. Cp. *The Waste Land*, 103: 'Jug Jug' and 203–4: 'Twit twit twit / Jug jug jug jug jug jug'; and among many similar, John Lyly, 'Spring's Welcome' from *Campaspe*, 3: 'Jug, jug, jug, jug, Tereu', no. 86 in Quiller-Couch's 1919 ed. of *The Oxford Book of English Verse, 1250–1900*; and Thomas Nashe, 'Spring', 4, 8, and 12: 'Cuckoo, jug-jug, pu-we, to-witta-woo', poem 1 in Book First of Palgrave's *Golden Treasury*;

also perhaps Skelton, 'To maystres Isabell Pennell', in *Garlande or Chapelet of Laurell*, 1000–4: 'Dug, dug, / Jug, jug, / Good yere and good luk, / With chuk, chuk, chuk, chuk.'

III. 22–3. Bellerophon . . . gelding. In Greek mythology, Bellerophon was 'castrated by the King of Argos because of false charges of improprieties toward the king's wife' (*Lesch*, 217). Cp. EP, *Homage to Sextus Propertius*, II. 2, 'The water dripping from Bellerophon's horse'.

III. 25. mansuetude. OED: 'Gentleness, meekness'. Citation for Chaucer, 'Parson's Tale', ¶580: 'The remedye agayns Ire is a vertue that men clepen Mansuetude.' Cp. Browning, *Ring and the Book*, VIII. 658: 'Our Lord Himself, made up of mansuetude'.

III. 28. Scamped. Spent negligently or hurriedly, as in *OED* v.2.1 and 3.

III. 33. Clap a clout on your jowl. EDD v.2.1: 'to beat, cuff, strike, *gen.*, about the head', giving a Northumberland usage, 'A a'll cloot yor jaw.' Here probably slang for 'shut your mouth.'

III. 34. Fy for shame! Fie. Cp. Chaucer, 'Nun's Priest's Tale', 71: 'Ye ben a very sleper, fy for shame'; Skelton, 'Skelton Laureat Upon the Dolorus Dethe and Muche Lamentable Chaunce of the Mooste Honorable Erle of Northumberlande', 42: 'Fy, fy, for shame, ther hartis wer to faynt'; and Thackeray, *Vanity Fair*, xvii: '"My relations won't cry fie upon me," Becky said.' 'Fie for shame' occurs years later in a translation of Aristophanes LZ quoted in his *Zukofsky*, 372, *Guedalla* B9.

III. 38. age of consent. Cp. T. S. Eliot, *The Waste Land*, 404: 'an age of prudence'.

III. 40. kecking. OED v.1: 'To make a sound as if about to vomit; to retch; to feel an inclination to vomit.' Cp. Milton, *An Apology for Smectymnuus*, Introduction: 'The worser stuffe she strongly keeps in her stomach, but the better she is ever kecking at, and is queasie.'

III. 44–45. Way-O! Bully boys blow! / Gadarene swihine have got us in tow. From a shanty called 'The Liverpool Girls' which exists in many variants, including one that contains the lines 'And it's blow, blow bullies blow / Them Liverpool Judies have got us in tow', or perhaps 'The Banks of Newfoundland', which begins 'You bully boys of Liverpool . . .' BB owned a 1921 volume called *The Shanty Book*. At readings, BB sang these lines, e.g. Riverside Studios, London, February 1982, in *Swigg*. Cp., in Matthew 8: 32, the demon-possessed swine that rushed into the sea. BB referred to these lines as a parody of a popular song in a letter to LZ (28 October 1935; mentioned *Forde*, 171). Also probably a reference to

Circe, who turned men into swine. Cp. Joyce, *Ulysses* II: 'On nags, hogs, bellhorses, Gadarene swine'. A controversial debate (1890–1) between Gladstone and T. H. Huxley on the miracle of the Gadarene swine took place in the monthly review, *Nineteenth Century*. BB's daughter Bourtai recalled her father singing shanties to her when she was a child (*Forde*, 40). Conceivably 'swihine' echoes Eliot's sing-spelling of 'Shakespeherian Rag' at *The Waste Land*, 128–30.

IV. In the longer draft sent to LZ, BB called this movement the **'Dead March and Polka'**. It was originally introduced by the line, **'Manly Mars for Coda!'** Among the lines omitted here are:

War
Natural, necessary, glorious war,
ennobles and elevates man. (*Forde*, 174)

[Epigraph] Ed anche vo' che tu per certo credi / che sotto l'acqua ha gente che sospira. From Dante, *Inferno*, VII. 117–18, at the fifth circle of Hell: 'the souls of the Gloomy – sluggish, gurgling in their throats a dismal chant'. BB's version of this epigraph appears in 40–2 of this section. Lines 1–6 of this section are a translation of Dante's 121–6. *Makin* (91, n. 51) notes that BB 'may well have mistranslated *l.* 123 as if the "fummo" were again "we were".'

IV. 7–8. Styx . . . rivers of Paradise. The river over which the shades of the dead are ferried by Charon. See BB's note to the poem, above. Cp. Genesis 2: 10–14, and perhaps also Dante, *Purgatorio* XXVIII. 130–1.

IV. 13. bright peaks. In the draft sent to LZ with the letter of 28 October 1935, these words are glossed by the following line: **'trivial ghosts'** (quoted *Makin*, 92).

IV. 14. love for love. Perhaps plays on the title of Congreve's comedy, *Love for Love*.

IV. 17. college of Muses. The nine sister goddesses in Greek mythology presiding over poetry and song.

IV. 19. bandy. As an adj. (*EDD* 7), it can mean 'knock-kneed'.

dot-and-carry-one. Cp. Kipling, 'Gunga Din', 35: ''E would dot an' carry one', and Stevenson, *Treasure Island* pt. IV, chap. XVI: 'I know my pulse went dot and carry one.' *EDD* 7, 'dot . . .': 'expressive of the walk of a lame person'. Cp. possibly Joyce, *Ulysses*, II, 'The Great Gallaher': 'Hop and carry one, is it? Myles Crawford said.'

IV. 21–3. Join the Royal Air Force . . . Flag. Slogans on military recruitment posters; at readings, BB recited these in a mock-emphatic voice, e.g. Riverside Studios, London, February 1982, in *Swigg*.

IV. 26. pox in Rouen. French pox? Venereal disease; see *OED*, 'pox', n.1.e, 'French' a. and n.6, and 'venereal,' 1.2.a. Mottram remarks that venereal disease 'gets you sent home from the Front but as a cure for self-doubt it is a fraud' ('"An Acknowledged Land": Love and Poetry in Bunting's Sonatas', *Poetry Information* 19 [Autumn 1978], 20). Rouen was a major British base in World War I, where there was ample opportunity to contract sexually transmitted diseases.

What a blighty! OED: 'n.c., Army slang: "In the war of 1914–18 applied to a wound that secured return to England."'

IV. 33. gaspers. OED 2: 'A cigarette, esp. a cheap or inferior one. *slang*.'

IV. 40–2. and besides I want you to know . . . with their sighs. BB's translation of Dante, *Inferno*, VII. 117–20. See also notes to 'Attis: Or, Something Missing', above. BB wrote to Forde, **'It might be worth noting that in Dante the boiling sighs of the Styx *are* presently submitted to a wind from Heaven, when the angel arrives to open the gate of Dis. The whole passage of the Inferno is indelibly in my mind. The gorgon in Attis is from the same page. (Whereas EP, who could remember the angel, had forgotten all the rest, which I think is bound up with the angel indissolubly)'** (BB to Forde, 4 July 1973; quoted *Forde*, 174). To Makin, BB wrote that **'in the Commedia, Medusa makes her appearance just after Dante has made acquaintance with the "accidiosi". Chaucer had the word, but it has vanished from modern English and all its very complex meaning is forgotten and no one takes any notice of it. It is essentially hopelessness, no longer a cardinal sin, perhaps because the industrial revolution has condemned so large a proportion of our population to wallow in it. In the Well of Lycopolis I have tried to turn Dante's contempt for it around, where I have Styx "silvered by a wind from Heaven" – ultimate hope rising from the helpless victims of accidie. You may reasonably conclude that it is a sin I feel myself much inclined to, to be cured or nullified by the epicurean slowworm, rather than by Alexander's heroics, though both have a place. Medusa hardly does more than confirm the accidie'** (BB to Makin, 3 December 1985; quoted *Makin*, 94–5). See also notes on 'slowworm' for *Briggflatts* I. 13.

The Spoils

BB had developed a working title, 'The Fifth Sonata' (*Lesch*, 233), and wrote to Peter Russell on 31 January 1951 that a new poem was **'getting onto paper in rough draft fairly fast as such things go with me – that is, twenty or even forty lines a week. I am pleased with some bits of it, and others will be alright after reshaping'** (quoted *Makin*, 108–9). Several drafts were sent to LZ beginning in 1948 (e.g. BB to LZ, 13 March 1951, held at HRC); some were originally in four movements like 'Well of Lycopolis,' but in the final version, the third and fourth movements were combined. A 1951 typescript (MS108, held at Durham) was marked up in pencil by BB to serve as the printer's copy for the Morden Tower edition; it contains a line dropped from all printed versions of the poem (see I. 17–18, below). As *Forde* observes (188), each section of the poem has 121 lines, which perhaps explains the deletion.

See BB's later foreword to *Arabic & Persian Poems in English* in Appendix II. B, and the list of books in BB's library generally pertaining to his interest in Arabic and Persian poetry, Appendix II. E.

The cover of the Morden Tower publication of *The Spoils* features a photograph of a Persian mosque; BB wrote to LZ (21 April 1965) recommending that he 'examine Upham Pope's beautifully illustrated book of Persian art, especially the pictures of the miniatures and the tile ceilings of domed mosques' (*Forde*, 123); Forde suggests that these can be considered 'a graphic design of a Persian poem'.

'Poem's title at last: The Spoils. Motto from Qor'an: Al-anfál li-llah, the spoils are for God. (to God, God's. God gets the booty). (Fifth Sonata wasnt intended for a permanent name, mere means of identification. But I do claim copyright, and bugger TSE. He was before me with Preludes, but I'd a bunch of Sonatas before he thought up his Quartets' (BB to LZ, 22 March 1951; quoted *Forde*, 177, and *Lesch*, 234, 236). When LZ responded with objections to the title, BB replied, **'If the title as set down sounds religiose, I'll not translate the Arabic motto, or even use the motto at all. But I don't see why the word "God", which has a million meanings, need be abandoned to the pious. The Spoils, all alone, is a little more enigmatic than I'd intended, but a title is nearly always an enigma anyway'** (19 April 1951; quoted *Forde*, 177).

On the poem's **'general intention'**, BB explained to LZ, **'If I could put it in prose I wouldnt take the trouble to write a poem'** (13 March 1951; quoted *Forde*, 178). EP did not like the poem, prompting an angry response to Dorothy Pound (11 December 1953; quoted *Burton*, 348): **'If Ole Ez had had time or inclination to read "The Spoils" attentively instead of being put off by the pair of Jews in part one of it, he might have noticed plumb in the middle of it is a remark that God is the dividing sword. It isn't there just for the noise. That's what I'm writing about, and that's why the spoils are for God in the epigraph from the**

Qor'an. It is shorthand for quite a lot, or if you like for something fundamental.'

▪ Let readers who lack Arabic forgive me for explaining that the epigraph, *al anfal li'llah*, is from the Qor'an, sura viii, and means 'The spoils are for God'. I named the sons of Shem at random from the Bible's list.

Some Persian words have no English equivalent. An *aivan* is a high arch backed by a shallow honeycomb half-dome or leading into a mosque. *Chenar*, Platanus orientalis, is grander than its London cousins; *tar*, a stringed instrument used in Persian classical music. *Vafur* signifies the apparatus of opium smoking, pipe, pricker, tongs, brazier, charcoal and the drug, shining like a stick of black sealing wax. The *azan* is the mo'ezzin's call to prayer. You hardly hear its delicate, wavering airs at other times, but an hour before sunrise it has such magic as no other music, unless perhaps the nightingale in lands where nightingales are rare.

Proper names explain themselves and can be found in books of reference. A few are not yet filed. *Hajji Mosavvor*, greatest of modern miniature painters, suffered from paralysis agitans. *Naystani*, a celebrated virtuoso of the nose-flute. *Taj* sings classical odes with authenticity; *Moluk-e Zarrabi* moulds them to her liking. *Shir-e Khoda* begins Teheran's radio day with a canto of the epic. *Sobhi* is the most perfect teller of tales, his own.

Gaiety and daring need no naming to those who remember others like *Flight-lieutenant Idema*.

Abu-Ali is, of course, Ibn Sina – Avicenna.

Despite these notes to accompany the poem, BB later remarked, 'I've found that some people seem to misunderstand what this poem's all about . . . It begins with the four sons of Shem, chosen entirely at random out of the list in the Bible, there's no significance whatever in their names. There is in the Bible, but not in my poem!' (Mottram, however, believes that the names 'correspond to cities of Abraham's world'. In his scheme, Lud is the ancient Luz, Asshur and Arpachshad are Mesopotamian towns, and Aram is Syrian, i.e. Damascus. See '"An Acknowledged Land": Love and Poetry in Bunting's Sonatas', *Poetry Information* 19 [Autumn 1978], 20.) 'And they are here to show four different aspects of the Semitic peoples. Arabs and Jews are very much alike, perhaps they wouldn't like to hear that in New York, but it is true. And not only in their language but in much of their habits and way of looking at things. So I have a rather militant Jew, and an Arab merchant, and a Badou, and a Zionist, not a modern Zionist, but just in general. And then go on in the second part to another fine thing, finer, than I think the Semitic thing, too, the civilization of Persia, for one part. But the poem became lopsided. It was intended to have four parts, as a sonata ought to have, of course. And I sent it all to Louis Zukofsky who wrote back and complained that the last two parts were pretty thin, and I read them through again and he was quite right.

They *were* pretty thin. And the only thing I could think to do about it was to shrink them both into one. So that the sonata is a lopsided affair, I'm afraid' (reading at Riverside Studios, London, February 1982, in *Swigg*).

BB told Edward Dahlberg that he was **'far from satisfied'** with *The Spoils*: **'The tension is often too low, the cadence is no more than competent. Still, there's something there and something that's not, I think, been said, at least recently'** (BB to Dahlberg, 30 June 1951; quoted *Lesch* 234). **'I reread Lycopolis and the Spoils and saw they arent good enough (questions of technique omitted); Rhone wine when I wanted Mouton. And still, let me boast, I dont think any of our contemporaries has got nearer'** (BB to LZ, 'June the New Moonth' 1953; quoted *Forde*, 207). **'*The Spoils* was planned in four movements and was first written so, in an interval between pretty strenuous doings in Italy which obliged me to hurry the last two movements far too much. Louis Zukofsky pointed out to me that the substance had run very thin in the last two movements, and as soon as I had time to consider them again I saw that he was right, but I had no leisure to rewrite them. So I cut away, probably more than Zukofsky wanted me to, and shrank the two movements into one, thus keeping a dense tissue, but losing the symmetry I had planned. That makes it lopsided. And too obscure'** (BB to Forde, 23 October 1972; quoted *Forde*, 205–6). BB felt that his condensing, in the final version of the poem, the last two sections **'of course spoils the symmetries . . . Zukofsky was rather distressed by that, he hadn't intended that at all! But it was the result, and consequently, "The Spoils" is a lopsided poem. I don't mean that it's a bad poem, it is [musically] lopsided, it's not, it's not got the symmetry it should have had and was planned to have.' '[It has] symmetries, but it is spoilt, is "The Spoils"'** (*Quartermain & Tallman*, 18).

Publication history

First published in *Poetry* 79, no. 2 (November 1951), 84–97, *Guedalla* D16, although sent to *Hudson Review* (BB to Dahlberg, 30 June 1951; *Lesch*, 234). The poem was broadcast by the BBC Third Programme, July 1957. Published in book form by Morden Tower Book Room, 1965, and in all editions of *CP*. Reprinted in *British Poetry Since 1945*, ed. Edward Lucie-Smith (London: Cox and Wyman, 1970), 37–48, *Guedalla* B14. Last twelve lines of section II also reprinted in a pamphlet distributed during BB's visit to St Andrews College, Laurinburg, North Carolina, 15–19 April 1976.

Notes

[I.] **'As the usual modern a priori theory, in all its varieties including Communism, is that man's highest aim is his physical comfort, or at least physical sufficiency, I would like to add that I had begun to**

doubt that before the war. Now I *know* it is quite untrue. Physical comfort is not even a remote aim of the Arab, and it takes quite a minor place amongst the aims of the Persians' (BB to LZ, 11 April 1946; quoted *Lesch*, 235). **'First movement, the anschauung or better the vorstellung, general no doubt, but more or less particularly characteristic of the Semitic peoples, which takes life as a journey (to Zion, to Jinnat) best performed with few impedimenta, and is indifferent to the furniture at the inn. (The second movement contrasts that with the people who go in for architecture and furnish as though they intended to live here forever). The advantage of the journey idea is that death becomes a familiar, almost a friend. No Lucretian cold-comfort required. Limits, their arts are those of the camp-fire (They write poetry and play the fiddle). They cannot share the illusion of tree-like semi-permanence needed by a good cultivator, and so when they cease to be shepherds they become merchants (Fundamentally, therefore, parasites, on beasts or on farmers, which may have something to do with the irritation they so commonly arouse: but I've not attempted to display that aspect.) This is alien to my bent, but I believe I see the good, and I think it idiotic to denounce (à la Voltaire–Ezra, as you observe) what has nobility and discipline. Within the [first] movement, the relief is the sensual counterpart (or counterpoint) of that way of life: which seems to me more needed in the modern west. You Ashkenazim have put [sexuality] partly aside because it shocks the people you live among: and since it is nevertheless a part of your inheritance, the effort to suppress it in an individual is apt to make a Jewish prude the most ticklish of all. We need sensuality because without it we stumble into the ways of hollering he-man Hemingway sentimentality, or else the medical text-book school which forces itself unwillingly to admit, item by item, what is really half our life. (The last I expressed my dislike for in "Lycopolis") Fucking on principle and fucking to keep one's courage up are both repulsive to me, and, I believe, damaging to mankind'** (BB to LZ, 13 March 1951; quoted *Forde*, 178, 185–6, and *Lesch*, 244, 246–7).

Epigraphs] *al anfal li'llah*. Transliteration of Arabic epigraph, taken, as BB noted, from the Koran, sura 8. 8.1. In its entirety this reads: 'They ask you about the spoils. Say: "The spoils belong to God and the Apostle. Therefore have fear of God and end your disputes. Obey God and His apostle, if you are true believers" (*The Koran*, trans. N. J. Dawood [London, 1990], 126).

These are the songs of Shem, after their families, after their tongues, in their lands, after their nations. Genesis 10: 31. BB wrote to LZ that the four speakers in the poem represent **'an arbitrary choice among the duly registered legitimate sons of Shem'** (13 March 1951; quoted *Forde*, 179, and *Lesch*, 236).

Before I. 5. ASSHUR. A son of Shem. Asshur **'suggests the merchant-soldier[,] the adventurer'** (BB to LZ, 13 March 1951; quoted *Forde*, 179 and *Lesch*, 237). **'Asshur is all one man . . . He sees himself as the other man sees him and leaves tax gathering or banking or what have you for soldiering. What he sees is "a man like me reckoning pence, / never having tasted bread / where there is ice in his flask etc." i.e., never having bivouacked in the desert, where the lack of moisture in the air makes the daily range of temperature extreme . . . And as Asshur realises what he's missing, the vision transforms itself into the reality without requiring the aid of a sentence to say so. Or so I hope . . . It is all happening to Asshur. Either he for[e]sees it or he lives it – the sequence in time hardly matters. Asshur, of course – biblically the father of the Assyrians – is here the restless, belligerent type of Jew'** (BB letter, 13 January 1965; quoted *Makin*, 110).

'[T]here are two separate movements in the breaking-camp sequence[.] Dawn, the camel wakes and lifts up his neck which has been stretched along the ground. There's no dung yet for the scarabs. That comes as the men saunter off after breakfast for a crap, pursued by scarabs, who cut the dung almost as it falls and shape it into balls with incredible speed and then roll it away, often before the man has finished. It is while this is at its height that the camels, now loaded, get up' (BB to LZ, 13 March 1951; quoted *Lesch*, 237–8).

I. 5. to assess the people. Cp. *FBO* 20 ('Vestiges'), stanza 5: 'taxation impoverishes the people'.

I. 10. Abdoel. Asshur's assistant.

I. 17–18. in his greaves I saw / in polished bronze. *OED* 1: 'Armour for the leg below the knee'. Cp. Tennyson, *Lady of Shalott* III. 4 'The sun came dazzling thro' the leaves, / And flamed upon the brazen greaves / Of bold Sir Lancelot'; and Symonds, *Greek Poets*, v. 133: 'The burnished brazen greaves that hang upon the wall'. In the marked-up TS used to publish the Morden Tower edition of the poem, a line appears which was never printed:

so in his greaves I saw
in polished bronze
linked between the dead and death-to-come,
a man like me . . .

I. 21. where there is ice in his flask. **'Mine froze at Wadi Mohammerah as late as March, and it's not uncommon either in the Syrian desert or that of Northern Arabia, let alone the high deserts of Persia'** (BB to LZ, 13 March 1951; quoted *Forde*, 181).

I. 39. Leah . . . Rachel. Reference to Genesis 29, in which Jacob is tricked by his uncle into working for fourteen years to win Rachel in marriage.

Before l. 43. LUD. BB relates the name to **'Lot, Sodom, the city Arab'** (BB to LZ, 13 March 1951; quoted *Forde*, 179, and *Lesch*, 238). Cp. Wordsworth, 'Humanity', 34: 'the field of Luz'; one of the sailors in Kipling's 'The Ballad of Fisher's Boarding-House' is named Luz; also Beddoes: 'So is there in such a man, a seed-shaped bone, / Aldabaron, called by the Hebrews Luz', *Death's Jest-Book* (1850) Act III, s. 3, 447–54, alluded to by EP in *Cantos* LXXX 90: 'The bone *luz*'.

l. 43. Tigris floods. **'The description of Bagdad in the spring floods would stand for Ctesiphon or Niniveh – the dead Kurds have floated down every year since before Xenophon at least'** (BB to LZ, 13 March 1951; quoted *Forde*, 183, and *Lesch*, 238–9). BB pronounced the name: 'Teegris'.

l. 46. Jerboas. Desert rodents.

Before l. 65. ARPACHSHAD. BB wrote to LZ, **'Lord knows who Arpachshad was. Glad to change any or all of the names for a fetching suggestion'** (13 March 1951; quoted *Makin*, 111). BB wrote to LZ later on that Arpachshad stands for **'the Bedoin'** and that it was not until the poem was nearing completion that he discovered Arpachshad's historical relation to the desert tribes. **'By the way, luck or instinct or what not, Arpachshad turns out to be claimed as an ancestor by the Harb, the Anaiza, and the Shammar (the three largest desert tribes) and also by the Koraish. Muse taking care of me?'** (BB to LZ, 19 April 1951; quoted *Forde*, 179, and *Lesch*, 239–40).

l. 73. Halt, both, lament . . . **'[The] opening words of two of the Mo'allaqat'** (BB to LZ, 7 February 1951; quoted *Lesch*, 240). **'*The mo'allaqat* (singular cat plural cart) were written in highly ornamented character on gilded scrolls to be hung at Mecca. "Halt, both, lament . . ." tries to give the Arabic dual while preserving the abruptness of that most celebrated opening, which is currently rendered (O ye Muses!) "Pause, O ye two, and let us bewail . . ." Incidentally the moon-silver pool on the sand-pale gold of the desert, below, is an imitation of Manuchehri's imitation of another line from this famous and lovely poem'** (BB to LZ, 13 March 1951; quoted *Forde*, 184, and *Lesch*, 241). Lesch explains that 'The Mo'allaqat is a collection which usually contains seven poems written between 545 and 605 AD in Arabia (in the first century before the rise of Islam). The tradition connected with these poems, each of which was written by a different author, is that "at the annual fair . . . each poet recited a set piece of verse, *Kásida*, it being put to the popular vote to decide upon their merits; and that afterwards those poems which had been judged the best were set down in golden manuscript and hung at the Káaba at Mecca, and so received the name of the

'Golden Odes' or 'The Suspended Poems'" (Lady Anne Blunt and W. S. Blunt, trans. *The Seven Golden Odes of Pagan Arabia, Known Also as the Mo'allakat* (London: Chiswick Press, 1903), xvi). After the rise of Islam, scholars collected these poems and preserved them in written form under the title, "Mo'allaqat"' (*Lesch*, 240). The anthology was compiled by Hammād ar-Rāwiyah, d. 772. LZ, perhaps stimulated by BB's interest in Persian poetry, quoted from the Mo'allaqat in his *Zukofsky*, 117, *Guedalla* B9. Manuchehri (Abu Najm Ahmad ibn Ahmad ibn Qaus Manuchehri, d. *ca.*1040) was a Persian poet who used Arabic words in his work; he was a protégé of 'Unsuri, also of interest to BB, as below.

Before I. 77. ARAM. Associated by BB with **'the later prophets, and hence may stand for later Judaism, down to the Zionists [. . .] the better modern Jewish mind (or emotions)'** (BB to LZ, 13 March 1951; quoted *Forde*, 179, and *Lesch*, 241). **'[Asshur] sets off the respectable Arab merchant [Lud], the badu [Bedouin] (Arpachshad) and the romantic, Zionist, mystical Jew, Aram'** (BB letter, 13 January 1965; quoted *Makin*, 111, n. 31).

I. 77–8. By the dategroves of Babylon / there we sat down and sulked. Burlesque of Psalm 137: 1: 'By the rivers of Babylon, there we sat down.' Cp. Shakespeare, *Merry Wives of Windsor* III. i. 23: 'Whenas I sat in Pabylon', quoted by LZ in his *Zukofsky*, 122, 390, *Guedalla* B9. Also T. S. Eliot, *The Waste Land*, 182: 'By the waters of Leman I sat down and wept.' Cp. 'Attis: Or, Something Missing', II. 2–4.

I. 81. Judah. David ruled over Judah for seven years before he was anointed king over all of Israel and captured Jerusalem, to which he brought the Ark and which he made his capital.

I. 82. vineyard. Cp. Matthew 20: 1–6, the parable of the hired labourers in the vineyard.

I. 87. hogg. Variant of hog. A young sheep of about nine to eighteen months of age (until it cuts two teeth).

I. 88. fullers. OED 'fuller', n.1.1 'full', v.3.1: 'One whose occupation is to full [to tread or beat] cloth [for the purpose of cleansing and thickening it].'

I. 89. David dancing before the Ark. Cp. 2 Samuel 6, especially 14–16. BB mentions the episode in a letter to Forde: **'Corelli should be the one for you, the Concerti Grossi, with jigs to play in the middle of Mass. I wonder whether the congregation was stirred to dance to the glory of God, like David before the Ark? I have seen a girl in Italy charlstoning up to the altar to get her Communion, and nobody seemed to think it odd. So, perhaps, should all worship be'** (BB to Forde, 23 October 1972; quoted *Forde*, 248).

I. 96. child cradled beside her sister silent and brown. Cp. *SBOO*, 3 ('Birthday Greeting'), and note.

I. 110, 115. Warmth of absent thighs . . . closing repugnant thighs. **'My Arab would describe his lady's cunt like a plum, like a ripe date. Since I'm not after notoriety and suppression I confine myself to thighs, since I can just get away with them. But all the same I'd far rather have the plum-cunt . . . What I mean can be presented, not said'** (BB to LZ, 13 March 1951; HRC).

I. 116. Who lent her warmth to dying David. Cp. 1 Kings 1: 1–4; verse 2: 'let her cherish him, and let her lie in thy bosom, that my lord the king may get heat'. See also *SBOO* 4: 'Did the girl shrink from David? Did she hug his / ribs, death shaking them, and milk dry / the slack teat from which Judah had sucked life?' BB recalled, late in life, his exposure to the Bible at Ackworth, a Quaker boarding school (1912–16): **'Every morning you had to get a large lump of the Bible by heart before breakfast. At breakfast the Bible was read to you. At dinner the Bible was read to you. At tea time, after tea, the Bible was read to you again. And on Sunday there were *very* large lumps of the Bible, besides Scripture lessons in between. And with that, and some other accidents, I came to be far better acquainted with the Bible than any of my juniors that I have come across. Although, there were other people mostly in Nonconformist schools of one sort or another of my own age who attained much the same grounding in the Holy Scriptures; the rhythms of the translation in the authorized version of Job, of the Song of Songs, some of the Prophets, all the extraordinary narrative skill of some of the chapters of the Book of Kings. I remember the early chapters of the Second Book of Kings in particular'** (*Descant*, [3–4]).

I. 117. Zion. Name for Jerusalem prior to David's capture of it.

II. **'Second movement. Begins with the Masjid-e Jom'a of Isfahan, a Seljuk building'** (BB to LZ, 7 February 1951; quoted *Forde*, 190–1). Erected in the eleventh century during the rule of Malek Shah, this mosque is the oldest dated monument in Isfahan, and a major example of Seljuk architecture in Iran (*Lesch*, 250, and *Forde*, 191). BB was Vice-Consul for the UK Foreign Office at Isfahan in late 1944; in *Descant* ([21]), he described it as **'the pleasantest city I've ever been in'**. To Dorothy Pound, he wrote, **'the city so full of gardens and orchards that from a mile or two away you see only a forest with a few domes and minarets sticking up from it'** (BB to Dorothy Pound, 27 November 1946; quoted *Makin*, 103). **'And part two, eastern also so as not to provoke irrelevant contrasts, as well as because the matter is fresh in my mind; life well-padded, itself a source of enjoyment, to which the thought of death comes** only close to the end, and which must then invent specious (though often beautiful) comforts. This is familiar enough and also a regular source of sentimentalities. To avoid them is not entirely easy, at least without sardonic remarks which would be out of tone and might seem to deny the general desirability of a good life' (BB to LZ, 13 March 1951; quoted *Forde*, 178, and partly *Lesch*, 249). Part II **'changes the scene from Arabia to Persia'** (BB reading, Air Gallery, 1977, in *Swigg*).

II. 2. alabaster. Summer mosques were constructed of alabaster 'in order to avoid excessive heat' (*Lesch*, 250).

II. 13. aivans. **'*Aivan*. Gigantic arch, pointed, apparently remotest ancestry of gothic: formerly framing the crowned King for audience, as the ruined specimen at Ctesiphon, early AD: later giving access to the covered parts of a mosque and the mihrab. Seljuk mosques have several, later mosques two or only one. Tile decorated, the tiles matched and renewed as they crack or fall. Sometimes there is decoration in raised brick; Safavi mosques have the upper part of the aivan often filled with honeycomb-work, and some have the honeycomb set with mirrors, very lovely when there is enough cash to keep the mirrors silvered, as at the shrine of Imam Reza at Meshhed'** (BB to LZ, 13 February 1951; quoted *Forde*, 192).

II. 15. Avicenna. Abū-a'Ali al-Husayn bin Sīna (980–1037), Persian physician known for commentaries on Aristotle and Galen. He was known to Chaucer's Physician and Pardoner in *Canterbury Tales*, and was placed by Dante with Averroës in the Limbo of the Philosophers. His views apparently influenced ideas of courtly love. Served as a Persian vizier. See BB's note to the poem, above. LZ discusses Avicenna in his *Zukofsky*, 121, *Guedalla* B9, in close proximity to having quoted BB's overdrafts of Rūdakī and Ferdowsī.

II. 16. Nezam-ol-Molk. Persian vizier in the reign of the Seljuks (see also note below).

II. 18. Taj-ol-Molk. Rival of Nezam-ol-Molk, and purported to be responsible for his death. See *Lesch*, 251, and *Forde*, 193, for a fuller discussion.

II. 22. Malekshah. Eleventh-century Persian ruler under whom the Seljuk empire reached its peak. BB pronounced the name 'Malekshắw'.

II. 24–5. who found Khayyam a better reckoner / than the Author of the Qor'an. Omar Khayyām, Persian poet, mathematician, astronomer, 1048–1131. 'As a friend of the vizier (Nezam-ol-Molk), he served in the court of Malek Shah. The sonata suggests that, in spite of the fact that during Malek Shah's reign religion was allowed to flourish, the Seljuk rulers were more interested in lasting monuments than in the religious implications of the construction of mosques . . . Thus, the Seljuks prized human reason (algebra) in an individual (Khayyam) above revelation both in terms of the teachings of the Prophet [Mohammed] and in terms of his design of mosques' *(Lesch*, 252). Forde suggests that the lines allude either to Khayyam's 'reform of the calendar which preceded the Gregorian reform by five centuries or to his sceptical outlook which stressed the importance of this life' (*Forde*, 193). Khayyam was apparently considered a better mathematician than poet. He is the subject of BB's 1935 typescript essay, 'The Lion and the Lizard', collected in *Three Essays*, in which BB remarked **'he is the astronomer in a world that has no ears except for quacks'** (30). LZ, perhaps stimulated by BB's interest in Persian poetry, quoted from Edward FitzGerald's translations of Omar in his *Zukofsky*, 122, 125, *Guedalla* B9.

II. 30–2. 'Lately a professor. . .' Lesch (253) identifies here 'an allusion to an incident that has been used as evidence that Khayyam believed in metempsychosis. Khayyam was walking with a group of students at an old college which was undergoing repairs. He encountered a donkey, being used to haul bricks, who would not enter the college grounds. Khayyam supposedly went up to the donkey and recited a quatrain to it extemporaneously, after which the donkey entered. Khayyam's students demanded an explanation. "He replied, 'The spirit which has now attached itself to the body of his ass [formerly] inhabited the body of a lecturer in this college, therefore it would not come in until now, when, perceiving that its colleagues had recognized it, it was obliged to step inside.'" The quatrain was: "O lost and now returned '*yet more astray*,' / Thy name from man's remembrance passed away, / Thy nails have now combined to form thy hoofs, / Thy tail's a beard turned round the other way!"' (See Edward G. Browne, *A Literary History of Persia*, 4 vols. [Cambridge, 1928–30], vol. 2, 254–5).

II. 34. absolute idiots. An 'overt reference to an incident in which one of Malek Shah's deputies refused to employ the son of a prominent man at court because he felt that the son was incompetent. Malek Shah, enraged by the man's "foolish" opposition, fired him and had the son, who was an "absolute idiot", take his place' (*Lesch*, 254).

II. 38. La Giralda. **'the belfry at Seville'** (BB to LZ, 7 February 1951; quoted *Forde*, 194). 'A minaret built in the twelfth century later used as a belfry' (*Lesch*, 254). BB pronounced the name 'Yiralda'.

II. 44. Seljuks. 'The Seljuks, who were the ruling family of a Turkish tribe, invaded and conquered most of Iran and Syria during the tenth century. They ruled, under the successive leadership of three great statesmen (Toghril Beg, Alp-Arslan and Malek Shah), until the empire was divided between Malek Shah's sons in the eleventh century. During their reign, Persian culture flourished and a series of institutions were established . . . with the intention of giving uniform training to the administrators and religious scholars who served the empire. In addition, the Seljuks were responsible for the building of numerous mosques, in part because it helped to promote religious unity, and also because it was a tangible and enduring sign of power' (*Lesch*, 249–50).

ll. 46. Abu Ali. Avicenna, as in BB's note to the poem, above.

ll. 48. Bokhara. A major centre of Islamic learning from the eighth century, from the sixteenth century to 1920 it was the capital of the khanate of Bukhara; among its monuments are the *madrassa* (an Islamic school) of Abdulaziz-Khan (1651–2), see BB's note to *SBOO* 5.

ll. 52. leaden mind of Egypt. **'I suppose no civilization ever failed to produce some delightful things. The Egyptians did in their off-moments when they werent attending to what they were doing. But pyramids, gigantic statues, (horrible huge statues of Zaghlul today too) buildings – Qasr-an-Nil for example – more hideous than any Europeans except the Germans can produce: Egyptian gestures are heavy, jowls heavy, they speak Arabic heavily, G for J, D for TH, B for W, their syntax, with the demonstrative after the noun, thickened in pronunciation and holding up the sense . . . Heavy wits, abuse and the cudgel; heavy lifeless spite. No Egyptian has managed to rule or even much influence the rulers of his country since Cambyses conquered it – Persian, Greek, Roman, Arab, Turk – even Zaghlul was part Turk. And their rulers have failed to influence them. The mosques, so famous, are all foreign, and everything light and pleasant in Egypt except what birds and foliage provide is foreign. Or sometimes Nubian'** (BB to LZ, 13 March 1951; quoted *Forde*, 195, and *Lesch*, 256).

ll. 58. God is the dividing sword. **'It isnt there just for the noise. That's what I'm writing about, and that's why the spoils are for God in the epigraph from the Qor'an. It is shorthand for quite a lot, or if you like, for something I think fundamental'** (BB to Dorothy Pound, 11 December 1953; quoted *Makin*, 107). BB quoted this phrase much later in his remembrance of Yeats: **'you must of course allow for my own conviction that "God is the dividing sword", and that order is no more than a rather unfortunate accident that sometimes hampers civilization'** ('Yeats Recollected', *Agenda* 12, no. 2 [1974], 46); he elaborated to Reagan that it **'means what it says, that all this sweet peace and brotherhood and so on is not the way things work,**

not by any wickedness of human kind, but by the way the world is organized. What progress is made is always made as the result of violent disturbances of one sort or another' (*Reagan*, 80).

ll. 61. murder more durable than mortar. Perhaps an echo of Horace, *Odes*, III. 30.

[Stanzas 4–6]. BB referred to these as **'public spirit triplets'** in BB to LZ, 13 March 1951 (quoted *Forde*, 201, and *Lesch*, 257).

ll. 65, 71, 73, 77, 79, 82, 85. Hajji Mosavvor; Naystani; Taj; Hafez; Moluk-e-Zarrabi; Shir-e Khoda; Sobhi. See BB's note to the poem, above. *Hajji* also means 'pilgrim', and is used to refer to a Muslim who has completed the pilgrimage to Mecca. *Hafez*, full name, Mohammad Shams od-Dīn Hāfez (1325/6–89/90), great Persian/Sufi poet. Shir-e Khoda's 'recitations of cantos from Ferdosi's *Shāh-nāmeh* . . . begin the radio day in Teheran' (*Lesch*, 259).

ll. 70. chenars. **'*Chenar.* The oriental plane, a splendid tree. A great double avenue of them runs through the centre of Isfahan. We were sitting under chenars at Shiraz when Naystani, in a hotel room, began to practice his flute, and the play of notes and the play of light through the leaves seemed to work in together'** (BB to LZ, 13 March 1951; quoted *Forde*, 196, and *Lesch*, 258).

ll. 71, 74. Naystani . . . tar and drum. **'A *tar* is a stringed instrument played with bow and pizzicato, the basis of Persian classical music as the fiddle is of ours. Borrowed by the Arabs, it was modified into the lute. Reduced to three strings (as tar) it re-evolved into zither and guitar by different roads. The word tar originally meant merely a gut string, but the present instrument must be at least as old as Hafez and probably a few centuries more.**

A *nay* is a flute (nose-flute) cut from a cane (nay) and is at least as old as the tar. Both are in use, apart and together, in unison and in a kind of counterpoint, as solo instruments, as accompaniment to dancing and as the preface and coda and intermezzos of classical singing. The voice itself is usually, but not always, accompanied by the drum alone, and almost always begins, after a rather long rest, without even drums. But when the singer pauses the instruments get going again. I have, however, sometimes heard the instruments accompanying the voice, quietly, the nay making a kind of subdued descant, very florid.

I remember escaping, vexed, from an overcrowded illtempered hotel in Shiraz into its lovely garden, and there, under the huge chenars (oriental plane trees) whose shadows were making a dance of sundapples on the ground, I found Naystani, the virtuoso, just taking his flute from his pocket, and he played most beautifully for a couple of hours, the flute music as kaleidoscopic as the shadow

pattern, getting in a single line that feeling of extreme multiplicity that Byrd gets in many parts, and that is nearer reflecting life than any simpler art. Nobody joined us, Naystani said nothing beyond "Salaam", it was unlike the same thing over the radio: not addressed to an audience, but almost as though addressed to the trees and the sun. The great player celebrating the first of spring in his own natural talent' (BB to LZ, 6 August 1953; quoted *Forde*, 189–90).

II. 93. scut. OED n.1.1.a: 'A short erect tail, esp. that of a hare, rabbit or deer.'

II. 97. vafur. See BB's note to poem, above.

II. 99. Onsori, Sa'di. Prominent Persian poets Abul Qasim Hassan ibn Ahmad 'Unsuri (d.1040 or 1049) and Abū-Muḥammad Muṣliḥ al-Dīn bin Abdallāh Shīrāzī, 1184–1283/1291?, native of Shiraz who pursued his education in Baghdad; known for his works *Bostan* ('The Orchard') and *Gulistan* ('The Rose Garden', from which BB translated tale I. 4; see Appendix II. F, below) as well as his aphorisms, lyrics and odes. His writing illustrated the virtues recommended to Muslims. His work drew the attention of Ralph Waldo Emerson, who compared it to the Bible for its wisdom and beauty. Bunting, however, felt that it was 'not mystical in the least' – not like Persian poetry in 'Swinburnean translations'. **'Sadi is a darling. I wish he had used a somewhat less arabicised vocabulary'** (BB to LZ, 1? December 1934; HRC).

II. 104. azan. See BB's note to poem, above.

II. 110. falcon. In a letter to LZ, BB worried, **'Is the falcon stuff too commonplace?'** (7 February 1951; quoted *Quartermain DP*, 144). **'The falcon has an echo probably unperceived by readers, since the name of Toghril, first Seljuk conqueror, means falcon'** (BB to LZ, 7 March 1951; quoted *Forde*, 197, and *Lesch*, 263).

III. Subtitled, in first draft sent to LZ, 22 March 1951, ***'Yet forty days'*** (*Makin*, 117, n. 36). See that draft for uncompressed version of opening; BB cut many lines to eliminate **'unwanted'** echoes of EP (BB to LZ, 25 June 1951; quoted *Forde*, 201).

This section relies heavily on BB's World War II experiences. **'I spent the whole war with the RAF, first as aircraftsman, then as corporal & finally as an officer – finishing up as Squadron Leader. Saw many fronts: North Sea – protecting convoys in a small yacht; Persia, before Alamein & Stalingrad, when it looked like being the next on the German list: Tripoli, the battle of Wadi Akarit: the last weeks of the Siege of Malta: I arranged the 'war room' for Eisenhower for the Sicilian Invasion, & then went over to Catania with a fighter-squadron, captured Cotrone [Crotone] on my own**

initiative: in Naples during the fighting north of the City – I just missed being blown up by the delay-action bomb which destroyed the Post Office there: back to England with the squadron to cover the invasion of Normandy: then out again to Persia with the Political Intelligence: lent to the Foreign Office as Vice-Consul at Isfahan – that was a grand job, often amongst the nomadic mountain-tribes, who taught me to ride & to shoot moufflon and ibex: and at last chief of all our Political Intelligence in Persia, Iraq, Saudi Arabia, etc.' (BB to Dorothy Pound, 22? November 1946; quoted *Makin*, 102). A more detailed account is given in *Descant*, [26–28]. **'I want also war: not as a horror, not as an opportunity for self-congratulatory glory (dear Hem[ingway] again, I'm afraid), but simply as an activity which has pleasures of its own, an exercise of certain faculties which need exercise: in which death is neither a bugbear nor a consummation, but just happens . . . part of the fun'** (BB to LZ, 13 March 1951; quoted *Forde*, 179, 201). **'People group bads and goods too easily, dont admit that heavy brutality may coexist with aesthetic merits, just as they dont admit that there may be merits in war, which is associated in their minds with the stupid slaughters of 1914–18 or the last battles of your Civil War to the exclusion of all virtue except endurance. But resolution and effort can be gay instead of grim, and the death and ruin have had their importance exaggerated. That is not to deny their existence nor to advocate multiplying wars. But freedom from war, like freedom from poverty, can be pursued at the expense of things better worth preserving than peace and plenty, of which, I would say, the most important, and most threatened, is personal autonomy. Freewill entails sin! I dont want my acts determined by any authority whatever'** (BB to LZ, 19 April 1951; quoted *Forde*, 201, and *Lesch*, 265–6).

III. 1. All things only of earth and water. **'[A]ll things only of earth and water is Xenophanes [*ca.*570–480 BCE], the four elements are Empedocles [*ca.*490–430 BCE]. The distinction is also a comment'** (BB to LZ, 19 April 1951; quoted *Forde*, 198, and *Lesch*, 282, n. 48). LZ later quoted Aristotle's discussion of Empedocles and the elements, *De Anima* I. 4, in *Zukofsky*, 59–60, *Guedalla* B9.

III. 9. chased. OED, ppl. a.2: 'Of plate, etc.: Ornamented with embossed work, engraved in relief.'

III. 15. shingle. OED n.2.1: 'Small roundish stones; loose waterworn pebbles such as are found collected upon the seashore.' The etymology says that *ch-* forms are Scottish and East Anglian, perhaps related to Norwegian *singl*, meaning coarse sand, small stones. A citation is given from Hakluyt's *Voyages*, I. 556: 'Chingle and great stones'.

III. 15, 18, 19. Lydian pebbles. The phrase is repeated to show **'their damn obsessiveness'** (BB to LZ, 25 June 1951; quoted *Forde*, 198, and *Lesch*, 267). *Alldritt* writes (125): 'The phrase "Lydian pebbles" that is insistently repeated in the passage alludes to an important moment in the history of the ancient world. The Lydians, whose king was Croesus, were, according to Herodotus in his account of what was for him a world war, the first people to introduce gold and silver coins and the first to sell goods by retail.' Mottram says that Lydian pebbles are 'plough-blunting stones' and that the adjective also implies 'a mode in ancient Greek music with a soft, so-called feminine character' (*Terrell*, 93). *OED* 'lydite' gives 'Lydian stone' (a black variety of jasper used by jewellers as a touchstone for testing gold), and gives a 1907 citation from the journal of the Geological Society: 'It is by no means a pure sand; there are no "lydite" or other pebbles.'

III. 17. Quarry and build, Solomon. Son of King David and King of Israel proverbially known for his wisdom and for building the Jews' first holy Temple in Jerusalem according to 1 Kings 6: 1.

III. 22. plowshare. Cp. Micah 4: 3–4.

III. 33. dytiscus beetles. Water-beetles.

III. 34–40. One cribbed in a madhouse ... **'The poets whose fates are listed in the "One cribbed in a madhouse" paragraph are not individuals in particular, but there are plenty of instances of poets who have been destroyed or hampered by all the means suggested. The reader can supply what name he pleases'** (BB to Forde, 23 October 1972; quoted *Forde*, 200, and *Lesch*, 269–70). Pound, Eliot and Auden are possibilities.

III. 40. iceblink. OED 1: 'A luminous appearance on the horizon, caused by the reflection of light from ice.' **'I think nearly everyone but you, my dear New York cockney, would know the iceblink by reputation without having to try the dictionary. I'm familiar with the thing itself, on the Banks, in the Gulf of St Lawrence, and "between Lofoten and Spitzbergen"'** (BB to LZ, 25 June 1951; quoted *Forde*, 200, and *Lesch*, 270). Cp. Kipling, 'The Last Chantey', 48: 'Oh, the ice-blink white and near'.

III. 42. magneto. An electrical generator that uses permanent magnets to produce periodic pulses of alternating current, providing a current pulse to the spark plugs in internal combustion engines.

III. 43. Flight-lieutenant Idema. Although an American, Idema had joined the Canadian Air Force. After serving in Malta he was shot down and killed in his Spitfire on 17 June 1944. **'Idema was the son of a smallish mid-western manufacturer who, like all his kind, hated**

[President] Roosevelt. He found an excuse for it when Churchill and Roosevelt successively visited Malta in the circumstances described' (BB to Forde, 4 July 1973; quoted *Forde*, 202). BB called Idema **'one of the bravest men I ever met and a particularly individual and picturesque one'** (BB to LZ, 18 June 1953; quoted *Burton*, 341).

III. 47–72. Malta's ruins . . . Tripoli dark / under a cone of tracers. In *Descant* ([22]), BB describes his journey across the desert to Tripoli to salvage materiel abandoned there by the Germans: **'A month of very hard fare, yet one of those I've enjoyed most in my life. Seeing vast stretches of the desert; and from El Alamein onwards there was this vast pile in all directions of abandoned, broken arms, broken guns, broken airplanes, broken cars and lorries, lying about. One of the two or three most astonishing things I've ever seen in my life – I've described it in "The Spoils"'** (see also BB to LZ, 9 May 1943 and 25 July 1944; quoted *Forde*, 48).

III. 55. littoral. OED: 'A littoral district; the region lying along the shore.'

III. 57. recognisance. Perhaps describes a painted recognition sign or identifying marking on the 'fragment of fuselage'.

III. 62. leaguered in lines. 'Leaguer' was the usual British term in North Africa in World war II for 'make an overnight camp' (both a verb for the process and noun for the camp itself), particularly for units with multiple vehicles, which would come together in one place to refuel etc.; 'leaguered in lines' in effect means parked in an orderly way. Cp. Keith Douglas, *Alamein to Zem Zem*, where the word appears in this sense several times, e.g. ch. 8: 'We leaguered at sundown in three long rows of squadrons.'

III. 74. Leptis. According to *Lesch* (271), the cemetery at Leptis can be dated from the fifth century. Leptis was, *Alldritt* writes (122), 'an important Carthaginian port and later a Roman city adorned by its conquerors with much imposing architecture'.

III. 75. Blind Bashshar bin Burd. **'An Arabic poet of Persian race who was put to death for heresy in the eighth or ninth century. It's not clear exactly what his heresy was, but it seems that he "glanced back" at the achievements of the Sassanian kings and the Zoroastrian religion, and in particular at the ideas of the communist rebellion of Mazdak which was put down after a temporary triumph in about 570 a.d. He was probably some kind of pantheist, though he didnt get as far as Hallaj, who said "Ana' l-hagg" ["I am the True One", or "the Fact", i.e. God] or some kind of Manichaean, but most likely a bit of both. He "speculated whither" by foreseeing only evil from the caliphate and rousing a rather vague spirit of rebellion.**

The first great Persian poets who wrote in Persian, a century or more later, thought well of Bashshar, at least as a poet. You'll find an adequate account of him in the first and second volumes of Browne's *Literary History of Persia* [vol. 2, 361]. **I forget now where my supplementary information came from, apart from mentions of him by the poets'** (BB to Forde, 23 October 1972; quoted *Forde*, 203, and partly *Lesch*, 272). In an earlier letter BB gave a different description of the poet's heresy, however. **'Bashshar bin Burd was executed for reminding the Caliph in a poem that fire had been worshipped for a considerable time and did the job pretty well. I dont expect you to like my undialectical interpretation of his story'** (BB to LZ, 22 March 1951; HRC).

III. 80. lie in wait for blood. From Micah 7: 2. 'The good man is perished out of the earth: and there is none upright among men: they all lie in wait for blood; they hunt every man his brother with a net.'

III. 82. Condole me with abundance of secret pleasure. From Swift, according to BB to LZ, 16 May 1951 (mentioned *Forde*, 203, and *Lesch*, 273), but untraced. Cp. Shakespeare, 'The Rape of Lucrece', 890: 'Thy secret pleasure turns to open shame.' Also possibly the last three lines of Thomas Campbell, 'Battle of the Baltic', which appears in Palgrave's *Golden Treasury*: 'the mermaid's song condoles / Singing glory to the souls / Of the brave!' Tennyson's comment on these lines was recorded by Palgrave: 'the infelicitous "mermaid's song *condoles*" . . . tempted him to a "How easily could a little blot like this be cured!"' (cited in C. Ricks's ed. [London: Penguin, 1991], 500).

III. 83–84. what we think in private / will be said in public. Lesch (273) compares this to Christ's criticism of the Pharisees in Matthew 10: 26 and Luke 12: 1–3.

III. 89. Staithes. A fishing village on the North Yorkshire coast. Note also *OED* n.1: 'The land bordering on water, a bank, shore,' with citation from Ælfred; 2: 'A landing stage, wharf'; 3: 'An embankment'.

III. 91. hard-lying money. British naval term for extra pay in consideration of special hardships.

III. 92. Rosyth guns sang. In 1940, BB joined 948 Squadron near Rosyth on Scotland's Firth of Forth, which was a wartime naval base. Guns on ships anchored near Rosyth responded to an air raid en route to Glasgow which BB witnessed; see note below. For details about his time at Rosyth, and his experiences aboard the *Golden Hind* on the North Sea, see *Burton* 271–5.

III. 93. Glasgow burning. **'Glasgow was burning in the west beyond**

the hills when the dawn came' (BB to LZ, 16 May 1951; quoted *Lesch*, 274).

III. 96. catfish on the sprool. A sprool is an instrument for single-line fishing with large hooks which foul the fish, according to Eric Mottram (*Terrell*, 93); not in *OED*; Bunting explained the word in a letter to LZ, 25 June 1951, as **'a bright piece of metal set with hooks, attached to a line and sinker and pulled smartly up and down in the water until it foul-hooks some fish. There are other names for it. In the Firth of Forth, where we've located the ship, sprool. I was trying to get the range of a German plane when Harry hooked the catfish.'**

III. 99. Chesapeake. A wartime naval base was located in Chesapeake Bay, an inlet of the Atlantic in the American states of Virginia and Maryland.

III. 100. bight of a warp no strong tide strains. 'Bight', the loop of a rope; *OED* 2 cites nautical usages, e.g. where the anchor hooks the bight of a cable; 'warp', *OED* n.II.3: 'a rope or light hawser attached at one end to a fixed object, used in hauling or in moving a ship from one place to another in harbour, road, or river', also an 'apparatus for hauling in vessels'. *OED* cites R. H. Dana, *Two Years Before the Mast*, chap. xxxvi.139: '[We] took the warp ashore, manned the capstan [etc.].' 'Bight' may also be a bend or curved indentation in coast line or recess of a bay; *OED* 3.a. cites Defoe, *Voyage Round the World*, 146: 'In the very bite or nook of the bay there was a great inlet of water.' Cp. Kipling, 'The Widow's Party', 40: 'As I lay in the bight of a canvas trough'; 'Mine Sweepers', 9: 'Lumpy and strong in the bight'; and "The Scholars', 5: 'from the Falklands to the Bight'.

III. 113. Largo Law . A hill overlooking the coastal village of Largo in Fife, a few miles east of Rosyth. BB remarked to Forde that the lines here are about **'what the tide says, rippling round the anchor chains of the ships assembling in the Firth of Forth for the Archangel convoy; the contrast of leisurely fishing with the need to prepare to face very ultimate things'** (BB to Forde, 23 October 1972, at Durham).

III. 117. Lofoten and Spitzbergen. Norwegian island groups.

BRIGGFLATTS

BB had written to LZ as early as 1953 that, **'I shall have to try again to write a QED sonata to earn the hatred of all the tasteful critics and a few centuries of misrepresentation *but* convince all candid listeners and so survive'** (BB to LZ, 'June the New Moonth' 1953; quoted *Lesch*, 307).

In mid-December 1964, BB wrote to an old friend, the actor and poet Denis Goacher, about his interest in the form of the long poem, which was **'much neglected'** (*Alldritt*, 151). Working on a draft of one while riding the train to and from his job as a subeditor at the Newcastle *Evening Chronicle*, he claimed to have **'two fat notebooks absolutely chocked full, front and back, both sides of the page'** (undated quotation, *Forde*, 58). Roy Fisher recalled BB telling him in the spring of 1965 that **'the music is complete; all I have to do is to make adjustments to the content'** and Gael Turnbull recorded in a journal entry for 15 May receipt of a letter announcing the poem's completion (*Alldritt*, 151–2). (Intriguingly, an early poem of Turnbull's published in 1956 was called, 'An Irish Monk on Lindisfarne, about 650 AD'; see notes on Lindisfarne and I. 14–37, below; BB owned several volumes by Turnbull, including *A Trampoline: Poems 1952–1964*). In June 1965, BB sent the finished poem to *Poetry*, where it was accepted for publication. It was read before the public for the first time at Tom and Connie Pickard's Morden Tower Bookroom in Newcastle in December 1965. *Poetry* 109, no. 2 (November 1966) announced that the poem had received 'The Levinson Prize'.

In an interview, BB remarked that he worked from **'one little notebook, two little notebooks, completely full both sides of each page, with the cuttings out and so forth. And I reckon roughly twenty-thousand words, twenty-thousand lines I mean, to get my seven hundred'** (*Quartermain & Tallman*, 17). The notebook material held by the Poetry/Rare Books Collection at the University of Buffalo, State University of New York, consists of one book as well a number of loose leaves which may or may not be from a second notebook. Bunting wrote first on recto pages, numbering them in the upper right-hand corner, then flipped the book over and wrote on verso pages, left unnumbered. He would try out a number of lines and expand these into sections of verse. Then he would rewrite the sections, incorporating revisions, and in some cases cancel the earlier sections. When a section had been finished, a new one was begun and worked on. At times, he drew scansion marks above or near certain lines. Some of the loose leaves can be interpolated successfully if either page numbers or repeated lines of verse make this possible; others seem orphaned, and may be from a second notebook of the same size. Bunting's handwriting in this material is at times quite difficult to decipher, although in other autograph manuscript material, for example fair copies of poems, it is usually quite clear; this may support Bunting's claim that he worked on the notebooks while he was commuting to work. Many cancellations of entire sections consist of single diagonal strokes; horizontal lines are often drawn through individual words or phrases, but when Bunting has scratched out words or phrases they are difficult to reconstruct. The redundancy of material makes it fairly straightforward to correlate it with the published version of the poem. The notebook material also includes a number of drawings and some incidental text, for example a letter of recommendation on behalf of Tom Pickard, a mailing address, etc. For a full discussion of notebook variants, see Peter Quartermain's 'Parataxis in Basil Bunting and Louis Zukofsky', in *Stubborn Poetries: Poetic Facticity and the Avant-Garde* (University of Alabama Press, 2013).

Guedalla (30–1) claims that 'the poem was written, so Bunting has wryly suggested, to show Tom Pickard how to write a long poem. It was originally 15,000 lines long and was reduced to its final 700 lines over a long period of time. The author prepared about twelve copies which he typed out and sent to various friends. This version is longer than the final published version.' However, Caddel notes that there is no evidence to support the claim of a longer version in typescript. The Olin Library at Washington University, St Louis, holds the carbon copy of the poem in typescript (*ca.*1965) that Bunting sent to Robert Creeley; it is not 'substantially different' from the printed version (Caddel, email to Don Share, 18 September 2000), and Creeley remembered no longer version of the poem.

On 10 August 1965, BB wrote to Henry Rago, the editor of *Poetry*: **'I know the difficulties of finding even a modest amount of space in a well-run magazine let alone about 750 lines; and you, no doubt, know the impatience of authors. There is a momentary spate of publicity about me in England at present and I would like to have taken advantage of it to get a good circulation for whoever presently makes a pamphlet of Briggflatts, particularly as several publishers seem determined to bring out my collected poems sometime next year, which will limit the time available for selling a pamphlet; but it is more important to me to appear in Poetry, which published my Villon 35 years ago and nearly everything considerable I have written since . . . I had also better say that I know there are inaccurate and incomplete mss copies floating around. It has been more copied by industrious penmen than any poem I ever heard of, Lord knows why, one copying down another's errors and so on. Over that I have no control. I suppose it is theoretically possible that some pirate might print one of these garbled copies without consulting me, but I don't** believe it. I'd make one hell of a fuss if it happened. But the existence of this curious mss circulation is another reason for hastening the printing as much as possible' (Joseph Parisi and Stephen Young, eds, *Between the Lines: a History of* Poetry *in Letters, 1962–2002* [Chicago: Ivan R. Dee, 2006], 75–6).

On the general composition of 'Briggflatts', BB told *Lesch* (310–11): 'I use anything as subject. Mostly I've written a poem that is concrete before I've got a subject. I know what shape it's going to be. I sometimes know, even in considerable detail, what the rhythm will be before I've got any notion of what is going to be said in it. *Briggflatts* began as a diagram on a piece of paper. I added a Latin motto to remind me of the kind of mood I wanted. It developed in that sort of way. In fact, the first line of the poem is the last, apart from the coda – it is a matter of filling out the form . . . My forms are . . . much larger, the architectonics are the poetry really . . . It's finding the actual building materials to suit the architect's design, not designing the building to suit the materials that happen to be lying around.' BB reproduced this diagram during an interview, and explained: 'You have a poem. You're going to have five parts because it's got to be an uneven number. So that the central one should be the one apex, there [pointing to diagram]. But what is new, the only new thing that I knew of in, in doing it, was that instead of having one climax in the other parts you have two. In the first two the climax is the less and another immediately comes out of it when you're not expecting it. So you have it for those two. In the others the first climax is the greater and it trails off . . . If you add to that the Coda which came accidentally more or less, you've got the diagram of the whole poem' (*Quartermain & Tallman*, 9). 'Once I had got the thing clear in my head as a diagram, I simply set to work and wrote it, writing when I could. Three lines in the train on the way to work, three lines on the way home from work. Saturday mornings when there was not much to do, because there's no stock exchange on Saturday morning [which would require BB to be at his newspaper job], I'd get perhaps ten or fifteen lines written – and always the cutting out and the buggering about and the buggering about and the rewriting and so on' (*Quartermain & Tallman*, 16).

BB told JW and Tom Meyer: 'There's several ways *Briggflatts* can be explained, but it's quite simple enough on the face of it, if you think that there are four seasons of the year, four times of life, grouped around another part making five principal parts – the other part being the journey of Alexander from the Medieval "Legend of Alexander", when he goes to the end of the world through the most awful, horrible things' (Jonathan Williams and Tom Meyer, 'A Conversation with Basil Bunting', *Poetry Information* 19 [Autumn 1978], 39).

About the geographical settings in the poem's structure: 'Spring is around Briggflatts, Summer is all over the place – London, the Arctic, the Mediterranean. Autumn is mostly in the Dales, and the last part is

mostly on the Northumberland coast' (*Quartermain & Tallman*, 15).

BB said in an interview late in his life that, **'A very short narrative – nine stanzas – was needed to set the key for *Briggflatts*. For the rest, I'd learned from Spenser that there's no need to tell the reader what he can see for himself'** (P. Craven and M. Heyward, 'An Interview with Basil Bunting', *Scripsi* 1, nos. 3–4 [1982], 30–1).

In a carbon copy of the TS sent to Robert Creeley (MS79 at Durham), as in the *Poetry* and Fulcrum versions of the poem, the notes are tellingly titled 'Afterthoughts'.

▪ **The Northumbrian tongue travel has not taken from me sometimes sounds strange to men used to the koiné or to Americans who may not know how much Northumberland differs from the Saxon south of England. Southrons would maul the music of many lines in *Briggflatts*.**

An autobiography, **but not a record of fact. The first movement is no more a chronicle than the third. The truth of the poem is of another kind.**

No notes are needed. A few may spare diligent readers the pains of research.

Publication history

First published in *Poetry* 107, no. 4 (January 1966), [213]–237. The first edition of *Briggflatts* was published in February 1966 by Fulcrum Press, London. A second edition was published in December 1966 and a second impression of this edition was published in November 1967, along with a paperback edition. The poem was included in all subsequent collections of BB's work. Stanzas 3–5 of section III were published in *Junior Voices: an Anthology of Poetry and Pictures* (London: Penguin, 1970), *Guedalla* B13; stanzas 13–16, Section II, and Coda published in *Georgia Straight*, n.pag., *Guedalla* D34; section I and Coda also published in *Tri-Quarterly* 21 (Spring 1971), 37–41, *Guedalla* D35, a special issue also published as *Contemporary British Poetry* (Chicago: Tri-Quarterly, 1971), ed. John Matthias and reissued as *23 Modern British Poets* (Chicago: Swallow Press, 1971), *Guedalla*, B15; last nineteen lines of stanza II and last six stanzas of section V in *Shake the Kaleidoscope*, 7–8, later issued as *The Best of Modern Poetry* (1975); stanzas 14–17 of section II, and the Coda were reprinted in a pamphlet distributed during BB's visit to St Andrews College, Laurinburg, North Carolina, 15–19 April 1976.

Notes

[Title] Briggflatts. Note the difference between Bunting's spelling, Briggflatts, and Brigflatts, the current name for both the Quaker meeting house and the name of the Cumbrian village in which it is located. *Burton* (531) remarks that Bunting 'might have argued that he was merely restoring a "g" that had been stolen from the hamlet by the Ordnance Survey after the 1950s series of maps.

Until then it had been "Briggflatts" since the beginning of organised government mapping of the country.' In fact the spelling had been inconsistent over time: Brigflatts, Brigflats, Briggflats, Briggflatts. According to *Lesch* (315), 'Although the village was originally in Yorkshire, it is now located in Cumbria as a result of boundary changes.' *Makin* (21) describes Brigflatts as lying 'where Garsdale (an extension of Wensleydale, which reaches right across the Pennines from the Roman road near Catterick) comes out by Sedbergh, on the edge of the Lake District. It is five solid whitewashed stone houses among the trees and fields between the Sedbergh road and the River Rawthey.' As *Lesch* describes it (315), 'the village consists of little more than four structures dating back to the early seventeenth century. The second oldest structure, built in 1675, is a Quaker meeting house. A somewhat more "modern" house, dating from 1725, is where Bunting spent his school holidays as a child.' At a reading (University of British Columbia, 20 November 1970), BB explained that the title **'comes from the name of a small hamlet in the Pennine mountains in a very beautiful situation in what you call a valley but which we call a dale'** (quoted *Forde*, 213). Cp. *Note*, [1]: **'The name "Briggflatts", that of a remote hamlet and a Quaker meeting house, ought to warn people not to look for philosophy.'** Also, [4]: **'In silence, having swept dust and litter from our minds, we can detect the pulse of God's blood in our veins, more persuasive than words, more demonstrative than a diagram. That is what a Quaker meeting tries to be, and that is why my poem is called *Briggflatts*.'** 'The affirmation of **"the ancient Quaker life accepted without thought and without suspicion that it might seem eccentric"** (BB to LZ, 16 September 1964) was one of Bunting's original aims in writing *Briggflatts*' (*Lesch*, 361). George Fox came to Brigflatts in 1652; his vision of 'a great people in white raiment by the river's side' came to pass when, the day after his visit, groups of Seekers in the vicinity of the River Rawthey gathered. Fox's message to them the following Sunday, delivered standing from a rock on Firbank Fell, in Lunedale, is acknowledged to be the founding event of Quakerism. (See *Makin* 21, 209.)

[Note] southrons. BB always read the poem aloud in a Northumbrian accent (but see Denis Goacher's comments on this, and BB's views on Northern – as opposed to 'southron' – speech, in note to *FBO* 14, 'Gin the Goodwife Stint'). BB also remarked about the poem's affinity with Northern prosody: **'You realise that a great deal of what people goggle at in *Briggflatts* is merely an undisciplined and indiscriminate use of Cynghanedd . . . Cynghanedd is of course all the things that hold poetry together by way of sound; various kinds of rhyme, real ordinary rhyme we are used to, the peculiar rhyme the Welsh like, when you come to the rhyme word and it doesn't rhyme but the next word rhymes instead, or when a rhyme goes in the**

middle of the next line, or the end of the line rhymes with the middle of the line before. And they like rhymes that don't have the same vowel, only the same consonants each side of it, and funny things like that, and a tremendous variety of possibilities in the alliteration and so on' (Sean Figgies and Andrew McAlister, 'Basil Bunting: The Last Interview', *Bête Noire* 2/3 [1987], 22–50; quoted by Richard Caddel, 'Bunting and Welsh', in *Locations of Literary Modernism*, ed. Alex Davis and Lee M. Jenkins [Cambridge, 2000], 61–2).

[Epigraph] Autobiography. As for the poem's being an 'autobiography', BB, in an introduction to a reading of the poem, said that *Briggflatts* follows the **'phases of a lifetime in line with the phases of a year without any attempt to bring in historical facts'** (20 April 1976 at Allentown Community Center, Buffalo, NY; quoted *Lesch*, 313).

[Dedication] For Peggy. Peggy Greenbank, BB's first love, sister of BB's schoolmate, John, at Ackworth School, Yorkshire. BB met Peggy in 1912 when he spent holidays at the Greenbank home in Brigflatts. There has been confusion between Peggy Greenbank and Peggy Mullett, to whom 'I am agog with foam' was dedicated. *Caddel & Flowers* (16) say that it was Greenbank to whom that poem was dedicated, as does *Alldritt* (12–13). *Alldritt* refers to Mullett as a later girlfriend (51). Yet *Forde* (212), giving no surname in her chapter on the poem, includes a photo confusingly captioned 'Peggy Mullett at Briggflatts farmhouse'.

BB wrote to Edward Lucie-Smith (11 July 1965): **'Yes, *Briggflatts* is now mentionable by name. My hand was forced by Tyne Tees Television, who smuggled it in, in a question in an interview to be shown sometime in August. So I took my courage in both hands and wrote to the person most concerned and she must put up with it, though she can still have her name removed from the dedication if she likes'** (*Forde*, 213). In a letter to LZ describing factors to be incorporated in this poem, BB includes **'Peggy Greenbank and her whole ambience, the Rawthey valley, the fells of Lunedale, the Viking inheritance all spent save the faint smell of it, the ancient Quaker life accepted without thought and without suspicion that it might seem eccentric: and what happens when one deliberately thrusts love aside, as I then did – it has its revenge. That must be a longish poem'** (BB to LZ 16 September 1964; quoted *Forde*, 207, and *Lesch*, 310).

[Epigraph] Son los pasariellos del mal pelo exidos. The notebook containing draft materials for *Briggflatts*: **'the sparrows have moulted'** (*Briggflatts notebook*, page facing 55, at SUNY Buffalo). From stanza 1954, 2, of *Libro de Alexandre*, a medieval Spanish epic poem in the *cuaderna via* form – monorhymed quatrains of fourteen-syllable lines – uncertainly attributed to Juan Lorenzo de Astorga (perhaps a scribe *fl.* mid 18th. c) or to the priest Gonzálo de Bérceo (*fl.* 1220–42); the poem recounts the life of Alexander

the Great in over 10,000 lines. For more on Alexander, see note to III. 72, below. *Forde* says (210) that BB originally used this verse for one of a series of mottoes, eventually omitted, for each section of *Briggflatts*. BB, introducing the poem at a reading, commented that the epigraph is **'from one of the Spanish troubadours'** (Poetry Room, Harvard University, 1976). **'Commonplaces provide the poem's structure: spring, summer, autumn, winter of the year and of man's life, interrupted in the middle and balanced around Alexander's trip to the limits of the world and its futility, and sealed and signed at the end by a confession of our ignorance'** (*Note*, [1]). In Longfellow's translation, "From the Poema de Alexandro," *l.*18, which BB possibly had seen: "The birds have ceased to moult and their mourning time is over."

The spuggies are fledged. ▪ *Spuggies:* **little sparrows.** *OED*, spug: '(sparrow): see sprug.' 'Sprug' is given as Scottish or Northern dialect, of obscure origin. *EDD*: 'house-sparrow'.

I. Original motto for this section was 'Son los pasariellos del mal pelo exidos', later the epigraph for the entire poem (*Forde*, 210). See note above.

I. 1. Brag, sweet tenor bull. **'. . . the bull had been in my mind for ages, but hadn't been put down as having anything to do with this poem until quite late in the process . . . The bull I noticed one day in a farm near Throckley where I was living at the moment; and, you know, it struck me, at once, nobody had noticed the bull has a *tenor* voice. You hear of the bull bellowing and this, that, and the other. But in fact he bellows in the most melodious tenor, a beautiful tenor voice. In spring, the bull does, in fact, if he's with the cows, dance on the tips of his toes, as part of the business of showing off, showing that he is protecting them, you see. He's not really doing anything, but he sees somebody walking by the hedge and he begins to dance at once, just to demonstrate to the cows what an indispensable creature he is. It is delightful, and it bears such a, a strong resemblance to the behaviour of young men in general and . . . well . . . all creatures. That came . . . it was there in my notebooks, but it had nothing to do with *Briggflatts* until a fairly late stage of the construction of the poem, when I actually began to write things down'** (*Quartermain & Tallman*, 11).

'. . . having got so far I had my Latin mottoes, I've forgotten what they were, except the one, and I had my seasons, and I had one or two other items that, that could be distributed symmetrically; what the hell were they now, I forget. Anyway, it then struck me that that bloody bull who'd been in my notebook for a long time was obviously Spring, so I started off with him and just wrote it in' (*Quartermain & Tallman*, 16). **'It first struck me that he's comically like a young man. And then it struck me that his voice was a tenor**

voice, which was more like a young man still, the attitude to a field full of heifers, his showing off all the time' (interview with Peter Bell, 3 September 1981, in *Swigg*). Cp. Spenser, *Faerie Queene* IV. x. 45–56, etc., especially: 'The raging Buls rebellow through the wood, / And breaking forth, dare tempt the deepest flood, / To come where thou dost draw them with desire', and Joyce, *Ulysses* II: 'he would rear up on his hind quarters to show their ladyships a mystery and roar and bellow out of him in bull's language and they all after him'.

I. 2. descant. To sing variations on. *OED* v.1.a: 'To play or sing an air in harmony with a fixed theme; *gen.* to warble, sing harmoniously.' Also perhaps 2, 'To make remarks, comments, or observations; to comment (*on, upon, of* a text, theme, etc.).' Cp. for this sense, among many, Shakespeare, *Richard III*, I. i. 26–7: 'to spy my shadow in the sun, / And descant on mine own deformity', and III. vii. 49: 'on that ground I'll build a holy descant'; Milton, *Eikonoklastes* B, 'To descant on the misfortunes of a Person fall'n from dignity is not commendable'; and Boswell's *Life of Johnson*, 5 Aug. 1763, 'He used to descant upon their very Hats and Habits.' Note also *OED* 3: 'To comment on, discourse about, discuss; *occas.* to criticize, carp at. *Obs.*' and 4: 'To work with intricate variation *on*; to fashion with artistic skill. *Obs. rare.*' As a noun, *OED* n.I.1: 'A melodious accompaniment to a simple musical theme (the *plainsong*), sung or played, and often merely extemporized, above it, and thus forming an air to its bass: the earliest form of counterpoint', and 3, 'A warbled song, a melodious strain'. 'Plainsong' occurs in line I. 63, below. Cp. in this sense Spenser, *Epithalamion*, V. 80, 'the Mauis descant playes'. (Wordsworth uses the word in *The Prelude* (1850), VI. 96, in close proximity to mention of Spenser in VI. 89.) Cp. also Campion, in whom BB was much interested (see notes on Helen for *Villon* III and *SBOO* 7), who wrote a treatise titled, 'The Art of Descant, or composing Musick in Parts'; Gascoigne, *Philomene* 6: 'To heare the descant of the Nightingale'; and Gray, 'Sonnet on the Death of Mr. Richard West', 3: 'The birds in vain their amorous descant join.' BB must have known Yeats's lines, apt in this context, from st. 2 of 'After Long Silence', section XVII of 'Words for Music Perhaps', 'That we descant and yet again descant / Upon the supreme theme of Art and Song: / Bodily decrepitude is wisdom; young / We loved each other and were ignorant.'

As for the relationship of descant to plainsong, BB had probably read LZ's *Bottom: On Shakespeare* (Austin, TX: Ark Press, 1963), *Guedalla* B9, in which descant and plainsong arise several times, e.g. vol. 1, 19: 'Scholarship dwelling on Shakespeare's awareness of contemporary musical terms has not emphasized that his development of plot and sub-plot is musical in the sense of plain-song and descant.' LZ quotes Shakespeare, *A Midsummer Night's*

Dream III. 1. 124–7: 'The finch, the sparrow, and the lark, / The plain-song cuckoo gray, / Whose note full many a man doth mark, / And dares not answer nay' (vol. 1, 48); and 'What a Character Is' by Sir Thomas Overbury (1581–1613): 'It is a quick and soft touch of many strings, all shutting up in one musical close; it is wit's descant on any plain song' (vol. 1, 177). The words are again conjoined in a discussion of *Pericles* (vol. 1, 332). In Skelton's 'Agaynste a Comely Coystrowne', the words occur in fairly close proximity, *ll.* 38 and 54, respectively: 'His descant is dasshed full of dyscordes', 'That neyther they synge wel prycke song nor playne'. Cp. perhaps the 'plaine-singing' poems of Sidney's *Arcadia*; also, generally the 1940 book, *Elizabethan Dances and Ayres for Descant Recorder and Piano*, which BB owned.

Rawthey. River Rawthey, near town of Sedbergh, in what is now Cumbria.

I. 3. pebble. See note to 'Lydian pebbles' in *The Spoils*, III.

I. 4. fells. *EDD* 1, 'fell': 'A hill, mountain; high, open, untilled ground; a moor, moorland.' *OED* 'fell', n.2.c: '*Sc.* "A field pretty level on the side or top of a hill" [from glossary in Burns, *Poems*, 1787].' Cp. Burns, 'Now Westlin Winds', ii: 'The partridge loves the fruitful fells.' B. Kirkby, *Lakeland Words* (Kendal?, 1898), 52: 'FELL – I'Lakeland o' t' moontains is fells, an' ther's a gay lot ta be gaan on wi', an' some o' them's a gay heet up. "Owt can I bide / But a cauld thow wind / On a hee fell side."' Cp. also Drayton, *The Poly-Olbion*, xvii, 388: 'Both in the tufty Frith, and in the mossy Fell'. Drayton introduced the idea of English 'odes' based on Horace, which may have influenced BB's own 'odes', heavily allusive to Horace. BB also used the word in I. 149, II. 58, IV. 54, V. 57, as well as in 'At Briggflatts meetinghouse', *SBOO* 11, and 'The Pious Cat', 171.

I. 6, 10, 12. ▪ *May* **the flower, as haw is the fruit, of the thorn.** Cp. (among many) Spenser, *The Shepheardes Calender*, May, 10: 'To gather may buskets and smelling brere'; Jonson, *Cynthia's Revels*, V. ii: 'your brests and forehead are whiter then gotes milke, or May-blossomes'; Shelley, 'The Question', 18: 'The moonlight-coloured may'; Arnold, 'Thrysis', 55: 'With blossoms red and white of fallen May'; Longfellow, *Golden Legends*, I: 'Court-yard of Castle', 'Fill me a goblet of May drink, / As aromatic as the May / From which it steals the breath away'; EP, 'Canzon: The Spear', VI. 5: 'No poppy in the May-glad mead'; Tennyson, 'Gareth and Lynette', 575: 'May-blossom, and a cheek of apple-blossom'; also Hopkins, 'The Starlight-Night', 10: 'Look, look: a May-mess, like on orchard boughs!'

I. 13. slowworm's way. Also called blind-worm. *Makin* (66) says, 'The slow-worm is a harmless, beautiful, and very shy lizard, who chiefly basks in the sun on heaths, or slips away, "flowing like a molten bronze rod" (in Colin Simms's words), under hedges.' BB was a friend of Simms and owned his book *Lives of British Lizards* (see particularly p. 108). Quartermain reports that 'the slow-worm (*Anguis fragilis*) grows to a length of several feet; male slow-worms turn brilliantly mottled blue on their backs, blue as the sky. They're very beautiful creatures' ('Parataxis in Basil Bunting and Louis Zukofsky', *Caddel*, 56; later in Quartermain's *Stubborn Poetries: Poetic Facticity and the Avant-Garde*). Suter notes that when asked 'what the slowworm suggests, Bunting relied that he could not "figure it out" precisely himself, except that it represents "the quietest attitude"' (Anthony Suter, '*Briggflatts* and the Resurrection of Basil Bunting', in *Terrell*, 219). Wordsworth's poems are replete with slow-worms, e.g. 'Written with a Slate Pencil Upon a Stone . . .', 34: 'There let the vernal slow-worm sun himself.' Also Tennyson, 'Aylmer's Field', 852: 'The slow-worm creeps . . . and all is open field'; Herrick, 'The Night-Piece, To Julia', 1, etc., 'Her eyes the slow-worm lend thee'; and Pope, 'To Mr. John Moore, Author of the celebrated Worm-Powder', 14, 'The Blockhead is a Slow-worm.' See also note to III. 68–71. For more on worms, see note to *FBO* 34.

I. 14–37. John Greenbank, Peggy's father, had a stonemason's business at High Brigflatts (*Caddel & Flowers*, 16; *Alldritt*, 12). BB affirmed that the figure of the mason was modelled on John Greenbank in *Quartermain & Tallman*, 12: '**[I] came to do mason's work . . . I've rubbed down gravestones and that's how I know how it feels to rub down a gravestone. And how your fingers ache on the damn job . . . and so on. I take care not to write anything that I don't bloody well know. And that is something that is different I think from a lot of poets who write. If I write about how it feels rubbing down a gravestone, well I have rubbed down a bloody gravestone.**' He also wrote to Forde of this: **'with [Greenbank's] sons [I] did a bit of rough work from time to time to help out'** (BB to Forde, 4 July 1973; quoted *Forde*, 216). See also V. 41–2. Cp. Gael Turnbull, 'An Irish Monk on Lindisfarne, about 650 AD', 'The patience of the bricklayer / is assumed in the dream of the architect.' (For more on Turnbull see headnote, above).

I. 25–6. On 16 September 1964, BB wrote to LZ about 'A Song for Rustam', a poem on the death of his son; in that letter, he'd written the couplet, **'In the grave's narrow slot / they lie: we rot.'** See notes to that poem.

I. 42. *lorry*. A cart.

I. 47. *stale*. Urinate (v.). Cp. Shakespeare, *Antony and Cleopatra*, I. iv. 62–3: 'Thou didst drink / The stale of horses'; Hardy, *Tess of the*

D'Urbervilles, lii: 'While the horses stood to stale and breathe themselves'; and Kipling, 'South Africa', 29: 'water where the mules had staled'.

I. 50. felloe. OED: 'The exterior rim, or part of the rim, of a wheel, supported by the spokes.' Citations from Ælfred's *Boethius* and Ælfric. Cp. Shakespeare, *Hamlet*, II. ii. 496: 'Break all the spokes and fellies from her wheel'; Sandys's version of Ovid's *Metamorphoses* II. 24: 'On silver Spokes the golden Fellies rol'd'; Chapman's *The Iliad*, IV. 525: 'The Fell'ffs, or out-parts of a wheele that compass the whole', and V. 732: 'The Axle-tree was steele, / The Felffes incorruptible gold.' Perhaps also Carlyle, *French Revolution*, I. v. vi, 'Never over nave or felloe did thy axe strike such a stroke.'

I. 53–9. The words, 'rain', 'hard' and 'marble' appear several times each in a description of travel through Hawes and Garsdale in Dorothy Wordsworth's journals, 4–8 October 1802 (*The Grasmere Journals*, ed. Pamela Woof [1991], 129–32; also *Journals of Dorothy Wordsworth*, ed. E. de Selincourt [1941], vol. 1, 176–83). Wordsworth mentions Hawes in 'Hart-Leap Well', 101.

I. 63. Baltic plainsong. For 'plainsong', see note to I. 2, above. Cp. Wordsworth, 'By the Sea-Side', 31–2: 'from the wide and open Baltic, rise / With punctual care, Lutherian harmonies.'

I. 65. ▪ **Northumbrians should know Eric *Bloodaxe* but seldom do, because all the school histories are written by or for southrons. Piece his story together from the Anglo-Saxon Chronicle, the Orkneyinga Saga, and Heimskringla, as you fancy.** See note to I. 133–4.

I. 68–9. Skulls cropped for steel caps / huddle round Stainmore. See note to I. 139. *Lesch* (324): 'The lines suggest the Vikings who cropped their hair in order to fit their heads into their helmets, as well as describing the hilltops around Stainmore Pass whose upper portions are barren of any vegetation.'

I. 70. ▪ **We have burns in the east, *becks* in the west, but no brooks or creeks.** *OED*: n.1.1: 'A brook or stream: the ordinary name in those parts of England from Lincolnshire to Cumbria which were occupied by the Danes or Norwegians; hence often used *spec.* in literature to connote a brook with stony bed, or rugged course, such as are those of the north country.' B. Kirkby, *Lakeland Words* (Kendal?, 1898), 13: 'BECK – Stream. A Lakeland lad'll know summat aboot a beck, Ah dar be bund, wharivver ye see him. "To think how poets wi' their sangs, / Their minds sud seea perplex, / 'Bout Eden, Lune, the Tyne, and Tees, / An' scwores o' mucky becks.["] – *Whitehead*.' BB used the word 'becks' in a comment about Ford Madox Ford's poetry: **'There are explorations that can never end in discovery, only in willingness to rest content with an unsure glimpse through mists, an uncertain sound of becks we shall never taste'** (*Selected Poems*, ed. BB, [Cambridge, MA: Pym-Randall, 1971], viii).

I. 77 and II. 159. fellside. See note to 'fells,' I. 4. The word also occurs in 'Snow's on the fellside . . .' in 'Uncollected Overdrafts'.

I. 78. peewit. Pewit. *OED* 1: 'A widely-diffused name of the Lapwing (*Vanellus vulgaris* or *cristatus*): the usual name in Scotland, and in Eng. Dial. Dict. cited as used from Northumberland to Berkshire.' Cp. Skelton, 'Phyllp Sparowe', 430: 'With puwyt the lapwyng'; Clare, 'The last of March', 41: 'The startling peewits, as they pass, / Scream joyous whirring over-head'; and Tennyson, 'Will Waterproof's Lyrical Monologue', 230, 'To come and go, and come again, / Returning like the pewit'. B. Kirkby, *Lakeland Words* (Kendal?, 1898), 113: 'PEE-WIT, TEA-FIT – "Pee-wit! Pee-wit! Ah lost mi nest an' Ah've rued it."' Probably also Edward Thomas, 'Two Pewits', e.g. 'Under the after-sunset sky / Two pewits sport and cry,' etc.

I. 93. streams. OED v.2.a: 'Of light, air, vapour, immaterial effluences, etc.: To be carried or emitted in a full and continuous current.' Cp. Shakespeare, *All's Well That Ends Well*, II. iii. 76–7: 'And to imperial Love, that god most high / Do my sighs streame.' Or perhaps *OED* 4.c: 'To go with a rush. *rare*.'

I. 99. tape. EDD 3: in weaving, 'a length of warp used for threading the machine'. *OED* n.1.1.a: 'A narrow woven strip of stout linen, cotton, silk, or other textile, used as a string for tying garments.' Citation for Ælfric, also Chaucer, 'The Miller's Tale', 55: 'The tapes of hir white voluper / Were of the same suyte of hir coler.'

I. 104. manhood's. Cp. 'Attis: Or, Something Missing', III. 30–1, **'The wraith of my manhood, / the cruel ghost of my manhood.'** In notebook of draft materials for *Briggflatts*, **'his soul's home'** (*Briggflatts notebook*, page facing 60, at SUNY Buffalo).

I. 117. Take a chisel to write. In a lecture, BB, quoting himself, commented that Milton is **'Most condensed – he "takes a chisel to write"'** (*BBP*, 61). EP, as BB knew, had long given this advice to poets, e.g. his letter of 27 July 1916 to Iris Barry: 'It is as simple as the sculptor's direction: "Take a chisel and cut away all the stone you don't want."' (*The Letters of Ezra Pound: 1907–1941*, ed. D. D. Paige, 91).

The complex designs of the *Codex Lindisfarnensis* 'are painstakingly built up over a measured geometric framework, traces of the construction work for which can be seen on the blank rectos of the leaves in the form of prick marks, compass holes, rulings and grid lines. It appears that, within this mathematical framework, the more subtle curves were then drawn purely by eye. It has been suggested that templates were used in the execution of some seventh- and eighth-century manuscripts, and there certainly seems to be evidence that templates were part of a pre-Conquest stone-carver's equipment' (Janet Backhouse, *The Lindisfarne Gospels* [London: Phaidon, 1987], 28). Cp. 'Isn't it poetical . . .', in 'Uncollected Overdrafts'.

I. 133–4. Bloodaxe, king of York, / king of Dublin, king of Orkney. *Lesch* (323) observes that, 'It is because of his method of killing his sibling rivals that he acquired the name "Bloodaxe".'

In a letter quoted by Makin (3 February 1978), BB wrote: **'Fifteen years earlier [than Eric Bloodaxe's death at Stainmore], at Brunanburgh, besides many earls, five Norse kings were slain, apparently all from Dublin . . . Eric of course was always king, wherever he went, and usually wherever he went he would be the effective king, because he had the most formidable war-band'** (*Makin*, 173). Eric had been king of Norway but, as his popularity diminished, he headed for Northumbria, about which BB wrote in a letter quoted by Makin (17 January 1978): **'He seems to have left the place to his brothers** *to avoid bloodshed*; **and if so, that must have weighed on his kingly god-descended conscience for the rest of his life'** (*Makin*, 173). Eric subsequently imposed himself as king of York in 948, but was driven out. He took over again in 952. Makin quotes Smyth, *Scandinavian York and Dublin*, 177–8: 'Eiríkr's arrival in the British Isles *ca.*946 can now be seen to have upset not only the calculations of the kings of Wessex but to have disturbed a political balance right across the British Isles . . . The Dublin and York axis . . . had been violently dismantled by Eiríkr and replaced by a north–south alliance based on York and the Isles. This arrangement threatened to destroy West Saxon hopes for the unification of England; reduced the political standing of the Orkney jarls; threatened the security of Hákon in Norway; usurped the political and economic rights enjoyed by the kings of Dublin; and antagonized the Scots and Strathclyde Britons who were regularly raided by Eiríkr to supplement his York income' (*Makin*, 172).

The Viking poet Egil Skallagramsson (*ca.*910–90) cursed Eric and killed his son; years later (*ca.*948), shipwrecked off the coast of Northumbria and having fallen into Eric's hands, he is said to have composed uniquely metred verse in Eric's honour in exchange for his life. Egil's verse and biography is preserved in *Egils Saga*, attributed to his descendant, Snorri Sturluson (1179–1241). Of Egil's praise-poem, BB wrote in letters quoted by Makin (17 January and 27 January 1978 – dating unclear in *Makin*): **'He praises qualities Eric more or less possessed and carefully avoids** *mere* **butter. No, I think**

Egil went to York of set purpose to patch things up with Eric, and the poem was in his satchel or in his memory before he ever sailed. Such a truce (or reconciliation) is well within the character of both of them' (*Makin*, 328).

In a letter quoted by Makin (18 May 1985) BB explained how he associated Eric with the relationship of the boy and girl in this section of the poem: **'[Eric's] linked lies weigh him into the mire and not only frustrate his ambition, but expose his emptiness at last. Eric has failed to admit his disaster in Norway [just as the poet] has failed to admit his continuing love for the girl'** (*Makin*, 170).

BB wrote letters on several occasions, quoted by Makin, about Eric Bloodaxe as a historical figure in *Briggflatts*: **'I wrote from memory and have checked nothing, though I did have a look one day for the Orkneyinga Saga; but found no version available . . . But my Eric has no need whatever to be authentic. He serves his purpose in the poem and would serve if I had to invent him'** (27 January 1978; *Makin* 329). The Orkneyinga saga is also known as *The History of the Earls of Orkney*, *ca.1192–1206*; an English version by Hermann Pálsson and Paul Edwards would appear in 1978. **'I am not troubled at all about lack of historicity in my Bloodaxe – his role in the poem is enough in itself'** (3 February 1978; *Makin*, 170). See also II. 193, below.

Cp. Wordsworth, *The Prelude* (1850) XIII. 320ff.: 'Our dim ancestral Past in vision clear; / Saw multitudes of men, and, here and there, / A single Briton clothed in wolf-skin vest, / With shield and stone-axe, stride across the wold,' etc.

I. 139. Stainmore. After his second expulsion from York, Eric was killed at Stainmore. Cp. Roger of Wendover; quoted in D. Whitelock (ed.), *English Historical Documents, c. 500–1042* (1955), 257: 'King Eric was treacherously killed by Earl Maccus in a certain lonely place called Stainmore, with his son Haeric and his brother Ragnald, betrayed by Earl Oswulf.'

II. Original motto for this section was 'Bloodaxe' (*Forde*, 210).

As for the sailing terms in section II, note that BB enrolled in a school for those seeking certification as mates or masters, the Nellist Nautical Academy, Newcastle, in 1938. For more on this, see *Descant*, [17–18]; for more on BB and sailing, see note to *SBOO* 12.

II. 4. toadies. Cp. Thackeray, *Vanity Fair*, XI: 'When I come into the country . . . I leave my toady, Miss Briggs, at home. My brothers are my toadies here.'

II. 10. blouse. Cp. 'That filly couldnt carry a rider nor', 11–12, 'Leslie who lets her blouse / slip from her shining shoulder'.

II. 11–15. Cp. BB's music column for September 1928 in *The Town Crier*, a London monthly (quoted *Caddel & Flowers*, 36): **'This is the close season for music. Theosophists and Spiritualists possess the halls. The virtuosi are on holiday or turning up at short notice to play unrehearsed concertos at the Proms . . . The critic, who has stoically endured for a whole year every kind of organised noise that man can hope to get his fellow man to pay for, has now suddenly found that the sounds that are supplied to Londoners gratis – to wit, motor-horns, accelerating 'buses, back-firing exhausts, drays, newsboys, street-organs and drunks, all restlessly modulating on a pedal-point of rubber-on-asphalt – are more than a mind with the acquired habit of listening can put up with for more than two years in succession without a break. There is a tale of a pianist who, having played a repeat passage as far as the double bars twice, forgot the bridge passage that followed and had to go on repeating and repeating until at last he broke down from sheer fatigue. London is such a pianist rendered tireless. The Traffic Symphony is not unstimulating to a country hearer; but after the seven hundredth and thirtieth repetition one prays for a transport workers' strike, a long one, or to become temporarily deaf. Therefore this is written from the country, where there is not silence, but a change of noise, a piano for a forte and an andante for a presto.'**

II. 19. left breast of a girl who bared it in Kleinfeldt's. Kleinfeldt's was the Fitzroy Tavern on the corner of Charlotte Street and Windmill Street, behind Tottenham Court Road in London. A well-known meeting place for artists and writers frequented by BB, it was run by Papa Judah Kleinfeldt, a Russian emigré. Alldritt writes: 'The process of entering the literary life of London got underway when, most probably in the Fitzroy Tavern, Basil began an important friendship. This was with the artist Nina Hamnett, a regular at the pub. Some ten years older than Basil, Nina knew just about everyone in the arts in both London and Paris, and after the war moved continually to and fro between the two cities. Though born into a middle-class family and with a colonel for a father, Nina quickly entered Bohemia via art schools in Dublin and London. By the time she was thirty and met Basil, Nina had had many great adventures. She had done paintings for, and then quarrelled with, Yeats's great enemy, the diabolist and magician Aleister Crowley. With the French sculptor Gaudier-Brzeska she had stolen marble so that he could make a carving of her shapely torso, which she was always ready to uncover and display on social occasions. The sculpture was eventually purchased for the Victoria and Albert Museum. Nina was very proud to be displayed there. When Dylan Thomas first introduced her to a friend in the Fitzroy she declared: "You know me, m'dear – I'm in the V and A with me left tit knocked off"'

(*Alldritt*, 24). BB owed his first encounter with T. S. Eliot's early work, and EP's early book, *Quia Pauper Amavi* (1919), to Hamnett: **'It was at that stage, when I was 19, that Nina Hamnett first showed me Eliot's early work and Pound's "Propertius". You can imagine my excitement . . . Ezra was using a rhythmical ease and freedom which put much within reach that had seemed out of reach before'** ('The Use of Poetry', ed. Peter Quartermain, *Writing* 12 [Summer 1985], 41).

II. 24–35. BB sent these stanzas to LZ on 10 November 1964 with a note: **'If you dont play bowls (not ten-pins, but on the grass with biased bowls) in America you may not quite get it'** (*Forde*, 221).

II. 29. woods. In draft to LZ, 'spheres' (*Forde*, 222) – *OED* n.1.7.f: 'Each of the bowls in the game of bowls.'

II. 36. ▪ ***Oxter*: armpit.** *OED* n.a: '*Sc., Irish*, and *north. dial.*' Cp. Allan Ramsay, 'Gentle Shepherd', III. ii: 'Aneath his oxter is the mark'; Scott, *The Bride of Lammermoor*, xxiv, 'Let her leddyship get his head ance under her oxter'; Shaw, *Admirable Bashville*, II. 304: 'with Bob Mellish tucked beneath his oxter'; Joyce, *Dubliners*, 206: 'many a good man went to the penny-a-week school with a sod of turf under his oxter'; *Ulysses* II: 'two bloody big books tucked under his oxter', 'passing the door with his books under his oxter', 'swaggersticks tight in their oxters', 'wedges it tight in his oxter'; and Auden, *The Orators*, II. 71: 'The madman keeper crawls through brushwood, / Axe under oxter.'

loom. *OED* n.1.5: 'The shaft, i.e. the part between the blade and the handle of an oar; also limited to the part of the oar between the rowlock and the hands in rowing; also, loosely, the handle.' Citation for Francis Marion Crawford, *The Children of the King*, i.5 (1893): 'Out go the sweeps . . . and the men throw themselves forward over the long slender loom, as they stand.' Mottram points out that the word also 'carries with it the sense of fabric-weaving machine' ('"An Acknowledged Land": Love and Poetry in Bunting's Sonatas', in *Terrell*, 99).

sweep. *OED* n.1.28: 'A long oar used to propel a ship, barge, etc. when becalmed, or to assist the work of steering.'

II. 37. wake. Mottram points out that the word can mean 'both a track and a funeral rite; both refer to the past and a possible future' ('"An Acknowledged Land": Love and Poetry in Bunting's Sonatas', in *Terrell*, 99).

II. 38. Thole-pins. *OED* 'thole', n.1: 'A vertical pin or peg in the side of a boat against which in rowing the oar presses as the fulcrum of its action; *esp.* one of a pair between which the oar works; hence, a rowlock.' Citation for Longfellow, *Evangeline*, II. ii. 102:

'The sound of their oars on their tholes had died in the distance.' Mottram points out that the word, 'thole', alone 'means to be exposed or subjected to evil, and thence to endure and suffer' ('"An Acknowledged Land": Love and Poetry in Bunting's Sonatas', in *Terrell* 99). Indeed, in a 1971 letter to JW, BB used the word: **'I find it possible – no, necessary – to laugh at all my friends and I presume, or hope, they laugh at me. How else are we to thole the ridiculous burden of human oddity I don't know'** (14 November 1971; quoted *McGonigal & Price*, 258). Cp. perhaps Joyce, *Ulysses* II: 'that they lie for to thole and bring forth bairns'.

oar. Cp. Kipling, 'Song of the Galley-Slaves', 10: 'The salt made the oar-handles like shark-skin', and 'Harp Song of the Dane Woman', 20: 'And the sound of your oar-blades, falling hollow'. Also Yeats, 'The Meditation of the Old Fisherman', 9–10: 'And ah, you proud maiden, you are not so fair when his oar / is heard on the water.' BB recited these poems in a lecture on precursors to modernism, in *BBP*, 109–10, 115.

II. 39. grommets. OED 2.1: 'A ring or wreath of rope, *spec.* one consisting of a single strand laid three times round. a. One of those used to secure the upper edge of a sail to its stay. b. A ring of rope used as a substitute for a rowlock in a boat.'

II. 40. halliards. OED 1: 'A rope or tackle used for raising or lowering a sail, yard, spar, or flag.' Cp. Kipling, 'The English Flag', 29: 'I have wrenched it free from the halliards.' BB uses the word in his introduction to the *Selected Poems* of Ford Madox Ford, which he edited (Cambridge, MA: Pym-Randall, 1971), vii: **'Ford sweated up his halliards like a sailor.'**

frapped. OED 'frap,' v.2.a: '*Naut.* To bind tightly.' Cp. Kipling, 'The Last Chantey', 32: "Once we frapped a ship, and she laboured woundidly'; also R. H. Dana, *Two Years Before the Mast*, chap. xxv: 'We succeeded . . . in smoothing it and frapping it [the sail] with long pieces of sinnet.' B. Kirkby, *Lakeland Words* (Kendal?, 1898), 57: 'FRAP – A sharp noise . . .'

shrouds. OED n.2.1: 'A set of ropes, usually in pairs, leading from the head of a mast and serving to relieve the latter of lateral strain; they form part of the standing rigging of a ship.' Cp. R. H. Dana, *Two Years Before the Mast*, chap. xxiii: 'In an instant every one sprung into the rigging, up the shrouds, and out on the yards.' Also Hakluyt, *Voyages* 282: 'Another walkes vpon the hatches, another climbes the shrowes' (BB owned a 1927 edition of Hakluyt's *The Principal Navigations, Voyages . . .*); and Dryden, 'Annus Mirabilis', 591: 'To try new shrouds one mounts into the wind.' Mottram remarks that the word 'is obviously a double word of support' ('"An Acknowledged Land": Love and Poetry in Bunting's Sonatas', in Bunting's Sonatas,' in *Terrell*, 99).

II. 49. steading. EDD: 'The site of anything; building land.' *OED*: '*Sc.* and *north.* 1. A farm-house and outbuildings; often the outbuildings in contrast to the farmhouse.'

II. 50. seracs. OED cites *Encyclopaedia of Sports* (1898): '*Serac*, a tower of ice on a glacier, formed by the intersection of crevasses.'

II. 55–60. Who sang . . . voices. A **'self-contained fragment'** of these verses exists which BB sent to LZ:

> Who sang, sea takes,
> flesh brine, bone grit.
> Keener the kittiwake.
> Fells forget him.
>
> Fathoms dull the dale,
> slime voices.
> Watchdog the whale,
> gulfweed curtain.

BB wrote that the way the stanza **'subsides to next to nothing is intentional'** (BB to LZ, 6 December 1964; quoted *Forde,* 223, and *Lesch*, 338).

II. 57. kittiwake. Common species of small gull. *OED*: 'Named in imitation of its cry.'

II. 63. ▪ ***Boiled louse:* coccus cacti, the cochineal, a parasite on opuntia.** At a reading, BB commented: **'The most beautiful of all the red dyes [It is] salutary to remember that one of the loveliest colours we possess comes from the louse'** (1976 Harvard reading).

II. 81–109. In 1950–1, BB lived with his wife and daughter in Lido di Camaiore, south of Rapallo and about four miles west of Lucca, in view of the Apuan Alps, where marble was quarried. His work for the Westminster Press and for an English paper, *Northern Echo* – and, Alldritt claims, as a spy for MI6 – took him to Parma, Milan, Siena, and Rome (*Alldritt*, 121). BB had also spent time in Rapallo with EP in 1924–5; see *Makin*, chap. 3.

II. 84. Lucca is the setting for events described in Dante, *Purgatorio* XXIV. Cp. Byron, *Don Juan,* XV st. 73: 'The simple olives, best allies of wine, / Must I pass over in my bill of fare? / I must, although a favourite "plat" of mine / In Spain, and Lucca, Athens, every where: / On them and bread twas oft my luck to dine, / The grass my table-cloth, in open air'. Also EP, *Cantos*, LXXVI, p. 459: 'The rain has fallen, the wind coming down / out of the mountain / Lucca, Forti dei Marmi, Berchthold after the other one', and LXXVIII, p. 483: 'The moon split, no cloud nearer than Lucca.'

II. 86. olives. Cp. 'Villon', III. 1–3, 'Under the olive trees / walking alone / on the green terrace' and *FBO* 8. 3, 'where the olive stirs and dozes'.

II. 90–2. Antonietta's . . . Amalfitan kisses. William Corbett, in his brief memoir of BB's 1976 reading at Harvard writes: 'Back at our house he spoke of the young Italian girl he must have remembered from these lines he had read in *Briggflatts* . . . He was over thirty at the time and she perhaps no older than sixteen. He would have married her but her family objected, and soon after their lovemaking in that Amalfi cave they parted. He paused to say, "I hope I'm not speaking too roughly"' (reprinted in William Corbett, *All Prose* [Cambridge, MA: Zoland Books, 2002], 160–1).

II. 104. cumber. *OED* v.1 cites *Alexander*. Cp. Swinburne, 'Evening on the Broads', 13: 'Cover the brood of her worlds that cumber the skies with their blossom.' Also Scott, *The Bridal of Triermain*, II. X, 'Cares, that cumber royal sway.' *EDD* cites George Eliot, *Adam Bede*, I. 159: 'I shall be nought but cumber, or a sittin' i' th' chimney-corner.'

II. 107. Garfagnana. Valley between the Apuan Alps and the Tuscan–Emilian Apennines created by the Serchio River and its tributaries.

II. 108. la Cisa. Sanctuary of La Mare de Déu de la Cisa, built in the eighteenth century.

II. 109. ▪ *Hillside fiddlers:* **Pianforini, for instance, or Manini.** Marco Pianforini (1795–1874?). Antony Manini (1750–86). *Lesch* (343): 'Manini, who lived in the late eighteenth century, was a violinist of some repute in England. Historians conjecture that he was a member of the Norfolk family of Mann whose name was italianized.' See *Dictionary of National Biography*, 12 (London: Oxford University Press, reprint 1937–8), 919–20. BB had written an article about Scarlatti sonatas, 'Recent Fiddlers', in *The Outlook* 61, no. 1568 (18 February 1928), 209.

II. 118. ▪ *Lindisfarne,* **the Holy Island, where the tracery of the Codex Lindisfarnensis was elaborated.** See notes to IV. 25–30 and V. 12.

II. 120–35. In a letter to LZ (6 December 1964; quoted *Forde*, 225, and *Lesch*, 345), BB calls this a **'self-contained fragment'** and remarks **'the debt (if any) to Kipling'**. Cp. 'Cities and Thrones and Powers', recited with other poems by Kipling in BB's lecture, 'Precursors', in which he comments, **'Some of Kipling's searching for the right form led him to kinds of pastiche, but pastiche done as well as he did it is poetry in its own right'** (*BBP*, 108).

II. 135. flawed fragments. In a letter quoted by Makin (13 January 1965), BB explains that the flawed fragments are (in Makin's paraphrase) 'not mere offcuts, but the sculptor's false starts, thrown aside because his chisel has slipped and spoiled them' (*Makin*, 133–4).

II. 140. pressed into the mire. Cp. among very many, especially Yeats, 'The Two Kings', 3–4: 'He had out-ridden his war-wasted men / That with empounded cattle trod the mire'; 'Byzantium', 8: 'The fury and the mire of human veins'; 24: And all complexities of mire or blood'; 33: 'Astraddle on the dolphin's mire and blood', etc. Also Milton, *Paradise Lost*, IV. 1010: 'To trample thee as mire'; Byron, *Don Juan*, VIII st. 20, 1: 'Thus on they wallowed in the bloody mire'; and Tennyson, *Idylls of the King*, 'Gareth and Lynette', 706–7: 'so my lance / Hold, by God's grace, he shall into the mire'; 'The Last Tournament', 470: 'And sank his head in mire, and slimed themselves'. The word also occurs often in Longfellow's version of Dante's *Divine Comedy*, e.g. *Inferno* VII. 124: 'Now we are sullen in this sable mire.'

II. 150. bent. Cp. BB's gloss in *P1950* for the word in 'Gin the Goodwife Stint': **tough, tussocky grass**. Cp. Spenser, *Faerie Queene* VI. iv. 4: 'stroke of strains or bents'; Scott, *Marmion* IX. xxv: 'Since Marmion saw that martial scene / Upon the bent so brown'; and Hardy, 'The Souls of the Slain', 10: 'the bent-bearded slope of the land'.

II. 161. Byrd. William Byrd, English composer (1543–1623). BB 'attended rehearsals of [neighbour and family friend William Giles] Whittaker's Newcastle Bach Choir, and was present at the memorable first performance of Byrd's *Great Service* given by the choir in Newcastle Cathedral on 31 May 1924. This important work was being performed for the first time in its entirety since the time of William Byrd, having recently been re-edited from parts discovered in Durham Cathedral by Dr. [Edmund H.] Fellowes . . . Bunting's Aunt Jennie Cheesman (Mrs Tom Lamb) was a long standing member of the Newcastle and Gateshead Choral Union under Whittaker, and as a member of the Newcastle Bach Choir sang in this and subsequent performances of the *Great Service*' (*Caddel & Flowers*, 29). **'Byrd was a mystic beyond question'** ('César Franck', *The Outlook* 61, no. 1569 [25 February 1928], 236; quoted *Makin*, 36). **'You and Louis [Zukofsky] . . . seem to think what people want and cant get can be expressed in terms of money. That is too single-minded and reminds one of Byrd's setting of the apostle's creed: "I believe in ONE god": I dont'** (BB to EP, 'Last of 1935'; quoted *Makin*, 79). **'English poets are too often on their dignity, they strive too constantly to be sublime and end by becoming monotonous and empty of lifegiving detail, like hymn-tunes. They have often been the slaves rather than the masters of their metres . . . This is partly because they have neglected the music of Byrd and Dowland so much more supple rhythmically than English poetry or than the**

music of the classical masters until recently most in favour' ('The Lion and the Lizard', unpublished MS, 1935; *Three Essays*, 30). LZ discussed Byrd in his *Bottom: On Shakespeare*, vol. 1, 420, *Guedalla* B9.

II. 171. Monteverdi. Claudio Giovanni Antonio Monteverdi (1567–1643), considered a master of the 'late' period of the madrigals, *ca.*1580–1620. Byrd, above, also composed madrigals.

II. 180. red against privet stems as a mazurka. Perhaps refers to a kind of heather, or Fuchsia 'Loxhore Mazurka', which has reddish flowers.

II. 183. Schoenberg's maze. BB had reviewed Schoenberg's *Gurrelieder* – a work which, according to *Alldritt* (53) requires 'five soloists, a speaker, three male choirs, a mixed choir and an orchestra' – in *The Outlook* 61, no. 1566 (1928). The words 'Schoenberg' and 'maze' occur in close proximity again in a 1974 lecture BB gave on LZ: **'Bach has always been a passion with Zukofsky; he studied the whole range of inversions and reversals, canon and what have you, used by Bach and exemplified in Bach's *Art of Fugue*, and the similar manipulations used by Schoenberg and his pupils on their tonerows, and he's tried them out, often very effectively, in rows of words. I'll try to find one of those, presently, in the maze of book-marks'** (*BBP*, 158). **'Even the cultured few limited their pleasures to Beethoven's successors or to Wagner and Verdi. Only the real intellectuals could put up with Debussy. Stravinsky was to be endured, but Schoenberg was merely a mad pedant'** (*BBP*, 121). On LZ changing meaning by altering punctuation: **'That's a trick of the sort I said he learned from people like Schoenberg'** (*BBP*, 169). **'I must have been one of the first people to be able to say in print in an English magazine that Schoenberg was the real noise, not some of the others who were being touted at the time'** (*Mottram*, 7).

The word *maze* invokes the labyrinth of Crete, as below.

II. 193. Pasiphae's. In Greek mythology, Pasiphae, wife of King Minos and sister of Circe, had intercourse with a sacred bull by entering a wooden cow constructed for her which the bull could mount; she subsequently gave birth to the Minotaur, half man, half bull, who was kept in the labyrinth made by Daedalus for Minos. Cp. Ovid, *Metamorphoses* VIII. 131–7, IX. 735–40, etc.; also Dante, *Inferno* XII. 12 and *Purgatorio* XXVI. 40–2; and EP's 'Prayer For His Lady's Life' (from Propertius, *Elegiae*, III. 26), 6: 'shameless Pasiphae' and *Cantos*, XXXIX. 22: 'That had Pasiphae for a twin', as well as LXXIV 'nec casta Pasiphaë', quoted from Propertius II. 38: 52; Swinburne's 'The Masque of Queen Bersabe', 258–66, as well as 'Phædra', 35; Joyce, *Ulysses* II: 'Remember Pasiphae for whose lust my grandoldgrossfather made the first confessionbox.' Perhaps also A. D. Hope's 'Pasiphae' and Robert Graves's 'Lament for Pasiphaë', and more generally, Yeats's 'Leda and the Swan'. **'Those fail who try to force their destiny, like Eric; but those who are resolute to submit, like my version of Pasiphae, may bring something new to birth, be it only a monster'** (*Note*, [1]). **'Perhaps again as in my poem, it is the need to write which comes first, and engenders the things it hardly dares to handle. So Pasiphae is the only myth adequate to the particular horror story I am engaged on. Oh, yes, I've taken care to make Bloodaxe as telling as I can: and another, abler age would have made a tragedy out of him as scarifying as anything the Greeks had; but in fact he is driven only by his own nature. Pasiphae has something more monstrous and more terrifying to submit to, of her own volition, but in the universe-busting mission that someone has to face – a few in each generation. In some degree I scorn Bloodaxe; but I do not scorn Pasiphae'** (BB letter, 13 January 1965; quoted *Makin*, 157).

II. 196. byre. OED 1: 'A cow-house. Perh. in OE times, more generally, "a shed".' Citation from Ælfric. Cp. Burns, 'A Dream', V. 7: 'barn or byre'; Scott, *Minstrelsy of the Scottish Border*, II. 79: 'My barns, my byres, and my faulds', and *Rob Roy* xxvi: 'my barn and byre'; Wordsworth, *The River Duddon*, XIII, 'Open Prospec', 3: 'with barn and byre, and spouting mill!' and *The Prelude* (1850), VIII. 21: 'From byre or field the kine were brought'; also Kipling, 'The Ballad of East and West', 54: 'The thatch of the byres'; 'The Ballad of Boh Da Thone', 13: 'camped in the byre'; 'The Lament of the Border Cattle Thief', 9: 'The steer may low within the byre'; 'The Only Son', 14: 'For I have dreamed of a youngling kid new-riven from the byre'; and chapter heading from 'Mowgli's Brothers' in *The Jungle Book*: 'The herds are shut in byre and hut.'

III. Original motto for this section was 'Processit longe flammantia moenia mundi', from Lucretius, *De rerum natura*, I. 73; in BB's translation, **'He went far beyond the flaming walls of the world'** (*Forde*, 210; Gilonis corrects Forde's citation, in *Caddel*, 157); Loeb: 'far beyond the flaming walls of the heavens'.

While composing the poem, BB wrote to Makin, **'I was never troubled by physical modesty, but I am unwilling to stand emotionally naked. I could not write, for instance, as Creeley does . . . The proper course would be to find things which reflect the simplicity I want indirectly. The bull [in Part I] is right. The cart ride to Bainbridge [with the tombstone] is probably right. But I can find nothing to do the same for the matter that should go into part three. And without that, the plan for part four would be no more than pornographic'** (BB letter, 4 January 1965; quoted *Makin*,

156). (Makin also quotes: **'Part Three wont come, perhaps because I find it impossible to abandon my lifelong reserve about myself, which I must do if the poem is to have the simplicity which must alternate with more complicated mental states to give it its shape'** (*Makin*, 155). Subsequently, he wrote, **'I have at last got what I believe will prove a fair start of Part Three . . . in fact based on Firdusi's version of the Alexander legend [see note to III. 72], though at some remove. It was to have been a short episode in Part four, but suddenly showed how it could expand to do just what I wanted for part three'** (BB letter, 20 January 1965; quoted *Makin*, 156).

III. 11. pebbles worn by tabulation. See note to *The Spoils*, III: 'Lydian pebbles'.

III. 21. scored by beaks. Cp. Villon, 'Ballade', 23–4: 'Pies, corbeaulx, nous ont les yeux cavez / Et arrachié la barbe et les sourcis.' ['Magpies and crows have carved out our eyes, / And torn off our beards and eyebrows.']

III. 28. ▪ *Hastor:* **a Cockney hero.** BB wrote to Makin (3 December 1984): **'the inhabitants of the world Alexander and his men pass through are not just people who wont try to excel, they include various who *choose* baseness, particularly "the Press" (with Hastor for president)'** (*Makin*, 147). In a subsequent letter to Makin (1 January 1985), BB explained that 'Hastor' is his **'private revenge'** on Hugh Astor of *The Times* (*Makin*, 147). BB had been a correspondent in Teheran for *The Times*, 1951–2. Hugh, younger son of Col. John Astor, the paper's chief proprietor, was also a *Times* correspondent in the Middle East (*Alldritt*, 158, however, says the reference is to the elder Astor). Expelled from Iran in April 1952, BB returned with his family to London, where he was unsuccessful in persuading the newspaper to give him further employment. BB wrote bitterly of this to Margaret de Silver (1 October 1952), claiming that *The Times* had promised to keep him on (*Alldritt* 141). In financial straits, BB wrote to BBC producer, D. G. Bridson (23 August 1955), **'I am perishing in the swamp still where Mossadeq threw me and *The Times* left me'** (*Alldritt*, 135). Regarding the lines 'there is no trash in the wheat / my loaf is kneaded from', see *Burton*'s account, p. 373 ff., which describes a sense in which this passage invokes a world in which 'turd bakers', i.e. those who adulterated bread in Teheran at the time, could flourish. Cp. EP's 'Salutation the Third': 'Let us deride the smugness of "The Times": / GUFFAW!'

III. 50. ▪ *Saltings:* **marshy pastures the sea floods at extraordinary springs.** *EDD*: 'land liable to be flooded by the sea'. Cp. Kipling, 'The Dykes', 21: 'At the bridge of the lower saltings the cattle gather and blare.'

III. 58. ▪ ***The Laughing Stone*** **stands in Tibet. Those who set eyes on it fall into violent laughter until they die. Tibetans are immune, because they have no humour. So the Persian tale relates.**

III. 62. ▪ **The male salmon after spawning is called a *kelt*.** *EDD*: 'A salmon three years old, after the male has deposited the milt, and the female the roe.' *OED* 1: 'A salmon, sea-trout, or herling, in bad condition after spawning, before returning to the sea.'

III. 68–71. In a letter to Forde (4 July 1973), BB glossed these lines: **'"Banners purple and green" etc. are the Northern Lights, Aurora Borealis, a formidable magnetic barrier which was until lately thought to "pen in mankind" and make moon voyages impossible'** (*Forde*, 230). Cp. Lucretius, *De rerum natura*, I. 73. In this passage, Lucretius praises Epicurus for a philosophy free from religion; this allows Epicurus, following the evidence of senses and reason, to pierce **'far beyond the flaming walls of the world'** (BB's translation); the flaming walls were **'of course, the aurora Borealis'** (BB to Makin, 3 December 1984; quoted *Makin*, 154). See note, above, on motto to section III. BB had translated Lucretius in the 1927 'Overdraft', 'Darling of Gods and Men, beneath the gliding stars'; see also notes on Lucretius for 'Attis' and *FBO* 34.

BB had written to LZ, **'we dont read Lucretius for a concourse of atoms, no fear!'** (BB to LZ, 10 May 1953; quoted *Makin* 65, n. 9). **'I read Lucretius quite early, and I have a very high respect for him both as a thinker and as a poet . . . Lucretius is very lucid, *very* lucid'** (*Mottram*, 9). **'It was such a long time ago that I was, so to speak, influenced by Lucretius, I hardly remember; but apart from the fact that, which of course doesn't show up in me at all, that he is almost the only poet, except recently Hugh MacDiarmid, to be able to make poetry out of scientific lingo, there is both a vividness in his description, a clarity in his setting forth of his problems, and a splendid dignity on the rare occasions where he breaks off to address the reader or the gods or somebody like that, something which is inherent in the way the consonants come, and so forth. He is nearer in time to the old Roman stuff than any of the classical writers, of course, by one full generation, just as Catullus is nearer than the other lyrical writers; and there is something more genuine, it's not been buggered about by literary guys taught in Greece so much as Virgil and Ovid and so forth'** (*Reagan*, 70). **'Lucretius made a text book sing'** (P. Craven and M. Heyward, 'An Interview with Basil Bunting', 28). **'Amongst philosophers I have most sympathy with Lucretius and his masters, content to explain the world an atom at a time'** (*Note*, [3]). BB had written to Makin that Lucretius was **'the only one of all the world's philosophers with whom I have much sympathy . . . by referring to it merely as a "Latin tag" you lose quite** a bit – the appeal to Epicurus, who was very like the slow-worm, unassuming, pacific, free of folly, (and exceedingly kind) for all his intellectual sophistication' (*Makin*, 154–5).

III. 72. But we desired Macedonia. **'You know the Alexander legend do you? Well, the Persian version of it was one of the very early ones, in Firdosi's *Shah Nameh*. Alexander wanders through country after country where the most horrible things are going on, and ultimately comes to the mountains of Gog and Magog on the edge of the world. And his troops refuse to follow him, but all alone he climbs up to the top of the mountain, and there he sees the Angel sitting exactly as in my poem, with the trumpet ready to his lips to blow, and looking anxiously to the east for the signal to, to blow the trumpet, and, and put an end to the world. And that of course does Alexander's business *for* him: he falls off the mountain, comes to, and leads everybody home in peace to Macedonia'** (*Quartermain & Tallman*, 9–10). See Appendix II. A. For Ferdowsī's version, see Reuben Levy, trans., *The Epic of Kings: Shah-Nama the National Epic of Persia by Ferdowsi* (London: Routledge & Kegan Paul, 1957), 244–5 (cited *Lesch*, 353). **'What Alexander learns when he has thrust his way through the degraded world is that man is contemptibly nothing and yet may live content in humility'** (*Note*, [2]). BB had written of Alexander years earlier to EP, saying that his **'attempt to make a whole civilization failed, but was a bloody good attempt, a real making: and what might have come of the union of polytheism's fluid alertness with the unshakeable availabil[i]ty of the gathas as foundation or ballast, might have saved you the trouble of studying Chinese'** (BB to EP, 11 November 1938; quoted *Makin*, 104). According to *Caddel & Flowers* (41), in December 1939 BB gave a lecture on Alexander for a WEA class at Morpeth in Northumberland. According to a wartime shipmate, BB remarked in the summer of 1942 that the 'East had not been given its rightful place by English historians on account of their ignorance of the languages of oriental sources. The hero of his account [a book BB said he intended to write] would be Alexander the Great and the villain the mosquito that stung him' (G. G. Evans, 'Basil Bunting – Summer 1942', *Stand* 33, no. 2 [Spring 1992], 70). Alexander appears in EP's *Cantos*, e.g. the 'Rock Drill' cantos, C, and CXIV.

Thom Gunn remarks: 'when Alexander falls stunned from the mountain, Bunting has him fall to a ground very like that of Northumberland' (*Shelf Life* [London: Faber, 1993], 61).

III. 79. ▪ ***Gabbro:*** **a volcanic rock.**

III. 90–5. Israfel. 'God created him at the beginning of time, and of all God's creatures, he possesses the most beautiful voice. He will sound the Resurrection Trump which will ravish the ears of the saints in paradise. He holds this trumpet at his mouth century after century, for at any time God could give him the signal to blow it. At the first blow, all the stars and the mountains will fall down: the world will be destroyed. The second blast will set in motion the resurrection, when all the people will rise from their graves. Israfel, Gabriel and Michael were the three angels that, according to legend, warned Abraham of Sodom's destruction. The angel of the trumpet in Islamic eschatology' (*Encyclopedia Mythica*, ed. M. F. Lindemans, online at www.pantheon.org, 1995–2000). See Arthur George Warner and Edward Warner, trans., *The Shāhnāma of Firdausí*, vol. 6 (London: Kegan Paul, Trench, Trubner, 1912), 78; also 160: 'Toil not so much, because some day a Call / Will reach thine ears' (cited *Lesch*, 353 and 359 respectively). Cp. Poe, 'Israfel' (1831), with epigraph, 'And the angel Israfel, whose heart-strings are lute, and who has the sweetest voice of all God's creatures. – Koran.' However, Israfel is not mentioned by name in the Koran. Cp. also perhaps Marian Osborne, also known as Marian Francis (1871–1931), 'The Song of Israfel'. Osborne was born in Canada, and lived in Wales in 1888–93; her book, *Poems*, was published in England in 1914, and was praised by *The Times*. The Israfel poem first appeared in *The University Magazine*. ('Marian Osborne', by John Garvin, in *Canadian Poets* [Toronto: McClelland, Goodchild & Stewart, 1916], 341–6.)

III. 100. rebate. OED n.3.b: 'An iron tool sharpened something like a chisel, and employed in dressing and polishing wood, etc.'

IV. Original motto for this section was 'Aneurin' (*Forde*, 210).

IV. 1. Grass caught in willow tells the flood's height that has subsided. BB told Tom Pickard that this line **'gets a landscape and a season before you even pass on to the next line. The "overfalls" in the next line tell you how to read the next page of the poem'** (BB to Pickard, 3 January 1980; quoted *Makin*, 228, n. 14).

IV. 2. overfalls. EDD: 'A dam or other obstruction in a stream.' *OED* n.1: '*Naut.* A turbulent surface of water with short breaking waves, caused by a strong current or tide setting over a submarine ridge or shoal, or by the meeting of contrary currents.' Cp. Hakluyt, *Voyages*, II. ii, 36: 'Certaine Currants, which did set to the West Southwestward so fast as if it had bene the ouerfall of a sand.'

IV. 4, 12, 16–17. ▪ ***Aneurin* celebrated in the Cymric language the men slain at Catterick by the sons of *Ida*, conquerors of Northumberland.** Aneurin, now usually spelled Aneirin, a renowned sixth-century Welsh poet, chronicles this event in *Y Gododdin*, considered the earliest extant Welsh text, preserved in a MS dated about 1250. By 'Cymric' BB means Celtic, or as he explained at a reading,

'proto-Welsh or Britonic' (1976 Harvard reading). Aneurin appears in Wordsworth's poems, e.g. *Ecclesiastical Sonnets* X. 1. At a reading given at the University of British Columbia (20 November 1970), BB describes Aneurin as someone who **'ought to be known to all, but probably isn't, the great Welsh poet of the early Dark Ages who left a splendid poem called *Gododdin*, mourning the men killed at the battle of Catterick by the newly arrived English'** (*Forde*, 233).

IV. 7. skald. Viking word for 'poet.' See note to I. 133–4 on Egil Skallagramsson.

IV. 9. ibex. According to *Makin* (184), BB describes being taught to hunt ibex, by mountain tribes in Isfahan, in a letter to Dorothy Pound (22? November 1946).

IV. 11. round. OED n.1.22.b: 'A single charge of ammunition for a firearm.'

IV. 17. Ida. Anglian king of Bernicia, a Dark Ages kingdom in northern England and southern Scotland.

IV. 22–4. See also note to IV. 4. Taliesin, like Aneurin a renowned Welsh poet (*fl.* sixth century). In a letter to LZ (6 August 1953), BB linked Aneurin and Taliesin as poets who **'belong with the best and straightest'** (*Forde*, 233). This judgement is consistent with that of the *Historia Brittonum* (attributed to Nennius), which lists both as among the five poets most prized by the Welsh. According to Brian Swann, BB believed that 'in a larger sense', the 'bards Aneurin and Taliesin, the former from the Edinburgh area, the latter from Cumberland', were actually Northumbrian (Brian Swann, 'Basil Bunting of Northumberland', *St Andrew's Review* 4, no. 2 [Spring–Summer 1977], 40; cited *Lesch*, 363). Taliesin appears in Wordsworth's poems, e.g. *Ecclesiastical Sonnets* V. 10, 'Taliesin's unforgotten lays', and XII. 3–4, 'The impetuous spirit that pervades / The song of Taliesin.'

IV. 25–30. In a letter quoted by Makin (18 May 1965), BB glossed this passage: **'I have been talking of the Anglo-Celtic saints who "put on daylight", represented as a brocade in which wires of "western metal" are woven. They rejected the Grecian god into which the Mediterranean had transformed Christ. Their god was no humanist. He was the god of the wolf as well as the sheep, "excepting nothing that is". Now the brocade is woven by shuttles, woven with extreme intricacy, for indeed it is nothing less than the whole universe: shuttles like midges darting, like drops from a fountain, like the dust of the little whirlwinds which continually form in the desert. It bears the rainbow and the moon's halo, things beautiful but hard to define, and it opposes the sharp sun that wants all things to be**

chained to the dictionary or the multiplication table. It gives, not so much tolerance as enthusiastic acceptance of a world in which things are not measured by their usefulness to man' (*Makin*, 146; sentence interpolated from quotation on 194; see also 238). V. Slade suggests that lines in this passage constitute a 'Northumbrian gloss of the Latin of the Lindisfarne Gospels' ('*Briggflatts*: A Criticism', *Tarasque* 3, n.d., n.pag.); when Eric Mottram said to BB, 'Another report is that the Lindisfarne lacings and plaitings were in your sensibility, quite consciously, when you were working on the interrelationship between parts of the poem,' BB replied: **'That is quite true'** (*Mottram*, 5). The *Codex Lindisfarnensis* was extremely important to BB; see his lecture on it, *BBP*, chap. 1.

G. Baldwin Brown (*The Arts in Early England* [New York, 1921], vol. 5) describes plaited patterns in the *Codex Lindisfarnensis*, tracing these back to Roman mosaic pavements: 'In the plait two or more filaments interlace, but not on straight lines, for each filament has to be pulled on one side to twine with its neighbor, and the diagonal lines thus generated are carried through the design' (380). 'Anybody who takes the trouble to follow out any one line in the pattern will find it lead him quite a long excursion into neighboring territory before it returns towards the point whence it started' (386).

BB wrote to JW: **'If those Hexham Abbey chantry carvings are 1491, it backs my assertion that culture – in this case Northumbrian Celto-Anglic – is far more durable than race. You may suppress it, but not continuously. I'm not likely to get a chance to ask any expert about them. Anyway, no expert has ever admitted the existence of a Northumbrian culture. Most experts don't even know that the Codex Lindisfarnensis and the Bewcastle Cross far ante-date the Irish things they derive them from, let alone that the same characteristics are there at Bywell, or on King Alfwulf (if that's the name)'s tomb in Hexham, or in Swinburne's, or, perhaps, underlying Spenser's, not to mention some poems by an impecunious friend of yours. Those carvings are hardly as grotesque and barbaric as geist Grendel and his mother, but it is compulsory to admire Beowulf, however little the critic understands it – or even reads it. I believe all that underlies the North is horrifying to our C. of E., Southron rulers and their academic sycophants'** (dated 'Guy Fawkes Day' 1984; quoted *McGonigal & Price*, 282).

Columba. Born in Ireland, 521. He established a monastery on Iona. According to *Makin* (191), 'He may have founded the line of calligraphy and illumination that led to the Lindisfarne Gospels.' Columba appears in Wordsworth's poems, e.g. 'The Highland Broach', 3; 'Homeward we turn', 1: 'Isle of Columba's cell'.

Columbanus. Born in Ireland, 543. Landed in Britain, probably on the Scottish coast, with his followers, *ca.*580.

Aidan. Born in Ireland, date unknown. Aidan brought Christianity from Columba's monastery on Iona to Northumbria in 634; first bishop and abbot of Lindisfarne, where he died in 651.

Cuthbert. Cuthbert was probably born in Northumberland, *ca.*634. Educated by Irish monks at Melrose Abbey, he was, at various times, a monk, solitary (on Farne Island), and bishop; he was known as a miracle worker. *Lesch* (370) discusses how under Cuthbert 'the change from Celtic to Roman Catholic Church customs was accomplished'. An anonymous *Life of Cuthbert* was written around 700, but discovery of his uncorrupt body gave new impetus to his cult; Bede used this *Life* as the basis for his own verse *Life of St. Cuthbert* (*ca.*716), as well as a later prose version (*ca.*721). After Cuthbert's death, his body was moved from Farne Island to Lindisfarne; relocated at several sites in Northumbria, it was eventually enshrined at Durham in 999, and moved later to Durham Cathedral. Cuthbert's cult, after his death, was responsible for the Lindisfarne Gospels, which BB called **'two-thirds Celtic and one-third Anglic'** (*Terrell*, 244). An Anglo-Saxon gloss (written in Northumbrian dialect) was added to the Lindisfarne Gospels in the late tenth century. In a letter to D. G. Bridson (20 April 1965), BB wrote that the final movement of *Briggflatts* showed **'St. Cuthbert in love with all creation'** (*Makin*, 199). **'Autumn is for reflexion, to set Aneurin's grim elegy against the legend of Cuthbert who saw God in everything, to love without expectation, wander without an inn, persist without hope'** (*Note*, [2]). **'If Saint Francis's praise of all creation in "Altissimu onnipotente bon signore" etc. or the ideas implied for Saint Cuthbert in the three lives of him can be reconciled in any way with what is commonly called religion, no doubt I am a religious poet. But I know of no church that would put up with either of them for a moment'** (P. Craven and M. Heyward, 'An Interview with Basil Bunting', 31) **'There's the contrast between Bloodaxe here and Saint Cuthbert here, the extreme opposite of each other in things'** (*Quartermain & Tallman*, 17). Cuthbert appears in Wordsworth's poems, e.g. 'The White Doe of Rylstone', 712 and 831; 'Grace Darling', 27; 'For the Spot Where the Hermitage Stood on St. Herbert's Island, Derwent-Water', 26.

IV. 33. sacred calves of the sea. Perhaps refers to seals, sometimes called sea-calves.

IV. 35. ■ ***Skerry:*** **O, come on, you know that one.** *OED* n.2: 'A rugged insulated sea-rock or stretch of rocks, covered by the sea at high water or in stormy weather; a reef.' Refers here to the island of Lindisfarne. BB explained this as **'a rock that gets covered at the top of the tide and uncovered the rest of the time'** (1976 Harvard reading). Cp. Kipling, 'The Coastwise Lights', 3: 'From reef and rock and skerry – over headland, ness, and voe.'

IV. 37. quoits. EDD 'quoit': 'A piece of broad thin stone or rock; a horseshoe used in playing quoits.' *OED* n.1.a: 'In orig. and widest sense (now only with ref. to the Greek and Roman discus), a flat disc of stone or metal, thrown as an exercise of strength or skill; *spec.* in mod. use, a heavy flattish ring of iron, slightly convex on the upper side and concave on the under, so as to give it an edge capable of cutting into the ground when it falls, if skilfully thrown.' Cp. translations of *The Iliad* XXIII by Chapman, 386–8: 'Nestors sonne . . . got as farre before / As any youth can cast a quoyte', and Pope, 712–13: 'Tho' 'tis not thine to hurl the distant dart, / The quoit to toss'. Cp. perhaps Joyce, *Ulysses* II: 'The quoits are loose.'

IV. 38. ▪ *Hoy:* **toss, hurl.**

IV. 40. Lice in its seams despise the jacket. BB glossed this in a letter quoted by Makin (18 May 1965): **'The lice on the brocaded jacket, of course, are those who can enjoy and understand nothing because they are determined not to look at the world itself'** (quoted *Makin*, 269).

IV. 43. ▪ *Skillet:* **An American frying pan; and** ***girdle*****, an English griddle.** See note to IV. 55, below.

IV. 44. ▪ *Fipple:* **the soft wood stop forming with part of the hard wood tube the wind passage of a recorder.** Bunting owned books such as *Elizabethan Dances and Ayres for Descant Recorder and Piano*, Edmund Priestley and Fred Fowler's *The School Recorder Book*, F. J. Giesbert's *Method for the Recorder (Blockflute)* and A. Rowland-Jones's *Recorder Technique*.

IV. 45. Domenico Scarlatti. BB claimed that Scarlatti's B minor fugato sonata (L.33/K.87) was in his mind as he developed the shape of the poem (*Agenda* 16, no. 1 [Spring 1978], 13); however, in a letter to Forde, he wrote (n.d).: **'(There's no one–one relationship between my movements and any of Scarlatti's)'** (*Terrell*, 269). He explained to Forde in 1972 that his adaptation of the sonata form was **'something not rigid, but capable of a kind of hidden continuity, and a string of movements made like Scarlatti's but unobtrusively linked seemed what was wanted . . . [M]usic has suggested certain forms and certain details to me, but I have not tried to be consistent about it. Rather, I've felt the spirit of a form, or of a procedure, without trying to reproduce it in any way that could be demonstrated on a blackboard'** (quoted *Lesch*, 150). At a reading in 1975, BB remarked: **'*****Briggflatts*** **was written with certain sonatas of Domenico Scarlatti in mind, and is heard best when those sonatas alternate with the movements of the poem'** (*Terrell*, 82).

BB's readings of *Briggflatts* were at times in fact accompanied by recordings of Scarlatti; there are varying accounts of which pieces were used. BB wrote to Forde (6 June 1971) that Scarlatti's B minor fugato sonata (L.33) was **'the key'** to *Briggflatts* (*Forde*, 213). Forde remarks that BB's 'plan for a full reading of *Briggflatts* included other sonatas between the movements: L.204 (1–2), L.25 (2–3), L.275 (3–4) and L.58 (4–5).' In the Bloodaxe Books record *Basil Bunting reads 'Briggflatts'*, L.33 accompanies his reading, and is allowed to finish before BB begins reading Part V. It is played a second time at the end of the Coda. Makin lists L.204 (K.105), L.25 (K.46), L.10 (K.84), L.275 (K.394), L.33 (K.87), L.58 (K.64), L.33 (K.87) repeated (*Makin*, 265). As best as I can determine, the scheme was typically L.204 to be played after the epigraph as an introduction to Part I; L.25 between I and II; L.10 between II and III; L.275 between III and IV; L.33 between IV and V. Mottram comments, 'In performance, the steady pace of Bunting's carefully inflected voice is contrasted with the different tempi of the six sonatas used. For example, the presto Longo 25 is played between Part Two and Three, the allegro Longo 252 between Three & Four, and the reading ends with a repetition of Longo 33, which acts as a sweet and tender farewell, after the concluding calm cadences' (*Terrell*, 102, n).

To Hugh Kenner, BB said: **'Music is organized in various ways, and one of the inventions – [an] eighteenth-century invention, for which I think the chief responsibilities lie with Domenico Scarlatti and John Christian Bach – [was] the notion of a sonata, where two themes at first appear quite separate, and all the better if they're strongly contrasted . . . gradually alter and weave together until at the end of your movement you've forgotten they are two themes, it's all one. And that struck me when I was very young, as a form that poetry could and should exploit. And I've tried to do it. And it's to that, and that kind of manœuvring, that I'm referring to when I talk about Domenico Scarlatti in *Briggflatts*'** (*Sound of Poetry*, National Public Radio, February 1980; quoted *Makin*, 258–9).

A sonata-like form for poetry gives the poet **'a chance to make shapes . . . though of course poetry has different problems than notes . . . I think that right from the start I did have things which had some of the simplicity of the Italian stuff without having its skill; and at the end I probably got something which has got the skill of the early Italian stuff, but perhaps not the simplicity'** (*Reagan*, 74). **'I had thought all along that the sonata was the more likely [musical form] to be of use. But I got off on the wrong foot trying to imitate Beethoven's sonatas, using extremely violent contrasts in tone and speed which don't actually carry well onto the page, and I had to puzzle about that for a while before I discovered it was better**

to go back to a simpler way of dealing with the two themes and to take the early or mid-eighteenth-century composers of sonatas – John Christian Bach and Scarlatti – as models to imitate' (*Descant*, [8]). In 1928, BB had described a Scarlatti sonata: **'Its themes are living things, not specimens pinned down for dissection . . . the development is as spontaneous as the movement of a beautiful living body. It is intricate as life is intricate: intricate but not involved. It is concise with something approaching the concision of life'** ('Recent Fiddlers', *The Outlook* 61, no. 1568 [18 February 1928], 209).

As for his BB's decision not to imitate Beethoven's sonatas, cp. preface to Palgrave, *Golden Treasury* (London, 1861): 'The development of the symphonies of Mozart and Beethoven has been here thought of as a model.' The *Golden Treasury* is not in the remnants of BB's library at Buffalo, but it is inconceivable that BB would not have been familiar with it; Palgrave modelling his anthology after complex musical compositions may have made an impression on BB.

BB claimed to find a sonata-like structure in Eliot's *The Waste Land* and *Four Quartets*: **'Eliot in "The Waste Land" stumbled by sheer accident on something very closely analogous to the form that musicians call the sonata, but he was surprisingly slow to realize what he had done – though in the end he proclaims it in the title of the "Four Quartets," a quartet being normally a sonata written for violins, viola and a cello'** (lecture on EP dated 1974; quoted *Terrell*, 256–7). **'Eliot accidentally made a very fine sonata in *The Waste Land*'** (Lesch interview, 24 April 1976; quoted *Lesch*, 181). **'I pointed out to him – he hadn't noticed it himself – in 1922 or 1923, that the form "The Wasteland" took, if you omitted the short fourth movement, is exactly that of a classical sonata. This seems to have stuck in his mind, so that when he wrote the "Four Quartets", each of them an exact copy of the shape of "The Wasteland", he calls them quartets – quartets being normally a sonata form'** (Jonathan Williams and Tom Meyer, 'A Conversation with Basil Bunting', *Poetry Information* 19 [Autumn 1978], 38). BB told Lesch, **'I think I was the first one that got the idea of imitating the form of the sonata and I have carried it to further lengths than any of the others.'** But he also said that Eliot's use of the sonata form in *The Waste Land* was **'partly due to inadvertence'** and that EP's **'pencil cutting'** removed much of it, though **'in fact Pound probably could see what he was doing'** (Lesch interview, 24 April 1976; quoted *Lesch*, 148); and later elaborated, **'We know now that that form was the almost accidental result of the cuts Pound made in Eliot's poem, but it didn't seem accidental to me then'** ('The Use of Poetry', ed. Peter Quartermain, *Writing* 12 [Summer 1985], 42).

To Forde (23 May 1972), BB wrote that Scarlatti's sonatas are

'single, except a few written late in his career, but it was an obvious development to link two or three of four of them together in an age that was making so much of the dance suite. Something very like that had already happened in J. C. Bach and others. The dance suite origin is made plain by the final movements, mostly minuets, rondos, etc. The thematic links in the earlier dance suites were attenuated or dropped: but 19th century composers often brought them back again in their sonatas. I wanted something not rigid, but capable of a kind of hidden continuity, and a string of movements made like Scarlatti's but unobtrusively linked seemed what was wanted' (*Forde*, 149). **'It is perhaps fortunate that though I knew Scarlatti well I did not then know much of Corelli, or I would have tried to emulate his aetherial largos and the way he makes the angels dance jigs, and I would have failed utterly instead of only relatively'** (*Forde*, 226). BB owned a copy of Arcangelo Corelli, *Eleven Pieces for Treble Recorder*.

For more on BB and the sonata form, see Anthony Suter, 'Musical Structure in the Poetry of Basil Bunting', *Agenda* 16, no. 1 (1978), 46–54, and D. M. Gordon, 'The Structure of Bunting's Sonatas', in *Terrell*, 107–23.

Cp. BB's views on music and poetry to EP's and Hulme's. See EP, *ABC of Reading* (New York: New Directions, 1960), 61; Samuel Hynes, ed., *Further Speculations of T. E. Hulme* (Lincoln, NE: University of Nebraska Press, 1962), 73.

IV. 49. copse. Cp. Milton, 'Lycidas', .42: 'The willows and the hazel copses green'.

IV. 52–63. My love is young but wise . . . Cp. generally Song of Solomon 1: 2, 15; 2: 2, 9; etc.; and Proverbs 31: 10–31.

IV. 55. girdle. See BB's note to IV. 43, above. *OED* n.2., '*north.* and *Sc.* A circular plate of iron which is suspended over the fire and upon which cakes are baked or toasted.' Cp. Burns, 'The Jolly Beggars', I.14: 'the verra girdle rang'; Scott, *The Antiquary*, xxv: 'I'll learn you to bake cold-water cakes on the girdle'; and Stevenson, *Kidnapped*, chap. XX: 'We lay on the bare top of a rock, like scones upon a girdle.'

IV. 56. settle. EDD: 'A long wooden bench with back and arms.' *OED* n.1.1: 'A sitting place', citations from *Beowulf*, Bede's *History* and Ælfric; 2: 'Something to sit upon; a chair, bench, stool, or the like. *Obs.*'; 2.b., high settle, 'an elevated seat, a chair of dignity or state; a seat of honour at table; a throne, seat of judgement. *Obs.* exc. *arch.* after OE use', with citations from Lindisfarne Gospels and Ælfric. Cp. also Dryden, 'Baucis and Philemon', 44: 'A common settle drew for either guest' and Tennyson, 'Geraint and Enid', 571–2: 'And cast him . . . / Down on an oaken settle in the hall.'

IV. 62. ▪ ***Scone:* rhyme it with 'on', not, for heaven's sake, 'own'.** See citation from Stevenson, *Kidnapped*, in note to IV. 55, above.

IV. 66. rive. OED v.1.10.b: 'Of wood or stone: To admit of splitting or cleaving.'

IV. 70. bent. See note to II. 150.

V. Original motto for this section was 'Nox est una perpetua dormienda' (*Forde*, 210). See note to V. 111. In an interview, BB suggested that this section is set **'mostly on the Northumberland coast'** (*Quartermain & Tallman*, 15).

V. 11. sea-crow. A cormorant, as in the next line; *OED* cites T. Stevens in *Hakluyt's Voyages* II. ii, 100: 'But sometimes his other enemy, the sea-crow, catcheth him [a fish] before he falleth.'

V. 12. cormorant. In a lecture, BB remarked, about the figure of the cormorant in patterns used to illuminate the *Codex Lindisfarnensis*: **'I have tried to suggest, in my poem *Briggflatts*, how the light reflected from the water at certain times does seem to clothe the cormorant's shining body in a variety of colours – I have seen it often in quiet harbours about dawn'** (*BBP*, 10). BB spoke to Terrell similarly about buzzards, remarking upon the 'beautiful heads, colours, wings, and eyes of buzzards and how graceful they are in flight' (*Terrell*, 31). BB also said that the cormorant was St Cuthbert's favourite bird. (Brian Swann, 'Basil Bunting of Northumberland', *St Andrew's Review* 4, no. 2 [Spring–Summer 1977], 39). See notes on Cuthbert above, IV. 25–30. Cormorants breed on the Farne Islands (www.nationaltrust.org/farne-islands).

V. 19. slew. OED v.1: '*trans.* To turn (a thing) round upon its own axis, or without shifting it from its place; also loosely, to swing round: a. *Naut.* and *Mil.*' 2. '*intr.* To turn about, to swing *round.*' *EDD* 1.v: 'To twist; to turn aside; to swerve, swing round; to reverse; to slip out of position.' Cp. R. H. Dana, *Two Years Before the Mast*, chap. xxv: 'The martingale had slued away off to leeward.'

V. 24. Conger. OED 1: 'A large species of eel living in salt water and attaining a length of from six to ten feet; it is caught for food, being common on the coasts of Britain and other European countries.' Cp. Walton, *Compleat Angler*, I. xiii: 'The mighty Conger, taken often in Severn about Gloucester', and Kipling, 'The English Flag', 62: 'I heave them whole to the conger.'

V. 27. ▪ ***Gentles:* maggots.** *OED* B.n.3. BB told Terrell that maggots are 'beautiful and remarkable: if watched closely they may be seen doing a sort of rhythmic ballet dance while they work' (*Terrell*, 31). At a reading, BB explained this as **'a fisherman's word . . . bait'** (1967 Harvard reading).

V. 28. brisk. OED v.2: 'to move about briskly'.

V. 43. links. OED n.1.b: '*pl. (Sc).* Comparatively level or gently undulating sandy ground near the sea-shore, covered with turf, coarse grass, etc.'

V. 44. thrift. OED n.1.4.b: 'The plant *Armeria maritima (vulgaris)*, a well-known sea-shore and alpine plant bearing rose-pink, white, or purple flowers on naked stems growing from a dense tuft of grass-like radical leaves.' Cp. Wordsworth, *The Excursion*, I. 722–3: 'Daisy-flowers and thrift / Had broken their trim border-lines.'

V. 47–9. Tweed and Till and Teviotdale . . . Redesdale and Coquetdale. These places are in what is now called Reiver Country – the river valleys of the Anglo-Scottish border region where feuding families known as the Border Reivers raided each others' homes in the fourteenth–sixteenth centuries; Sir Walter Scott lived in the area, and refers to Teviotdale in his Border marching song, 'Blue Bonnets Over the Border'. The River Till is a tributary to the River Tweed. BB would probably have known the anonymous poem, 'Two Rivers', in Quiller-Couch's *Oxford Book of English Verse* (1919), dated there to the seventeenth century:

> Says Tweed to Till –
> 'What gars ye rin sae still?'
> Says Till to Tweed –
> 'Though ye rin with speed
> And I rin slaw,
> For ae man that ye droon
> I droon twa.'

Cp. also, among many, Wordsworth, 'Yarrow Revisited', I. 49–56, in which Scott is 'compelled to change . . . Cheviot . . . And leave thy Tweed and Tiviot', and II. 6; 'White Doe of Rylstone', 689, 'from Tweed to Tyne', and 1099; 'View from the Top of Black Comb', 10, 'Tiviot's stream, to Annan, Tweed, and Clyde', among others; and Kipling, 'Sussex', 61: 'Choose ye your need from Thames to Tweed'; chapter heading from 'The Light That Failed', 24–5: 'And towers nine upon the Tyne, / And three upon the Till'; and 'The English Way', 16: 'flood along the Tweed'.

V. 50. ▪ ***Wilson* was less known than *Telfer*, but not less skilful.** Names of Newcastle sheepdog trainers who were winners in local competitions. J. M. Wilson is pictured in an October 1928 newspaper photo headlined, 'Coquetdale Sheep Dog Trials', reproduced in *Caddel & Flowers*, 38. While living in **'a shepherd's cottage in the hills in central Northumberland'** in 1929, BB **'learned a little about how they train sheepdogs'** (*Descant*, [12]). The

Redesdale and Coquetdale area is well-known for the Border terriers originated there. The name, Telfer – as well as the place-name, 'Tividale' – appears in the poem 'Jamie Telfer of the Fair Dodhead'.

V. 55. Hedgehope. Hedgehope Hill.

V. 60. Then is diffused in Now. Cp., as John Seed observed, BB on EP: **'His Now is so penetrated by Then it is sometimes hard to separate them; and this is as it is in life for all of us'** (*The Cantos of Ezra Pound: Some Testimonies by Hemingway, Ford, Eliot, Walpole, Macleish, Joyce and Others*, ed. Ford Madox Ford [New York, 1933]; quoted in John Seed, 'An English Objectivist? Basil Bunting's Other England', *Chicago Review* 44, no. 3/4, 119).

V. 62. rowan. The mountain ash. Cp. 'The Complaint of the Morpethshire Farmer', 17, and Scott, *The Lady of the Lake*, III. iv. 1–2: 'A heap of wither'd boughs was piled, / Of juniper and rowan wild.'

V. 70. Aldebaran. See note to V. 104–5, below.

V. 75. occulted. Cp. Shakespeare, *Hamlet*, III. ii. 81: 'his occulted guilt'.

V. 75–6. ▪ **Sailors pronounce** *Betelgeuse* **'Beetle juice' and so do I. His companion is 'Ridgel', not 'Rhy-ghel'.** At a reading, BB glossed Betelgeuse as **'the star in Arabic'** (1976 Harvard reading).

V. 81. Orion. See note to V. 104–5, below.

Farne. St Cuthbert died on Farne Island; see note to IV. 25–30. **'I think people see that one has taken care to write about things one knows about, or to make damned sure they are correct, and so forth, even if one has thereupon afterwards twisted them and altered them, as Pound twisted and altered things that he knew perfectly well what the exact thing was. I take care, for instance, if I say that a certain star is rising over the Farne Islands, at the moment in question that star is rising and the other stars will correspond in their positions, and so forth'** (interview in *meantime*, 1977; quoted *Terrell*, 269–70).

V. 84. Capella. See note to V. 104–5, below.

V. 85. Procyon. See note to V. 104–5, below.

V. 100. combe. OED 'coomb' 2.c: 'In the south of Scotland and in the English Lake district, "[in] such hills as are scooped out on one side in form of a crescent, the bosom of the hill, or that portion which lies within the lunated verge, is always denominated the coomb". (Hogg, *Queen's Wake*, 1813, *Notes*, xxiv).' The entry notes that 'in Cumbria it appears on some local names'. *EDD* 1: 'A narrow valley, between two hills, with only one inlet; the head of a valley'; 3: 'A hollow scooped out of the side of a mountain; the bosom of a hill having a semicircular form'; 4: 'The wooded side of a hill.' Cp. Hardy, *Wessex*

Cp. Hardy, *Wessex Tales* I. 3: 'and furzy downs, combs, or ewe-leases'. Puns here with 'silent but for bees'. BB's pronunciation of the word when reading this poem was ''küm', e.g. Morden Tower reading, 27 February 1965, on Harvard Poetry Room disc.

V. 104–5. ▪ ***Sirius* is too young to remember because the light we call by his name left its star only eight years ago; but the light from *Capella*, now in the zenith, set out 45 years ago – as near fifty as makes no difference to a poet.** *Lesch* (397), citing Samuel G. Barton and William H. Barton, *A Guide to the Constellations* (New York: McGraw Hill, 1928), 20–1, says that if one 'were to consult an astronomical chart, it would confirm that the sequence of the rising of the stars which is presented – first Aldebaran, a star in Taurus; then Capella, a star in Auriga; then Betelgeuse and Rigel, both located in Orion – is comparable to that which might be viewed at the year's end in this northern location'. **'They came in first as a means of fixing the time and date. If you notice where the stars are at the beginning of the star passages, and where they are at the end of them, go to a nautical almanac, and work things out backwards. You'll find that you must be at approximately the latitude of Farne Islands, at approximately New Year's Eve . . . That idea, of course, is an old one, and is taken in my case from Chaucer, who always fixes the time wherever he goes in Hell, Purgatory, and Heaven by means of solar sidereal navigation'** (interview with Peter Bell, 3 September 1981; in *Swigg*). BB probably also knew that Dante had consulted star charts in Prophacius Judaeus' *Almanach* for the year 1301 in order to establish the dates on which events occur in the *Divine Comedy* (see Robert Hollander, *Dante* [New Haven: Yale University Press, 2001], 93, and 196, n. 120).

Sirius glows. Cp. Pope, 'Summer, The Second Pastoral, or Alexis', 21: 'sultry Sirius burns'; and 'The First Book of Statius his Thebais', 748: 'raging Sirius blasts'. For more on Sirius, see note to 'The Well of Lycopolis', III. 11.

V. 107–9. Fifty years a letter unanswered; / a visit postponed for fifty years. // She has been with me fifty years. The light from Capella originating at the time BB was involved with Peggy Greenbank would be seen fifty years later, as *Briggflatts* was being composed. Cp. Jonson, 'His Excuse for Loving', 1–4: 'Let it not your wonder move, / Less your laughter; that I love. / Though I now write fifty years, / I have had, and have my peers . . .'

V. 111. For love uninterrupted night. Catullus V, 6. Originally the motto for part V. Loeb: 'For us, when the short light has once set, remains to be slept the sleep of one unbroken night.' Cp. Campion's version, 'Then must we sleepe one ever-during night,' etc. BB was much interested in Campion; see notes on Helen for *Villon* III and

SBOO 7. Also EP's 'Translations and Adaptations from Heine', VIII, 'Night Song', 7–8: 'In an uninterrupted night one can / Get a good deal of kissing done.' Cp. also Jonson's version of the Catullus in *Volpone*, act 3, which includes the line, '"Tis with us perpetuall night"'; and Samuel Daniel's in the last three lines of 'A Pastoral' – possibly the first translation into English. **'But you see the Catullus line here, *nox est perpetua una dormienda*. It is a much more complex line than any of the translators has ever got across. The *una* is never given its full value. . . . *Nox est perpetua:* there is an everlasting night. *Una dormienda* doesn't mean *one* night, it means a night that is *all one*, that never varies. That is the important point in the Catullus line, you see. And that sets you thinking, and that sets you going, and things come into your mind. It is from that, I should think – though I'm not sure at this stage, time has passed – I think that it's probably from that line that the whole train of thought started, that brought back the various things that become matter in the poem. But the poem starts merely as a shape; the matter comes after'** (*Quartermain & Tallman*, 12–13). **'Whether Catullus is being ornamental or direct, he uses invariably the most straightforward Latin syntax, the language of a man talking'** (*BBP*, 160). BB said in an interview that, **'The first line I wrote [of *Briggflatts*] was the last line of the poem, apart from the Coda'** (*Quartermain & Tallman*, 10).

CODA. **'As for the Coda, you will never believe it, but this is the truth. I'd written three-quarters of *Briggflatts*, was busy in fact on the last part, when I had to turn over papers on my desk to get something for the bloody income tax commissioners, and on the back of an old bill I found a poem that I'd written long before and forgotten when I wrote it, which required three or four lines cut out, and with those three or four lines cut out it was the Coda, and was obviously part of *Briggflatts*'** (*Quartermain & Tallman*, 14). BB told Reagan that the Coda is **'carefully arranged as far as vowel sounds go to be very singable, but the stanzas do not repeat themselves exactly'** (*Reagan*, 79). BB explained in an interview that a pun in this section title hinges on the fact that **'coda means tail – just to wag its tail at the end of it'** (Jonathan Williams and Tom Meyer, 'A Conversation with Basil Bunting', *Poetry Information* 19 [1978], 40). *OED* notes, under entry 2, '*Ballet*: The sense "tail of a note" is only Italian.' EP had a poem entitled 'Coda' in *Lustra*, included in *Personae*.

CODA. 2. *earsick*. Not in *OED* or *EDD*.

CODA. *12–17*. Cp. 'Chomei at Toyama', 17–18: 'Whence comes man at his birth? or where / does death lead him? Whom do you mourn?'

When Forde suggested that 'the final stoic expression of [*Briggflatts*] is the underlying pain of inevitable death,' BB wrote back, **'The pain, yes – not of death, but of wrong unrighted or unrightable'** (4 July 1973; quoted *Forde*, 107, 209).

1965. Dated 15 May 1965 in the *Poetry* and Fulcrum Press versions.

CHOMEI AT TOYAMA

About the editing of the poem for publication, BB wrote to Morton Dauwen Zabel, then associate editor of *Poetry*, on 4 January 1933: **'First: re Chomei, I'll wait and see the extracts you suggest before making a definitive answer . . . of course I'd best like it to be printed whole, since to me it seems to depend in a high degree on the general design: the balance of the calamities and consolations pivoted on the little central satire, the transmogrification of the house throughout, the earth, air, fire and water, pieces, first physical then spiritual make up an elaborate design, which I've tried not to underline so that it might be felt rather than pedantically counted up. Also the old boy's superficial religion breaking down to anchor it in its proper place'** (quoted *Forde*, 135–6). He wrote again on 24 March: **'All right, you must do as you think best in all the circumstances. I hate to see *Chomei* cut up, because I think it depends mainly on the balance of parts throughout and the picking out of four somewhat "poetical" bits rather misrepresents the very simpatico ole Jap'** (quoted *Forde*, 136).

▪ Kamo-no-Chomei flourished somewhat over a hundred years before Dante. He belonged to the minor nobility of Japan and held various offices in the civil service. He applied for a fat job in a Shinto temple, was turned down, and next day announced his conversion to Buddhism. He wrote critical essays, tales and poems; collected an anthology of poems composed at the moment of conversion by Buddhist proselytes (one suspects irony); and was for a while secretary to the editors of the Imperial Anthology.

He retired from public life to a kind of mixture of hermitage and country cottage at Toyama on Mount Hino and there, when he was getting old, he wrote the Ho-Jo-Ki in prose, of which my poem is in the main a condensation. The careful proportion and balance he keeps, the recurrent motif of the house and some other indications suggest to me that he intended a poem more or less elegiac but had not the time nor possibly energy at his then age to invent what would have been for Japan, an entire new form, nor to condense his material sufficiently. I have taken advantage of Professor Muccioli's Italian version, together with his learned notes, to try to complete Chomei's work for him. I cannot take his Buddhism solemnly considering the manner of his conversion, the nature of his anthology, and his whole urbane, sceptical and ironical temper. If this annoys anybody I cannot help it.

Variant notes as below in *Poetry* 42, no. 6 (September 1933), 356–7, with slight variants in *CE* (given fully in Textual Variants):

Kamo-no-Chomei, i.e. Chomei of Kamo, flourished somewhat over a hundred years before Dante. He belonged to the minor Japanese nobility, and held various offices in the civil service. He applied for a fat job in a Shinto temple, was turned down, and the next day announced his conversion to Buddhism.

He wrote: *Tales of the Four Seasons*; *Notes with no Title* (critical essays); and a quantity of poems; edited an anthology of poems composed at the moment of conversion by Buddhist proselytes (one suspects irony); and was for a while secretary to the editors of the imperial anthology.

He was as modern as, say, Cummings. His Kyoto had a number of curiously detailed parallels with modern New York and Chicago.

He got sick of public life and retired to a kind of mixture of hermitage and country cottage at Toyama on Mount Hino, and there, when he was getting old, he wrote his celebrated *Ho-Jo-Ki*, of which my poem is, in the main, a condensation. The *Ho-Jo-Ki* is in prose, but the careful proportion and balance of its parts, the leit-motif of the House running through it, and some other indications, suggest that he intended a poem, more or less elegiac; but had not time, nor possibly energy, at his then age, to work out what would have been for Japan an entirely new form, nor to condense his material sufficiently. This I have attempted to do for him.

[In *CE:* **He was quite up to date: and up-to-date is always *contemporary* with us.**]

I cannot take his Buddhism solemnly, considering the manner of his conversion, the suspect nature of his anthology, and his whole urbane, sceptical and ironical temperament. If this annoys [anybody *CE*] **the kind of scholar who likes to make out every celebrated writer as dull and respectable as himself, I cannot help it.**

I am indebted to Professor Muccioli's Italian version of the *Ho-Jo-Ki*, and especially to his learned notes. Professor Muccioli does not[**, as far as I can learn,** *CE*] **take my view of Chomei's religious opinions.**

Additional notes as below.

BB wrote to Harriet Monroe: '**Re Chomei: Ezra likes it and so does Yeats, but Eliot speaks ill of it because I haven't been to Japan, which seems irrelevant, and because he says it echoes Pound, which, if true, would be a count against it. But Pound supposes it to contain echoes of Eliot. I'm not aware of echoing anybody. Except Chomei: his book was in prose and four to five times as long as my poem. But I think everything relevant in Chomei has been got into the poem**' (20 November 1933; quoted *Forde*, 146). BB wrote to James G. Leippert that the poem was '**a poem which whatever its worth or worthlessness in itself, might have a useful influence: showing, for instance, that poetry can be intelligible and still be poetry: a fact that came to be doubted by the generation that took most of its ideas indirectly from Eliot**' (Leippert, 26 September 1932;

quoted *Forde*, 134). Mottram quotes BB saying of the poem that there was 'merit in the shape of the thing, and very little in the line by line run of it' (*Terrell*, 96).

BB told JW and Tom Meyer in 1976: 'I'm not sure how Japanese ["Chomei at Toyama"] is, for I know no Japanese and nothing about Japan. Long ago I came across a little volume which included an Italian prose translation of a prose book of essays written by a Japanese who died about the year 1200 and it had notes to it, learned notes. As I read it, it seemed to me that Chomei had so shaped his volume of essays that it was equivalent to an elegiac poem – but, of course, such a thing would have been quite outside any tradition he knew of, and when he wrote it he was, for those ages, an old man, well over sixty and without the energy to invent a new form. I thought "oh well now I'll do what Chomei would have done if he could, and I'll write a poem of it." So I made a poem and altered it a good deal here and there and transferred some of the learned notes into the poem itself . . . In recent years, very surprisingly to me, the Japanese have suddenly taken a great interest in this poem. A Japanese professor who came over from Tokyo to see me a couple of years ago told me there had been some kind of centenary celebration of Chomei which had caused them all to take a new interest in his writings, and someone had noticed that I had done this poem based on his book of essays, and all the Japanese professors have been busy ever since trying to compare the two to see what I have done to them. That surprises me very much, but still, there it is' (Jonathan Williams and Tom Meyer, 'A Conversation with Basil Bunting', 37).

For more on Chomei, see *Burton*, 194–6; also Roger Bersihand, *Japanese Literature*, trans. Unity Evans (New York, 1965).

At a reading in London, on 1 February 1982, BB commented that the poem is written in an 'upside-down quantitative verse' (quoted *Forde*, 146). 'I tried, at various times, partly because I knew Ezra Pound tried it, too, and Pound, I don't think, ever brought it off, but I again and again tried quantitative metres in English. They are very rarely Greek metres, they are mostly metres that are quite different from Greek. In fact, once I wrote a poem which Ezra was very puzzled by because on the page it looked like Sapphics, but in fact it was Sapphics with short syllables where the long are in Sappho, and long syllables where the short are in Sappho. And this worked quite well, and [fitted?] in tolerably well into English. And so you have to invent your own metres for anything quantitative in English. But I did write a number of quantitative poems, and in fact I wrote one long poem which, not all, but three-quarters of it, is in quantitative metres, in that case nearly all of them altered Greek metres, which is "Chomei at Toyama". And nobody, for all these many many years, nobody has ever observed that this is a quantitative poem, is organized by quantity. Perhaps because when this was done, the line endings seemed to come in odd places. And so I changed the line endings,

and they come rather where it helps a person to read it, instead of where the metre comes' (reading, Riverside Studios, February 1982, in *Swigg*). In 1983, he wrote to Tom Pickard that the poem **'was first written in very strict quantitative metres, and these of course dictated a line length; but I found I'd let the metres distort my English here and there and also I didnt want disputes with professors about longs and shorts, so I rearranged it'** (BB to Pickard, 19 March 1983; quoted *Makin*, 49).

As for the use of quotations in the poem, BB remarked: **'Where Chomei merely refers to a Chinese quotation you or I wouldn't get at all without the notes I translated the Chinese from the Italian into English'** (Williams and Meyer, 'A Conversation with Basil Bunting', 37). He wrote to Makin, **'I try to persuade myself that *I* never wrote out of books, only out of what I knew for myself. Its not quite true, and there is one big exception (Chomei at Toyama), but on the whole I think it is so'** (BB to Makin, 1 April 1985; quoted *Makin*, 70). For more on BB's use of Muccioli's translation of Chomei, including incorporating material from Muccioli's footnotes, see *Makin*, chap. 4, and Nicoleta Asciutto, 'A Japan of the Mind: Basil Bunting's Modernist Adaptation of Chomei's "Hojoki"', in *Postgraduate English (Durham University)* 25 (September 2012). Examples of BB's use of the footnotes are given in the annotations below, in Makin's translation.

Publication history

Written in Rapallo, 1931–2, after BB discovered and purchased a copy of Marcello Muccioli's 1930 translation of *Hōjōki* (*ca.*1212) by the major Japanese poet Kamo Chōmei (1155–1216) in a bookstall on the harbour quays of Genoa. *Hōjōki* is usually translated as *An Account of My Hut* or sometimes *The Ten Foot Square Hut*, and is a poetic diary of Buddhist renunciation and meditation, reflecting the transience of life, evidenced by natural disasters and human conflict. BB's version was first published in excerpted form in seven sections, *Poetry* 42, no. 6 (September 1933), 301–7, *Guedalla* D8, with variant notes, 356–7. EP included it in *Act. Ant.*, *Guedalla* B4, and Guedalla's revision of his bibliography suggests possible publication of an extract, untraced, in *The Observer* (Memphis, TN), October/November 1933. In *CE*, with dedication: **for William Butler Yeats**. Also published in *P1950*, *Loquitur*, and all editions of *CP*. Also in *Tri-Quarterly* 21 (Spring 1971), 42–51, *Guedalla* D35, a special issue reprinted as *Contemporary British Poetry* (Chicago: Tri-Quarterly, 1971), ed. John Matthias and reissued as *23 Modern British Poets* (Chicago: Swallow Press, 1971), *Guedalla*. B15; and *The Oxford Book of Twentieth Century English Verse*, ed. Philip Larkin (Oxford: Oxford University Press, 1973), 322–31, *Guedalla* B18.

Notes

5. Kyoto. Former capital city of Japan (794–1869). It suffered many disasters in Chomei's lifetime: a great fire in 1177 (particularly disastrous since most of Kyoto was built of wood), a whirlwind in 1180, a sudden removal of the court from Kyoto in 1180 (which lasted only six months before it moved back to Kyoto), famine in 1181, and an earthquake in 1185.

14–15. Whence comes man at his birth? or where / does death lead him? Cp. *Briggflatts*, 'Coda', 12–17: 'Where are we who knows / of kings who sup / while day fails? Who, / swinging his axe / to fell kings, guesses / where we go?'

34. Men are fools to invest in real estate. This perhaps owes something to EP's views.

48. bufera infernal! Dante, *Inferno* V. 30: 'La bufera infernal' ['The stormy blast of Hell'].

87. Riverside Drive. Located on west side of Manhattan in New York. Cp. BB's note in *Poetry* that Chomei **'was as modern as, say, Cummings. His Kyoto had a number of curiously detailed parallels with modern New York and Chicago.'**

92. Hoshi. Hoshi means 'priest'. A poem of Sora's about visiting Matsushima (in the collection *Sarumino*) can be found in Chōmei's *Mumyōshō*, where it is attributed to Sukemori Hoshi.

93–5. A, Amida . . . fortythree thousand A's. Note in *Poetry* and *CE*: **'*Amida:* in the more or less polytheistic Buddhism of medieval Japan, Amida presides over the earthly paradise, where the souls of decent dead men repose for a while. He was reverenced about as widely as Mary is by Catholics, and Chomei, probably attracted by the poetic qualities of the Amida myth, professed a special devotion for him.'** Buddhism spread from China to Japan from about 950, and became very popular in the twelfth century, especially the following of a Buddha called Amida Buddha, said to dwell in a divine 'Pure Land'. 'Pure Land Buddhism' promised salvation through faithfulness to the Amida Buddha, and eventual rebirth in the Pure Land; it focused on charity, humility and devotion rather than individual enlightenment.

In later life BB owned Donald Keene's *Anthology of Japanese Literature from the Earliest Era to the Mid-Nineteenth Century*. In Keene's prose translation, Chomei writes that priests 'went about writing the letter A on the forehead of every corpse they saw, thus establishing communion with Buddha. In an attempt to determine how many people had died, they made a count during the fourth and fifth months [of the famine], and found within the boundaries of the capital over 42,300 corpses lying in the streets.' In a note to this passage, Keene writes that 'great significance is given to *A*, the first letter of the Sanskrit alphabet, the beginning of things, and it is believed that all afflictions can be ended by contemplating this letter' (Keene, 203).

94. *East End.* East End of London? Cp. BB's note in *Poetry* that Chomei **'was as modern as, say, Cummings. His Kyoto had a number of curiously detailed parallels with modern New York and Chicago.'**

96. *Crack, rush, ye mountains, bury your rills! OED* n.1.2: 'A small narrow trench; a drill. Now *dial.*' But cp. Tennyson, *In Memoriam*, XXXVII. 5: 'Go down beside thy native rill.'

102. *great earthquake of Genrayku.* ▪ **The earth quaked in the second year of Genryaku, 1185.**

108–9. *hung / from their orbits like two tassels.* Cp. Tennyson, *In Memoriam*, CII. 11–12: 'The low love-language of the bird / In native hazels tassel-hung.'

114. *tertian ague of tremors. OED* A.1.: '*Path.* Of a fever or ague: Characterized by the occurrence of a paroxysm every third (i.e. every alternate) day.' Cp. Chaucer, 'Nun's Priest Tale', 139–40: Ye shul haue a ffeuere terciane / Or an Agu.'

123. *A poor man living amongst the rich.* BB explained to Forde that **'the real balancing point of the Hojoki is the bit that begins "A poor man living amongst the rich" to "if he doesnt he passes for mad"'** (BB to Forde, 4 July 1973; quoted *Forde*, 136).

136. *Inland Revenue.* Until 2005 the British government department responsible for the collection of direct taxes.

138–9. *Whoever helps him enslaves him / and follows him crying out: Gratitude!* 'Bunting has made a very characteristic mistake, for Muccioli, 44, says: "If one is dependent on others, one is their slave; if one has helped someone, one is pursued by his gratitude and devotion"' (*Makin*, 72, n. 24).

151–2. *And that quarter / is also flooded with gangsters.* 'The thieves, Muccioli tells us (48, n)., were called "White Waves"; that is the only name Chomei gives them. Bunting picks up the humour with "flooded"' (*Makin*, 70, n. 18).

161. *The dew evaporates from my sixty years.* Cp. Muccioli, 51: 'And now, having reached the point at which the dew of my sixty years is about to evaporate' (*Makin*, 72, n. 26).

189. *westward whence the dead ride out of Eden.* Cp. Milton, *Paradise Lost*, V. 142–3: 'Discovering in wide landscape all the east / Of Paradise and Eden's happy plains.'

191. Amida. See note to 93–5.

192–3. Summer? Cuckoo's Follow, follow – to / harvest Purgatory hill! 'This is a very compressed suggestion of what Muccioli has. Text (63): "In summer I hear the cuckoo which, with its calling, promises me the path of Mt Shide." Note: "*Shide no yamaji* is, according to Buddhist beliefs, a road and a mountain that each person must follow and pass over after death. The expression has become a synonym of the hereafter, the beyond and so on . . . [The travails of multiple lives on earth, for the person not yet worthy of paradise, are compared to] a mountain road and their bitternesses to its roughnesses. [In the classics, the cuckoo is called Lord of the fields from Mt Shide] because, according to a popular tradition, this creature lives on Mt Shide, and appears in the fields at the time of the harvest, encouraging the peasants to their work"' (*Makin*, 70, n. 18).

194. nightgrasshopper. Not in *OED*.

200. a Lent of commandments. OED n.1.3.a: 'a period of forty days'. Cp. Milton, *Free Commonwealth*, V. 421: 'Before so long a Lent of Servitude'.

202–5. A ripple of white water after a boat, / shining water after the boats Mansami saw / rowing at daybreak / at Okinoya. Note in *Poetry* and *CE*: ***Mansami:* celebrated Japanese poet.** In Keene's translation (208), the name is rendered 'Priest Mansei'. The phrase about the white wake behind a boat is apparently an allusion to a poem of Manei's.

206–7. Between the maple leaf and the caneflower . . . Po Lo-tien. Note in *Poetry*: ***Po Lo-Tien:* celebrated Chinese poet, better known in the West as *Po Chui*.** This line is an allusion to the 'Lute Song' of Po Chü-i (772–846), a poet and a government official, and one of the great writers of the Tang dynasty.

209. (I am playing scales on my mandolin.) In Keene's translation (208): 'I . . . play the lute in the manner of Minamoto no Tsuenenobu.' Keene's note explains that 'Minamoto no Tsuenenobu (1016–97) was a famous musician and poet.'

210–11. Autumn Wind . . . Hastening Brook. Cp. Muccioli, 67: 'If I feel more in the vein than usual, I play the air of "Wind of Autumn" to the echo of the pines"' (*Makin*, 71, n. 23). Keene (208) renders these song titles as 'Song of the Autumn Wind' and 'Melody of the Flowing Stream'.

216. tsubana buds. Reed ears; the open seed clusters of reeds. One of the essential 'season words' used in Japanese poetry, the Japanese word, *tsubana*, is used to signify mid-spring.

218–22. *Valley Farm . . . Fushimi and Toba . . . Sumiyama.* There are no direct equivalents for these names in Keene's translation.

223. *beyond Kasatori it visits the great church.* In Keene's translation (208): 'I follow along the peaks to worship at the Iwama or Ishiyama Temple.'

224. *foot it!* Cp. Shakespeare, *The Tempest*, I. ii. 380: 'Foot it featly here and there', and the hymn 'Courage brother, do not stumble': 'Let the road be rough and dreary, / And its end far out of sight, / Foot it bravely'.

225. *Semimaru.* Legendary poet and musician *ca.* second half of the ninth century, possibly blind and royal by birth; skilled in playing the *biwa* (a Japanese lute), he lived as a recluse in a small hut. See Susan Matisoff, *The Legend of Semimaru: Blind Musician of Japan* (New York, 1978).

226ff. *Somehow or other / we scuttle through a lifetime. / Somehow or other / neither palace nor straw-hut / is quite satisfactory . . . Whenever a monkey howls there are tears on my cuff // There are fireflies that seem / the fishermen's lights / off Maki island*, etc. Forde says of these lines (142) that BB here 'deliberately underscores the central satire [BB quote *Forde*, 135–6, 139] by adding lines of a poet Chomei only mentions but does not quote'. Keene's note (209, n. 17) reads: 'This paragraph is full of allusions to old poems which it would be tedious to explain.'

243–4. *At the pheasant's chirr I recall / my father and mother uncertainly.* Cp. Browning, *Sordello*, VI. 788: 'Rustles the lizard, and the cushats chirr.' Also Tennyson, *In Memoriam*, XCV. 6: 'Not a cricket chirred.'

246–8. *Chattering fire / soon kindled, soon burned out, / fit wife for an old man!* Makin compares Muccioli, 43–4: 'Sometimes, stirring the ashes, the fire seems to me like a companion of the slumbers of my old age' (*Makin*, 72, n. 24).

256. *Soanso's dead.* So-and-so. Cp. BB's 'Many well-known people have been packed away in cemeteries', 8: 'What's-his-name's dead.'

263. *Imperial Anthology.* The first official collection of classical Japanese poems, in the *tanka* form, was produced during the Heian era, *ca.*905.

274–5. *If you keep straight you will have no friends / but catgut and blossom in season.* Makin: '[Cp. Muccioli, 81–2]: "Friends of men are those who esteem the rich and give preference to those from whom they can obtain something. Certainly they do not love men who are upright and men of heart. Therefore it is better to have, as one's only friends, music and nature"; and Muccioli's gloss: "*Shichiku kwa-getsu*, literally strings and bamboo, flowers and the moon." (Bamboo stands for woodwind instruments)' (*Makin*, 72, n. 24).

296. *I am shifting rivermist, not to be trusted.* Cp. Muccioli, 86: 'I compare my character to a floating cloud; I do not trust it, I expect nothing from it' (*Makin*, 72, n. 25).

300, 307. *Hankering, vexation and apathy.* This 'derives from a footnote in Muccioli which interprets a disputed passage as referring to the Three Obstacles to Salvation' (*Makin*, 69).

316. *Buddha says: 'None of the world is good.'* See note to Amida, above. Keene's translation (211): 'The essence of the Buddha's teaching to man is that we must not have attachment for any object.'

322. *I've a passionate nature.* Makin: 'The corresponding passage is in Muccioli, 92, where Chomei reproaches his heart for being even now immersed in worldly impurity, and asks: "Is this perhaps because my *karma* of poverty afflicts me, or because I rave, assaulted by the passions of the world?" His heart has no answer. He thus criticizes himself for what is (in Buddhist terms) a fundamental flaw: he is still attached to the world, though his "world" is only his hut. But in Bunting, "I've a passionate nature . . ." is merely part of his disclaimer of any special status or virtue' (*Makin*, 71, n. 22).

FIRST BOOK OF ODES

▪ **I have taken my chance to insert a couplet in the First Book of Odes and promote *The Orotava Road* from limbo to its chronological place amongst them, which has obliged me to renumber many.**

Dedication in *CE*: **'Of those not particularly dedicated, let Ezra Pound take all that are good in his opinion.'**

There are no poems in this section dated before 1924; BB claimed to have destroyed all poems composed prior to 1923 without showing them to anyone (*Descant*, [5]).

The 'odes' were so named following the publication of *RM*; the poems in this section which originally appeared in *RM* were there called 'carmina', after the Latin title for Horace's poems. The titles used for these in *RM* were subsequently replaced with numbers, and first called 'odes' in *CE*. They were first published as 'odes' in *P1950*, and a volume of them titled, *First Book of Odes* (*FBO*) was published by Fulcrum Press in 1965.

The **'odes are called odes because Horace called his odes. An ode is essentially a sonnet to be sung, not all of mine are meant to be sung; most of them are'** (Lesch interview, 24 April 1976; quoted *Lesch*, 36). However, according to J. B. Leishman (*Translating Horace* [Oxford: Bruno Cassirer, 1956], 38; quoted *Forde*, 84), 'the term *odae* . . . was not used to describe Horace's lyrical poetry until some centuries after his death. He himself called them *carmina*, songs.' BB clearly knew Ronsard's work, and it may be that the designation 'First Book of Odes' owes something to that poet's 'Le premier livre des amours', 'Le second livre des amours', 'Le premier livre des sonnets pour Helene', 'Le seconde livre des sonnets pour Helene', and 'Les Odes'. The *qasidas* BB translated (see 'Overdrafts' and 'Uncollected Overdrafts' below) may perhaps also be considered odes.

1 'Weeping oaks grieve, chestnuts raise'

Cp. T. S. Eliot, *The Waste Land*, 1–4; Makin compares st. 2 to Tennyson, 'The Lotos-Eaters', 42 and 94–5 (*Makin*, 303).

'This is the oldest fraction that I've preserved. It's only a little bit of what was a poem. But the rest of it was too dreadful to preserve at all. And really, it concerns Regent's Park. You know, I used to live just around

the corner from Regent's Park, in a little garret . . . And that avenue of chestnut, horse-chestnut trees is, in the spring, so magnificent. I was in love with Regent's Park, and once wrote a poem to say, quite falsely, that it was the finest park in all Europe . . . It had to be abolished, that poem. It wasn't good enough' (reading, London, 1980, in *Swigg*).

Publication history

Titled 'Sad Spring' in *RM*, where it was included in the 'Carmina' section. EP included it, unnumbered, in *Act. Ant.*, *Guedalla* B4. In *CE* as Ode II. As Ode I in *P1950*, *FBO*, *Loquitur* and all editions of *CP*. Reprinted in *Georgia Straight*, n.pag., *Guedalla* D34. Variant in letter to Basilio Fernández; see Appendix VII. The poem is mentioned in a letter from LZ to EP dated 9 November 1930. It was considered, along with 'Against the Tricks of Time, 'While Shepherds Watched', 'Chorus of Furies' and 'To Venus' ['Darling of Gods and men, beneath the gliding stars'], for *Poetry*'s 'Objectivists' issue which LZ was to edit (*Pound/Zukofsky: Selected Letters of Ezra Pound and Louis Zukofsky*).

2 'Farewell ye sequent graces'

Revised version of 'Against the Tricks of Time', which appeared in a different version in *RM* and *CE*; that version presented in *UO*, below. Published in *P1950*, *FBO*, *Loquitur* and all editions of *CP*. Variant in letter to Basilio Fernández; see Appendix VII.

Notes

1. Farewell ye sequent graces. Cp. Shakespeare, Sonnet 60, 4: 'In sequent toil all forwards do contend', and 'nature finds itself scourged by the sequent effects', *King Lear*, I. ii; Milton, *Paradise Lost*, XII. 165: 'There he dies, and leaves his Race / Growing into a Nation, and now grown / Suspected to a sequent king.'

3–10. Silent leavetaking . . . fantom dancers. Cp. T. S. Eliot, 'Preludes', III. **'I had some knowledge of music and I had arrived via a somewhat strange route at the conclusion that poetry should try to take over some of the techniques that I only knew in music. So that when I discovered Eliot writing poems and calling them "Preludes", even though the resemblance, to say, Chopin's Preludes was slight and superficial, I was extremely interested. He was obviously thinking on lines not dissimilar from my own'** (*Descant*, [6]).

10. fantom. *OED* n.6. ('*appositive* or *adj.*') cites St Cuthbert for 'fantom'. Cp. Dryden, translation of the fourth book of Lucretius, *Concerning the Nature of Love*, 67: 'So Love with fantomes cheats our longing eyes'. BB also uses the word in 'Overdrafts', 'Last night without sight of you my brain was ablaze', 12.

11. Airlapped. Not in *OED* or *EDD*.

3 'I am agog for foam. Tumultuous come'

BB called this a poem for which Yeats had a **'particular fancy'** (BB to LZ, 9 September 1953; quoted *Forde*, 85). **'When Yeats first met me, he confided to his diary and to his letters that he had just met the most terrible anarchist and frightful person that Pound had ever acquired as a disciple. But shortly afterwards, he asked me to dinner, and meanwhile he had taken the trouble to look at what little work I had available. And you know, the old man had – it's mere decency, of course, to learn two or three lines out of the poet you're entertaining and quote them, it shows you have read the thing – but he read all the twenty-odd lines of this poem, he spouted them off by heart. And much later again he referred to it, and obviously Yeats liked it. So though it's early stuff and not the stuff I have devoted myself to trying to make, it has his sanction'** (reading, London, 1980, in *Swigg*). Burton (132) notes that the poem draws 'heavily' on Mallarmé's 'Les Fenêtres' and echoes Matthew Arnold's 'Dover Beach'. But in a letter to Guedalla (6 May 1969, held at Durham), BB said: **'Every time it's reprinted I've wondered whether to drop it. I kept it, I suppose, mainly because Yeats liked it, but he liked it because it was so clearly the attempt to assimilate Mallarmé (not Coup de Dés, but Las du triste hospital), or so I imagine.'**

Publication history

Titled 'Foam' in *RM*, where it was included in the 'Carmina' section. In *CE* as Ode III. In *P1950* as Ode 4. In *FBO*, *Loquitur* and all editions of *CP*. Reprinted in *Georgia Straight*, n.pag., *Guedalla* D34. Variant in letter to Basilio Fernández; see Appendix VII.

Notes

[Dedication] Peggy Mullett. A girlfriend of BB's. See note to dedication of *Briggflatts*; not Peggy Greenbank.

1. I am agog for foam. Cp. Keats, letter to J. H. Reynolds, 14 March 1818, 'Being agog to see some Devonshire . . .' (*Letters of John Keats*, ed. Robert Gittings [Oxford, 1970], 74).

3. tidelong. Not in *OED* or *EDD*.

15. sprayblown. Not in *OED* or *EDD*.

18. braceletted. Cp. T. S. Eliot, 'The Love Song of J. Alfred Prufrock',

64: 'Arms that are braceletted and white and bare', and Joyce, *Ulysses*, Bello speaking in the Circe episode: 'your wellcreamed braceletted hands'.

4 'After the grimaces of capitulation'

In late 1928, BB sent the poem to EP, asking, **'Is this a poem? Have I found my voice? Everybody says it is exceedingly disagreeable of me to be unpleasant about sunrise and the loud chorus of complaints encourages me to think that I must have done something of my own at last'** (*Caddel & Flowers*; quoted *Burton*, [151]).

Publication history

Titled 'Aubade' in *RM*, where it was included in the 'Carmina' section, and divided into stanzas of 3, 5, 4, and 4 lines. In *CE* as Ode XXV, with title or sub-heading, 'Aubade'. In *P1950* as Ode 3. In *FBO*, *Loquitur* and all editions of *CP*. Variant in letter to Basilio Fernández; see Appendix VII.

Note

15. noctambulistic. A noctambulist is a sleepwalker. Cp. Donne, *Sermons*, xlvi. 467: 'That our Noctambulones, men that walke in their sleepe, will wake if they be called by their names.'

5 'Empty vast days built in the waste memory seem a jail for'

'This is another quantitative one, which in this case is in fact Greek metres taken literally and without change into English' (reading, Riverside Studios, London, February 1982, in *Swigg*).

Publication history

Titled 'Against Memory' in *RM*, where it was included in the 'Carmina' section. In *CE* as Ode VI. Also in *P1950*, *FBO*, *Loquitur* and all editions of *CP*. In *Fragmente* 1, no. 1 (Freiburg im Breisgau, Germany, 1951), 7, *Guedalla* D15, translated into German by Rainer M. Gerhardt, the journal's editor (and EP's translator); the first published translation of a poem by BB. Reprinted in *Georgia Straight*, n.pag., *Guedalla* D34.

Notes

[Dedication] Helen Egli. Née Helen Rowe, with whom BB had an affair, in London, around 1921. See *Burton*, 135–6.

4. *whimper*. Cp. T. S. Eliot, 'The Hollow Men', V. 31: 'Not with a bang but a whimper.'

6. *Polyhymnia*. Muse of sacred hymns and poetry; see note to 'Attis: Or, Something Missing', II. 56–7.

6 *Personal Column /* '. . . As to my heart, that may as well be forgotten'

In *RM*, where it is the book's last poem; included in the 'ETCETERA' section, followed by three asterisks and an indented, italicized couplet: *Bournons* [*sic.*: *Bornons*] *ici cette carrière, / Les longs ouvrages me font peur.* (From Jean de la Fontaine, *Fables*, Book 6, Epilogue); *translation*: 'Here check we our career: / Long works I greatly fear' (Elizur Wright). Amusingly, Marianne Moore rendered it 'Our peregrination must end there. / One's skin creeps when poets persevere.' In *CE* as Ode XII. Also in *P1950*, *FBO*, *Loquitur* and all editions of *CP*.

Notes

3. *refs. exchgd.* References exchanged. This part of the poem is done in the style of a newspaper classified advertisement, as the title indicates.
   h.&c. Hot and cold. Abbreviation used in accommodation rental advertisements in newspapers.

7 'The day being Whitsun we had pigeon for dinner'

Titled 'Whitsunday Ode' in version sent to LZ in 1935.

Publication history

In *CE* as Ode VII. First published in *P1950*. Also in *FBO*, *Loquitur* and all editions of *CP*. Reprinted in *Georgia Straight*, n.pag., *Guedalla* D34.

Notes

1. *Whitsun*. Feast day usually celebrated on the seventh Sunday after Easter; marks the descent of the Holy Spirit upon the Apostles.
   pigeon. Associated with the dove and the Holy Ghost; *Lesch* (50) observes that pigeon is also an inexpensive game bird for the working-class table.

6. *Wimbledon, Wandsworth, Clapham, the Oval. Lesch* (51) suggests that this follows a bus route. *OED*: 'Kennington Oval, in athletics

"the Oval", an open space at Kennington in South London (opened in 1846), where cricket-matches, etc., are played.'

6–7. Lo, / Westminster Palace where the asses jaw!' Contemptuous reference to the Houses of Parliament. Cp. Judges 15: 16: 'And Samson said, With the jawbone of an ass, heaps upon heaps, with the jaw of an ass have I slain a thousand men'; also Ben Jonson, 'Bellum scribentium' in *Explorata: or Discoveries*: 'loud brayings under their asses' skins!'

8. buckshee-hunt! OED: '*slang* (orig. Army). [Alteration of baksheesh; cf. bukshi.] A.*n.* Something extra, free, or to spare; an allowance above the usual amount. B. *adj.* Free; spare, extra. Hence as *adv.*' Earliest citation from 1916.

11–12. rei novae / inter rudes artium homines. 'He ruled more through personal influence than sovereign power.' Peter Quartermain suggests an alternate reading: 'a new thing to [*or* among] men unacquainted with the arts'; as he points out, the TS of *CE* 'places the final two lines at the bottom of the page, suggestive of a footnote and implying their status as translation of Livy'; see his 'Take Oil / and Hum: Niedecker/Bunting', in *Radical Vernacular: Lorine Niedecker and the Poetics of Place*, ed. Elizabeth Willis (Iowa City: University of Iowa Press, 2008), 281, n. 3. ▪ **The quotation might not be readily identified without a hint. It is from Livy.** From Livy (59/64 BCE–17 CE), *Ab Urbe Condita*, I. vii. 8, which refers to an encounter between Hercules and Evander, revered for his invention of the Roman alphabet. Makin remarks that K. Müller, in a PhD dissertation, 'tells us that the context there adds nothing to the meaning' of the poem (*Makin*, 58, n. 56).

8 *Each fettered ghost slips to his several grave. /* 'Loud intolerant bells (the shrinking nightflower closes'

The poem's original title, 'While Shepherds Watched', was taken from the Christmas carol 'While Shepherds Watched their Flocks by Night', whose words were composed by Nahum Tate (1652–1715; Poet Laureate of England from 1692) around 1700; the carol is based on Luke 2: 8–14. Handel set the words to music adapted from his 1728 opera, *Siroe, King of Persia*. Both this carol and work by Joseph Skipsey (1832–1903), a Northumbrian poet BB admired and edited, appear together in *The Home Book of Verse* (1912, many later editions; ed. Burton Egbert Stevenson), which BB may have seen. BB owned the 1888 ed. of Skipsey's *Carols, Songs, and Ballads*.

Publication history

Titled 'While Shepherds Watched' in *RM*, where it was included in the 'ETCETERA' section. In *CE* as Ode XXIX with title, 'While Shepherds Watched'. Also in *P1950*, *FBO*, *Loquitur* and all editions of *CP*. The poem is mentioned in a letter from LZ to EP dated 9 November 1930. It was considered, along with 'Against the Tricks of Time, 'Sad Spring', 'Chorus of Furies' and 'To Venus' ['Darling of Gods and men, beneath the gliding stars'], for *Poetry*'s 'Objectivists' issue which LZ was to edit (*Pound/Zukofsky: Selected Letters of Ezra Pound and Louis Zukofsky*).

Notes

[Epigraph] Each fettered ghost slips to his several grave. Cp. Milton, 'On the Morning of Christ's Nativity', 234.

2. *baulk*. *OED* v.1.III.5. *trans.* d: 'To frustrate, foil, render unsuccessful.' Citation for Swift, *Censure*, Misc. (1735) V. 104: 'The most effectual Way to baulk Their Malice, is – to let them talk.' *EDD* III, *Fig.* 1: 'To hinder, prevent, thwart, impede.' Cp. Kipling, 'A Song in Storm', 26: 'Each billow's baulked career', and 'England's Answer', 28: 'Baulking the end'. Perhaps *EDD* 3: 'to balk a thing and not to speak to it, or to leave it unanswered' as in Marlowe, *Edward III*, II. v: 'We . . . must not come so near to baulk their lips.'

8. *shoddy*. *OED* n.2: 'A cloth composed of shoddy wool'; n.1.a: 'Woollen yarn obtained by tearing to shreds refuse woollen rags, which, with the addition of some new wool, is made into a kind of cloth.' Cp. st. 4 of the carol: 'swaddling bands'.

9. *enorbed*. Not in *OED*, but entries for orb (v). and orbed (a.). Cp. Shakespeare, 'A Lover's Complaint', 25: 'th'orbed', and *Twelfth Night* v. i. 278: 'that orbed continent'. Also Milton, 'On the Morning of Christ's Nativity', xv, 143: 'Orbed in a rainbow', *Paradise Lost*, V. 42: 'Full orbed the moon', and VI. 543: 'his orbèd shield'; Shelley, 'The Cloud', 45: 'That orbèd maiden with white fire laden, / Whom mortals call the Moon'; and Tennyson, 'The Princess', vi. 153: 'Orbed in your isolation'.

9 'Dear be still! Time's start of us lengthens slowly'

'This . . . is a poem which is quantitative.' That is, in quantitative verse; see note on metre in 'Chomei at Toyama' (reading, Riverside Studios, London, February 1982, in *Swigg*).

Cp. generally Marvell, 'To His Coy Mistress'.

Publication history

Titled 'Advice to a Lady' in *RM*, where it was included in the 'ETCETERA' section. In *CE* as Ode XXIV. Also in *P1950*, *FBO*, *Loquitur* and all editions of *CP*. Reprinted in *King Ida's Watch Chain*, n.pag., *Guedalla* D22, as 'Ode 9'; also in *Georgia Straight*, n.pag., *Guedalla* D34.

10 Chorus of Furies

Titled 'Chorus of Furies (Overheard)' in *RM*, where it was included in the 'ETCETERA' section; in *CE* as Ode XVII with sub-heading, *Chorus of Furies: / overheard. // Guarda, mi disse, le / feroce Erine.* In *P1950* as Ode 11. In *FBO*, *Loquitur* and all editions of *CP*. The poem is mentioned in a letter from LZ to EP dated 9 November 1930. It was considered, along with 'Against the Tricks of Time, 'Sad Spring', 'While Shepherds Watched' and 'To Venus' ['Darling of Gods and men, beneath the gliding stars'], for *Poetry*'s 'Objectivists' issue which LZ was to edit (*Pound/Zukofsky: Selected Letters of Ezra Pound and Louis Zukofsky*).

Note

[Epigraph] Guarda, mi disse, le feroce Erine. From Dante, *Inferno*, IX. 'Mark the fierce Erinnyes' (Temple Dante). The Furies, at the entrance to the sixth circle of Hell, threaten Dante with Medusa's head, the sight of which would have turned him into stone; Virgil protects him, however. See also notes to 'Attis', II.

11 *To a Poet who advised me to preserve my fragments and false starts* / 'Narciss, my numerous cancellations prefer'

At a 1970 reading (in *Swigg*), BB explained that the poet who so advised him had done so in Rapallo.

Publication history

Listed as 'To Narciss' in table of contents, but not in text of poem in *RM*, where it was included in the 'Carmina' section under the title or sub-heading, 'To a POET who Advised me to PRESERVE my Fragments and False Starts'. In *CE* as Ode XXIII with same title or sub-heading. Published in *Whips & Scorpions*, 97, *Guedalla* B2. In *P1950* as Ode 10. In *FBO*, *Loquitur* and all editions of *CP*.

Notes

1. Narciss. Narcissus, who in Greek mythology pined away for love of his own reflection.
cancellations. BB frequently destroyed the drafts of his poems.

2–5. damp dustbins . . . miscellaneous garbage. Cp. Yeats, 'The Circus Animals' Desertion', 35–7: 'A mound of refuse or the sweepings of a street, / Old kettles, old bottles, and a broken can, / Old iron, old bones, old rags'.

12 'An arles, an arles for my hiring'

Titled 'Sonnet' in *RM*, where it was included in the 'ETCETERA' section, and in *CE* as Ode IV, with title, 'Sonnet'. Also in *P1950*, *FBO*, *Loquitur* and all editions of *CP*.

Notes

1–2. arles . . . arlespenny. Small change; but also an advance payment on a signed contract. Cp. Burns, 'My Tocher's the Jewel', 9: 'Your profeer o' luve's an airle-penny.' Also Wordsworth, *The Prelude* (1850), III. 476–7: '"An obolus, a penny give / To a poor scholar!"' In Greek mythology, a penny was Charon's fare for crossing the Styx.

3. Apollo. Greek God whose lyre associated him with music, poetry and dance.

14. Quaeret in trivio vocationem. Loeb: 'to hunt for an invitation' from Catullus XLVII, 7, in Loeb as *quaerunt in trivio vocationes*. The last line of BB's poem is a translated version of this, and was printed as a note at the foot of the text in *RM*. Cp. Celia Zukofsky and LZ's version of the Catullus poem in Celia Zukofsky and LZ, trans., *Catullus* (London, 1969), n.pag. Cp. also EP, *Hugh Selwyn Mauberley*, I. 1–3: 'For three years, out of key with his time, / He strove to resuscitate the dead art / Of poetry; to maintain "the sublime" / In the old sense.'

15. cadging for drinks. Years later, in a notebook of draft materials for *Briggflatts*, BB wrote the lines, eventually discarded: **'touching his acquaintances for food and / [dinner, for] tobacco'** (*Briggflatts notebook*, page facing 17, at SUNY Buffalo).

13 *Fearful symmetry* / 'Muzzle and jowl and beastly brow'

First published in *Poetry* 32, no. 5 (February 1932), 251, *Guedalla* D6. In *CE* as Ode XVIII. Also in *P1950*, *FBO*, *Loquitur* and all editions of *CP*.

Notes

[Epigraph] Fearful symmetry. From Blake, 'Tyger, tyger'. According to *Alldritt* (18), when BB was a schoolboy at Leighton Park, the school magazine, *The Leightonian*, noted that he had read publicly an essay on Blake, 'whom he admired as a prophet rather than a poet'.

6. Kuala Lumpur. Capital city of Malaysia.

8. profitable likeness. Cp. EP, *Hugh Selwyn Mauberley*, II. 9–12: 'The "age demanded" chiefly a mould in plaster, / Made with no loss of time, / A prose kinema, not, not assuredly, alabaster / Or the "sculpture" of rhyme.'

R.A. Royal Academician.

15. ♂. Male symbol. BB wrote to Harriet Monroe that the printer's omission of this symbol destroyed the poem's rhythm (undated letter, late 1931, held at the University of Chicago).

Felis Tigris (Straits Settlements) (Bobo) Wording which might be used on the plaque of a cage at a zoo; Bobo would be the tiger's name. *Felis tigris* was formerly the Linnaean designation for the tiger (now *Panthera tigris*). In 1826, Malacca, Singapore and Penang, former British colonies in the Malay Peninsula, were unified administratively and called the Straits Settlements, under the control of British India. Years later, in a notebook of draft materials for *Briggflatts*, BB wrote the lines, eventually discarded: **'Fame exhibits a tiger caged.'** and **'Men cage tigers.'** (*Briggflatts notebook*, 42 and 43, at SUNY Buffalo).

14 Gin the Goodwife Stint

BB remarked that this poem and 'Complaint of the Morpethshire Farmer' were **'attempts to make use of the ballad form'** (interview with Tom Pickard, June 1981, in *Swigg*).

Cp., generally, Wordsworth's preface to the second edition of *Lyrical Ballads*, re 'the language really used by men'; BB admired Wordsworth's ballad-like poems, the Lucy poems especially: **'he attempted in Lucy etc the simplicity which is commonly recommended as the nearest road to the sublime, and sometimes came within sight of the distant peak:**

and he attempted the Lucretian manner, not without successful pages' (BB to LZ, 3 November 1948; quoted *Forde*, 90). **'All my life the most important English poet for me was Wordsworth, whom Pound despised'** (Lesch interview, 24 April 1976; quoted *Lesch*, 26). Cp. also Tennyson's 'Northern Farmer' poems, D. H. Lawrence's Nottinghamshire dialect poems, which EP had praised, e.g. 'Whether or Not' and 'Violets'; and also many of Kipling's poems.

On the spoken dialect of Northumbrian, BB said, **'Burns had a language and a whole literature of forerunners, an album of tunes to find words for an output of very sophisticated satire to underpin his songs; but Northumbrian is only a spoken language, with no recognizable spelling . . . and no literature of its own within the last four centuries, except anonymous ballads . . . the process of balladry had ended, at least in the pit villages, before Skipsey's time. He had to speak with his own mouth even when he meant to speak for all his people'** (Joseph Skipsey, *Selected Poems*, 7). Skipsey (1832–1903) was a Northumbrian colliery worker and self-educated poet. When Mottram asked, 'Did you ever think of writing in a transcription of something like Northumberland dialect?' BB replied, **'It's been tried but it's unworkable because there is no spelling convention that will fit it. Swinburne made a serious attempt to write ballads in Northumbrian, failed, and translated them into Scots – lowland Scots . . . The occasional dialect word in the midst of ordinary English is quite enough to give the atmosphere, as you'll see if you read the two ballads I did about 1930'** (*Mottram*, 3; quoted with different wording in *The Listener*, 28 August 1975, 274). BB introduced a radio broadcast reading Wordsworth's 'The Brothers' by explaining: **'I am a Northumberland man and all I can claim for my reading [aloud] is that my vowels are nearer to those Wordsworth uttered than a Londoner's might be, and my intonation perhaps less foreign to his. Nobody had thought of standard English in Wordsworth's time. He spoke as a Northerner, in spite of the years spent in Cambridge, London and Somerset. In such a Northern way that Keats and Hazlitt found it hard to follow his conversation, and though he did not compose in dialect, he composed in his own voice aloud. His music is lost if his poems are read in Southern English, and no doubt that is why so many critics imagine he had none'** (quoted in *The Listener* [8 October 1970], 484). Years later he remarked to Peter Bell: **'I suppose that the conception of Standard English is only a little older than Wordsworth, and it had not gained, I wouldn't say universal, but even common acceptance within Wordsworth's lifetime. By 1850, I daresay, middle-class people expected to find that other middle-class people spoke like London or Oxford or Cambridge, but not until just about the time that Wordsworth died. And it's a great addition to some of those Romantics if you know where they came from. Some of Keats, read in what is now called Standard English, is absolutely unbearable. But he was a Cockney, and if you will read it in Old Cockney, such as he spoke, it would be now** the Cockney of southeast London, I think, verging on Kentish, if you read his poems in that, quite a lot of that oversweetness vanishes. Keats becomes much more tolerable. And the same way with Wordsworth. The ordinary southern Englishman or the Englishman brought up in middle classes, who would speak Standard English, is simply unaware that there is any music in Wordsworth, whereas he is one of those musical poets, if you will give his vowels full Northern strength. And you remember that "r" is a letter which was pronounced in his talk. Somewhere about 1820, Keats was asked to dinner where Wordsworth was to be one of the guests. And he went along hoping to get a lot of wisdom from the great poet, but for most of the time he couldn't understand what on earth Wordsworth was saying. The Cockney couldn't *hear* the Cumbrian. At the end of the evening Keats was just beginning to get something from it. And similarly, at an earlier date, Hazlitt went to Somerset to interview Wordsworth and Coleridge in the days when they lived there, but he was defeated because he couldn't understand Wordsworth. Standard English is a very modern conception, it is a narrowing one, the standard changes and gets narrower and narrower, and what you now hear from a large percentage of BBC announcers, a large percentage of the people they interview, is a hateful narrow-vowelled affair which sometimes becomes as excessive, this narrowing, as South African, Rhodesian did. Northumbrian has kept most of its vowels. And though its "r" has become less conspicuous in my lifetime, it's still there as a gutteral, not a rolled "r", Wordsworth's "r" was a rolled "r" as it still is in Cumberland. [Northumbrian speech] changes, and the next generation, brought up on television, will have changed it more, still. There must have been bigger changes last century. What is called "Geordie" is a bastard language, it's a mixture mainly of south Northumbrian with the Irish that was brought in by the labourers who came first to dig canals, then to build railways, and finally settled down largely in the coal mines. So that a man from Jarrow is speaking what has a double origin in Northumbrian and in northern Irish' (interview, 3 September 1981, in *Swigg*).

'Wordsworth did not write dialect; but he composed aloud, very loud according to the anecdotes, in the language he spoke, and that was not the Koiné we are all taught to use now. Read him aloud, with R's and broad vowels. Remember that the word "water" was unknown to him. He rhymes it with "chatter" and "shatter" because he pronounced it "watter"; and though he spells Yarrow with OW, as the map does, he rhymes it with the word he (and we) pronounce "marra", and rhyme with "Jarra", down the river there' (*BBP*, 103). ('Jarrow is on the Tyne, downriver from Newcastle.' [*BBP*, 201, n. 9]).

Denis Goacher, thinking particularly about *Briggflatts*, remarked that BB's 'Northumbrian accent was a manufactured one. He had, in fact, a very refined voice but had two things in mind when reading his poetry aloud. He was very careful to keep the flat A's and a bit likely to roll his R's, but he certainly did not, in normal speech, roll his R's to the prodigious extent that he did when reading his poems. I never heard any sort of Northumbrian sound like that! There was also a slight over-emphasis on wanting to bring back the valuable consonants and, in particular, to make up for the elision of the R in English Southern speech. I thought he had a point there – that we have lost something, as indeed modern French has done. But the self-conscious rolling of his R's, I thought, slowed up the actual course of the line . . . He is really tracing back his past, recovering the accent he was born with, with a layer of nostalgia. But, I repeat, there is an over-emphasis on regionality, because he wished to make a point *against* Southern speech' ('Denis Goacher Talks about Basil Bunting', *Caddel*, 204). For more on BB, Wordsworth, and Northern accents, see Kenneth Cox, 'Basil Bunting Reading Wordsworth', *Jacket* 28, online at: http://jacketmagazine.com/28/cox-bunt.html.

Publication history

First published by EP in *Act. Ant.*, *Guedalla* B4. In *CE*. Also in *P1950*, *FBO*, *Loquitur* and all editions of *CP*. Reprinted, with BB's glosses and note, by EP in *Conf. Cumm*, *Guedalla* B10; also in *Sum* 5 (April 1965), n.pag., *Guedalla* D19, with credit line, 'From "Poems: 1950", The Cleaners' Press, Galveston.'

Notes

1. bent ▪ [note, *P1950*] **tough, tussocky grass.** See note to *Briggflatts* II. 150.

3. Gin. ▪ [note, *P1950*] **if [conjunction].** *EDD* 3. Cp. Burns, among others 'The Shepherd's Wife': 'What will I get to my supper, / Gin I come hame, gin I come hame? / What will I get to my supper / Gin I come hame again een, jo?', and 'Collier Laddie,' iii. 1–4: 'Ye shall gang in gay attire . . . / Gin ye'll leave your Collier Laddie'; Scott, *Old Mortality*, xliv, 'Follow me, gin ye please, sir'; and Tennyson, 'Northern Farmer, Old Style', xvii. 4: 'an' gin I mun doy I mun doy'. B. Kirkby, *Lakeland Words* (Kendal?, 1898), 61: 'GIN – If; in case.'

stint. *OED* v.14 cites *Northumbrian Glossary*, 'stent', 'to limit. "Aa's stented tiv an oor at dinner."' See also c., 'To "pinch", go short. *? dial.*' *EDD* 1.v: 'To limit, restrict, esp. with regard to food; to abstain; to deprive.'

6. bairns. Small children. Cp. Joseph Skipsey, 'Get Up': '"Get up!" the caller calls, "Get up!" / And in the dead of night, / To win the bairns their bite and sup, / I rise a weary wight.' *OED* citations include *Beowulf*.

11. twa pund . . . C.P.R. ▪ [note, *P1950*] **It was recently, and may still be, possible for an emigrant pledged to agricultural labour to cross to**

Canada on C.P.R. boats for two pounds. (C.P.R. = Canadian Pacific Railway). Cp. Burns, 'Tam O'Shanter', 177: 'Wi' twa pund Scots, ('twas a' her riches)'.

12. *packet*. Packet-boat.

15 'Nothing'

In *CE* as Ode XIII. Titled 'The Word', first published in *Poetry* 37, no. 5 (February 1931), 260–1, issue ed. by LZ and commonly known as 'The Objectivist Issue', *Guedalla* D2. Ode 16 ('Molten pool, incandescent spilth of') appears in this publication as the last stanza of 15, under the heading '*Appendix: Iron*'. EP included Ode 15, unnumbered, in *Act. Ant.*, *Guedalla* B4. Also in *P1950*, *FBO*, *Loquitur* and all editions of *CP*. Reprinted in *Granta* 71, no. 12457 (6 November 1965), 13, *Guedalla* D24.

Notes

6–7, 12. *thought's intricate polyphonic / score . . . sharp tool paring away*. Polyphonic music and the mason's chisel with its waste leavings are concerns in *Briggflatts*; cp. respectively *Briggflatts* II. 161–83, IV. 45; and I. 14–37, 114–17, II. 131–5.

20. *condensed*. Cp. EP, *The ABC of Reading* (1934), 92: 'DICHTEN= CONDENSARE. This chapter heading is Mr. Bunting's discovery and his prime contribution to contemporary criticism, but the idea is far from new.'

32. *ictus*. *OED* 1: '*Pros*. Stress on a particular syllable of a foot or verse; rhythmical or metrical stress. Used of Old English verse.'

16 'Molten pool, incandescent spilth of'

In *CE* as Ode XIV. For publication history, see note to Ode 15.

Note

1. *spilth*. *OED*: 'That which is spilled; the action or fact of spilling.' Cp. Shakespeare, *Timon of Athens*, II. ii. 164–5: 'our vaults have wept / With drunken spilth of wine'.

17 *To Mina Loy* / 'Now that sea's over that island'

BB called this poem his attempt at Mallarmé, in 'Yeats Recollected', *Agenda* 12, no. 2 (1974), 37–8.

Publication history

In *CE* as Ode XVI without dedication to Mina Loy. First published in *P1950*. Also in *P1950*, *FBO*, *Loquitur* and all editions of *CP*. In *Imagi* 14, vol. 5, no. 3 (1951), n.pag., *Guedalla* D17, as '1' of 'two poems'. Reprinted in the *Newcastle Journal* (17 July 1965), 7, *Guedalla* D21; this periodical was owned by the same company as the Newcastle *Evening Chronicle* which employed BB in 1954–66; and in *Granta* 71, no. 12457 (6 November 1965), 13, *Guedalla* D24.

Notes

[Dedication] Mina Loy. Painter and poet (1882–1966), praised by EP, mostly known for her book *Lunar Baedecker*, published by Contact. David Annwn reports Carolyn Burke's reading of this poem 'as pretty straight biography: memories of Loy's drowned husband, Arthur Cravan, mingling with perceptions of her present state of grieving and an apartment filled with "flea market finds". There is, she implies, also a layer of amorous feelings mixed with shame over a famous drunken evening' ('Her Pulse Their Pace: Women Poets and Basil Bunting', *McGonigal & Price,* 126). See also Jim Powell, 'Basil Bunting and Mina Loy', *Chicago Review* 37, no. 1 (1990), 13.

2. sleeks. *EDD* 6.v.: 'to make level and even'. Cp., among many: Drayton, *The Barrons Warres*, III. 47: 'Sleek ev'ry little Dimple of the Lake / Sweet Syrens, and be readie with your Song'; Pope, *The Iliad* XXIII. 349–50: 'that wont to deck / Their flowing manes, and sleek their glossy neck'; and Tennyson, 'Merlin and Vivien', 897: 'To sleek her ruffled peace of mind.'

31. latch. Cp. *OED* n.2: '*Naut. Obs.*' Perhaps from 'lurch'. Citation given from Sir William Petty, *Political Arithmetick* . . ., iii. (1691), 51: 'Such [ships] as draw much Water, and have a deep Latch in the Sea.'

18 The Complaint of the Morpethshire Farmer

▪ **The war and the Forestry Commission have outdated this complaint. *Cowpit* means overturned.**

Note in *CE*: **'The Duke of Northumberland, like many Scottish landlords and a few other northern English ones, finds it pays better to let his land run wild and take what foolish "sportsmen" will pay for almost**

non-existent shooting, than to keep the ditches clean so that sheep may thrive and his farmers be able to pay their rent regularly. Yet the cost of putting in sheep-drain, even new, is very small and wherever the farmer has been able to do it himself the land is reclaimed. Some of it is even arable. In these cases the Duke at once raises the rent, the farmer is ruined, and the land reverts to heather.'

As *Lesch* explains (74), 'During the earlier part of the century, large tracts of land in northern England were purchased for raising grouse for hunting. Grouse thrive on land which is overrun and marshy, the occasion for the farmer's complaint.' In 1928, BB shared quarters with Ned Wilson, a shepherd for a farmer whose landlord was the Duke of Northumberland; see *Caddel & Flowers*, 35–7.

The poem's appearance prompted a signed letter from William Carlos Williams, published in *Four Pages* 8 (August 1948): 'ON BASIL BUNTING'S POEM IN FOUR PAGES: (1) Read, as I was told to do recently, Crabbe's Village. (2) Two summers ago at Wilmington, Vermont, I was told of the impossibility of getting anyone to gather sap for sugar or to do any farm work at any price, for the most part. Why? $5,000,000 worth of real estate, farm land, had been bought up by wealth during the preceding year. And why, again? Top executives of the usual corporations have to show a loss in their income. What better vehicle than a farm? And with what disastrous effect on local farm-labor, since the more they pay (the owner) the more loss they can show. Thus if they produce maple sugar at $2 a pint, minimum, it means nothing but benefit to them though it is disaster to everyone in the neighborhood, except, of course the farm-laborer who grabs for the pennies while his own land runs down. Such artificial manipulation of prices, as our present income tax laws permit and even foster, tend inevitably toward such abuses.'

BB wrote to Dorothy Pound that, **'I began with a wish to limit my aims (abolish the protection of "game" in England and extend the range of black-faced sheep), and they [the poems] were still far too abstract and ambitious to do anything but harm if I persisted'** (11 December 1954; quoted *Caddel*, [173]).

At a reading late in his life, BB remarked of the poem that **'the matters it deals with were cleared up long ago . . . The Forestry Commission came and took all the land and drained it. And then the war came and all the farmers got rich instead of being extremely poor'** (London, 1980, in *Swigg*).

BB remarked that this poem and 'Gin the Goodwife Stint' were **'attempts to make use of the ballad form'** (interview with Tom Pickard, June 1981, in *Swigg*). At readings, BB customarily read the poem in a Northumbrian accent, e.g. London, 1980, in *Swigg*.

In a letter to LZ (10 November 1964; mentioned *Forde*, 88), BB complained that he was as tired of this much-anthologized poem as Yeats was of 'The Lake Isle of Innisfree'.

Publication history

In *CE*. First published by EP, unnumbered, in *Act. Ant.*, *Guedalla* B4. Also in *Four Pages* 5 (May 1948), 3, *Guedalla* D13. (*Four Pages* was edited by Dallam Flynn, who also published *P1950*). In *P1950*, *FBO*, *Loquitur* and all editions of *CP*. Included by EP in *Conf. Cumm*, *Guedalla* B10.

Notes

[Title] Complaint of. Peter Robinson notes that 'This generic title has a long lineage including poems by Chaucer and Villon, a lineage modishly revived by Jules Laforgue in *Les Complaintes* (1885) and so having its echo in poems of Pound and Eliot. It is also used to entitle a literary ballad in Wordsworth's "The Complaint of a Forsaken Indian Woman", a poem which like "The Last of the Flock" may have helped Bunting to an awareness of what poetry is when young. Both poems appeared in the *Lyrical Ballads* (1798)' (Peter Robinson, 'Bunting's Ballads', *Caddel*, 180, n. 27).

1. Morpeth. County town of Northumberland, which lies fifteen miles to the north of Newcastle Upon Tyne.

5. bide. *OED* v.2, 'To remain or continue *in* some state or action', and 3, 'To remain in a place, or with a person', citing Ælfred; v. II. trans. 6, 'To wait for, await', cites *Lindisfarne Gospels*. Cp., among many, Shakespeare, *Twelfth Night*, II. iv. 94–5: 'There is no woman's sides / Can bide the beating of so strong a passion'; Donne, Elegy 3. 31: 'Waters stink soon, if in one place they bide'; Milton, *Paradise Regained*, I. 58–9: 'wherein we / Must bide the stroke of that long-threatened wound'; Scott, *Old Mortality*, xxiii: '"Bide a wee, bide a wee", said Cuddie'; and Tennyson, 'Enoch Arden', 435: 'Will you not bide your year as I bide mine?'

8. kye ▪ [note, *P1950*] **cattle.** Burns uses the word frequently, among many, his song to the air 'Invercald's reel', ('Tibby I hae seen the day'), 28. Cp. also '"Hae back the kye!" the Captain said,' etc., in the poem 'Jamie Telfer in the Fair Dodhead', in the 1919 *Oxford Book of Ballads*; and Scott, *Midlothian* xxv: 'she's gawn to look after the kye'.

10. coulter ▪ [note, *P1950*] **plowshare.** *OED* citations include Ælfric and Chaucer.

11. neebody. Nobody. (Not *EDD*).

12. burn. Cp. BB's note to *Briggflatts* I. 70: **We have burns in the east, *becks* in the west, but no brooks or creeks.** *OED*: n.1.1: 'In OE.: A spring, fountain; a stream or river. In later use: A small stream or brook. Now (exc. in the form Bourne n.1) chiefly *north*.' Also used in 'Stones trip Coquet burn', in *SBOO* 10, and 'You've come! O how flustered and anxious I've been', in 'Uncollected Overdrafts'; also 'burns' in 'Snow's on the fellside . . .', in 'Uncollected Overdrafts'. BB used the word 'becks' in a comment about Ford Madox Ford's poetry: **'There are explorations that can never end in discovery, only in willingness to rest content with an unsure glimpse through mists, an uncertain sound of becks we shall never taste'** (Ford, *Selected Poems*, viii).

14. braes. *OED* 1: 'The steep bank bounding a river valley.' *EDD* 1: 'A declivity, hillside, steep bank; the broken bank of a river.' Cp. among many, Burns, 'The Banks o' Doon', 1: 'Ye banks and braes o' bonnie Doon'; Scott, *Midlothian*, ix: 'The elfin knight sate on the brae'; Wordsworth, 'Ellen Irwin', 2: 'Upon the braes of Kirtle'.

17. rowan. The mountain ash. Cp. *Briggflatts* V. 62.

19. cowpit ▪ [note, *P1950*] **overturned.** See BB's note, above. *OED* 'coup', v.3: 'To be overturned or upset; to fall or tumble over; to capsize.' Cp. Burns, 'Death and Dr. Hornbook', 103: 'I drew my scythe in sic a fury, / I near-hand cowpit wi' my hurry', and Scott, *Old Mortality*, xxxviii: 'The bairns would be left to . . . coup aen anither into the fire', and *Redgauntlet*, Letter XI, 'Wandering Willie's Tale': 'Over he cowped as if he had been dead.'

24. hire. *OED* v.3.b: 'To engage oneself as a servant for payment. Chiefly *N. Amer.*'

27. hind ▪ [note, *P1950*] **farm labourer.** *OED* n.2 citations compare *Rushworth Gospels*' use of the word with *Lindisfarne Gospels*. *EDD* 1: 'A farm-labourer or ploughman; a farm servant'; 2: 'An upper farm-servant hired yearly and provided with a house; a married farm servant', with Northumbrian usage: 'A farm-servant hired by the year at so much per week. Hinds formerly had "corn wages", and were mostly paid in kind by the produce of the farm . . . Money wages are now general. At present sixteen to eighteen shillings per week, with house free, coals carted, a garden, and generally some potatoes planted on the farm or "found" for him. At the hiring a stipulation is often made by the farmer that the hind must furnish a female hind-worker at a stipulated price per day, with extra wage in harvest time.'

37. Clyde. River Clyde, from which ships would depart to cross the Atlantic.

19 'Fruits breaking the branches'

First published, unnumbered, by EP in *Act. Ant.*, *Guedalla* B4. In *CE* as Ode XXXIV. Also in *P1950*, *FBO*, *Loquitur* and all editions of *CP*. Reprinted in *Sum* 5 (April 1965), n.pag., *Guedalla* D19, with credit line, 'From "Poems: 1950", The Cleaners' Press, Galveston'; and in *Georgia Straight*, n.pag., *Guedalla* D34.

Notes

2. rift. OED n.2.2.b: 'An opening or break in clouds or mist'. Citation for Mandeville. Cp. Milton, *Paradise Regained*, IV. 410–13: 'the clouds / From many a horrid rift abortive poured / Fierce rain with lightning mixed.'

11. Elysium. Homeric Elysian fields, a land to which heroes pass without dying; or the lower world described by Latin poets where the good spirits of the dead reside.

20 Vestiges

BB's daughter Bourtai, born in Rapallo in 1932, was named after the wife of Genghis Khan, betrothed to him while still young, whose name (also rendered Börte) is said to mean 'grey-eyed'.

▪ **A presumably exact version of Jengiz Khan's correspondence with Chang Chun exists in Bretschneider's *Mediaeval Researches from Eastern Asiatic Sources*. Others more competent than I may prefer to investigate it in the Si-Yu-Ki of Li Chi Chang, one of Chang Chun's disciples who made the journey with him and recorded the correspondence. Pauthier rendered that work, according to Bretschneider, very imperfectly into French.** BB owned Bretschneider's book.

Publication history

Written in Rapallo, 1931. Titled 'Jenghis' in *CE*. Published in *P1950*, *FBO*, *Loquitur* and all editions of *CP*. Reprinted in *The Art of Poetry*, ed. Hugh Kenner (New York: Holt, Rinehart, and Winston, 1959), 106, *Guedalla* B7; and *Tri-Quarterly* 21 (Spring 1971), 34–5, *Guedalla* D35, a special issue reprinted as *Contemporary British Poetry* (Chicago: Tri-Quarterly, 1971), ed. John Matthias and reissued as *23 Modern British Poets* (Chicago: Swallow Press, 1971), *Guedalla*. B15.

Notes

I. 3. chivvied. Harassed. Cp. Joyce, *Ulysses* II: 'a pen chivvying her brood of cygnets'; and Kipling, 'The Lost Legion', 11: 'So some of us chivvy the slaver'. BB described the police chivvying Tom Pickard in an unpublished letter dated May Day 1970, quoted in a bookseller's catalogue.

I. 5. Franks. BB owned a copy of Lewis Sergeant, *The Franks.*

I. 6. Yellow River. Chutsai (see below) collected taxes on the north side of the Yellow River.

I. 7. Temuchin. Genghis; see below.

I. 13. Chin. The Chin (now more usually spelled Jin) Dynasty (1115–1234), ravaged by the Mongols under Genghis Khan between 1205 and 1209.

I. 15. Jengiz. Genghis Khan (1162–1227), Mongolian conqueror.

I. 16. Yen. Beijing.

Windy Shore. Cp. Matthew Arnold's 'The Forsaken Merman', 26.

I. 17. Chutsai. Chinese statesman captured by Genghis during the occupation of Beijing in 1215.

I. 18. That Baghdad banker. See *Makin*, 61, and n. 66 on that page, comparing EP's attacks on usury with this poem's attack on greed. BB sent a TS entitled 'Local Credit' to Harriet Monroe in 1933 or 1934. Many years later, in a notebook of draft materials for *Briggflatts*, BB wrote variations on the lines, eventually discarded:

> Cash corrodes scalpels, credit diverts
> prognosis, gain is a load on the wrist

(*Briggflatts notebook*, 42, 43, 44 at SUNY Buffalo). Cp. *FBO* 32.

II. 1. Chang Chun. According to BB's source, Bretschneider, Ch'ang Ch'un was 'a Taoist monk of great repute for wisdom and sanctity. He was born A.D. 1148' in Shan tung. 'In the beginning of the thirteenth century he was held in great respect in the courts.' Genghis, 'after his invasion of Northern China, heard of the great sage, and sent him a flattering invitation to come to his court. In the meanwhile, the Mongol chief undertook his expedition to Western Asia, and Ch'ang Ch'un was obliged, not withstanding his advanced age, to abandon his recluse life in the mountains of Shan tung, and expose himself to the dangers of a long journey through Central Asia to Persia and the frontiers of India, where he met the great conqueror. The journey there and back occupied three years, 1221–1224' (Bretschneider, vol. 1, 35).

Genghis's 15 May 1219 letter to Ch'ang Ch'un – probably written by Chutsai – is quoted in Bretschneider (excerpted here; emphasis mine, to indicate words or wording used by BB):

'Heaven has abandoned China owing to its haughtiness and extravagant luxury. But I, living in the northern wilderness, have not inordinate passions. I hate luxury and exercise moderation. I have only one coat and one *food*. I eat the same *food* and am dressed in the same tatters as my humble herdsmen. I consider the people my children, and take an interest in *talent*ed men as if they were my brothers. We always agree in our principles, and we are always united by mutual affection. At military exercises I am always in the front, and in time of battle am never behind. In the space of *seven years* I have succeeded in accomplishing a great work and uniting the whole world in *one empire*. I have not myself distinguished qualities . . . To *cross a river* we make *boats and rudders*. Likewise we invite *sage* men, and choose out [our] assistants for *keep*ing the *empire* in good *order*. Since the time I came to the throne I have always taken to heart the ruling of my people; but I could not find worthy men to occupy the places of the *three* (kung) and the *nine* (k'ing). With respect to these circumstances I inquired, and heard that thou, master, hast penetrated the truth, and that thou walkest in the path of right. Deeply learned and much experienced, thou hast much explored the laws. Thy sanctity is become manifest. Thou hast conserved the rigorous rules of the ancient *sages*. Thou art endowed with the eminent *talent*s of celebrated men . . . We are separated by mountains and plains of great extent, and I cannot meet thee. I can only descend from the throne and stand by the side. I have *fasted and washed*. *I have* ordered my adjutant, *Lui Chung Lu* . . . to prepare an *escort and a cart* for thee. . . . I hope that at least thou wilt leave me a trifle of thy wisdom . . . Given on the 1st day of the 5th month [15 May], 1219' (Bretschneider, vol. 1, 37–9).

II. 7. Lords of Cathay. Mandeville describes the lords of Cathay in his *Travels*, 'The Great Khan of Cathay', chap. 23.

II. 18, 23. Chang; Liu Chung Lu. Genghis's adjutant; variant spelling from source (see above).

Chang: I am old. Cp. Bretschneider, vol. 1, 40–1: 'I confess that in worldly matters I am dull, and have not succeeded in investigating the *tao*, although I tried hard in every possible way. I have grown old and am not yet dead . . . I am old and infirm and fear that I shall be unable to endure the pains of such a long journey, and that perhaps I cannot reach your majesty; and even should I reach, I would not be good for anything . . . My appearance is parched, my body is weak. I am waiting for your majesty's order. Written in the 3rd month [April] of 1220.'

II. 25. girls. Cp. Bretschneider, vol.1, 43–4: 'Although I am only a savage of the mountains, how can I travel in the company of girls?'

21 Two Photographs

In *CE* as Ode XXXV. First published in *P1950*. Also in *FBO*, *Loquitur* and all editions of *CP*. Reprinted in *King Ida's Watch Chain* (Link One, n.d., ?1965), *Guedalla* D22, n.pag.; in *Georgia Straight*, n.pag., *Guedalla* D34; and in a pamphlet edited by Guedalla, distributed at the Modern British Poetry Conference, 18–20 October 1974, Polytechnic of Central London, *Guedalla* B21.

22 'Mesh cast for mackerel'

In *CE* as Ode VIII. First published in *Poetry* 45, no. 1 (October 1934), 13, *Guedalla* D9, under title, 'Fishermen'. Also in *P1950*, *FBO*, *Loquitur* and all editions of *CP*. Reprinted in *Sum* 5 (April 1965), n.pag., *Guedalla* D19, with credit line, 'From "Poems: 1950", The Cleaners' Press, Galveston'; in *King Ida's Watch Chain*, n.pag., *Guedalla* D22, without a title; in *Georgia Straight*, n.pag., *Guedalla* D34; and in *The Ubyssey* 52, no. 19 (20 November 1970), 13, a student newspaper at the University of British Columbia, Vancouver, *Guedalla* D33.

Note

1. mackerel. Cp. the conclusion of Swift's *Tale of a Tub*: 'I am living fast to see the time, when a book that misses its tide, shall be neglected, as the moon by day, or like mackerel a week after the season.'

23 The Passport Officer

In *CE* as Ode XXXII. First published by EP in *Act. Ant.*, *Guedalla* B4. Also in *P1950*, *FBO*, *Loquitur* and all editions of *CP*. Reprinted in *King Ida's Watch Chain* (Link One, n.d., ?1965), *Guedalla* D22, n.pag.

24 'Vessels thrown awry by strong gusts'

▪ **The case was tried in 1917 or 1919, I forget.** [*CE*: **'The case referred to was tried in 1918.'**] In an introduction to the poem at a reading given on 20 April 1976 at Allentown Community Center, Buffalo, NY, BB remarked that the poem is based on a **'piece of litigation . . . in the House of Lords in 1919'** (*Lesch*, 98).

Publication history

In *CE* as Ode IX, with title, 'Shipping Intelligence'. First published in *P1950*. Also in *FBO*, *Loquitur* and all editions of *CP*. Rejected by *Poetry* in 1932.

Notes

2. *broach to*. *OED* v.2.1: 'To veer suddenly so as to turn the side to windward, or to meet the sea.' Cp. R. H. Dana, *Two Years Before the Mast*, xxxii, 126: 'They hove the wheel up just in time to save her from broaching to.'

4. *flotsam*. *OED* 1: '*Law*. Such part of the wreckage of a ship or its cargo as is found floating on the surface of the sea.'

16. *purlieus*. Outskirts; outside of official jurisdiction, as opposed to the *precincts*. BB wrote to Harriet Monroe on 27 September 1932 that, in Makin's summary, 'He has heard argued in the Lords a case concerning a ship torpedoed by a U-boat at the entrance to Le Havre harbour; payment of the insurance depended on whether the ship was in the "purlieus" or the "precincts." Bunting notes that he has dropped the U-boat, as irrelevant to his purposes, and relocated the incident in the Aegean or the Ionian Sea' (*Makin*, 256, n. 38). Cp. Milton, *Paradise Lost*, II. 832–3: 'A place of bliss / In the purlieus of Heav'n'; Tennyson, *In Memoriam*, LXXXIX. 12: 'dusty purlieus of the law'; and Wordsworth, 'Peter Bell', 86–7: 'These nether precincts do not lack / Charms of their own'; *The Excursion*, VIII. 369: 'forest purlieus'.

7. *Lord Shaw had it argued / a week in the Lords*. Thomas Shaw, Lord Shaw of Dunfermline (1850–1937), noted lawyer and jurist.

19. *donkeyman*. Man in charge of a donkey-engine, a steam-powered winch used for hoisting or pumping.

24. *Kingsway*. Former location, in London, of the Meteorological Office, originally formed as a department of the Board of Trade and brought under the auspices of the Air Ministry during World War I.

25. *Epicurus*. *Lesch* (99) remarks: 'Forces beyond the control of men performing their duty mock the belief of Epicuru[s], that the practice of virtue leads to happiness.'

28. *Lord Carson*. Baron Edward Henry Carson, MP in the British parliament (1892–1921); he successfully defended Lord Queensberry in the Oscar Wilde libel case, and also led the opposition to the Irish Home Rule bill.

32. *gardens sacred to Tethys*. The sea is compared here to the gardens of the Titaness who was Oceanus' consort and progenitor of the gods.

25 'As appleblossom to crocus'

In *CE* as Ode XIX. First published in *P1950*. Also in *FBO*, *Loquitur* and all editions of *CP*.

Note

17–18. Postume. Reference to Horace, *Odes*, II. 14 ('Eheu fugaces, Postume, Postume') – cp. BB's version of that poem in 'Overdrafts'.

26 'Two hundred and seven paces'

In an introduction to the poem at a reading given on 20 April 1976 at Allentown Community Center, Buffalo, NY, BB remarked that the poem is about a **'gentleman whom I observed in a pub at the Kensington Road in about 1924 or 25'** (*Lesch*, 102). In 1979, he said that this took place **'in about 1926 or so'** (reading, Keats House, London, in *Swigg*).

Publication history

In *CE* as Ode XXVI. Also in *P1950*, *FBO*, *Loquitur* and all editions of *CP*. Reprinted in *Granta* 71, no. 12457 (6 November 1965), 14, *Guedalla* D24.

Note

19. fire-extinguisher. Jazz-age slang for chaperone.

27 'On highest summits dawn comes soonest'

Cp. EP's experiments with Japanese poetic forms in *Lustra* (1915), e.g. 'In a Station of the Metro' and 'Alba'.

Publication history

Originally section 3 of 'Trinacria' (in *UO*, below). First published as a separate poem in *FBO*. Also in *Loquitur* and all editions of *CP*.

28/29

These poems were each attributed to 'Hafiz' when first published in *Bozart-Westminster* (Oglethorpe University, GA), 1935, *Guedalla* D10. The issue was titled 'A Collection of English and American Poetry collected by T. C.

Wilson, John Drummond and Ezra Pound'. BB deleted the attributions in subsequent publications of the poems, and responded to a query about this: **'If I'd thought there was very much of Hafez left in the product, I'd have put it with the other translations'** (BB to Forde, 23 May 1972; quoted *Forde*, 131). Hafez (Khwāja Šamsu d-Dīn Muḥammad Hāfez-e Šīrāzī, 1315–90) was one of the most popular of all the Persian poets. He perfected the *ghazal* and influenced Western poets as various as Goethe and Robert Bly. His poems describe the intoxications of love and wine, which some interpret mystically. It is conceivable that BB was aware of James Clarence Mangan's versions and imitations of Persian *ghazals* and other poems, including those of Hafiz; more certainly Kipling's 'Certain Maxims of Hafiz' and Goethe's *Westöstlicher Divan* (1814–18), the latter inspired by, yet not translations of, Hafiz. See Appendix II. B., Bunting's foreword to Omar Pound's *Arabic & Persian Poems in English*.

28 'You leave'

In a letter to LZ, 29 September 1935 (held at HRC; quoted *Forde*, 129), BB sent a version of the poem with the attribution: '(Hafiz, a rubay)'. The *rubai*, an invention of the Persian poets (possibly Rūdakī), was introduced to the West by Edward FitzGerald's *The Rubáiyát of Omar Khayyám*. (BB felt that FitzGerald's version was **'splendid and inadequate'** – limited by **'certain shortcomings of English poetry in general'** and called him **'a great adapter of a greater poet'** ('The Lion and Lizard', *Three Essays*, 30); Quartermain comments that BB 'found its loftiness of language a betrayal of the perceived world as well as of Omar' (*Quartermain*, 13). Forde characterizes the form of the *rubai* as 'four half-lines of which line 1, 2, and 4 are in monorhyme; line 3 usually outside the rhyme pattern marks an anticipatory pause before the climactic last line' (*Forde*, 129). BB retains the practice of introducing the *rubai* with two or three long syllables; BB described the form to LZ as **'epigrammatic in character, severe and Gregorian in effect'** BB's letter to LZ of 30 August 1933 included a transliterated and untranslated version of a *rubai* by Khayyam (given in *Forde*, 131). LZ, perhaps stimulated by BB's interest in Persian poetry, quoted from Hafiz in his *Zukofsky*, 141–2, and from FitzGerald's *Rubáiyát of Omar Khayyám*, 122, *Guedalla* B9.

Publication history

In *CE* as Ode XXII with title, 'The Shirazi Blues' and attribution to 'Hafiz' at foot of poem; Hafez was from Shiraz, Persia's capital city. First published in *Boz-West*, 10–11, *Guedalla* D10, with title, 'The Shirazi Blues', and attribution, at the foot of the poem, to 'Muhammad Shams-ud-Din Hafiz'. No attribution in later published versions. In *P1950* as Ode 27. Also in *FBO*, *Loquitur* and all editions of *CP*. Reprinted in *King*

Ida's Watch Chain, n.pag., *Guedalla* D22, without a title. The poem also was used, without attribution to BB, in Kenneth Patchen's *The Journal of Albion Moonlight* (New Directions, 1941), 26.

29 'Southwind, tell her what'

Cp. generally Shelley, 'Ode to the West Wind'.

Publication history

In *CE* as Ode XX, with attribution, 'Hafiz', at foot of poem. First published in *Boz-West*, 10, *Guedalla* D10, as 'III' in a numbered group, with attribution to 'Hafiz' at foot of poem. No attribution in later published versions. In *P1950* as Ode 28. Also in *FBO*, *Loquitur* and all editions of *CP*. Reprinted in *King Ida's Watch Chain*, n.pag., *Guedalla* D22, without a title; and *Georgia Straight*, n.pag., *Guedalla* D34. Published in English in *Anglia* 36, no. 4 (October 1970), 54–5, *Guedalla* D32; *Anglia* was 'a quarterly magazine in the Russian language prepared for the Foreign Office by the Central Office of Information, for sale throughout the USSR'.

Note

1. *Southwind*. BB also uses the word in 'Overdrafts', 'Darling of Gods and Men . . .'

30 The Orotava Road

Titled 'Traffic: Santa Cruz de Tenerife' in draft sent to LZ (MS *ca.*1935; held at HRC). BB introduced the poem at a reading by saying that it was written **'to see how much I could annex of Dr Carlos Williams's early technique about the year 1935, before he started writing *Paterson*'** (Morden Tower reading, 27 February 1965, on Harvard Poetry Room disc).

Publication history

First published in *P1950*, not as an Ode, but in a section by itself. Also in *FBO*, *Loquitur* and all editions of *CP*. Reprinted in *King Ida's Watch Chain*, n.pag., *Guedalla* D22; in *Cambridge Opinion* 41 (n.d. [?1965 or 1966]), 21, *Guedalla* D25; in *Georgia Straight*, n.pag., *Guedalla* D34; and *Shake the Kaleidoscope*, 6–7, later issued as *The Best of Modern Poetry* (1975).

Notes

[Title] Orotava Road. Located on Tenerife, in the Canary Islands, where BB lived in 1933–6; see *Makin*, chap. 5. BB wrote to EP, **'The people on this island so unspeakable, and the food so uneatable, they make prolonged residence impossible, in spite of such great cash saving . . . One village on the south hasnt had a drop of rain for over five years now. A lot of the people live in caves, murder each other constantly . . . In the mountains east of Santa Cruz they . . . eat semi-ground wheat dampened with a little water or spittle: and a couple of handfuls does them'** ('Twentyumph' January 1934; Yale). **'Population of uncivil lunatics, unclean moreover'** (8 February 1934; Yale). **'Nothing but a tentpeg through the skull could distract me more completely than the sort of life we've had to live [here]'** (Undated [1935/6?]; Yale). Letters quoted *Makin*, 74–5. **'I don't like Spaniards at all as a rule. I like them better than Germans, but they are a cruel people, the Spaniards. One gets tired of their cruelty, one gets tired of the neglect of comfort, of the horrible food the Spaniards find good enough for themselves even when they're rich enough to afford very decent food. But, the climate in the Canaries is delightful. The scenery is very good. The girls are very pretty'** (*Descant*, [15]).

2. *waggon*. A typical Northumbrian spelling (*EDD* 1 [9]).

9–10. In margin of MS sent to LZ (held at HRC), beside 9–10, BB wrote **'cf. a line of yours'**. But *Lesch* (111) finds no parallel line in LZ's *55 Poems* (1923–35).

11, 13. *'Hu! vaca! Hu! vaca! . . . 'Adios caballero'*. Roughly, Spanish for 'Where are you going, cow!' and 'Good-bye, sir.' BB wrote to EP, **'the natives are so disgusting I refuse to learn Spanish'** (8 February 1934, Yale; quoted *Makin*, 75).

34. *wimple*. Cp. *Gesta Romanorum*, LXIX, 317: 'The emperesse hydde hire face with a wympill' (BB owned an 1877 ed. of *Gesta Romanorum*); also Scott, *The Lay of the Last Minstrel*, V. , xvii. 4, 'White was her whimple, and her veil', and *Ivanhoe*, XLII, 'Her flowing wimple of black cypress'.

36–7. In the margin of the MS sent to LZ, beside 36–7, BB wrote **'cf. W.C.W.'** (*Lesch*, 113). No direct allusion has been traced, but Charles Tomlinson and Anthony Suter suggest that the poem's structure is indebted to William Carlos Williams's triplets, e.g. 'To Elsie' (1922).

At the end of the MS sent to LZ, BB wrote: **'Altogether, it doesn't answer! Wont do! To hell with all these legacies of that ass Flaubert'** (*Lesch*, 111).

31 *O ubi campi!* / 'The soil sandy and the plow light, neither'

Titled 'Farmer' in draft to LZ *(ca.*1935; held at HRC). In an introduction to the poem at a reading recorded at Harvard University in 1976 BB said, **'Here's the American farmer in the 1930s. Middlewestern farmer whose fields have been blown away by the wind.'**

Publication history

First published as Ode 29 in *P1950*. Published in *Nine* 4, vol. 2, no. 3 (August 1950), 217–19, *Guedalla* D14, and *Imagi* 14, vol. 5, no. 3 (1951), n.pag., *Guedalla* D17, as '2' of 'two poems'. Also in *FBO*, *Loquitur* and all editions of *CP*. Reprinted in *King Ida's Watch Chain*, n.pag., *Guedalla* D22, as 'O ubi campi'; and in *Granta* 71, no. 12457 (6 November 1965), 14, *Guedalla* D24.

Notes

[Epigraph] O ubi campi! 'O where are those fields!' From Virgil's *Georgics*, II, 486. In the draft sent to LZ, the inscription reads **'*O fortunatos nimium:* / also: *O ubi campi!*'** *O fortunatos nimium, sua si bona norint, agricolas*: 'O farmers, happy beyond measure, could they but know their blessings!' (Loeb, rev. ed.).

3. cropping. Cp. Milton, *Paradise Lost*, V. 67–8: 'O fruit divine, / Sweet of thyself, but much more sweet thus cropped.' Since the poem is about the American farmer, note *OED* v., 6.a: '*trans.* To cause to bear a crop; to sow or plant with a crop; to raise crops on. Also *intr.*, to cultivate land; to work as a farmer. Chiefly *U.S.*'

13. full-close. Musical term referring to the 'perfect' or 'authentic' cadence in ecclesiastical music.

16. doss-and-grub. A cheap lodging house.

32 'Let them remember Samangan, the bridge and tower'

▪ **In Samangan Rustam begot Sohrab.** Reference to classical Persian epic, Ferdowsī's *Shāh-nāma* (completed 1010), which elaborated legendary adventures of Rustam, son of Queen Roudaba, over a period of three centuries. In the *Shāh-nāma*, Rustam marries the daughter of the king of Samangan, a border province of Turán. BB had found a French translation of the epic in a bookstall on the quays of Genoa in the early 1930s; see Appendix II. Cp. Matthew Arnold, 'Sohrab and Rustum', and note to 'A Song for Rustam'. BB named two of his children for figures in Ferdowsī: daughter Roudaba (b. 1934) and his son Rustam (b. 1937, d. 1953). In the *Shāh-nāma* Roudaba is the mother of Rustam, its main hero. LZ, perhaps stimulated by BB's interest in the *Shāh-nāma*, quoted from translations of the work in his *Zukofsky*, vol. 1, 121, *Guedalla* B9. See also notes to 'A Song for Rustam' in *UO*, below, a poem on the death of his son.

Publication history

First published as Ode 30 in *P1950*. Also in *FBO*, *Loquitur* and all editions of *CP*. Reprinted in *The Art of Poetry*, ed. Hugh Kenner (New York: Holt, Rinehart, and Winston, 1959), 117, *Guedalla* B7, and *Inquiry* 1, no. 22 (October 30, 1978), 27 (accompanying Kenner's review of *CP1978*).

Note

9. *usurers*. Makin compares EP's views on usury to BB's, *Makin*, 61, and n. 66 on that page. Several years later, in a notebook of draft materials for *Briggflatts*, BB wrote variations on the lines, eventually discarded:

> Cash corrodes scalpels, credit diverts
> prognosis, gain is a load on the wrist.'

(*Briggflatts notebook*, 42, 43, 44 at SUNY Buffalo). Cp. BB's 'Vestiges'. Also Kipling, 'The Peace of Dives', 45: 'And the blood of Man to filthy usury!'

33 *To Anne de Silver* / 'Not to thank dogwood nor'

▪ **The cool breeze of a pure, uncomprehending rendering of Handel's best known aria.**

Suter suggests the poem imitates LZ. See *Lesch*, 124.

Publication history

First published as Ode 31 in *P1950*. Also in *FBO*, *Loquitur* and all editions of *CP*. Reprinted in *Sum* 5 (April 1965), n.pag., *Guedalla* D19, as Ode 31, with credit line, 'From "Poems: 1950", The Cleaners' Press, Galveston'; in *King Ida's Watch Chain* (Link One, n.d., ?1965), n.pag., *Guedalla* D22, titled 'Ode 31'; and in *Makaris* (Christmas 1969, published at Durham University), *Guedalla* D30a.

[Dedication] Anne de Silver. Daughter (b. 1917) of Margaret de Silver. BB had an affair with Margaret in London in the late 1920s and thanks her in the preface to *RM* **'for bailing me out of Fleet Street'**. In an interview, he elaborated: **'She had been left a great deal of money by her husband. She was the widow of one of the founders of the Civil Liberties Union, and she spent this money in the course of her lifetime very largely on subsidizing artists, poets, politicians, lawyers, civil liberties, etc. Before she died, I believe she got rid of practically all of it, just giving it away in this very wonderful and rather discriminating generosity. I met her and found when she had left London that she had left word with Otto Theiss [literary editor of *The Outlook*] that I was to have a subsidy of 200 pounds a year for two years to give me a chance to get going writing. I could hardly refuse! It was the greatest possible help'** (*Descant*, [11–12]). The subsidy terminated with his marriage to Marian Gray Culver in 1930 (see *Burton*, 149–51, 223, 228, 259, 343–5). BB had heard Anne, aged twenty, sing Handel's 'Largo' in one of Margaret's luxurious homes; years later, describing the writing of this poem, he recalled how Anne's singing **'in a light sweet insufficient voice . . . moved me as a clear block of marble must move a sculptor'** (quoted *Alldritt*, 93, apparently from a letter to Margaret dated 28 August 1948; see *Alldritt*, 204, n. 2, in which it is speculated that BB had somehow offended Anne).

34 *To Violet, with prewar poems. /* 'These tracings from a world that's dead'

Draft sent to LZ (held at HRC).

▪ **Perhaps it is superfluous to mention Darwin's *Formation of Vegetable Mould*.** The full title of Darwin's book, a copy of which BB owned, is *The Formation of Vegetable Mould Through the Action of Worms, with Observations on Their Habits*. In a 1970 review, BB wrote that Hugh MacDiarmid **'sees things washed clean of irrelevancies as Darwin did. Suckling poets should be fed on Darwin till they are filled with the elegance of things seen or heard or touched. Words cannot come near it, though they name things'** (BB review, 'Thanks to the Guinea Worm', of MacDiarmid's *More Collected Poems* and *A Clyack-Sheaf*, *Agenda* 8, nos. 3–4 [Autumn–Winter 1970], 119). In 1978, BB said: **'I think that a man who wants to write in the 20th century makes a great mistake if he doesn't begin by reading *The Origin of Species*, where he will find the most magnificent example of the building up and testing of [a] hypothesis . . . And Darwin was a very good prose writer. He does not of course go**

in for purple patches, but for what he wants to do, his prose is not only adequate, it's very hard indeed to think of any way of improving it. There are many books that are neglected and that ought to be read continually by literary men, but probably the thing which sixth forms, let us say, who are going in for the literary sides of the curriculum, should all be able to do, is to read *The Origin of Species*' (*Mottram*, 9). In an interview, BB said, **'I have tried off and on to get English departments to make *The Origin of Species* a set book, but they scoff. So no Lucretius for our literature'** (P. Craven and M. Heyward, 'An Interview with Basil Bunting', 30). A song gently lampooning Darwin appears in a book BB owned, an 1897 ed. of *The Scottish Students' Song Book*, 52; note also Kipling, 'Our Fathers of Old', 9–10: 'Anything green that grew out of the mould / Was an excellent herb to our fathers of old.'

Publication history

First published in *Poetry* 58, no. 6 (September 1941), 304, *Guedalla* D12, with title, 'To Violet', with subheading, '*with prewar poems*'. In *P1950* as Ode 32. Also in *FBO*, *Loquitur* and all editions of *CP*. Published in English in *Anglia* 36, no. 4 (October 1970), 54–5, *Guedalla* D32.

Notes

[Dedication] Violet. While stationed in Scotland at the beginning of World War II, BB became fond of a young woman named Violet Harris, a local secretary who typed up his poems and to whom BB became deeply attached; see *Burton*, 273–4. When the poem was accepted by *Poetry*, he wrote to LZ that he was pleased that Violet would **'see *her* poem in print'** (BB to LZ, 9 Sept. 1941).

4. *pavements laid for worms to soil*. Introducing a 1981 reading of the poem, BB said, **'That refers to Darwin's book about earthworms'** (quoted Eric Mottram, 'Basil Bunting: Human Framework and "Nature"', *Caddel*, 81); see note above about Darwin. Gilonis compares this line to a sentence from *Formation of Vegetable Mould*: 'In the morning, after there has been heavy rain, the film of mud or of very fine sand over gravel-walks is often plainly marked with [worm] tracks' [London, 1881, 14–15] – and with lines from Lucretius's *De rerum natura* – 'we perceive . . . worms to teem when excessive rains bring rottenness over the earth' (Loeb). For more on Lucretius, see also notes to 'Attis' and *Briggflatts* III. 68–71.

9–10. *this unread memento be / the only lasting part of me*. **'I've no longings for personal immortality, and if there were a reasonable system of publishing anonymously, anonymous my stuff would be. What the hell has posterity to do with me?'** (BB to LZ, 5 March 1949; quoted *Lesch*, 127).

Forde (96) suggests that the form of this poem is derived from the odes of François de Malherbe (1555–1628) (cp. *A La Reine, sur les heureux succès de sa régence*, discussed *Lesch*, 128), and quotes BB to LZ, 6 August 1953: **'I've been thinking when worries let me about how and where I got whatever I know and feel about poetry, and the more I think the bigger Malherbe's part in it seems . . . Horace gave me the first inkling of how it was done (odes). Malherbe produced all I afterwards found in Ez's writing except what I'd already got from Horace [Malherbe was] the man who never forgot music for a moment and who, for all his determination to eat more toads than the next fellow, ate 'em with such a clean melody and so little mumbo-jumbo that he stands inspection still without any allowances for period etc.'** (*Forde*, 96 and 250; *Lesch*, 127). A number of Malherbe's lyrics were composed to fit, or were later given, musical settings, which would have been significant to BB. In 1934, BB had written to LZ that he admired Malherbe because whenever he had written anything **'he would go down to the market and get the women there to read it to him, and he would pay them if there were any words they didn't know. He didn't expect them to understand what he was aiming at or even enjoy the poem, but he wished above all things to be meticulous about keeping his language clear and plain'** (27 April 1934; quoted *Quartermain*, 13).

See also note to 'A Song for Rustam', below.

35 'Search under every veil'

Draft sent to LZ (held by HRC).

'[T]he change of weight in the middle of "Search under every veil" is very deliberate: up till then I have only a stock sentimental poem which I attempt to raise suddenly onto another level altogether. The fact that you dont grumble at the sentimental beginning is quite possibly due to what is thus reflected back from the end, which I think I couldnt have got in the same light movement' (BB to LZ, 28 July 1949; quoted *Forde*, 92, and *Lesch*, 132).

Publication history

First published as Ode 33 in *P1950*. Also in *FBO*, *Loquitur* and all editions of *CP*. Reprinted in *King Ida's Watch Chain*, n.pag., *Guedalla* D22, as 'Ode 33'.

36 'See! Their verses are laid'

▪ **A friend's misunderstanding obliges me to declare that the implausible optics of this poem are not intended as an argument for the existence of God, but only suggest that the result of a successful work of art is more than the sum of its meanings and differs from them in kind.** The friend was probably LZ, to whom BB had written: **'The words that bother you in "See their verses are laid": "impending" is weak, but I couldnt find what's wanted – what's the word for quarter of the solid formed by the rotation of an ellipse on its axis, and has it an adjective? "shouldering" probably has for you moral echoes which havent worried me. I meant it just physically, in which sense it is exact. Neatness: the civil service air of an embassy overcoming my natural untidiness? Energy? Of a kind. Both [Odes 36 and 35] are attempts to concentrate a lot of weight behind one punch. The first is artful – makes a feint to deceive the reader: the other "comes out fighting". There's nothing more to it. One could easily have said as much in a page and a half'** (BB to LZ, 28 July 1949; quoted *Forde*, 95, and *Lesch*, 134–5).

Cp. EP, Canto 45, 1–5. Also *Briggflatts* I. 114–17 and II. 130–5.

Publication history

First published as Ode 34 in *P1950*. Also in *FBO*, *Loquitur* and all editions of *CP*. Reprinted in *King Ida's Watch Chain*, n.pag., *Guedalla* D22, as 'Ode 34'. Published in English in *Anglia* 36, no. 4 (October 1970), 54–5, *Guedalla* D32.

Note

3–4. lapis lazuli / white marble. Cp. Yeats, 'Lapis Lazuli', especially 30: 'Who handled marble as if it were bronze.'

37 On the Fly-Leaf of Pound's Cantos

Lesch (137) points out that BB had received EP's Pisan Cantos in June 1949, and discussed them in letters to LZ (reproduced in *Lesch*, 428–30). *Forde* observes (93) that the poem was written during the time of EP's commitment to St Elizabeths Hospital.

'Once, in the period when he was supposed not to say a word to anybody for many years, Pound sent me a little tape which he had spoken. It had a small amount of letter on it, and then having exhausted what he had to say, I suppose, it wasn't much, he started reading my poems. He read them very well. And he read right through until he came to "[On] the Fly-Leaf of Pound's Cantos." And then he started it. Half-way, he got stuck. He started again and he got stuck half-way, he started the third

time, he said, "God dammit, I cahn't!" And he stopped. And I never felt so much moved, he had obviously felt this as an enormous compliment' (reading, Riverside Studios, London, February 1982, in *Swigg*). Denis Goacher remembered a conversation with EP in 1954: 'He said, "Basil wrote a small amount of extremely good poetry, some of which I even remember." Then he brought out his copy of the collected *Cantos* up to that date, because he had been re-reading them for the purposes of *Rock Drill*. There was, in front, a letter from Basil Bunting containing his poem "On the fly-leaf of Pound's 'Cantos'", which begins '"There are the Alps". Pound took out this letter, in which Basil had typed out his poem, and when he read this to me, he broke down in the middle of it. He couldn't finish it because he was so upset. It is not often that one poet gives another poet as great a compliment as that' ('Denis Goacher Talks about Basil Bunting', *Caddel*, 207). The letter, dated 12 January 1951, contains a somewhat longer version of the poem (printed above, in *Fragments and False Starts*, p. 255); it is held by the Lilly Library, Indiana University.

Publication history

First published in *Agenda* 4, no. 2 (October–November 1965), 28, *Guedalla* D23 (an issue dedicated to EP), and *FBO*. Also in *Loquitur* and all editions of *CP*. Reprinted in *The Oxford Book of Twentieth Century English Verse*, ed. Philip Larkin (Oxford: Oxford University Press, 1973), 322, *Guedalla* B18, and *The Faber Book of Twentieth-Century Verse*, 3rd ed., ed. John Heath-Stubbs and David Wright (London: Faber & Faber, 1975), 68, *Guedalla* B22.

Notes

1. Alps. The year after this poem was written, BB declined Peter Russell's request for work to be included in a volume dedicated to EP: **'The Cantos are as much a fact as the Alps & as little likely to be lost sight of, so that I just dont have anything to say. There they are'** (BB to Russell, 28 February 1950; quoted *Lesch*, 137–8). Cp. EP on Villon: 'Villon is no theorist, he is an objective fact' (*The Spirit of Romance* [London: J. M. Dent, 1910], 187). Also Pope, 'An Essay on Criticism', 225–32: 'So pleas'd at first, the towering *Alps* we try, / Mount o'er the Vales, and seem to tread the Sky . . . Th' *increasing* Prospect *tires* our wandring Eyes, / Hills peep o'er Hills, and *Alps* on *Alps* arise!' an image probably derived from Silus Italicus, *Punica* III. 528–35; Wordsworth, 'Peter Bell', 59–60: 'the Alps are here / Like waters in commotion', and *Memorials of a Tour of Italy, 1837*, XXVI. 11: 'the far winding barrier Alps'. Also Wordsworth's note to 'Descriptive Sketches', 347: 'Whoever, in attempting to describe their sublime features, should confine himself to the cold rules of painting would give his reader but a very imperfect idea of those emotions which they have the irresistible power of communicating to the most impassive imaginations', and 593: 'endless Alp of life'. Also *The Prelude* VI, 'Cambridge and the Alps'. Note also Cowley, 'The Motto', 17–18: 'Unpassed Alps stop me, but I'll cut through all, / And march, the Muses' Hannibal.'

4. *et l'on entend . . . le refrain joyeux et leger*. 'And one hears it, maybe, the joyous and light refrain.' From a French–Italian folksong, 'Le Soir à la Montagne'. Alex Niven speculates that the song is alluded to because BB and EP knew it from their time together in Rapallo in the 1930s. (See Niven, 'Towards a New Architecture: Basil Bunting's Postwar Reconstruction').

SECOND BOOK OF ODES

1 'A thrush in the syringa sings'

Draft sent to LZ (held by HRC).

Publication history

First published in *Paris Review* 34 (Summer 1965), 92–3, *Guedalla* D20, and in *CP1968*. In all editions of *CP*, but dated 1964, as is the autograph MS reproduced in *King Ida's Watch Chain*, n.pag., *Guedalla* D22. However, the *Paris Review* version gives the date 1949 beneath the poem. Also published in the *Newcastle Journal* (17 July 1965), 7, *Guedalla* D21; this periodical was owned by the same company as the Newcastle *Evening Chronicle* which employed BB in 1954–66; published in English in *Anglia* 36, no. 4 (October 1970), 54–5, *Guedalla* D32; in *Poetry Brief: an Anthology of Short Poems*, ed. William Cole (New York: Macmillan, 1971), 32; and under title, 'Ode', in *Shake the Kaleidoscope*, 1, later issued as *The Best of Modern Poetry* (1975).

Notes

1. thrush. Cp. Spenser, *The Faerie Queene*, VI. iv. 17–18: 'Abrode to wend, / To take the ayre and heare the thrushes song'; also Scott, *The Lady of the Lake*, III. ii, 18–19: 'The blackbird and the speckled thrush / Good-morrow gave from brake and bush.'

syringa. Or common lilac. Cp. Cowper, *Task* VI. 150: 'Laburnum, rich / In streaming gold; syringa, iv'ry pure.' Jane Austen writes, in a letter (8 February 1807) to her sister, Cassandra, 'I could not do without a syringa, for the sake of Cowper's line.'

2 'Three Michaelmas daisies'

Used for Fulcrum Press's Christmas Card, 1965. First collected in *CP1968*, and included in all subsequent editions.

Note

1. *Michaelmas daisies*. Feast of St Michael, celebrated on 29 September; in England, one of the four quarter days on which payments traditionally fell due. A species of wild aster blooms at Michaelmas. *Burton* (410) remarks that 'Michaelmas represents the fading of the year and a gift of a Michaelmas daisy has traditionally been a way of saying goodbye. But Michaelmas daisies are one of nature's final acts of defiance of winter, providing colour and life deep into the autumn months, and the second stanza is a rousing affirmation of life even as death beckons.'

3 Birthday Greeting

In an introduction to the poem at a reading recorded at Harvard University in 1976 BB said, **'Here's a young lady I met in the Bakhtiari mountains once.'** The Bhaktiari are a nomadic tribe in Iran; BB's second wife, Sima, was a Bakhtiari, and a teenage girl when they married. BB, while serving in the RAF in Persia, wrote to LZ: **'My men became the envy of other units. And out of hours (and out of bounds) they entertained me every now and then as Bakhtiari's should, with pipes and drums, dancers and singers, sweetmeats and rice and strong drink, and a man to fan me all the evening – very welcome in the terrific heat of Khuzistan (139° in the shade – and it had been 145° a little earlier)'** (BB to LZ, 9 May 1943; quoted *Forde*, 47). BB told LZ that he loved the Bakhtiari **'as burningly as ever I loved'** (25 July 1944; quoted *Makin*, 104).

Publication history

First published in *Agenda* 4, nos. 5–6 (Autumn 1966), 3, *Guedalla* D27, with title, 'Birthday Greetings', and dated 'II, 3.1965', and in all editions of *CP*. Dated '1964' in *CP1994/2000*. The *Agenda* text features a hand-cut paper correction, pasted over the last line, to amend an indentation of the line. The poem was issued, with *SBOO* 8, by Unicorn Press as *Two Poems*. Reprinted in *Makaris* (Christmas 1969, published at Durham University), *Guedalla* D30a; in *Georgia Straight*, n.pag., *Guedalla* D34; and in a pamphlet distributed during BB's visit to St Andrews College, Laurinburg, North Carolina, 15–19 April 1976.

Note

10. *fourteen years old*. Cp. Marvell, 'Young Love', 9: 'Common beauties stay fifteen.'

4 'You idiot! What makes you think decay will'

First published in *CP1968*; in all subsequent editions.

Notes

13. unslaked. Cp. Byron, *Childe Harold's Pilgrimage*, IV. cxxiv, 2: 'We gasp away . . . unfound the boon, unslaked the thirst.' (The word occurs, with a different meaning, in Scott, *Old Mortality*, st. xxi: 'Would ye build a wall with unslaked mortar?')

14–16. David . . . Judah. Reference to I Kings 1: 1–4; verse 4: 'And the damsel *was* very fair, and cherished the king, and ministered to him: but the king knew her not.' See also note to *The Spoils*, I. 116, 'Who lent her warmth to dying David'.

5 'Under sand clay. Dig, wait'

▪ ***Canvas udders*, motarekeh mal moy, the cooling water bags carried through the desert. *Dynast*, Abdulaziz Ibn Saud, of the tribe Aneiza.** *Lesch* (294–5): 'Ibn Saud (*ca.*1880–1953) is the man responsible for the formation of the modern state of Saudi Arabia and for initiating the exploitation of its oil. At the turn of the century, he regained his family lands from the tribe which ousted his father from them. He also revived the practice of Wahhābism, an extremist Moslem puritanical movement, in part because he could use this religious fanaticism to his own ends. It allowed him to bring many of the nomadic tribesmen under his control, for he decreed that it was their religious duty to abandon their nomadic existence and build houses at the desert wells.'

Publication history

First published in *CP1968*; in all subsequent editions.

Notes

2. *Billy.* A lightweight metal pot used for boiling water or cooking over a fire, or to carry water.

4. *ice.* On the line, **'where there is ice in his flask'** in *The Spoils* [I], BB had written to LZ (13 March 1951): **'Mine froze at Wadi Mohammerah as late as March, and it's not uncommon in the Syrian desert or that of Northern Arabia, let alone the high desert of Persia.'**

10. *Aneiza, kin.* A kinsman of Ibn Saud, as above; the Anaiza were one of the three largest desert tribes, according to BB (letter to LZ, 19 March 1951).

12. *slaked*. See note to 'unslaked' in *SBOO* 4. *OED* 'slake' v.1 includes citations for Ælfric, St Cuthbert, and *Alexander*. Cp. Spenser, *The Faerie Queene*, III. i. 52–3: 'They slaked had the fervent heat / Of appetite'; Shakespeare, 'The Rape of Lucrece', 424–5: 'His rage of lust by gazing qualified, – / Slak'd not suppress'd'; Chapman, *Odyssey*, XI. 796–7: 'Tormented Tantalus yet could not slake / His burning thirst'; and Scott, *The Lady of the Lake*, II. xiv. 16: 'A mass of ashes slaked with blood.'

6 What the Chairman Told Tom

First published in a limited edition by Pym-Randall, Cambridge, MA (1967). In all editions of *CP*. Reprinted in *Makaris* (8 October 1969, published at Durham University), *Guedalla* D28a/29a; *Georgia Straight*, n.pag., *Guedalla* D34; and in *Tri-Quarterly* 21 (Spring 1971), 35–6, *Guedalla* D35, a special issue reprinted as *Contemporary British Poetry* (Chicago: Tri-Quarterly, 1971), ed. John Matthias and reissued as *23 Modern British Poets* (Chicago: Swallow Press, 1971), *Guedalla*. B15. Appears in *Say It Aloud*, ed. Norman Hidder (London: Hutchinson, 1972), 162–3, *Guedalla* B17, and *The Oxford Book of Twentieth Century English Verse*, 332, *Guedalla* B18. Reprinted in a pamphlet distributed during BB's visit to St Andrews College, Laurinburg, North Carolina, 15–19 April 1976.

Notes

[Title] Tom. Tom Pickard. BB wrote to John Matthias that the poem is a joke (*Forde thesis*, 44). When he read the poem (e.g. Keats House, London, 1979, and Riverside Studios, London, February 1982, in *Swigg*), he used what Caddel characterizes as an 'urban middleclass Tyneside – High Fenham, perhaps, or Gosforth' accent ('Frankly on the Air: A Consideration of Bunting's Readings', *McGonigal & Price*, 60). Pickard claimed in 'Rough Music (Ruff Muzhik)', which appeared in the Spring 2000 issue of *Chicago Review* (15), that the Chairman was based on the Lord Mayor of Newcastle City Council and chairman of the Cultural Activities Committee, Mrs Gladys Robson, 'magistrate, leader of the council'.

7. *opera*. Since the word 'opera' is derived from the Latin word for work, there is perhaps a play on 'work' in 4.

repertory. Mr Shaw, in *Shaw on Theatre*: 'All the players in the country, whether they are British Drama League players or Repertory players or regular professional players' (ed. E. J. West, New York, 1958, 235).

8. *The Desert Song. Desert Song* was a musical play with music by Sigmund Romberg and lyrics by Otto Harbach, Oscar Hammerstein II and Frank Mandel. It opened 30 November 1926 in New York and was produced at the Theatre Royal, Drury Lane [7 April?] 1927; film versions were produced in 1929, 1943 and 1953. A romance set in Morocco, it includes the song, 'The Desert Song'.

28. *Reds*. Communists.

7 *Ille mi par esse deo videtur* / 'O, it is godlike to sit selfpossessed'

'There is a poem, first written by Sappho, one of the two or three poems left us, which was translated, and altered a bit by Catullus. The only place that I know of where the translation seems to me better than the original. Mr. Pound would be angry if he heard me say that, but he is no longer able to hear. Many people have tried to do it, but those who made a good job of the first two lines never succeeded in getting the third . . . So, I have failed as did Ben Jonson. I too have got the first two lines and then had to go off on my own' (introduction to the poem at a reading given on 20 April 1976 at Allentown Community Center, Buffalo, NY; quoted *Lesch*, 298–9). **'Ben Jonson . . . got through the first few lines and then had to go off on something of his own because he couldn't follow the Catullus. And the same thing happened to Campion; he got so far he was going on the Greek, and got lost again, and had to do something else. So I'm not ashamed that the same thing happened to me'** (reading, Keats House, London, 1979, in *Swigg*).

BB wrote to Forde that he intended **'some distant kinship with the Sapphic stanza'** (4 July 1973; quoted *Forde*, 114). Cp. BB's 'Please stop gushing about his pink' in 'Overdrafts'. Also cp. Campion's versions of Catullus V ('My sweetest Lesbia') and VII ('Harden now thy tyred hart . . .' and 'Come, you pretty false-ey'd wanton . . .'); Jonson's of V. 4–6 in 'Song. To Celia', and V. 7–11 and VII in 'To the Same' from *The Forest* V and VI, respectively. Campion and Jonson did not attempt versions of LI, however. Cp. also Byron, 'Translation from Catullus: Ad Lesbiam'.

Publication history

First published in *CP1968*; in all subsequent editions. Also published in English in *Anglia* 36, no. 4 (October 1970), 54–5, *Guedalla* D32; and in *Inquiry* 1, no. 22 (October 30, 1978), 27.

Notes

[Epigraph/title] Ille mi par esse deo videtur. From first line of Catullus LI: 'He seems to me to be equal to a god . . .' (Loeb); note that LZ and Celia Zukofsky also produced versions of Catullus.

8. furlongs. A furlong is an eighth of a mile, roughly 200 metres. Cp. George Eliot, *Daniel Deronda*, II. IV. xxxi: 'She was really getting somewhat febrile in her excitement . . . Was it at the novelty simply, or the almost incredible fulfilment about to be given to her girlish dreams of being "somebody" – walking through her own furlongs of corridor and under her own ceilings of an out-of-sight loftiness.'

8 *All you Spanish ladies* / 'Carmencita's tawny paps'

BB introduced the poem at a reading given on 20 April 1976 at Allentown Community Center, Buffalo, NY, by saying that it is based on a young lady whom he observed in Spain (*Lesch*, 300).

Publication history

First published in *Agenda* 4, nos. 5–6, (Autumn 1966), 3, *Guedalla* D27, with title, 'All you Spanish ladies', and dated 'II. 8. 1965'. Also issued with *SBOO* 3 by Unicorn Press in *Two Poems* (Santa Barbara, CA, 1967). Reprinted in *Makaris* (Christmas 1969, published at Durham University), *Guedalla* D30a. Reprinted in a pamphlet edited by Guedalla, distributed at the Modern British Poetry Conference, 18–20 October 1974, Polytechnic of Central London, *Guedalla* B21. In all editions of *CP*.

Notes

1. tawny. *OED* a. and n.B cites *Alexander*; cp. Thackeray, *Vanity Fair*, chap. xxiv: 'I ain't particular about a shade or so of tawny.'

5, 14. Ay de mi chica! . . . Ay de mi muchachita! 'Woe is me, little child!' . . . 'Woe is me, little girl!' Cp. Rossetti's translation of Cino's 'IX Canzione: His Lament for Selvaggia', in which the phrase 'Ay me!' is repeated several times; also Kipling, 'One Viceroy Resigns', 8: '*Ay de mí!*'

9 'All the cants they peddle'

▪ Whoever has been conned, however briefly, into visiting a 'poets' conference' will need no explanation of this ode.

Publication history

First published in *CP1978*; in all subsequent editions. Reprinted in *Georgia Straight*, n.pag., *Guedalla* D34.

Notes

1. cants. EDD v.[1] and *sb.*[1], 5: 'Gossip, tattle; merry tales; malicious talk'; cp. Burns, 'Epistle to J. Rankine, Enclosing some Poems', 7: 'Ye hae sae monie cracks an' cants'; also 6: 'A tattler, gossip, tale-bearer.' The word also evokes, as the *OED* gives in sb.3, II 'the speech or phraseology of beggars, etc.'; pet phrases, 'a trick of words, esp. a stock phrase that is much affected at the time, or is repeated as a matter of habit of form', 'phraseology taken up and used for fashion's sake, without being a genuine expression of sentiment', etc.

5. stipendiary. OED A.1: 'That receives a stipend.'

15–16. each dancer alone / with his foolhardy feet. Cp. Yeats, 'Mohini Chatterjee', 28: 'Men dance on deathless feet'; also 'Among School Children', 64, 'How can we know the dancer from the dance?'

10 'Stones trip Coquet burn'

'It's a poem about the upper waters of the Coquet River . . . [I]t's only when the lines are put together that it turns into something erotic. And that only because you feel this poem and attribute feeling to the river' (Lesch interview, 24 April 1976; quoted *Lesch*, 302). BB had written to Guedalla earlier: **'Naive people who have seen it rejoice to find me reverting to nature in the neo-Georgian sense; others unnaive complain of my eroticism. Brrr'** (BB to G, 'May day 1970'; held at Durham).

Cp. Horace, *Odes*, III. 13, 'O fons bandusiae.' **'I did a year or two ago a translation of Horace which I think is very much like the tone of Horace's words. But all my life, since I was a youngster, I wanted to do the "*O fons bandusiae*" and I can't even get the first line. Like nearly all of the great poets, Horace depended on sound and the "*O fons bandusiae*" creates throughout, but especially in the first lines, the actual sound of the running water of a stream. You might be able to create a spring in English, perhaps if you were very skilful and able, but it wouldn't bear any resemblance, however unique, to Horace's sounds'** (Lesch interview, 24 April 1976; quoted *Lesch*, 303). (Horace's first lines are: 'O fons Bandusiae, splendidior vitro, / dulci digne mero non sine floribus, / cras donaberis haedo, / cui frons turgida cornibus.') In an interview, BB referred to **'the matchless onomatopoeia of "*O fons bandusiae*"'** (P. Craven and M. Heyward, 'An Interview with Basil Bunting', 30).

'It occurred to me a year or two ago that the Greeks filled their rivers with nymphs. So did the Elizabethans, imitating them. But that the little burns from which the rivers grow are not usually supplied with nymphets. And I love the Coquet River, so there you are!' (reading, Keats House, London, 1979, in *Swigg*). **'[I]f you go near the fountains of the river, where it is very little, it must have nymphettes'** (reading, 1982, in *Swigg*). Nereids, who were saltwater and freshwater nymphs, appear in 'Once, so they say . . .', in 'Overdrafts'.

Cp. also Ronsard's ode, 'Ô Fontaine Bellerie', which is also an adaptation of Horace; and Wordsworth, 'There is a little unpretending Rill'.

Publication history

First published in *Agenda* 8, nos. 3–4 (Autumn–Winter, 1970), 62, *Guedalla* D31, with title, 'Coquet Burn', and *Georgia Straight*, n.pag., *Guedalla* D34. Reprinted in a pamphlet edited by Guedalla, distributed at the Modern British Poetry Conference, 18–20 October 1974, Polytechnic of Central London, *Guedalla* B21. In all editions of *CP* from 1978.

Notes

1. burn. Cp. BB's note to *Briggflatts* I. 70: **We have burns in the east, *becks* in the west, but no brooks or creeks.** See also note to 'The Complaint of the Morpethshire Farmer', 12.

7. midgy. OED cites J. Grahame, *Birds of Scotland*, II. 143: 'The swallow . . . Skims 'long the brook, . . . / Where dance the midgy clouds in warping maze / Confused.'

16. plodge. EDD gives the Northumbrian usage: 'generally used for wading in water'. *OED*: 'Chiefly *dial. Intr.* To wade or walk heavily in water, soft ground, or anything in which the feet sink.' Cp. Robson, *Bards of Tyne* 27, 'To see the folks a' duckin; men an' wives together pludg'd.' Also used in 'That filly couldnt carry a rider nor' in 'Uncollected Overdrafts'. Cp. also possibly Joyce, *Ulysses*, II: 'He plodges through their sump', 'Bloom plodges forward again'.

11 At Briggflatts meetinghouse

'It took me four months to get it right' (BB to JW, 16 March 1975; quoted *Quartermain*, 18). BB wrote to Forde: **'I've written almost nothing for a long time. You will easily imagine that inflation on the scale we are enduring leaves no peace to a man whose income is fixed and very small. More and more has to be done without. I never know two months in advance how we shall live. That is not a circumstance favourable to reflection, let**

alone steady craftsmanship. But I'll put a little bit into the envelope that I concocted for the tercentenary of Briggflatts meeting house, which is being celebrated this spring. It is not easy to write "religious" poetry without falling into a dozen traps: but perhaps I have avoided most of them' (BB to Forde, 11 May 1975; quoted *Forde*, 103–4, 244). **'It's the only time I've ever been able to write a poem for a particular occasion . . . It took me about six months to do it . . . I don't know whether you dislike Roman immensity and exaggeration and Egyptian immensity and exaggeration as much as I do, but I hope you do'** (reading, Riverside Studios, London, February 1982, in *Swigg*).

Publication history

First issued as a broadside in 1975, when BB gave a reading on 20 April at Allentown Community Center, Buffalo, NY. Also published in *Montemora* 2 (Summer 1976), 7, where it is dated 1975, and *Poetry Review* 65, no. 4 (1975), [1], both with subheading, 'Tercentenary'. In all editions of *CP* from 1978.

Notes

[Title] Briggflatts meetinghouse. See headnote for *Briggflatts*.

1. Caddel glosses the first line: 'Boasts (noun, plural) [at which] time mocks [en]cumber Rome'; or, 'The boasts which Rome [metonymically, the culture of ancient Rome, or perhaps the Roman Catholic Church] once made about its permanence now encumber it, and are mocked by the passage of time' (http://www.jacket.zip.com.au/jacket10/bunting-briggflats.html).

cumber. BB uses the word in *Briggflatts* II. 104. *OED* v.1 cites *Alexander*. Cp. Swinburne, 'Evening on the Broads', 13: 'Cover the brood of her worlds that cumber the skies with their blossom'; also Scott, *The Bridal of Triermain*, II. X, 'Cares, that cumber royal sway.' *EDD* cites George Eliot, *Adam Bede*, I. 159: 'I shall be nought but cumber, or a sittin' i' th' chimney-corner.'

Wren. Sir Christopher Wren (1632–1723), English architect who designed St Paul's Cathedral in London, among other buildings of worship.

3. *fells*. See note to *Briggflatts* I. 4.

6. *saints' bones*. Cp. *Briggflatts*, IV. 25–30.

9–10. *we ask nothing / but silence*. Cp. *Note*, [4]: **'In silence, having swept dust and litter from our minds, we can detect the pulse of God's blood in our veins, more persuasive than words, more demonstrative than a diagram. That is what a Quaker meeting tries to be, and that is why my poem is called *Briggflatts*.'**

12 *Perche no spero* / 'Now we've no hope of going back'

Quartermain says that BB felt that the poem would be **'better lost'** and notes that it 'originally formed the opening lines of a longer and untitled poem, itself destroyed'; this longer poem ended with 'a bit of Hadrian's hymn, "anima [*sic*], blandula, vagula"' (*Quartermain DP*, 144) – 'Poor soul! Softly, whisperer . . .' (see Loeb vol. 284: *Minor Latin Poets*, 1934) – published by Caddel as a separate *Uncollected Overdraft*; see note to that poem, below. BB used variations of the phrase **'since I've no hope of ever going back'** in a notebook of draft materials for *Briggflatts* (*Briggflatts notebook*, pages facing 32, 37, 50, 56, 58, 59, at SUNY Buffalo).

BB introduced the poem on television as words a man might speak to his yacht (*Forde*, 104). In an interview, he said, **'I take care not to write anything that I don't bloody well know. And that is something that is different I think from a lot of poets who write . . . If I write nautical technicalities, they're those of a guy who's sailed a lot'** (*Georgia Straight*, n.pag.; *Agenda*, 16, no. 1 [1978], 12). In a letter to LZ concerning *The Spoils*, BB 'indicates that his terminology is probably no more complicated than that used by other poets (**"lets say, with TSE and his garboard-strakes"**). He felt that **"most people know something about the sea from reading or imaginary adventures"**' (*Lesch*, 335–6, quoting BB to LZ, 25 June 1951; also *Forde*, 223). BB owned quite a number of sailing-related books, e.g. R. H. Dana, *Two Years Before the Mast;* Joseph Conrad, *Tales of the Fish Patrol* and *Within the Tides*; James Inman's *Nautical Tables*; Hilaire Belloc, *The Cruise of the Nona* and *On Sailing the Sea*; Stephen M. Burton, *A Set of Nautical Tables for General Navigation*; Richard Walter, *A Voyage Round the World*; Francis B. Cooke, *Yachting Yarns*; Maurice Griffiths, *Post-war Yachting*; Conor O'Brien, *Yacht Gear and Gadgets*; Eric C. Hiscock, *Let's Go Cruising*; Francis B. Cooke, *Practical Yachting Hints*; and D. R. Collins, *Sailing in Helen*.

Publication history

First published in *Agenda* 16, no. 1 (Spring 1978), 5, under title 'Per che no spero' and dated 1977; the poem was read in 1979 at Keats House, London (in *Swigg*). First added to *CP* in 1985. In *CP1985*, the title was made an epigraph and corrected to 'Perche no spero' and the first line was then given as the title in the table of contents. In spite of the poem's publication history, editions of *CP* from 1985 on date the poem as 1980.

Notes

[Epigraph/title] Perche no spero. 'Because I do not hope.' From Cavalcanti's Sonetto VIII ('Perch'i' no spero di tornar giammai'). Cp. T. S. Eliot, 'Ash-Wednesday', I. 1–3: 'Because I do not hope

to turn again / Because I do not hope / Because I do not hope to turn', and 'East Coker,' III. 23–4: 'I said to my soul, be still, and wait without hope / For hope would be hope for the wrong thing', and Rossetti's translation, 'Because I think not ever to return', numbered XXV and titled, 'Ballata. In Exile at Sarzana'. Also EP's translation of the sonnet, 'Ballata XI', ('Because no hope is left me, Ballatetta . . .') in *Ezra Pound: Translations*, ed. Hugh Kenner (New York, 1963), 121, and detailed discussion in his essay, 'Cavalcanti', in *Make It New* (London: Faber & Faber, 1934), chap. 7. LZ, too, imitated the Cavalcanti poem in 'A'-9, which attempts to retain the formal qualities of the original; and in a version done in what Mark Scroggins calls 'Brooklyn Irish slang', 'A foin lass bodders me' (Scroggins, *Louis Zukofsky and the Poetry of Knowledge* [Tuscaloosa: University of Alabama Press, 1998], 351–2, n. 9).

2, 9, 16. cutter. Small single-masted boat, rigged as a sloop.

6. leach. OED n.1.1? Perhaps a slice of meat being cured in the brine of the sea. Perhaps also referring to a leech [*sic*], the edge of a sail; if it is incorrectly tensioned, the leech of a sail may 'stutter' noisily.

8. swatchways. OED 'swash' n.1.III. 9: 'swash-way, "a channel across a bank, or among shoals, as the noted instance between the Goodwin Sands" (Smyth, *Sailor's Word-bk.*, 1867).'

13. gut. OED n.5: 'A narrow passage. a. A channel or run of water, a branch of a stream; a sound, strait.'

18. shrouds. Ropes leading from the head of a mast, part of a ship's rigging. Cp. Dana, *Two Years Before the Mast*, chap. xxiii: 'In an instant every one sprung into the rigging, up the shrouds, and out on the yards.'

19. riding light. OED 'riding' *vbl. n.* 7: 'a special light displayed by a ship when riding at anchor'.

20. too long, watch too glumly. Forde notes that when he read the poem BB 'emphasised a pause between each "too" in the second last line which further solemnised the ending' (*Forde*, 105).

OVERDRAFTS

▪ **It would be gratuitous to assume that a mistranslation is unintentional.**

Cp. BB's note, 'Translation', in Appendix 1 of *CE*, 118: **'A good translator intends to make the same impression on his readers as the original poet made on his. He will not employ archaisms unless the original employed them, which is hardly ever the case. He will employ anachronisms as often as seems needful to avoid the kind of obscurity that gives footnotes an excuse. He will never write as the contemporary of an antique original but will try to make an antique original write like the best of our contemporaries.**

A poet, however, is concerned only to make a good poem. He owes no fidelity at all to former poets. They are there to be pillaged and altered at discretion since all alike, we share the legacy. They are in any case out of copyright.

Let no one presume to rely on anything of mine that looks like a translation. In this volume I have rarely translated except what I thought I could improve. Even the Machiavelli narrative, which is fairly close to the Italian, has been raised from prose to verse. If my Horace can be deemed Horatian it is not because of verbal accuracy. I have erected some poems on a basis robbed from Hafiz rather than translated any of his ghazals. I have improved the rubai, ode XX, so much that I hesitated to set Hafiz's name under it, but upon reflection thought best to associate all extensive borrowings with the lender's name and content myself with disclaiming in an appendix any intention of flattering, belittling, misrepresenting, or, in the current sense, translating any of them.'

In an interview with Lesch, BB remarked, **'One of the best practices you can have, in simply learning to handle words, to get them in the right order, is translating.'** BB's own translations **'were merely for the purpose of studying something or other'** (Lesch interview, 24 April 1976; quoted *Lesch*, 14).

See also Appendix II. B, Bunting's foreword to Omar Pound's *Arabic & Persian Poems in English*..

Richard Price remarks, 'By calling these works "Overdrafts" Bunting publicly affirms that he has come to an understanding of indebtedness with the poets who, as it were, underwrite him. On that basis, he can only supply what is provisional – a draft – and must also in some sense obscure, write "over", the work of his poetic betters. But to take out an overdraft is usually to smoothen cash flow problems: in this case by translating these works, the poet keeps his own poetry moving, in currency, in credit' ('Basil Bunting and the Problem of Patronage', in *McGonigal & Price*, 97).

'Darling of Gods and Men, beneath the gliding stars'

Cp. generally Lucretius, *De rerum natura* I; also Spenser's adaptation of Lucretius in *Faerie Queene* IV.

Publication history

Titled 'To Venus' in *RM*, where it was included in the 'ETCETERA' section, with subheading, 'after Lucretius', and in *CE* as Ode I, without title, but dedication 'to Venus' and attribution at foot of poem, 'Lucretius'. Published in LZ's *A Test of Poetry* (New York, 1948), *Guedalla* B6, 108. Also in *P1950*, *Loquitur*, and all editions of *CP*. Reprinted in *Poetry for Pleasure: The Hallmark Book of Poetry* (Garden City, NY: Doubleday, 1960), 338–9, *Guedalla* B8, as a translation of Lucretius, *De rerum natura* I. 1–24; under title, 'Hymn to Venus', in *The Crystal Cabinet*, ed. Horace Gregory and Marya Zaturenska (New York: Holt, Rinehart, and Winston, 1962), 96, *Guedalla* B8a; *Grok* 2 (19 May 1967), 5, *Guedalla* D28; in *Georgia Straight*, n.pag., *Guedalla* D34. The poem is mentioned in a letter from LZ to EP dated 9 November 1930. It was considered, along with 'Against the Tricks of Time', 'Sad Spring', 'While Shepherds Watched' and 'Chorus of Furies', for *Poetry*'s 'Objectivists' issue which LZ was to edit (*Pound/Zukofsky: Selected Letters of Ezra Pound and Louis Zukofsky*).

Notes

8. southwind. From *De rerum natura* I. 11, Loeb: 'teeming south wind'. Gilonis identifies this as 'a mistranslation of *favoni*, the *west* wind which blew "at the commencement of spring, and promoted vegetation" (Lewis & Short, *A Latin Dictionary*)' (Gilonis, 'The Forms Cut Out of the Mystery', *Caddel*, 151). BB also uses the word in *FBO* 29.

17. Alma Venus. Mother Venus is invoked at the beginning of Lucretius' *De rerum natura*. Venus was seen by Romans to be related to them through her son Aeneas; but she was also considered to be *Venus physica*, the generative force behind nature.

trim. Perhaps as in trimming sails; also *OED* v.1.a: 'To make firm or strong; to strengthen, confirm; to give as security; to arm or array (a force); to settle, arrange; to encourage, comfort, exhort.' Citations for King Ælfred, and *Lindisfarne Gospel*, John v. 31. BB wrote in 1933 that **'the minimum requirement of a poem is that it should trim**

some known thought to a greater precision, or note comprehensibly and communicably some previously unknown thought' (*The Cantos of Ezra Pound: Some Testimonials*, quoted by Reagan in 'Basil Bunting, *obiter dicta*', *Terrell*, 230).

'Yes, it's slow, docked of amours'

Published in *Whips & Scorpions*, 42, *Guedalla* B2, as 'Number Two' of a pair of poems – the other being 'Please stop gushing', below – under the title 'Crackt Records'. Sub-heading, '*Miserarum est neque amori dare ludum* . . .' (Loeb, 'Wretched the maids who may not give play to love nor drown their cares in sweet wine . . .'), from Horace, *Odes*, III. 12, of which this poem is a version; Sappho fragment 102 lies behind Horace's poem. Also published by EP in *Act. Ant.*, *Guedalla* B4, with subheading and attribution **'– Q.H.F.'** In *CE* as Ode XXXVIII with attribution to 'Horace' at foot of poem. In *P1950*, *Loquitur*, and all editions of *CP*. Reprinted in *Erotic Lyrics*, ed. Anthony Howell (London: Penguin, 1970), 12, *Guedalla* B12, under heading, 'Overdraft from Horace'.

Notes

1. docked. EDD 4: '*Fig.* To abridge, diminish; to reduce a man's wages, lower the price.' Cp. ' I'm the worse for drink again, its' in 'Uncollected Overdrafts', 7: ' You'd dock my drink for the fast, you!'

4. father's. BB changes Horace's *patruus*, for paternal uncle, to 'father'.

6. Cytherea. Venus, Roman goddess of love; named for the Peloponnesian island, Cythera, associated with Venus, both the goddess and the planet. Cythera is, in effect, the realm of gratified desire. Gilonis remarks that Cytherea is 'Aphrodite, wave-born, wave-washed onto the isle of Cythera – but she should have her son Cupid with her, not some "lad"' (in 'Soiled Mosaic: Bunting's Horace Translations', *McGonigal & Price*, 211). Cp. Samuel Daniel, *Delia* XVIII (1592 version), 2: 'Yeelde Cithereas sonne those Arkes of loue'; Swinburne, 'Siena', 182–4: 'what a Grace, / Where no Greek worships her shrined limbs / With wreaths and Cytherean hymns?' Also Byron, 'Translation from Anacreon', 15: 'When Cytherea's blooming Boy'; Wordsworth, 'The Birth of Love', 2–4: 'What dire intrigues disturbed Cythera's joy! / Till Venus cried, 'A mother's heart is mine; / None but myself shall nurse my boy'; and the opening of his translation of the *Aeneid*, Bk. I.

Minerva. Roman goddess of wisdom.

12. pug. Slang term for boxer; plays on Horace's *pugno*, 'fist'.

13. He can shoot straight from the butts. OED: n.4, II: 'A mark for shooting.' 2.a.: 'For the purposes of archery there were usually two butts, one at each extremity of the range; hence . . . the use of *the butts* for "the archery-ground".' Cp. Dryden, Virgil's Georgics II. 773: 'The groom his fellow-groom at butts defies.' The hides from which hunters do their shooting also come to mind here.

15. *daylong*. Cp. Tennyson, 'The Brook', 53: 'His weary daylong chirping.'

16. *tiger*. Plays on Horace's *catus*, 'clever'.
arms'-length. Also used in *The Pious Cat*, 114.

'Please stop gushing about his pink'

Cp. Kipling, 'Carmen Circulare', especially 6–7: 'Though reckless Lydia bid thee fly, / And Telephus o'ertaking jeer'.

Publication history

First published in *Pagany* 2, no. 3 (July–September 1931), 125, with title, 'A Cracked Record', and subheading, '(CUM TU LYDIA TELEPHI)', *Guedalla* D3; and *The New Review* 1, no. 4 (Winter 1931–2), 385, *Guedalla* D4. Also in *Whips & Scorpions*, 41, *Guedalla* B2, as 'Number One' of a pair of poems titled 'Crackt Records', with subheading, '*Cum tu Lydia Telephi. . . .*' (Loeb, 'When thou, O Lydia, praisest Telephus') from Horace, *Odes*, I. 13, of which this poem is a version; Sappho fragment 51 lies behind Horace's poem. Cp. *SBOO* 7, based on Catullus' version of the poem. In *CE* as XXVIII. Also in *P1950*, *Loquitur*, and all editions of *CP*.

Notes

2. *Dulcie*. Based on the Latin word, *dulcis*, meaning 'sweet'. Dulcibella, also based on this word, was used as a generic name for an idealized, virtuous sweetheart in poetry from medieval literature through the eighteenth century. Cp. Horace, *Odes*, I. 13: 'dulcia barbare / laedentem oscula quae Venus' (Loeb: 'him who savagely profanes the sweet lips that Venus has imbued with the quintessence of her own nectar'), and its use by BB in *SBOO* 10; also III. xii: 'Miserarum est neque amori dare ludum neque dulci' (Loeb: 'Wretched the maids who may not give play to love nor drown their cares in sweet wine'). Also cp. Dulcinea in Cervantes' *Don Quixote*. And possibly Marc Connelly and George S. Kaufman's play, *Dulcy* (1921); they also wrote a musical, *Helen of Troy, New York* (1923).

10. *thrice blest*. Cp. Tennyson, *In Memoriam*, XXXII. 13: 'Thrice blest whose lives are faithful prayers.'

Verse and Version

Translation into Latin of LZ's tribute to EP. The version of LZ's poem (number 13 in his '29 Songs') reproduced from *Loquitur* on differs from the text as published in LZ's *55 Poems* (Prairie City, IL: J. A. Decker, 1941), 79, and *ANEW: Complete Shorter Poetry* (New York: New Directions, 2011), 46–7. These versions begin in lower case ('in that . . .') and conclude with a semi-colon ('. . . kindness;').

'First yr poem: I am no hand at Italian and intended sending it to Monotti; but in the mean time tried what I could do with it in Latin, which seemed to me more suited than modern Italian (not Dante's) to the monumental terseness, especially when dealing in relatives without antecedents – this? Italian reader inquires Which? So I showed my version to Ezra and he seems to intend to print it, and that will be all right, seeing that most edicated Eyetalians read Latin alright, provided I havent made any egregious errors, which is quite possible, and I am not certain Ezra would detect them though he knows more about Latin than I do.

But since Latin is in some ways more precise than our own lingo, there were places where I was in doubt and may have got yr meaning a few shades out, shades not delicate as the difference of pale pink and paler, but properly Cimmerian, catastrophic indigoes. In the second stanza, what tense is *put*? I have made it present, rejecting past or perfect not from any ability to penetrate the ambiguity of the English, but because superimponunt sounds better than superimponebant or superimposuerunt. And in the last line of the poem, is *every kindness* object or subject? Before happening for every kindness, or before every kindness happens? I have made it nominative. If ablative, then "prius quam pro omnibus mitioris". Or maybe omitting "pro" . . .

As for the difference of Verba and dicta, tristitiam and maestitiam, I chose by the noise they make; though I rejected luctus as being too definitely funereal. Dicta perhaps connects with mens as well as ora. Id for *this* rather than istud because I conceived you to be avoiding rather than courting emphasis on the pronoun; the horum of line 5 being plural is not likely to cause confusion. *Its* in line 8 may refer either to *sorrow* or to *this*: so might eius, though I think it would be more natural to take it with id. The dislocation of omnia in line 10 avoids the ugliness of -que quam and of course is not, in Latin, an inversion, that is, a *per*version. The only other liberty with your word order is tristitiam before superimponunt, which is more natural in Latin, makes a better rhythm, and avoids the possible ambiguity that might arise from setting tristitiam and eius together. Punctuation supplied, concession to the deadness of the dead language' (BB to LZ, September 1932; quoted *Forde*, 111–12).

BB would later write to LZ that **'Horace works wonders with a word order which was crabbed even to his contemporaries, as one may see by**

reading Lucretius and Ovid on either side of him in time. It is not right to banish such effects, which have their place, one I think too much neglected now, even though we and especially I follow Yeats's example of plain diction and plain syntax' (3 November 1948; quoted *Forde*, 118).

Publication history

First published in *Il Mare* 1229 (1 October 1932), 3, *Guedalla* D7. In *Loquitur* and all editions of *CP*.

'Once, so they say, pinetrees seeded on Pelion's peak swam'

Version of Catullus LXIV, that poet's longest poem, 1–25; Loeb: 'Pinetrees of old, born on the top of Pelion', etc.

Publication history

Published in *Loquitur* and all editions of *CP*.

Notes

1. pinetrees seeded on Pelion's peak. From 'Peliaco' in LXIV, 1. D. H. Garrison, in *The Student's Catullus* (Norman, OK, 1989, 134) comments: 'Peliaco is adjectival . . . We are expected to know that the pines begot on Pelion's peak sail Neptune's clear waves in the form of a ship named the Argo.'

1–3. Perhaps an attempt to recreate alliterative use of 'p' sounds in LXIV, 1–3: 'Peliaco quondam prognatae vertice pinus / dicuntur liquidas Neptuni nasse per undas / Phasidos ad fluctus et fines Aeëteos . . .'

2. Phasis. River in Colchis, on the eastern shore of the Black Sea, and homeland of Medea. In LXIV, 3, from 'Phasidos', the Greek genitive of Phasis.

3. gamesome. Cp. Coleridge, 'To a young Ass', 31: 'How thou wouldst toss thy heels in gamesome play'; Browning, 'Pippa Passes', 24: 'As if earth turned from work in gamesome mood.'

Argos. Ancient Greek city, birthplace of Perseus, a son of Zeus.

4. deal sweeps. Long wooden oars.

5. Lady of Citadels. Pallas, who guarded the citadels of town-dwellers, helped build the ship, *Argo*, for Jason's companions; the story of the departure of Jason and the Argonauts is told in LXIV, 1–21.

7. *Amphitrite*. In Greek myth, a sea goddess, daughter of Nereus and Doris, and one of the Nereids listed in Hesiod's *Theogony*. In LXIV, 11, 'Amphitriten' is, by metonymy, the sea.

8. *spindrift. OED*: 'Orig. *Sc.* Continuous driving of spray.' Cp. Kipling, 'The Last Chantey', 62: 'Stinging, ringing spindrift', and 'The Coastwise Lights', 1: 'Our brows are bound with spindrift.' BB also uses the word in 'You can't grip years, Postume', below.

12. *Thetis . . . Peleus*. In Greek myth, Thetis, a Nereid loved by both Zeus and Poseidon (god of the sea), was (according to Prometheus) destined to bear a son greater than his father. The two gods consequently decide to marry her to Peleus, king of the Myrmidons.

13. *Thetis took Peleus spite of the briefness of man's lifetime*. Thetis, unwilling to wed a mortal (cp. *The Iliad* 18. 434), resisted Peleus by changing into a variety of shapes – but Peleus caught her with the help of a centaur, Chiron. Peleus and Thetis would become the parents of Achilles.

18. *pinebrands*. Wedding torches. In LXIV, 25, the torches, by metonymy, are marriage. *OED* earliest citation for this meaning under 'brand' is from the *Lindisfarne Gospel*, John xviii. 3. Cp. Shakespeare, *Cymbeline*, II. iv. 89–91: 'Two winking Cupids . . . nicely / Depending on their brands.'

Thessaly. Peleus (see above) was king of the Myrmidons in Thessaly, where Achilles would grow up.

19. *Jove*. Jupiter, chief Roman god, giver of victory; associated with lightning and thunderbolts. Corresponds with Greek Zeus.

— *and why Catullus bothered to write pages and pages of this drivel mystifies me*. LXIV is Catullus' longest poem; Garrison (*The Student's Catullus*, 133) explains that poets who dissented from the old epic style, which was 'overworked by the hacks of Alexandria, Athens, and Rome', wrote 'mini-epics that were subdivided into a story within a story'.

'When the sword of sixty comes nigh his head'

Translation of excerpt from Ferdowsī's *Shāh-nāmeh* ('Book of Kings'). Loloi and Pursglove remark that this passage functions in the original 'in something like the manner of, say, the autobiographical passage which opens Book III of *Paradise Lost*' (*Terrell*, 345; see this article also for a detailed comparison of BB's version with the original). Asked in an interview whether he had attempted a large-scale translation of Ferdowsī – presumably the *Shāh-nāmeh* – BB replied: **'Yes. It was no good'**

(P. Craven and M. Heyward, 'An Interview with Basil Bunting', 29). LZ quoted parts of the poem in his *Zukofsky*, vol. 1, 121, *Guedalla* B9.

Publication history

Last poem in 'Overdrafts' section in *P1950*. Also in *Loquitur*, and all editions of *CP*.

Notes

11. *couriers*. *OED* n.2 cites Hakluyt's *Voyages*, I. 21.

14. *bulbul*. A thrush, or oriental bird, sometimes called nightingale of the East, admired for its song; *OED* cites Sir W. Jones's *Memoirs* (1784), II. 37: 'We . . . cease to wonder that the Bulbul, with a thousand tales, makes such a figure in Persian poetry.' *OED* gives 'a sweet singer' and cites Thackeray, *Vanity Fair*, lxii: 'You must belong to the Bulbul faction'; cp. also Kipling, 'Army Headquarters', 11: 'He warbled like a *bul-bul*.'

'All the teeth ever I had are worn down and fallen out'

Translation of Rūdakī's 'Lament in Old Age.' See Loloi and Pursglove's detailed comparison of BB's version with the original in *Terrell*, 346–7. **'Rudaki's qasidas have given me great delight, especially the wonderful one about all his teeth falling out. One must certainly add his name to the list of the world's very great poets, even though the remains are so few and fragmentary. I will perhaps send you a prose translation if I ever finish it. I have taken a great liking also to Persian classical music and wish I could get some records of it'** (BB to LZ, 28 August 1948; quoted *Forde*, 124). BB later sent a draft of the poem to LZ (held at HRC), and commented that this translation **'gives some idea of the way a Khorassani mind worked in 950 ad – I mean, in my English. Rudaki's Persian is delightful.'** In this draft, the following note appears after the title: **'(Monorhyme – every second line – with a good deal of internal rhyming and alliteration. The vocabulary exceedingly simple, the main effects being got by the cross-beat of ictus and stress in an elaborate quantitative measure)'** (BB to LZ, 2 December 1948; quoted *Forde*, 124). LZ quoted parts of the poem in his *Zukofsky*, 120–1, *Guedalla* B9. Cp. perhaps James Elroy Flecker, *Golden Journey to Samarkand*.

Publication history

First published in *Nine* 4 (Summer 1950), 2, no. 3 (August 1950), 217–18, *Guedalla* D14, under title, 'A Qasida of Rudaki's'. In *P1950*, *Loquitur*, and all editions of *CP*.

Notes

13. *makes new what was worn threadbare*. Cp. title of EP's *Make It New* (London: Faber & Faber, 1934).

52. *Poet of Khorassan*. Rūdakī (Abū 'Abdi'llāh Ja'far ibn Mohammad, *ca*.859–940) was the first important poet to write poems in the 'New Persian' that used the Arabic alphabet. He was from Rudak in Khorassan, now Tajikistan, hence the name by which he is commonly known. Popular tradition holds that he, like Homer, was blind.

57. *dirhems*. A dirhem was a small silver coin. *OED* cites Burton's *Arabian Nights* (1887) III. 36: 'I now adjudge him the sum of ten thousand dirhams.'

58. *Prince Makan*. Rendered 'Prince of the Pure and Brave' in A. V. William Jackson's translation of Rūdakī's poem, (in *Early Persian Poetry*, 44), with note: 'This line is a difficult one . . . I prefer to regard the allusion as being to some one of the Abbasid Caliphs of Rudagi's time . . .'

'Shall I sulk because my love has a double heart?'

Translation of a *qasida* by Manuchehri; see Loloi and Pursglove's detailed comparison of BB's version with the original in *Terrell*, 347–9. Manuchehri was an eleventh-century Persian poet who used Arabic words in his work; he was a protégé of 'Unsuri, also of interest to BB. **'Manuchehri? Haven't I ever pestered you with him? If one puts Homer and Firdosi carefully in one place and then looks for the three or four greatest poets remaining I don't see how anyone who has the luck to read him can omit Manuchehri. His variety is enormous and everything he did he did better than anyone else. You want the directness of some Catullus? Go to Manuchehri. You want the swiftness of Anacreon? Manuchehri. The elaborate music of Spenser? Go to Manuchehri. The formal, fulldress ode with every circumstance of solemnity and splendor? Not Pindar, Manuchehri. Satire direct and overwhelming, Manuchehri all alone – no competitor. He was a younger contemporary of Firdosi, and like him went to the Ghaznavi Court – I think probably after Firdosi had left it, for most of Manuchehri is addressed not to Mahmud but his successor. But at that time one man might well have heard both of them, to say nothing of Unsuri and Farrukhi, both also very great poets. I dont know where else at any time a man could have had such an experience. I think Manuchehri very likely began by imitating the great Arabic poet then still recent, Al-Motanabbi, and found he could do it standing on his head. So first he set himself difficult technical problems and solved them, then he**

began inventing new forms, finally he found he could say what was in him without any elaboration at all and have a great poem' (BB to LZ, 28 July 1949; quoted *Forde*, 127). **'. . . the finest Persian carpets could never have been designed except in the same culture which produced the qasidas of Manuchehri'** (*BBP*, 19).

An undated notebook held at Durham contains BB's annotated transcriptions of poems from Kazimirski's edition of Manuchehri (Paris, 1886).

Publication history

Published in *Loquitur*, and all editions of *CP*. A longer version, 'The thundercloud fills meadows with heavenly beauty', appears in 'Uncollected Overdrafts'.

Note

[Attribution] qasida. A carefully constructed ode-like lyric 'of at least twelve lines generally, each unit (*bayt* or distich) is composed of two balanced halves (*misra*) corresponding to each other in metre and parallel in theme. The *qasida* is in monorhyme introduced in the opening *bayt*, the only unit in which both halves are rhymed. All the remaining *bayts* repeat this rhyme, but only at the end of the unit. Since the poetry was meant to be sung or recited, the monorhyme could be made acceptable to the ear, although it seems wearisome to the eye. To compose a *qasida* tests the poet's skill in adapting the metre to the theme and rhyming ingeniously' (*Forde*, 122).

'Came to me —'

Version of a poem by Rūdakī. In an introduction to the poem at a reading recorded at Harvard University in 1976 BB explained that it is **'a poem of rudities which is a dialogue; a gentleman is confiding with a friend of his'.**

Publication history

First published in *Paris Review* 34 (Summer 1965), 92–3, *Guedalla* D20 and in *Loquitur*. Also published in all editions of *CP*. Reprinted in *Georgia Straight*, n.pag., *Guedalla* D34; and under title 'Rudaki', in *The Penguin Book of Love Poetry*, ed. Jon Stallworthy (London: Allen Lane, 1973), 111, *Guedalla* B19.

Note

17. Cornelian. Suggestively, the reddish berry-like fruit of the cornel-tree (said to be common in Persia), a cornelian cherry. (In the sense of *OED* 1, 'A variety of chalcedony, a semi-transparent quartz, of a deep dull red, flesh, or reddish white colour; used for seals, etc.,' there is a citation for Mandeville, and a usage in Byron, *Don Juan*, I, st. 198, 7: 'The motto, cut upon a white cornelian'. *The Book of the Thousand Nights and One* (London: privately printed, 1901), p. 223, refers to 'verses in praise of a mole upon the cheek', one of which is: 'O thou, the moles upon whose cheek recall Globules of musk upon cornelian strewed . . .'

'This I write, mix ink with tears'

See Loloi and Pursglove's detailed comparison of BB's version with the original in *Terrell*, 349–50. BB wrote to LZ on 28 July 1949: **'The most important of Unsuri's [Abul Qasim Hassan ibn Ahmad 'Unsuri (d. 1040 or 1049)] poems are lost – they were romances, the first to exist in any language unless we count the Greek novels – but there are a good many qasidas left, and, I think, a powerful short poem which is printed amongst the poems "attributed" to Sa'di. I will try to translate it for you.'** When he sent the translation to LZ on 6 August, he wrote, **'Attributed to Sa'di: But, I think, possibly by the much earlier and greater poet Unsuri. Unsuri wrote "Vamiq and Azra" (or translated it from Pahlevi) and may have been the first to write a "Laila and Majnun". Sa'di wrote neither.'** In pencil at the end of the poem, he added, **'This last poem is song in fullest sense: hope my rendering would be singable. Last line a bit Jacobean, lute cadences all ready for it.'** (All letters quoted *Forde*, 132).

Responding to a suggestion by LZ, he wrote back on 5 September: **'You're right, no doubt, about the comma after Azra and Laila in the little Unsuri piece. Too familiar myself, I thought that "everybody" was familiar with the names and the outline of the story of Laila and Majnun, and that that would explain the preceding verse about Vamiq and Azra. I even thought you had referred to it in your first long work . . . Laila's parents refused to let her marry him and he went mad, the stereotype of the lovers who go mad all through romantic poetry in Europe as well as the East. Nearly all the main romantic themes seem to come from a group of now lost Pahlevi poems of the fifth and sixth century, of which Vamiq and Azra is one, Xosro and Shirin another, Vis and Ramin the most closely preserved in its Persian version: and Laila and Majnun may or may not have been another: as a source of the romantic subjects it should, by analogy, be one, but it is barely possible that Nezami of Ganjeh invented it in the twelfth century.'** (Quoted *Forde*, 132). LZ, perhaps stimulated by BB's interest in Persian poetry, quoted from Nizami's version of 'Laila and Majnun' and from works by Sa'di in his *Zukofsky*, 126–8, *Guedalla* B9.

Publication history

Published in *Nine* (no. 11, April 1956 / vol. 4, no. 2, 9), *Guedalla* D18, under title, 'A qit'a wrongly attributed to Sa'di'. Also in *Loquitur*, and all editions of *CP*.

Note

3–4. *to tell Azra Vamiq's pain . . . Laila Majnun's plight*. Vamiq and Azra, legendary lovers – see BB's comment above; *Laila Majnun* is a tragic Persian love story, along the lines of Romeo and Juliet; the classic version was by the Persian poet, Nizami, and the story also occurs in the discourses of Maulana Jalalu-'d-din Muhammad Rumi.

'Last night without sight of you my brain was ablaze'

A translation of a *ghazal* by Sa'di; see Loloi and Pursglove's detailed comparison of BB's version with the original in *Terrell*, 350–1. 'The most general explanation of the *ghazal* . . . which has something of the character of the European sonnet, is that although it follows the *qasida* in structure and rhythms, it seems more a Persian outgrowth of the fixed Arabic erotic prelude of the *qasida* . . . In distinction to this Arabic court poetry form, the *ghazal* . . . more radically Persian, from the cultural life of the town, speaks chiefly of love, human or mystical, although anything might be added to the subject matter that stirred the emotions. Of all the types of Persian poetry that Bunting translated, the most numerous are the *ghazal*; and these are the works of the greatest writers of the form, Manuchehri, Sa'di, and Hafez' (*Forde*, 125–6). Sent to LZ with the comment, **'I'll type out my last translation, one of the most famous poems in the language in mediaeval times, imitated by Hafez, but now less heard of, one of the finest of Sa'di's long lines in Persian. This prevents the translation being line for line, but doesn't prevent it being almost literal'** (28 July 1949; quoted *Forde*, 126). At a reading of the poem, BB remarked that Sa'di was **'not mystical in the least'** – not like Persian poetry in **'Swinburnean translations'** (University of British Columbia, 9 December 1970, in *Swigg*).

Publication history

First published in *Nine* 4 (Summer 1950), 2, no. 3 (August 1950), 219, *Guedalla* D14, under title, 'A ghazel of Sa'di's'. Also published in *Loquitur*, and all editions of *CP*. Reprinted in *Georgia Straight*, n.pag., *Guedalla* D34.

Notes

10. Laila Majnun. See note to previous poem, 3–4.

12. fantom. BB also uses the word in *FBO* 2.

16. Pleiades. Loose cluster of stars in the constellation Taurus, six of which are visible to the naked eye; named for Atlas' seven daughters who, in Greek mythology, were turned into a group of stars.

'You can't grip years, Postume'

Version of Horace, *Odes*, II. 14. BB wrote to Forde, **'The only [Latin translation by BB] worth keeping is the *Eheu fugaces*'** (23 February 1973; quoted, *Forde*, 105). BB remarked at a reading of the poem: **'I think that gets about as close to Horace as it's possible in English'** (Keats House, London, 1979, in *Swigg*).

Publication history

Added to 'Overdrafts' in *CP1978*; this and subsequent editions of *CP* use BB's date of 1971, but this is incorrect as the poem was published, in variant form, earlier – three times: in *Make* 9 (n.d. [?1969]), n.pag., *Guedalla* D29, *Sunday Times* 7646 (14 December 1969), 51, *Guedalla* D30 (reproduction of autograph MS with heading, 'A new poem by Basil Bunting', and title in parentheses, 'Version of Horace', dated 1969), and *Agenda* 8, nos. 3–4 (Autumn–Winter, 1970), 61, *Guedalla* D31, (with title, 'Eheu fugaces, Postume, Postume', and attribution at foot of poem, 'from Horace'). Published as a broadside (London, 1972) by 'Guido Londinensis', i.e. Guido Morris, who ran the Latin Press in London from the 1930s to the 1950s; and also by Sterling Memorial Library's Bibliographical Press (New Haven, 1976). Reprinted in a pamphlet edited by Guedalla, distributed at the Modern British Poetry Conference, 18–20 October 1974, Polytechnic of Central London, *Guedalla* B21.

Notes

1. Postume. Reference to Horace, *Odes*, II. 14 ('Eheu fugaces, Postume, Postume . . .'). Cp. *FBO* 25. Gilonis notes that this is 'the only Latin name Bunting takes over into an overdraft' ('Soiled Mosaic: Bunting's Horace Translations', *McGonigal & Price*, 226).

7. Pluto. In Greek myth, Pluto, brother of the gods Zeus and Poseidon, ruled over the dead in the underworld with his queen, Persephone.

14. spindrift. See note to 'Once, so they say . . .', 8, above.

28. pope. For Horace's Latin *pontifex*, a member of the college of priests. Gilonis remarks that BB 'modernizes the referent etymologically, and makes a wonderful – if subliminal – reference to Chateauneuf du Pape, neat parallel to Horace's Caecuban' ('Soiled Mosaic: Bunting's Horace Translations', *McGonigal & Price*, 226–7, n. 69).

How Duke Valentine Contrived

Based on Niccolò Machiavelli (1469–1527), 'A Description of the Method Used by Duke Valentino in Killing Vitellozzo Vitelli, Oliverotto da Fermo and Others' ('Descritione del modo tenuto dal duca Valentino nello ammazzare Vitellozzo Vitelli, Oliverotto da Fermo, il signor Pagolo e il Duca di Gravina'), an account of events which took place during 1502–3; it was appended much later to *The Prince* (chap. XXVI). The account is based on Machiavelli's service as the Florentine Republic's agent to Cesare Borgia (1478–1507), son of Pope Alexander VI, who used trickery and murder to subjugate his rivals for power. The numerous names of people and places BB took wholesale from the account are not glossed here; information about these can easily be found in sources on Machiavelli. BB called his version an **'adaptation . . . a pretty raw one'** (BB to John Matthias, 23 March 1970; quoted *Forde*, 120). Forde quotes (119) an observation of Allan Gilbert, who translated the worknotes, that in the original Machiavelli 'subtly exploited the possibilities, including colloquial qualities, of Florentine speech'; she adds that BB tries to do the same in English with his version. BB had written at about the time of the poem's composition, in 'Some Limitations of English', that **'Machiavelli was the last Italian writer to concern himself with the language'** (*Three Essays*, 24–5). Quartermain quotes BB, in Vancouver (1970): **'"How Duke Valentine Contrived" is not worth keeping; it's got a few good lines but it's an exercise. Its main if not its only virtue is Machiavelli's. I'm sure when Shelley drowned he thought, "If only I could get my hands on the works. So I could destroy them. They're no good"'** (*Quartermain DP*, 144). In a copy of *Act. Ant.* apparently presented to Violet Harris (see 'To Violet with prewar poems'), he wrote above the poem: **'Dull poem'** (Pamela Coren, 'Bunting's own *Active Anthology*', *PN Review* 40, no. 4 [March/April 2014], 13).

Publication history

First published by EP in *Act. Ant.*, *Guedalla* B4. In *CE*. Published in *P1950*, but in a separate section, and not as an 'Overdraft'. In 'Overdraft' section of *Loquitur*, all editions of *CP*.

UNCOLLECTED POEMS

The Pious Cat

According to Caddel (*UP*, 64), BB 'intended this fable to be published as an illustrated book for children'. BB began it in 1937 – the year his wife Marian left him, taking their two children. (BB's daughter Bourtai told Forde (40) that she remembered her parents reading Kipling's 'The Cat Who Walked by Himself' from *Just So Stories* to her at about this time.) An undated notebook is held at Durham containing BB's annotated transcriptions of the Persian original.

A translation of *Mush va gurbah* ('*Mouse and Cat*') by 'Ubayd-i Zakani (d. 1371), like Hafiz, a Persian poet of the Timurid period. The poem is sometimes said to be a political satire, using a pastiche of styles, whose subject is a warlord who destroyed a ruler of Shiraz. 'Ubayd was apparently from Qazwin, whose inhabitants he ridiculed, and later lived impoverished in Shiraz. He turned from straightforward literary work to the skilful satire, parody – often incorporating the serious verse of other poets – and ribaldry for which he would become well-known. BB introduced the poem at a reading by saying that **'It was seized upon not so much by the politicians as by the children, and it has remained for now 600 years the principal children's book of Persia. When I left Persia less than thirty years ago, it was still the book which children first read, about the age of twelve or so'** (Leeds, 1978, in *Swigg*).

Publication history

This poem was first published posthumously by Bertram Rota, in a 1986 limited edition. That edition presents two versions: one set from BB's TS, which includes BB's note dating the poem '1939–77' – which may be a transcription error; and a facsimile autograph MS version which includes BB's note dating the poem '1937–77'. (Another slightly variant MS, MS8, is held at Durham; a note by BB indicates that illustrations by his daughter Maria were to have been included, but they were not.) For *UP* and *CP1994/2000* Caddel followed the MS version Rota used. A 1978 recording of BB reading the poem (in *Swigg*), however, generally conforms with the TS version and so, reflecting his latest known intentions, it is presented here.

Notes

[Title] The Pious Cat. Cp. Kipling, 'Verses on Games', 41: 'The Pious Horse to church may trot.'

[Attribution] by Obaid-e Zakani (and Basil Bunting) 'Ubayd-i Zakani (Nezam od-Din Ubeydollah Zâkâni, *ca.* fourteenth century) was a court poet in Shiraz at the same time as the young Hafiz; best known for his bawdy satires and political poems. In a 1978 reading recorded at Leeds (in *Swigg*), BB read this poem as being **'by Obaid-e Zakani, hampered somewhat by Basil Bunting'. ▪ You must call him 'Obeyed', like the English word 'obeyed a command', 'obeyed a zaw-kaw-nee'; and save most of your breath for the 'nee'. He wrote this story about six hundred years ago, and Persian children still read it at school, or they used to, twenty years since. Any story that lasts as long as that is worth listening to, I think. Perhaps not everything in it is true, but bits of it are very true indeed. 1937–77.** (In the Rota TS version, this note appears as the 'Post Script'). The title page of the MS copy at Durham adds: 'with pictures by Sima-Maria', BB's daughter (b. 1950), but the illustrations are not included. BB was hesitant to see the poem published; see *Burton*, 500–1.

11. Haltwhistle. Town in Tynedale, Northumberland, near Hadrian's Wall.

19, 82. Tibbald . . . St. Tibbald. OED, under Tibert, identifies this name with the cat in the apologue of Reynard the Fox, and hence 'used as a quasi-proper name for any cat, and (as a common noun), a cat'. The entry contains citations for variants of the name in Caxton's version of Reynard, Shakespeare (*Romeo and Juliet*, II. iv. 18, and II. i. 78), Jonson, Dryden and Collins. Cp. Pope's Tibbald, the pseudo-poet, in *The Dunciad* (Lewis Theobald, 1688–1744).

86. bottle of Schiedam. A malt wine made from fermented grain (usually barley); there were hundreds of factories producing this wine in Schiedam, Holland, in the nineteenth century, but far fewer after World War I.

105. Reward of Abstinence. Cp. Henry George, *Progress and Poverty*, III. 3. 09: 'Interest, we are told, in all the standard works, is the reward of abstinence.' Also G. B. Shaw, *An Unsocial Socialist* (a book BB owned) chap. IV: 'But all I ask is the ninepence, and let the lady keep the one and threepence as the reward of abstinence'; chap. V: 'At Cambridge they taught me that his profits were the reward of abstinence – the abstinence which enabled him to save.'

109. daily bread. Matthew 6: 12: 'Give us this day our daily bread'; and version in Luke 11: 3: 'Give us day by day our daily bread.'

114. arm's length. Also used in 'Yes, it's slow, docked of amours', 16.

151. rat-bane. Rat poison.

173. fells. See note to *Briggflatts* I. 4.

176. Solway coast. Cp. Kipling, 'The Rhyme of the Three Captains', 3: 'And one was Admiral of the North from Solway Firth to Skye.'

206. Obaid-e Zakani. See note, above. BB's final lines play on 'Ubayd's lines, 'And all that's left is this peculiar story / Bestowing posthumous, poetic glory / On old Obayed-e Zakani' (trans. Dick Davis, from 'Spells to Fascinate the Angel Gabriel', *Parnassus* 25, nos. 1–2 (2001), 169–70).

They Say Etna

BB's father had been a member of the Fabian Society; Alldritt comments that the 'left-wing views that Basil heard argued and repeated in his father's circle had a strong effect on him' (*Alldritt*, 7). BB critiqued the legal system of capitalism in a schoolboy paper presented to Leighton Park School's Senior Essay Society, entitled 'The Relation of the State and Individual Liberty and Law'. In this talk he asked, **'what profit we if the spirit of the law is liberty while the letter of it is not so? It is by the letter of the law that the Englishman is ruled; and letters may be differently read . . . Let us return to the spirit. That may lighten the burden of the poor'** (quoted *Alldritt*, 17–18).

Publication history

Caddel writes that from 'internal evidence' the poem was written after 1929 'and from the preponderance of 1932 news-events . . . we could surmise an editing process around 1932'. Included in *CE*, and quoted by EP in his letter from Rapallo for the *Japan Times* (18 April 1940). (Richard Caddel, 'Acknowledged Land: a Biography of "They Say Etna" and a Debate between Bunting and Pound', in *Ezra Pound and Europe*, ed. Richard Taylor and Claus Melchior [Amsterdam, 1993], 69). First published in EP's *Act. Ant.*, *Guedalla* B4, with joke names replacing the real ones subsequently restored in BB's *CE* version, which appears as Ode XXI, untitled. The substitutions were presumably made, Makin speculates, 'because of the British libel laws' (*Makin*, 56, n. 54). Published in a corrupt version in *P1950*. BB excluded the poem from all later volumes, and in a copy of *Act. Ant.* apparently presented to Violet Harris (see 'To Violet with prewar poems'), he crossed out the poem and wrote above it: **'Bad poem – forget it'** (Pamela Coren, 'Bunting's own *Active Anthology*', *PN Review* 40, no. 4, [March/April 2014], 12). *UP* and *CP1994/2000* present the *Act. Ant.* version;

Caddel explained that 'faced with three versions', he chose 'that which seems the most self-contained and complete: in this case, the earliest' (*CP2000*, 229). Because they are different enough to require separate consideration, the *Act. Ant.* and *CE* versions are both presented here; the unreliable *P1950* version is also included separately as an anomaly. The penultimate stanza and its headline-tag are quoted in *Conf. Cumm, Guedalla* B10.

Notes

[Title] Etna. Cp. Milton, *Paradise Lost*, I. 232–7: 'shattered side / Of thund'ring Etna, whose combustible / And fuelled entrails thence conceiving fire, / Sublimed with mineral fury, aid the winds, / And leave a singèd bottom all involved / With stench and smoke', and III. 470–1: 'A god, leaped fondly into Etna flames, / Empedocles'. Also Arnold, *Empedocles on Etna*, especially II. 3, 'Etna's great mouth', and stage direction, 'Smoke and fire break forth with a loud noise.' In Arnold's poem, the Greek philosopher and statesman Empedocles is no longer able to experience joy; he considers himself to be useless, and intends to kill himself by leaping into the crater of Mount Etna despite the arguments of two friends that life is worth living.

2. *belches*. Cp. Milton, *Paradise Lost*, I. 671: 'Belching outrageous flame.'

3. *Duisburg's pudenda*. Duisburg, Germany, is a port at the confluence of the Rhine and Ruhr rivers, and a longtime centre for coal, iron and steel production.

6, 19, 36, 39. Gear and gear. EDD 4 gives a Northumbrian usage meaning 'apparatus', including mining gear: 'The pit gear means the winding pulleys, ropes, and fittings. "A set o' gear" is the pitman's set of working tools. Any complicated outfit is called gear . . .' Also 1. clothing; 9. household goods; 10. property, effects, wealth, money; and 16. an affair, business, matter; a circumstance – e.g. Scott, *Rob Roy*, xxii: 'This gear's mine and I must manage it'; and *OED n.*5.b, the organs of generation, as in Swift's *Tale of a Tub*, xi. 202; 6 and 7, machinery, and wheels working one upon another, by means of teeth; 11, stuff and nonsense. Caddel (in essay cited above, 73) says that gear is: 'winding machinery at the pithead; goods, moveable property, wealth (Northern, scarce); timberwork supporting a pit (see also Gallows timber); the loop of rope in which the feet were placed to descend into the pit; the last extractions from a dead working (Hooson's mining dictionary); harness, trappings of pit horses (Nicholson's dictionary of the coal trade); equipment, apparatus, *stuff*'. Shakespeare uses the word a number of times to mean a purpose, some matter, business; but see especially *OED*

9.b: in Scottish and Northern dialect, wealth, money, e.g. 'goods and gear' in Arbuthnot's *John Bull* III. iv; 10, rubbish, including material drawn out of mines. B. Kirkby, *Lakeland Words*, 59–60: 'GEAR – What's o' this gear? T' lad's mudder ass'd him that, as she was emptyen his pocket, an' aboot a swillful o' stuff – string, marvels, knives, bits o' iron, indy-rubber, pencils, an' seea on com oot. Annudder 'll say he's oot o' gear when he's gadly; an' a chap's badly geared up when his gallases breck, er his shirt button comes off, er his dicky flees lowse.' Cp. Kipling, 'The Benefactors', 9: 'It is not learning, grace nor gear'; 'My Lady's Law', 15–16: 'desiring less / Great gear than her delight'.

7, 10. Ergot and Appiol. Ergot is a fungal disease of the seeds of rye and grasses; apiol (with one p) is a medicinal substance obtained by distilling parsley seeds with water, also known as parsley camphor, used to induce abortions. Ergot here may also be a play on argot, the jargon or slang of thieves and rogues, since such are those named below, or perhaps even ergo as a noun, of which the *OED* has a nonce instance defined as a 'logic-chopper'; in Chaucer's 'The Physician's Tale', Appius is an evil judge who lusts for the chaste and beautiful Virginia. Perhaps BB's use of the words intends to echo the names of the characters in T. S. Eliot's prose dialogue 'Eeldrop and Appleplex', published by the *Little Review* in its May 1917 and September 1917 numbers.

9, 10. Mr Reader. Presumably addressing the reader.

13. Popone or Kreuger? [*Act. Ant.*]. 'Popone' is Italian for melon, and encodes the name of Andrew Mellon, as in the later *CE* version, see note below; perhaps also a play on 'pop you one', to strike somebody, as *OED* v.1. (Cp. epigraph, chap. 7, George Eliot, *Middlemarch*: '*Piacer e popone / Vuol la sua stagione.*' [Italian proverb: 'Pleasure and melons / Want the same weather.']) Kreuger was Ivar Kreuger (1880–1932), Swedish industrialist known as 'The Match King', who attempted to acquire a monopoly to sell matches worldwide through a fraudulent scheme which collapsed in the 1929 stock market crash; he committed suicide in 1932; a biography by E. Sterner was published in 1930. He appears in EP's *Cantos*, CIII; EP also mentions him in his 'National Culture: a Manifesto' (1938): 'Ivar Kreuger was boomed in the Sat. Ev. Post as more than a financial titan. And that state of belly tickling sycophancy still festers.'

Mellon or Kreuger? [*CE*]. Mellon was Andrew Mellon (1855–1937), US financier and philanthropist who served as Secretary of the Treasury (1921–32), thus associated with the Wall Street Crash, and later Ambassador to Great Britain (1932–3). EP mentions him in *Cantos* XXXVIII, and in his 'Murder by Capital' (1933): 'What has capital done that I should hate Andy Mellon as a symbol or a reality?'

14. *Middle Passage*. The sea journey between West Africa and the West Indies, used in the slave trade.

20. *Hatry's case*. Clarence Hatry, London industrial financier who formed the Austin Friars Trust; he was ruined in 1929 when it was revealed that he had used forged securities as loan collateral, court cases relating to which began in 1932. Appears in EP's *Jefferson and/or Mussolini* (New York, 1936).

21. *Lord Bunting* [*Act. Ant.*]. Lord Bunting is presumably BB himself.
Lord Reading [*CE*]. Lord Reading was Sir Rufus Daniel Issacs, 1st Marquess of Reading (1860–1935), among other things the presiding judge in the case of Roger Casement, and eventually Lord Chief Justice of England, with connections to the coal industry.

22. *UKASE*. An edict of the tsarist or Soviet government.

30. *Boris Godunof*. A character in Pushkin's drama, later adapted for opera by Mussorgsky; Godunof murders Dmitri, rightful heir to the throne, to rule Russia, but frightened by the appearance of 'false Dmitri', actually a monk, he admits his guilt and dies, leaving the crown to his son, Feodor.

32. *Duke of Slumberwear* [*Act. Ant.*]. Slumberwear, *OED* n., 'night clothes'. For this and the other invented names cp. perhaps a passage in a 1935 letter from BB to EP: **'But I will try to insinuate here and there [into the *New English Weekly*] that the workingman might have some look in other than what amounts to a larger dole: including the man who works at writing poetry, and even though the life said workingman wants is incompatible with nearly every law in the country and certainly with all those Lord Bankerville and Lady Whatshername want to bolster'** (quoted Reagan, 'Basil Bunting obiter dicta', in *Terrell*, 274). Years later LZ referred to a similarly constructed 'Lord Bicarbonate of Soda' in his *Zukofsky*, 348, *Guedalla* B9. The disguised reference is to the Duke of Northumberland, as in the *CE* version of the poem.
Duke of Northumberland [*CE*]. See note to 'The Complaint of the Morpethshire Farmer'.

32–3. *can get more / by letting the shooting*. See note to 'The Complaint of the Morpethshire Farmer', on the Duke of Northumberland and land drainage.

34. *leveret*. *OED* 1: 'A young hare, strictly one in its first year.'

36. *Lord Cummingway* [*Act. Ant.*]. Perhaps E. E. Cummings; possibly also a sexual pun.

Lord Tommanjerry [*Act. Ant.*]. *OED*, Tom-and-Jerry, 'to drink and indulge in riotous behaviour', also a 'low drinking shop'. Also a citation from 1894 *Northumberland Glossary* for 'Tom-and-Jerry, a catcall'. Perhaps refers to book by Pierce Egan (1772–1849), *Life in London; or, the Day and Night Scenes of Jerry Hawthorn, Esq., and his elegant friend, Corinthian Tom, accompanied by Bob Logic, the Oxonian, in their Rambles and Sprees through the Metropolis* (1821) and its sequel, *Finish to the Adventures of Tom, Jerry, and Logic, in their Pursuits through Life in and out of London* (1829); illustrated by Cruikshank, the books underwent a number of stage adaptations during the nineteenth century. 'Jerry' is slang for German soldier, perhaps pertinent here because of the German connections of the earlier version's Lord Londonderry; see next note.

Lord Joicey [*CE*]. Principal shareholder of the Great Northern Coal Company, who lost several sons killed in the early part of World War I.

Lord Londonderry [*CE*]. The seventh Marquess of Londonderry (1878–1949), a County Durham coal owner. He was Britain's Air Minister in the early 1930s and was also known for his controversial contacts with Hitler and other leading Nazis later in that decade. An earlier Lord Londonderry was among the objects of Byron's scorn in *Don Juan*.

37. *Lord St Thomas* [*Act. Ant.*] St Thomas perhaps plays on Timothy Dwight's hymn, 'I Love Thy Lord – St Thomas', on the name of St Thomas Aquinas, St Thomas à Beckett or perhaps even on that of T. S. Eliot.

Duke of Oppenham [*Act. Ant.*]. Oppenham perhaps evokes George Oppen (1908–84), closely associated with LZ and Objectivism; Oppen was Jewish, so perhaps 'ham' was an additional jest. Perhaps also E. Phillips Oppenheim (1866–1946), British author of fiction about intrigue and espionage, who was subsidized by a wealthy New York businessman.

Lord St Oswald [*CE*]. Title named for St Oswald (d. 642, King of Northumberland 633–42, who revived Christianity by inviting Aidan to be bishop of Lindisfarne), patron saint of the medieval priory in the grounds of the family seat of the first Lord St Oswald, Rowland Winn (1820–93), at Nostell Priory.

Duke of Hamilton [*CE*]. The Dukes of Hamilton were a line of Scottish nobility; much of their wealth came from coal mines. Beatrix becomes engaged to a Duke of Hamilton in Thackeray's *History of Henry Esmond, Esquire*.

38. *too dear.* Followed in *CE* by the additional lines:

Steel, steal: steal, steel, Lord Weir.
(An exercise in free association).

Andrew Weir, later Lord Inverforth (1865–1955), worked in a shipping office in Glasgow as a young man and bought his first ship at age twenty; the firm he founded was one of Britain's largest owners of ships. He became air minister during World War I and later a government adviser on armaments. A Lord Weir was also a nineteenth-century hanging judge in R. L. Stevenson's *Weir of Hermiston* (1896). Cp. T. S. Eliot, 'Coriolan', 'I. Triumphal March', 1–2: 'Stone, bronze, stone, steel, stone, oakleaves, horses' heels / Over the paving.'

41. *governor*. *OED* 8: 'A self-acting contrivance for regulating the passage of gas, steam, water, etc., esp. the supply of any one of these to a machine, in order to ensure an even and regular motion.' According to Caddel (see essay cited in 'Publication history', above, 73), the 'control mechanism on the engine for the pit winding gear'.

44. *Davy lamps*. Safety lamps used in coal mining, invented by Sir Humphry Davy.

52. *pownies*. Ponies. 'The curious spelling of *pownies* is interesting: this is a direct transliteration of the local Throckley dialect . . . Bunting's much-loved grandfather Isaac Taylor Cheesman and his uncle Matthew Taylor Cheesman (both Throckley men) would have used this dialect, and Bunting would have grown up used to hearing it being spoken' (*Caddel & Flowers*, 33). *OED*: 'pony' probably Scottish in origin, from 'powney'. Cp. Burns, 'Second Epistle to J. Lapraik', 2: 'An' pownies reek in pleugh or braik . . .' Also Trollope, *The Eustace Diamonds*: 'Oh, ay – there's shelter, na doubt, for mair pownies than they'll ride . . .', and Wilkie Collins, *The Two Destinies*, chap. 17: '"Just leave it to the pownies," the guide says.'

57–61. *The water rose . . . widows were provided for.* BB wrote to EP (21 March 1934; quoted *Quartermain*, 11–12): **'I was on the spot when the View Pit was flooded and forty-five men drowned, I heard what the men had to say about it and the whole cursed system.'** The account in BB's letter 'closely matches accounts of the disaster at View Pit, or "Low Monty", on 30 March 1925, when miners broke through into the disused workings of the neighbouring Paradise Pit in Benwell' (*Caddel & Flowers*, 33). BB's father, Thomas Lowe Bunting, had been a pit doctor for Montague Colliery in Scottswood-on-Tyne, where BB was born, while his maternal grandfather, Isaac Taylor Cheesman, was manager for the Throckley Coal Company's Isabella, Derwentwater and Blucher Pits (*Caddel & Flowers*, 11).

54. *stife*. *OED*: 'Chiefly *dial.* A suffocating fume or vapour.'

74–5. *'The sea is his and he / who made it'*. Psalm 95, verse 5: 'The sea *is* his, and he made it: and his hands formed the dry *land*.'

75–6. Who / made Holland. Cp. Marvell, 'The Character of Holland', 1: 'Holland, that scarce deserves the name of land.'

78. MAGGOT. See Caddel essay (74–5): 'At the end of his life, lice maggots and gentles . . . are repeatedly used by Bunting as images of human ignorance: "Old age", he wrote in his note on *Briggflatts*, "can see at last the loveliness of things overlooked or despised, frost, the dancing maggots, sheepdogs . . . And still we know neither where we are nor why." In *Briggflatts* itself, the maggots are at work,' etc. [*Briggflatts* II. 145; V. 127].

84. BOLSHEVIK. Member of the Lenin-led revolutionary faction of the Social Democratic Party in Russia from 1903; this group seized complete control of the country after the Russian Revolution in 1917, and was renamed the Communist Party.

[After 84]. In margin of *CE*, with arrows pointing to headings, BB's handwritten circled note: **'heavy leaded type, newspaper headline style'**.

UNCOLLECTED ODES

1 'Coryphée gravefooted precise, dance to the gracious music'

Published as an epigraph in the 'Carmina' section of *RM*. In *UP* and *CP1994/2000*.

Notes

1. Coryphée. A ballet-dancer who ranks higher than a member of the corps de ballet but below a soloist, and who performs in small ensembles.

gravefooted. Not in *OED*.

2 Against the Tricks of Time

Published in *RM*, where it was included in the 'Carmina' section; this version presented in *UP* and *CP1994/2000*. But in *CE* as XXXIX, untitled, with variants; this version is presented here. A revision of 12–31 became 'Farewell ye sequent graces' (*FBO* 2, above) from *P1950* onwards. The poem is mentioned in a letter from LZ to EP dated 9 November 1930. It was considered, along with 'Sad Spring', 'While Shepherds Watched', 'Chorus of Furies' and 'To Venus' ['Darling of Gods and men, beneath the gliding stars'], for *Poetry*'s 'Objectivists' issue which LZ was to edit (*Pound/Zukofsky: Selected Letters of Ezra Pound and Louis Zukofsky*).

Notes

12. Farewell ye sequent graces. Cp. Milton, *Paradise Lost*, XII. 165: 'There he dies, and leaves his Race / Growing into a Nation, and now grown / Suspected to a sequent king.'

14–23. Silent be our leave-taking . . . fantom dancers. Cp. T. S. Eliot, 'Preludes', III. **'I had some knowledge of music and I had arrived via a somewhat strange route at the conclusion that poetry should try to take over some of the techniques that I only knew in music. So that when I discovered Eliot writing poems and calling them "Preludes", even though the resemblance, to say, Chopin's Preludes was slight**

and superficial, I was extremely interested. He was obviously thinking on lines not dissimilar from my own' (*Descant*, [6]).

23. *fantom. OED* n.6. ('*appositive* or *adj.*') cites St Cuthbert for 'fantom'. Cp. Dryden, translation of the fourth book of Lucretius, 'Concerning the Nature of Love', 67: 'So Love with fantomes cheats our longing eyes . . .' BB also uses the word in 'Overdrafts', 'Last night without sight of you my brain was ablaze', 12.

24. *Airlapped.* Not in *OED* or *EDD*.

37–8. *PROPTER NOS HOMINES ET PROPTER / NOSTRAM SALUTEM.* 'For us men, and for our salvation descended from Heaven'. From the Nicene creed, a text in the Ordinary of the Latin Mass; in the Missal of the *Book of Common Prayer*, sung in the Eucharist service; also in Bach's *Mass in B minor*, Mozart's *Mass in C minor*, and in Beethoven's *Mass in C.*

3 Reading X's 'Collected Poems'

Published in *Whips & Scorpions*, 43, *Guedalla* B2, as 'Reading X's "Collected Works"' and printed in *UP* and *CP1994/2000*. The version presented here is the later version BB used in *CE*, where it is Ode XXXVII.

Note

7. *versicles.* Little verses. Cp. Byron, letter to Moore, 25 March 1817: 'Here are some versicles.'

4 Hymn To Alias Thor

In *CE* as Ode X, with subheading, 'Hymn to alias Thor'. In *UP* and *CP1994/2000*.

Notes

[Title] Thor. Pagan warrior-deity of Scandinavia; the name derives from a Germanic word for thunder. Thor was foe to a race of giants, but benevolent to mortals.

21–22. *bloom / snot.* The conjunction of these perhaps invites a comparison to the end of chap. 3, Joyce's *Ulysses*, in which Stephen Dedalus wipes his snot on a rock. BB called 1922, the year he discovered *The Waste Land* and *Ulysses*, **'a great year'** (P. Craven and M. Heyward, 'An Interview with Basil Bunting', 29).

5 'The flat land lies under water'

In *CE* as Ode XI. In *UP* and *CP1994/2000*.

Note

2. *chequer*. Cp. Keats, *Endymion*, II. 287: 'hill-flowers running wild / In pink and purple chequer'. Also Ruskin, *Modern Painters*, I. II. VI. i. ¶18: 'The shadows of the upper boughs . . . resting in quiet chequers upon the glittering earth.'

6 'Gertie Gitana's hymn to waltzing'

A separate poem titled 'Sonnet II', reworked for this poem, was sent to LZ in a letter dated 29 September 1935 (held at HRC), published in *Makin*, 81. It was accompanied by versions of 'Isn't it poetical . . .', a variant 'Gertie Gitana's hymn to waiting', 'Envoi to the Reader' and 'You leave / nobody else / without a bed'.

Publication history

In *CE* as Ode XXXI. In *UP* and *CP1994/2000*.

Notes

1. *Gertie Gitana's hymn to waltzing*. Gertie Gitana was a popular early twentieth-century British music-hall star (1887–1957); a *gitana* is a female Spanish gypsy (Gitano, *OED*). Cp. EP's ' To a Friend Writing on Cabaret Dancers', 24–5: '"CARMEN EST MAIGRE, UN TRAIT DE BISTRE / CERNE SON ŒIL DE GITANA".'

3. *Polymnia-alias-Echo*. Muse of sacred hymns and poetry; see note to 'Attis: Or, Something Missing', II. 56–7.

5. *Waterloo Road*. A low-rent area, near London's Waterloo Station.

7–8. *Erasmus and other idiots / nuts on the classics*. Desiderius Erasmus (1469–1536), Dutch humanist and scholar, who compiled the first printed and distributed version of the New Testament. He collected over 3,000 proverbs from the work of classical authors for his *Adagia* (1500).

14. *kerb*. More familiar to American readers as 'curb', the edge of a sidewalk.

15. *Sadi's right*. Reference to a poem by the Persian poet, Sa'di, translated by BB: 'Many well-known people have been packed

away in cemeteries'. Appears as the second poem in 'Uncollected Overdrafts'.

21. *mugs game*. Cp. T. S. Eliot: 'As things are, and as fundamentally they must always be, poetry is not a career, but a mug's game. No honest poet can ever feel quite sure of the permanent value of what he has written: He may have wasted his time and messed up his life for nothing' (*The Use of Poetry and the Use of Criticism*, 1933).

22. *selva oscura*. 'Dark wood', from Dante, *Inferno* I. 2.

23. *swanking*. *EDD vbl. sb.*: 'Pretense, shamming, fooling.'

24. *Omar*. Omar Khayyām; see note on Omar in *The Spoils*, II, and BB's 1935 typescript essay 'The Lion and the Lizard', collected in *Three Essays*, 28–31. Paraphrase of sentiments found in FitzGerald's *Rubáiyát of Omar Khayyám*. Note EP's lines in *Hugh Selwyn Mauberley* ('Yeux Glauques'): 'The English Rubaiyat was still-born / in those days.'

28. *Barbara*. Unidentified.

30. *Bank of Aeolus*. In Greek mythology, Aeolus was the god of the winds.

33. *sundry*. *OED* 'sundry *a*.' has citations for Ælfric and Bede. Cp. Dryden, *Ovid's Art of Love*, I. 863: 'sundry women are of sundry minds'.

38. *Muleteers*. Cp. Evelyn's diary (which BB had read), 11 April 1645: 'On May-day the greate procession of the Universitie and the Mulatiers at St. Antonie's'.

Firdusi. Also spelled Ferdowsī, Firdawsi, or Firdousi. Pseud. Abū ol-Qasem Mansūr (*ca.*940–1020), Persian poet, author of Persian national epic, *Shāh-nāmeh*; see Appendix II. A, and note to *FBO* 32.

Burns. Robert Burns, Scottish poet (1759–96).

40. *a moder-rate kettledr-rum r-r-roulade*. Perhaps reproduces Scots accent.

46–7. *Double-tonguing a corked flute / descant to the bass*. Cp. *Briggflatts*, I. 2, IV. 44, etc.

49. *Superannuation Fund*. A retirement savings fund.

50–2. *count upon it . . . good of his country*. In a letter to Dorothy Pound years later, BB wrote: **'Every time I call at the [British] Embassy [in Persia] or have anything to do with them I am reminded of my old quotation from Swift: "Count upon it as a truth next to your creed that no one man in office of which he is master for life will ever hazard that office for the good of his country"'** (9 June 1949; quoted *Makin*, 120).

7 Envoi to the Reader

TS (held at HRC) sent in 1935 to LZ among a group of poems (including sections of *UO* 6 and 'Isnt it poetical . . .'); appended to the title is the note: '**(It don't apply to you, Louis)**'. Other draft versions exist, e.g. variant in letter to EP (dated 'Day after saint bloody John' [25 June] 1935), at Beinecke: '**Incidentally, if nobody else thanks you for not being in last Faber anthology, if it is such as you imply and I imagine, please accept mine. If say Mr Spender were incredibly to invite me to contrib to such, I wd send in my fart poem.**'

Publication history

In *UP* and *CP1994/2000*.

8 Trinacria

Note in *CE*: '**Only 2 & 4 are Sicilian: the other two are from North Italy.**'

Publication history

In *CE* as Ode XXXVI. In *UP* and *CP1994/2000*. Though calling this an 'Uncollected Ode' – it was an Ode in *CE* – Caddel wonders whether the poem should not be 'an overdraft' (*CP2000*, 180). Part 3 became *FBO* 27 from 1965 onwards.

Note

[Title] Trinacria. Sicily. Dante referred to his exile in *De vulgari Eloquentia* (II. vi. 4) – a work about which BB said, '**I think that a man who will read *De vulgari Eloquentia* will have got most of the literary criticism he's ever going to require**' (*Mottram*, 8) – in an example of a Latin sentence: 'Eiecta maxima parte florum de sinu tuo, Florentia, nequicquam Trinacriuam Totila secundus adivit.' ('Once the greater part of your blossoms, Florence, were torn from your breast, in vain did the second Totila make his way to Sicily.')

9 A Song for Rustam

TS at SUNY Buffalo dated 1952–1964 (the first date added in ink, possibly in another hand). Also TS sent to LZ with letter of 7 September 1964 (held at HRC).

Rustam was BB's first son, d. 1952, born in 1937 after his separation from his first wife. BB heard about the death from his eldest daughter. Cp. Matthew Arnold, 'Sohrab and Rustum'. BB and Arnold used the same translation; see notes to Arnold's *Poems*, 1854 (*McGonigal & Price*, [185]). Also, in each poem, a father laments the loss of a son he did not see grow up (Arnold himself lost two sons). Cp. 'corn' in 294–5 of the Arnold with 8, and thematically Arnold's 'And his soul set to grief, as the vast tide / Of the bright rocking Ocean sets to shore / At the full moon; tears gathered in his eyes', 616–18) to the first stanza of this poem. Also, while Kenneth Allott finds unconvincing the suggestion that Arnold got some of the details of his poem from *The Travels of Marco Polo*, tr. Hugh Murray (1844), BB had in his library *Il libri di messer Marco Polo* . . . (1932), and *Il milione di Marco Polo* . . . (1928). See also notes to *FBO* 32, above. According to Colin Simms, BB said in conversation: **'Matthew Arnold didn't know any Persian. He got his *Sohrab and Rustum* story, the synopsis of the *Shahnamé*, out of General Malcolm. His version is misleading. Arnold took it from Malcolm's very inaccurate translation and embroidered on that. He made a very good thing out of it . . . The end of Arnold's *Sohrab* is very tricky and surprising but the end of Firdosi's is such that it brings tears to your eyes . . . a really tricky thing! And you get no idea, in Arnold, that Sohrab is anything but a character from an epic. He is in the Firdosi; he has indeed young ladies . . . Arnold might have thought that it would take away from the epic! Of course, he didn't know, Malcolm hadn't put that in his synopsis!'** (BB to Simms, 5 May 1983, in 'From "The Bunting Tapes"', *Chicago Review* 44, no. 3/4 [1998], 98–9).

On the composition of the poem generally, BB remarked, **'Perhaps it is enough to say that between you and Tom Pickard . . . somehow the old machine has been set to work again, and I have actually been writing. Therefore I send you the first fruits'** (quoted *Forde*, 58). **'It is hard for me to estimate how much, if any, of the old skill is left, and whether a decade of foul drudgery after a decade of absorbing action has reduced me to imbecility. Moreover, facing at last the death of my elder son, I have courted the risk of platitude and even cliche by trying to banish "literature" as far as I can from the statement of what I feel, or felt: for you will say that I am as slow as Malherbe, whose ode on the death of somebody's wife was not ready until the man had been remarried several years and was rearing a new family. It has made me very sad, unwrapping this, and I hope I have clipped something out of it that has shape and grace: but I feel incompetent to judge'** (BB to LZ, 7 September 1964; quoted *Lesch*, 309). (For more on BB and Malherbe, see note to *FBO* 34).

'Anyway, its all for long consideration, I suppose. That "long" is the trouble. I've a feeling that there isnt so long to write what I want to write. I'll die or petrify, or my disgusting drudgery will make me imbecile. Still, better silence than rubbish.

> **In the grave's narrow slot**
> **they lie: we rot.**

[Cp. *Briggflatts*, I. 25–6: 'In the grave's slot / he lies. We rot.']

The we doesnt mean you, whose work for a living is merely dull, not stultifying. Worms dont eat you alive . . . Well, that looks like the programme of an old man revisiting the scenes of his youth, casting up his accounts, as my father did in the few months before he died. I have no means to carry it out, but I must try.

We are all very little more than turds. I've said more here than I ever said to anybody, Louis, at least since I grew up. YOU wont dive after useless salvage, but chuck this flotsam back into the ocean to sink. And having no even approximate equal to talk to, its a relief to write it to you' (BB to LZ, 16 September 1964; quoted *Makin*, 123).

Publication history

First reproduced in an appendix to *Lesch* (426). Published in a corrupt version, and dated 7 : IX : 64 in *Sulfur* 14 (1985), 7. In *UP* and *CP1994/2000*.

10 'To abate what swells'

TS at SUNY Buffalo, dated 1971.

BB admired Lorine Niedecker's poetry, and they met in 1967. In a letter to Cid Corman, she wrote of their meeting, 'Basil came! With two daughters . . .. Have you ever met him? His manner is timid and tender. Withal so kindly. O lovely day for me' ('Letters of Lorine Niedecker to Cid Corman 1961–1970', ed. Lisa Pater Faranda, *Conjunctions*, 5 (1983), 156; quoted *Forde*, 60). Niedecker wrote a poem about BB, 'The Ballad of Basil'.

Publication history

Published in *Epitaphs for Lorine*, ed. Jonathan Williams (Penland, NC: Jargon Society, 1973), *Guedalla* B20. In *UP* and *CP1994/2000*.

Note

7. *swathe*. *OED* citations for 'swath', 1: 'Track, trace', include Beowulf, Ælfric, and Bede.

11 'Such syllables flicker out of grass'

In an earlier letter to Forde (23 May 1972; quoted *Forde*, 242–3), BB had written: **'It may illuminate what I've said about sonata form or any other form if I tell you what happened on the voyage home [from British Columbia through the Panama Canal]. I'd a number of themes in my**

head for at least three years, some longer, but could do nothing with them because they didnt seem to join together or oppose each other in any way that suggested their proper shape. The one night I saw the new moon, the very first new moon, emerging from the old moon as Helen, Selanna, the new moon, must have emerged from Leda's egg; and the next night I watched Jupiter as a drop of molten silver sliding down the flank of the new moon. And as I turned away from this marvellous sight I caught a glimpse of a very young girl who seemed obviously the new moon in flesh, slim, graceful, blonde; and instantly many old themes began to assemble themselves as though this were the keystone enabling them to form an arch, themes of renewal, mainly, closely bound, though I had never perceived it. And this was wonderfully reinforced when I spoke to the girl and found her name was Linnaea and she a descendant of Linnaeus who named all the flowers, as though she were Persephone as well as Selanna. There was even the germ of an anti-theme ready to fit in, though that needs more perception before I can use it. I cannot say more yet; but it seems to me that I shall soon be able to begin work on a sonata, or what is more likely to prove a sonata than not, with the transformations of the first theme all worked out though those of the second one may delay me.' In a similar letter to Quartermain (9 April 1973), he wrote that he'd **'been looking at the new moon, the April new moon that takes the attitude of Wordsworth's "little boat" in *Peter Bell*, Ezra's barge of Ra-Set'** (quoted *Quartermain DP*, 144).

The poem was never completed, though it went through a number of drafts, apart from the thirty lines given here. Quartermain commented that the 'drafts of "A New Moon" that [BB] destroyed were good enough for most poets of his time, indeed better' (*Quartermain DP*, 146).

Publication history

According to Caddel (*UP*, 62 / *CP2000*, 230; *Caddel & Flowers*, 54), some copies were typeset and printed by BB on an Adana press and circulated to friends *ca.*1972 (copy at Durham). Sent in a letter to Forde dated 26 February 1973 and reprinted in *Forde thesis*, later *Forde*, 243–4, with the comment, **'*First* draft – many errors and clumsinesses to be cut out or changed.'** Also sent as a 'working draft of the opening lines of "A New Moon"' to Quartermain, 9 April 1973, quoted in *Quartermain DP* (146); a variant MS notebook version of the first ten lines is reproduced on the inside back cover of *Caddel & Flowers* (I present this text in the 'Fragments' section). In *UP* and *CP1994/2000*.

Notes

4. *paeonies*. Var. of peonies.

6. *carves my stone*. Cp. *Briggflatts*, I. 14–37, 114–17, II. 131–5.

7. *haugh*. *OED*: 'Sc. and north. dial. A piece of flat alluvial land by the side of a river, forming part of the floor of the river valley.' Cp. Burns, 'Scotch Drink', 13, 'Let husky wheat the haughs adorn.'

14. *stots*. *OED* v.: '*Sc.* and *north*. 1: To rebound, bounce (from, off); to fall or impinge with a bounce (on against); to jump, start, spring.'
kerf. *OED* 2: 'The result of cutting; the incision, notch, slit, etc., made by cutting, esp. by a saw.' (Citations for *OED* 1. 'The act of cutting or carving; a cut, stroke', include Ælfric, *Gawain and the Green Knight*, and Gower. Note also 2.b.: '*fig*. The furrow made by a ship's keel.'); also *EDD* 1. Or perhaps *EDD* 2: 'A layer of earth; a solid piece cut or carved out by the spade.'

18. *Uber sophiae sugens*. A Latin phrase, source untraced, meaning 'sucking [at] the breast of wisdom'. In Greek mythology, a smear of milk was left after the infant Hercules suckled milk from Hera to obtain her wisdom. Discovering that the baby was Zeus' bastard son by a mortal woman, she pushed him from her breast and the spurting milk became the Milky Way, the *Kiklios Galaxios*, from which the word 'galaxy' is said to be derived. Cp. Shakespeare, *Romeo and Juliet*, I. iii. 68: 'I would say thou hadst suck'd wisdom from thy teat'; Massinger, *The Unnatural Combat*, I. i: 'I think they suck this knowledge from their milk'; T. S. Eliot mentions the play in his essay on Massinger in *The Sacred Wood*; Landor, 'They are not weak, suckled by Wisdom', cited *Webster's Revised Unabridged Dictionary* (1913), 1527.

21. *Loki's daughter*. Cp. *Egil's Saga*, chap. 60. In Norse mythology, Loki's daughter, Hel or Hella, is ruler of the Underworld, with the status of goddess and queen; sister of the Wolf Fenrir and the Middle-Garth's Wyrm, she is considered a demonic figure.

23. *goaf*. *EDD sb*. 2: 'The space left in a coal-mine after the whole of the coal has been extracted.' *OED* 2 cites entry for 'Goave' from *Northumberland Glossary* (1893): 'space cleared of coal. Usually printed, but inaccurately, as *goaf*.' *Caddel & Flowers* (63) identifies the goaf in the poem as a slag heap of the Percy Pit at Newburn nicknamed 'The Black Alp'; it supposedly once reached a height of 150 feet.

27. *foss*. Var. of fosse. *OED* 'fosse' 1: 'An excavation narrow in proportion to its length; a canal, ditch or trench; a cart-rut' 2: 'A ditch or dike formed to serve as a barrier against an advancing foe, a moat surrounding a fortified place,' with citation for Mandeville. *EDD* 1: 'A trench, a bank with a ditch.'

29. *shammy*. *EDD*: 'A wash-leather.' From chamois or shamoy, to prepare leather by working oil or grease into the skin.

12 *Dentdale conversation* / 'Yan tan tethera pethera pimp'

Published in *Truck* 21 (1979). In *UP* and *CP1994/2000*, where Caddel says it can be dated 1978.

Notes

[Title/subheading] Dentdale. In Cumbria; name recorded from 1577, contains Old Scandinavian word, *dalr*, 'valley'. Dent, possibly an old river-name, origin and meaning uncertain, dates from the thirteenth century (*A Dictionary of English Place-Names*, A. D. Mills [Oxford, 1998]).

1. Yan tan tethera pethera pimp. Northern dialect for 'One two three four five.' B. Kirkby, *Lakeland Words* (Kendal?, 1898), 161: 'YAH, YAN – One. When yan's deun what yan can, what mair can yan deea?' The table of 'scoring numerals' on p. 163, under 'Westmoreland', gives Yan, Tahn, Teddera, Meddera, Pimp, and under 'Coniston and District' gives Yan, Taen, Tedderte, Medderte, Pimp. This type of numbering is traditionally used for counting sheep.

3. gimmers. *OED* 1: '*Sc.* and *north.* dial.: A ewe between the first and second shearing.' Citation for Scott, letter to Ellis, 19 May 1804 (in Lockhart): 'Long sheep and short sheep and tups and gimmers and hogs and dinmonts had made a perfect sheep fold of my understanding.' *EDD* 1: 'A young female sheep, *gen.* from one to two years old, or between the first and second shearing; a ewe that has not borne young.' Cp. Scott, *Waverley* xi: 'gimmers and dinmonts, and stots, and runts, and kyloes'.

wethers. *OED* 1: 'A male sheep, a ram; esp. a castrated ram.' Citations include Ælfric; cp. Crabbe, *The Parish Register*, II. 343: 'Two pigs, a cow, and wethers half a score, / Increased his stock.' Also *EDD* 1. Cp. Burns, 'Ken ye ought o' Captain Grose?', 11: 'And eaten like a wether-haggis?'

UNCOLLECTED OVERDRAFTS

See Appendix II. B, Bunting's foreword to Omar Pound's *Arabic & Persian Poems in English*..

'Night swallowed the sun as'

The couplet appears as part of a TS held by the HRC, titled 'The Rosegarden, Part One: The Habits of Kings. Tale Number Four'. This prose piece, first published in *Bunting's Persia*, is punctuated by verse fragments, including the following:

> Noah's son took to low company:
> him prophecy ceased to illumine.
> The dog of the Seven Sleepers became,
> by prolonged good company, human.

At the foot of the TS, BB wrote, **'I am very fond of Noah's son and always recite it whenever there's an opportunity.'** The above lines were sent to LZ in a letter of [1?] December 1934. According to Caddel, BB 'would still recite it on occasion towards the end of his life' (*UP*, 62 / *CP*, 230). Peter Quartermain recorded a slight variant of the couplet in a notebook entry dated 23 October 1971 when he was staying with BB in Victoria: 'The night swallowed the sun as / the whale swallowed Jonas.'

According to Caddel, a version of Sa'di's *Gulistan*, I. iv.

Publication history

Published in LZ's *A Test of Poetry* (New York, 1948), 107, *Guedalla* B6. Dated there by LZ '*c.* 1935'. In *UP* and *CP1994/2000*.

Notes

2. *Jonas*. From the New Testament Greek form, Ionas, of Jonah, whose story is told in the Old Testament Book of Jonah.

'Many well-known people have been packed away in cemeteries'

According to Caddel, a version of Sa'di's *Gulistan*, I. ii.

Publication history

In *CE* as Ode XXVII with attribution to 'Sadi' at foot of poem. In *UP* and *CP1994/2000*.

Notes

5. *Naushervan*. The sixth-century pre-Islamic Iranian emperor Nausherwan was known as the model of a just ruler.

8. *'What's-his-name's dead.'* Cp. Kipling, 'Pharoah and the Sergeant', in which 'Sergeant Whatsisname' figures. Cp. also BB's 'Chomei at Toyama', 256: 'Soandso's dead.'

'Light of my eyes, there *is* something to be said'

Version of poem from *Diwan-i Hafiz* (Caddel cites H. S. Jarrett's ed. [Calcutta, 1881], no. 444; *UP*, 62/*CP2000*, 230).

Publication history

First published in *Boz-West*, 10, *Guedalla* D10, as 'II' in numbered group; this version presented here. In *CE* as Ode V; that version in *UP* and *CP1994/2000*.

Notes

8. *Send for the wine-merchant*. Typed in margin of *CE*: (bootlegger).

18–19. *gold-scattering gown* . . . Hafiz *in his flannel shirt*. Loloi and Pursglove point out that the parallel in the original is between a golden gown and a woollen gown, Hafiz identifying the latter with himself; he does so because it 'makes possible – indeed invites – identification of him, as speaker of this poem, as a Sufi'. The nickname Sufi, according to A. J. Arberry as quoted by them, 'is undoubtedly derived from the Arabic word for wool' (Parvin Loloi and Glyn Pursglove, 'Basil Bunting's Translations of Hafiz', in *McGonigal & Price*, 192).

Desinas ineptire / 'O everlastingly self-deluded!'

Version of Hafiz (Caddel cites Jarrett ed., no. 503; *UP* 62/*CP2000*, 230).

Publication history

In *CE* as Ode XV. In *UP* and *CP1994/2000*.

Note

[Title] Desinas ineptire. Catullus VIII, 1–2, 'Miser Catulle, desinas ineptire . . .' Loeb: 'Poor Catullus, 'tis time you should ease your folly, and account as lost what you see as lost.' Cp. LZ's version, 'Miserable Catullus . . .' and LZ and Celia Zukofsky's version, 'Miss her, Catullus? . . .' Also Campion's, 'Harden now thy tyred hart with more than flinty rage.'

'Isnt it poetical, a chap's mind in the dumps?'

Version of Hafiz (Caddel cites Jarrett ed., no. 226; *UP*, 62/*CP2000*, 230). Variant TS in HRC (see note to *UO* 7, above).

Publication history

In *CE* as Ode XXXIII. In *UP* and *CP1994/2000*.

Note

8. his marble was hacked out in haste. Loloi and Pursglove observe that 'an allusion to "a painter from China" [in Hafiz's original] is transmuted into a quasi-sculptural conceit about the carving of marble' ('Basil Bunting's Translations of Hafiz', *McGonigal & Price*, 200). Cp. *Briggflatts* I. 117.

'I'm the worse for drink again, it's'

Variant TS sent to LZ (held by HRC). Version of Hafiz (Caddel cites Jarrett ed., no. 225; *UP*, 63/*CP2000*, 230).

Publication history

Included in *CE* as Ode XL, without attribution to Hafiz. In *UP* and *CP1994/2000*.

The Beginning of the Stories

TS held by the HRC. 'etc etc etc' at the foot of the text is handwritten.

Publication history

First published in *Bunting's Persia*.

Note

11. Kayumart. A Persian figure similar, or identical to, the Biblical Adam.

From 'Faridun's Sons'

As Caddel notes, a 'rough version exists as section 7 of a TS headed (in ink) "About 1/3 of the story of Faridun's Sons"' held at the HRC, 'together with related Firdosi material in draft form' (*UP*, 63/*CP2000*, 230). This material was incorporated into the work titled 'From Faridun's Sons' in *Bunting's Persia*, where it was first published. The full sequence is a version of Ferdowsī's *Shāh-nāmeh*, 'Faridun', 543–92 (Caddel cites edition from Tehran, 1934; *UP*, 63/*CP2000*, 230). BB wrote to LZ, **'I am just about sending Ezra some fourteen Cantos of Fariduns sons. But I must deal with seven more before I can send it to a publisher. IT aint good enough, I regret to say. It makes me uneasy, and I can only hope to deceive people who cant read Poishyan. Luckily there are lots of them'** (BB to LZ, 1 December 1934; HRC).

Publication history

First published in *The Criterion* 15, no. 40 (April 1936), 421–3, *Guedalla* D11, with title, 'From "Faridun's Sons", by Firdusi'. In *UP* and *CP1994/2000*.

Notes

1 ff. Faridun (or *Afaridun*), *Salm, Tur, Iraj, Turan.* Legendary Persian King whose story is told in Ferdowsī's epic poem *Shāh-nāmeh*, the 'Book of Kings'. BB's own handwritten note to the typescript of 'The beginning of the stories' explains: **'Faridun was the 6th king. After overthrowing a fearful tyrant & getting wives for his sons, he caused the wars of Iran & Turan which lasted off & on for centuries.'** Faridun's sons were Salm, Tur and Iraj. He divided up the world by giving central Asia to Tur, after whom the land was named Turan, and Iran to his youngest son, Iraj. Tur was jealous of Iraj and killed him in order to seize Iran; Iraj was avenged by his grandson, Manuchehri, and from then on Iran and Turan were at war.

146. *Ahrimans.* The Zoroastrian epitome of evil, a devil; juxtaposed with Ahura Mazda or Ohrmuxd, the epitome of good, though this dualism was toned down somewhat by Ferdowsī, who was Muslim.

236. *Jamshed.* Legendary Persian king said to have lived for a thousand years and ruled for many hundreds during the golden age; he had command over angels and demons. Near the end of his rule, he sat on a jewelled throne and was raised to the heavens; for this and other kinds of hubris he eventually fell out of favour with the Creator.

Baudelaire in Cythera

Version of Baudelaire, *Un Voyage à Cythère.*

Publication history

In *CE* as Ode XXX. In *UP* and *CP1994/2000*. Caddel, wondering whether BB's Baudelaire is 'too free to be regarded as translation', categorizes the poem uncertainly as an 'overdraft' (*CP2000*, 180).

Notes

1. *trapezing. OED* 'trapeze' cites G. du Maurier's *Trilby*, I. 70: 'Fencing and boxing and trapezing seemed to be more in her line.'

4. *Songfamous Cythera.* The Peloponnesian island, Cythera, is associated with the goddess Venus.

11. *ringdove.* Wood pigeon.

13. *Baedeker.* A popular series of travel guide-books, with a system of star ratings. Cp. T. S. Eliot, 'Burbank with a Baedeker: Bleistein with a Cigar'.

15. *slacking.* To loosen, make slack. Cp. Scott, *Old Mortality*, xli: 'Tak the gentleman's horse to the stable, and slack his girths.'

27. *Venus' land.* See note to Cythera, above.

28. *through the looking-glass.* Title of Lewis Carroll book.

'Amru'l Qais and Labīd and Ahktal and blind A'sha and Qais'

Fragment from a MS letter to LZ (held at the HRC) dated 'May Day 1939'. Version of Manuchehri (Caddel cites A. Kazimirkski's ed. [Paris, 1886], no. 87, 9–21; *UP*, 63/*CP2000*, 231). Manuchehri was an eleventh-century Persian poet who used Arabic words in his work; he was a protégé of 'Unsuri, also of interest to BB. **'So! I have been reading Manuchehri: bloody fine poet too. The bird that preens its feathers many times a day, going over and over them "like a petty clerk who has made a mistake in his accounts". And the sonority of his musammats. And the abrupt and wonderful transitions. And his observation of deer & flowers & cameldrivers & girls. The tulips that "are a row of parrots asleep with their head under their wing". The names of the ancient Arab poets, in a satire'** (BB to LZ, May Day 1939; quoted *Forde*, 128).

The poem, in BB's version as in the original, mentions by name a number of renowned classical Arabic and Persian poets, notably: *Amru'l Qais* (Imru'l-Qays, d. *ca.*540), one of the greatest Arab poets of the pre-Islamic period; *Qais* (*ca.* seventh century), Bedouin poet who fell in love with Laia, and became known as Majnun, or 'madman'; Labīd (Labīd ibn Rabi'a, 550–*ca.*661), known for his *qasidas*; *Akhtal* (al-Akhtal, *ca.* 640–*ca.*710), Christian poet and anthologist; *blind A'sha* (**Maymun Ibn Qays Al-a'sha, 570–*ca.*625), whose name means 'the night-blind'**; *Bu Nuvās* (Abū Nuwās, *ca.*747–62–*ca.*813–15, whose name means 'the man with the forelock'), a poet of mixed Arab and Persian ancestry who appears in the *The Thousand and One Nights*; *Bu Shakūr of Balkh* (Abū Shakūr of Balkh, *fl. ca.*941), whose work seems to have influenced Omar Khayyām. The work of some of the poets mentioned, e.g. *Bu Salaik* (Abu Salik?, *fl. ca.*900), *Bu'l Abbās* and *Bu'l Fath*, survives only in fragments.

Publication history

Included in *Forde thesis*; printed in *Terrell*, 322–3. In *UP* and *CP1994/2000*.

'Night is hard by. I am vexed and bothered by sleep'

TS send to LZ (held by HRC) in 1949. Version of Manuchehri (Caddel cites Jarrett ed., no. 6; *UP*, 63/*CP2000*, 231). Manuchehri was an eleventh-century Persian poet who used Arabic words in his work; he was a protégé of 'Unsuri, also of interest to BB. **'I am going to enclose . . . a literal version of one of Manuchehri's ghazals. The last couplet is very famous and has been quoted or imitated by nearly every notable ghazal writer in Persian history. But the characteristic of the original is**

vigour, which has evaporated in the translation and I dont know how to get it back. I think my own have energy. Whether they have anything else I'm more doubtful' (BB to LZ, 28 May 1949; quoted *Forde*, 127–8, and *Lesch*, 131).

Publication history

First published in *Nine* 4 (Summer 1950), 2, no. 3 (August 1950), 218–19, *Guedalla* D14, under title, 'A ghazel of Manuchehri's'. In *UP* and *CP1994/2000*.

'You, with my enemy, strolling down my street'

MS with slight variations at Durham dated 1949. Version of Manuchehri (Caddel cites Jarrett ed., no. 91; *UP*, 63/*CP2000*, 231).

Publication history

First published in *Nine* 11 (April 1956), 4, no. 2, 9, *Guedalla* D18, under title, 'A ghazal of Manuchehri'. Revised version published in *Agenda* 16 (no. 1, Spring 1978), 7, where it is dated 1949. In *UP* and *CP1994/2000*.

'The thundercloud fills meadows with heavenly beauty'

Version of Manuchehri (Caddel cites Jarrett ed., no. 14, 1–12; *UP*, 63/*CP2000*, 231). Manuchehri was an eleventh-century Persian poet who used Arabic words in his work; he was a protégé of 'Unsuri, also of interest to BB.

Publication history

First published in *Nine* 11 / vol. 4, no. 2 (April 1956), 10, *Guedalla* D18, under title, 'From a qasida of Manuchehri'. The second section, beginning 'Shall I sulk', dated 1949, appears as an *Overdraft* (see above) from *Loquitur* onwards. In *UP* and *CP1994/2000*.

Note

5. San'a. Ancient city in Yemen, now its capital.

'Hi, tent-boy, get that tent down'

TS with MS alterations, dated 1949, at Durham. Version of Manuchehri (Caddel cites Jarrett ed., no. 29, 1–46; *UP*, 63 / *CP2000*, 231). Manuchehri was an eleventh-century Persian poet who used Arabic words in his work; he was a protégé of 'Unsuri, also of interest to BB.

Publication history

In *UP* and *CP1994/2000*.

Notes

5. *Babyl*. Babylon?

6. *Sanubar.* Any cone-bearing tree; a fir. Often used metaphorically in Persian to mean an attractive young person of either sex.

18. *tyro*. *OED*: 'A beginner or learner in anything; one who is learning or who has mastered the rudiments only of any branch of knowledge; a novice.' Cp. Scott, *Redgauntlet*, letter XIII: 'A subject upon whilk all the tyrones have been trying their whittles.' Also Ruskin, *Modern Painters*, 2nd ed., I. Preface, 36: 'The merest tyro in art knows that'.

23. *Najib*. His horse.

24. *hobbles*. *OED* n.3: 'A rope, strap, clog, or other apparatus used for hobbling a horse or other beast.' Also *EDD* 5.

26. *headstall*. *OED*: 'The part of a bridle or halter that fits round the head.' Cp. Pope's *The Iliad*, VIII. 676: 'And fix'd their headstalls to his chariot-side.'

37. *fishglue*. *OED* n.1.7: 'fish-glue, glue obtained from the bladders and sounds of fish, isinglass.'

39. *Dogstar*. The star Sirius; see note to 'The Well of Lycopolis,' III. 11. Cp. Pope, 'On the Statue of Cleopatra', 64: 'the Dogstar burns'; Byron, *Don Juan*, Dedication st. 4, 6: 'when the dogstar rages'.

40. *Mosul's mound*. The ruined Assyrian capital, Nineveh, founded by Nimrod (see Jonah 3, in the Bible), is thought to be located beneath a large mound called Nimrud on the Tigris River opposite Mosul, in present-day Iraq; cp. Austen Henry Layard's *Nineveh and Its Remains* (London, 1849) or his *A Popular Account of Discoveries at Nineveh* (London, 1853).

41. *Great Bear*. Ursa Major.

'You've come! O how flustered and anxious I've been'

TS with MS alterations, dated 1974, at Durham.

Publication history

In *UP* and *CP1994/2000*.

Notes

6. flock. OED n.2, e.g. Pope, 'Epistle to Allen Lord Bathurst', 301: 'a flock-bed, but repair'd with straw'.

20. burn. Cp. BB's note to *Briggflatts* I. 70: **We have burns in the east, *becks* in the west, but no brooks or creeks.** See also note to 'The Complaint of the Morpethshire Farmer', 12.

'Ginger, who are you going with?'

Version of Horace, *Odes*, I. 5.

Publication history

TS with MS revisions, dated 1969, at Durham, published in facsimile in Harry Gilonis, ed., *Horace Whom I Hated So* (London: Five Eyes of Wiwaxia, 1992), n.pag. Version with revisions presented in *UP* and *CP1994/2000* and here.

Notes

1. Ginger. OED n. and a.1, B.: '*adj. dial.* Of hair: Having the colour of ginger. Of a person: Sandy-haired'. Gilonis remarks that this 'parallels the Roman call-girl name "Glycera" (roughly "Sweetie," but ginger's more spicy); and echoes the colour word for her hair, *flava*, which can mean anything from flaxen blonde to auburn or full redhead' (Harry Gilonis, 'Soiled Mosaic: Bunting's Horace Translations', *McGonigal & Price*, 220).

3. meadowsweet. A fragrant flowering plant which grows alongside streams. In TS the third sentence reads,

> One who snuffs may now,
> soon dogroses, then meadowsweet?

Gilonis comments: 'There is a consensus among botanists that these three wildflowers bloom in the order in which their names appear here, overlapping only slightly – May–June, June–July, June–August.

Summer's lease, then, has all too short an ending' (*McGonigal & Price*, 221).

'Like a fawn you dodge me, Molly'

TS with MS alteration, undated, at Durham. Version of Horace, *Odes*, I. 23.

Publication history

In *UP* and *CP1994/2000*.

Notes

1. Molly. OED n.1: 'A familiar pet-form of the name Mary; often applied contemptuously to a "lass", "wench", and occas. to a prostitute. (Cf. Moll).'

'That filly couldnt carry a rider nor'

TS, undated, at Durham. Version of Horace, *Odes*, II. 5. Cp. Ronsard's ode 'Pourquoy comme une jeune poutre' ['Why, like a young mare'], a version of the Horace poem.

Publication history

In *UP* and *CP1994/2000*.

Notes

1. filly. Gilonis remarks that Horace used *iuvenca*, 'heifer' or 'young girl,' not *equula* (as in English, a stock term for 'young girl') in his poem, but that 'filly' is the exact equivalent for the Greek πωλή in Horace's own model, Anacreon fragment 417. 'Bunting's poem shares with Anacreon a lightness and delicacy, in contrast to the blunt, even distasteful explicitness of the Horace. Horace writes thus to *dissuade* his addressee from pursuing a too-young girl; Bunting shies away from pursuing even the implications (his "stallion" behaves periphrastically in comparison to Horace's bull). The reticence goes further: Jimmy-who-can't-be-told-from-a-girl is the Gyges with the unguessable face, *ambiguoque voltu*, from "The Well of Lycopolis"' (in 'Soiled Mosaic: Bunting's Horace Translations', *McGonigal & Price*, 225).

5. plodge. See note to 'Stones trip Coquet burn', *SBOO* 10.

10. *besom. OED* n.7: 'A contemptuous or jocular designation for a woman. *Sc.* and *dial.* (Pronounced 'biz m . . .)' Cp. Scott, *Old Mortality*, viii: 'To set up to be sae muckle better than ither folk, the auld besom', and *Redgauntlet* xx: 'the auld besom'; also Kipling, 'The Wishing-Caps', 20: 'And the besom won't board you next time.'

Dante: *Inferno* XXIX

TS included in letter to Denis Goacher dated 21 August 1964. In the letter, BB says, **'This isnt Dante, no. I dont know the Binyons and the predecessors of Binyon (except Warren Vernon, who stuck to prose). Force and directness are, as you say, the things to preserve. I believe if you keep as close to Dante's own words as is compatible with simple, spoken English you will find the movement almost takes care of itself. A minimum of manoeuvring will preserve it fast and hard, as the Italian is. I have spent exactly forty minutes doing the first page or two, to give you some notion of what I mean. Obviously, in that time, one cannot clean up at all. Only five lines have been altered from what I put down in the first motion, and about five or six words cut out or replaced by simpler words. (The few lines embodied in the Well of Lycopolis Part Three took me days to do).'**

Publication history

Previously unpublished.

Notes

7. *bolge.* Italian for 'ditch'. In the *Inferno*, bolges are part of the concentric circles of Hell, e.g. the Malebolge in this canto, the evil trench or ditch.

27. *Geri del Bello.* Cousin of Dante's father, whose killing obliged the Alighieri family to avenge his murder. Virgil sees this shade threaten Dante while he is occupied with talking to another shade from Altaforte, Bertrand de Born.

29. *Altaforte.* Cp. EP's 'Sestina: Altaforte', in which de Born is called a 'stirrer up of strife'.

'Snow's on the fellside, look! How deep'

Version of Horace, *Odes*, I. 9. Cp. Housman's version of Horace, *Odes*, IV. 12, 'The snows are fled away . . .'

Publication history

From MS at Durham dated 1977; this version used – with corrections – in *UP* and *CP1994/2000*. The MS is reproduced on the inside front cover of *Caddel & Flowers*. Published in *Agenda* 16, no. 1 (Spring 1978), 6, with variants.

Notes

1. fellside. The word also occurs in *Briggflatts* I. 77 (see note) and II. 159.

3. burns. Cp. BB's note to *Briggflatts* I. 70: **'We have burns in the east, *becks* in the west, but no brooks or creeks.'** See also note to 'The Complaint of the Morpethshire Farmer', 12.

'Poor soul! Softy, whisperer'

Quartermain reports (as cited above) that this was intended as an ending for an uncompleted longer poem of which *SBOO* 12 (*Perche no spero* / 'Now we've no hope of going back') was at one point the opening. Version of a fragment by Emperor Hadrian (*ca.*117–38), his dying address to his soul: '*Animula vagula blandula / hospes comesque corporis / quae nunc abibis / in loca pallidula rigida nudula / nec ut soles dabis iocos*' (Loeb vol. 284: *Minor Latin Poets*, 1934). Cp. EP's 'Blandula, Tenulla, Vagula', in his *Canzoni* (1911) and in the *Cantos*, CV; also T. S. Eliot's 'Animula'. Note also Thomas Hardy's interest in the fragment; John Bayley, in *An Essay on Hardy* (Cambridge: Cambridge University Press, 1978), writes that the opening phrase 'must have held an appeal for Hardy, for he quotes it more than once'. Bayley is quoted by Robert Mezey in his edition of Hardy's *Selected Poems* (New York: Penguin Classics, 1998), who adds: 'This phrase, essentially untranslatable, might possibly be rendered as "little charmer, wayward little soul of mine"' (xxxv). Also Byron's version, 'Adrian's Address to His Soul, When Dying'; also Stevie Smith, 'Animula, vagula blandula'. BB knew Smith's work, writing to JW about her death, **'Sorry to know I shan't hear Stevie Smith again: little stuff, but honest done, worked on . . .'** (Jonathan Williams, 'Some Jazz from the Baz', in *McGonigal & Price*, 257).

Publication history

Originally published when quoted in Quartermain's 'Six Plaints and a Lament for Basil Bunting', *Conjunctions* 8 (1985), reprinted as chap. 8 of *Quartermain DP*, 144. In *UP* and *CP1994/2000*.

SCHOOL POEMS

According to Caddel, in 1916 BB published these two poems, which are his only surviving juvenilia. Forde remarks that a 'prize-winning poem and essay, published probably in 1916 or 1917 in the Leeds evening paper, the *Mercury*, has never been found' (*Forde*, 23).

The Song of the Ackworth Clock

Published in the *Annual Report of the Headmaster of the Ackworth School* for 1916, where it was attributed to 'Basil C. Bunting, leaver July 1916'. In *UP* and *CP1994/2000*.

Keep Troth

This poem very strongly resembles Kipling's 1913 poem, 'A Boy Scouts' Patrol Song', whose refrain is 'look out!' Cp. also Sir Henry Newbolt, *Vitaï Lampada*, refrain: 'Play up! play up! and play the game', and perhaps James Clarence Mangan's 1849 poem 'Bear Up!', e.g. 'Though thou hast drained, even to its lees, / Life's bitter cup – / Though Death and Hell be round thee, still / Place faith in GOD! He hears! He sees! / Bear up! Bear up!'

Publication history

Published in *The Leightonian* at Leighton Park School in December 1916, under the name B. C. Bunting. BB attended the school from September 1916 until 1918. In *UP* and *CP1994/2000*.

Notes

3. the war. In spite of, or perhaps in keeping with, the patriotic sentiments of this poem, during World War I BB was a conscientious objector. *The Leightonian* for December 1918 would report: 'B. C. Bunting is serving a sentence of 112 days at Wormwood Scrubs, after refusing agricultural work on the ground that in effect that was sending another man to fight for him'; in July 1919, it would report that 'B. C. Bunting visited the school in person [on June 24th] and informed us cheerfully that he was now living in London and avoiding the police.' See *Burton* and *Forde* for details of this period of BB's life.

LIMERICKS

Caddel claims that BB had great enthusiasm for limericks, and that a number of them have been brought to Caddel's attention as having been written by BB for which no authentication was possible. In addition to the two limericks published by BB during his lifetime, Caddel notes a third 'which has reputedly passed into the koine' and which remains untraced (*CP2000*, 238). *Forde* (17) describes BB's sister Joyce's fondness for limericks, apparently influenced by their father reading Edward Lear to them when they were children.

'What a pity that Bela Bartok'

Published in *Truck* 21 (1979). From a letter to EP, undated but early 1935, held at the Beinecke, in which he claims that the limerick (as he calls it) **'got itself collected some years ago & privately printed in Wien'**. That publication has not been traced. In *UP* and *CP1994/2000*, but printed incorrectly. The final line ('Yes, obviously.') was omitted. There also should have been inserted '11 [*sic*] character spaces and a full stop at the end . . . so that it ends "And conducting the piece with   ."' The character spacing corresponds to the missing words "his cock"' (Neil Astley to Paul Keegan, email, 13 June 2006; Astley had tried to correct the misprinting in *CP2000*, but though the typesetting was correct, the printer deleted the full-stop, thinking it was a mistake). A version printed without the indents appears in *Burton*, 197.

'That volatile poet called Jonathan'

Published in *62 Climerikews to amuse Mr Lear*, ed. Jonathan Williams (Denver: DBA/JCA Editions, 1983). In *UP* and *CP1994/2000*.

Notes

1. Jonathan. Jonathan Williams?

‘An overfat guest at the Ritz’

Postscript to a letter from BB to JW dated 15 May 1984, published in a selection of their correspondence in *McGonigal & Price*, 279.

FRAGMENTS AND FALSE STARTS

'Do not think that I am contented here'

From an unpublished letter to Otto Theis, 28 September 1929, sold at auction by Bonhams in 2013. Otto Theis was sometime literary editor of *The Outlook*, for which BB was music critic; he also administered the fund that Margaret de Silver created for him. BB's note: **'Counting syllables is the only way [to] write!'**

'Powder and lipstick and lace on their drawers'

First published in *Burton*, 184. From BB to EP, 'Twentyumph' January 1934, held at Beinecke.

Sonnet II

Sent to LZ in letter of 29 September 1935; published in *Makin*, 81. Lines from this poem were incorporated into the published version of 'Gertie Gitana's hymn to waltzing', *UO* 6.

The Well of Lycopolis [variant]

This variant text of 'The Well of Lycopolis' was sent to LZ in a letter dated 28 October 1935 and can be found in the LZ archive at HRC. The TS is marked, apparently in LZ's handwriting, 'This is original. Printed ed. (revised) (ca.1950.)' In this letter, BB remarked, **'NO one will publish the W of L. Perhaps as well, not sure I want it published.'** This feeling about the poem persisted; as late as 1982 he felt it was **'the most disgruntled of all my works, the one which takes the gloomiest view of everything . . .'** (reading at Riverside Studios, London, February 1982, in *Swigg*).

Notes

l. 56. Labour of Love. Unidentified, but a manual or tract for women containing information about sex and contraception.

2. 31. *a poetico sermone plane abhorret*. Phrase taken from Gottfried Hermann's eight-volume *Opuscula* (1827–77), 'De Aeschyli Trilogiis Thebanis', v. 7, 195 (Leipzig: E. Fleischer, 1839); Hermann (1772–1848) was known for his philological work on Greek metrics and his editions of Aeschylus, Euripides and others. The phrase means roughly: 'one clearly shudders at poetic language'. *Sermones* is also the title of Horace's Satires, and it is a word that suggests conversation.

2. 35. *Mr Hampstead . . . Mr 14th Street*. No doubt these are meant to signify urban types generally, but a John Hampstead is the protagonist in Peter Clark MacFarlane's 1916 novel *Held to Answer*, in which Hampstead, an actor, ends up in a ruinous relationship with a disreputable actress.

3. 55. *Mazdak*. Zoroastrian prophet (died *c.* 524 or 528 CE) whose teachings, regarded as heretical, were intended to purify and reform Zoroastrianism. Like Zoroastrianism and Manichaeism, Mazdakism taught that there were two original principles of the universe: Light, which is good, and Darkness, which is evil. Cp. note to *The Spoils*, III. 75.

3. 59. *Mani*. See note immediately above. Mani (*c.* 216–74 CE) was the prophet founder of Manichaeism, which identified a rigid dualism of good and evil, locked in eternal struggle.

3. 64. *Zarathustra Spitama*. (*c.* tenth century BCE, though traditionally dated 628–551 BCE); founder of Zoroastrianism. His teachings were collected in the Gathas and the Avesta; lines 65–74 are derived from the former. **'Zarathustra anticipated Voltaire and other rationalists: "Digging is better than prayer" is in the Gathas'** (BB to Dorothy Pound, 6 January 1951; Lilly Library, University of Indiana, Bloomington).

4. 1. *P–K4*. Notation for a common first move in a game of chess, pawn to the fourth square on the king's file. Cp. Eliot's 'Game of Chess' in *The Waste Land*, especially 137–8, which alludes to Middleton's *A Game at Chesse*; the play, a political allegory, tells of the attempted rape of a White Virgin by a Black Bishop's Pawn. Note also EP's 'A Dogmatic Statement Concerning the Game of Chess: Theme for a Series of Pictures', published in *Poetry* (March 1915, 257) and later *Lustra*.

4. 19. *Zamzam*. The Well of Zamzam, at Mecca, the holiest place in Islam. According to Islamic tradition the Well was revealed to Hagar, Abraham's wife and Ishmael's mother. After Abraham was instructed by God to leave his wife and son, Hagar sought water for the thirsting infant but could not find any. Hagar climbed two hills to

ask Allah for water, after which he sent the angel Jibreel (or Gabriel), who scraped the ground with his wing, causing water miraculously to spring out.

4. 22. *Helicon.* In Greek mythology, two springs sacred to the Muses were located at Mount Helicon: the Aganippe and the Hippocrene, the latter considered a source of poetic inspiration. Helicon as a river is mentioned in some stories about Orpheus; after Dionysus' followers killed him, they tried to wash their hands in its waters, but the river sank underground so as not to become tainted with Orpheus' blood.

4. 25. *Hippocrates.* Hippocrates (*c.* 460–*c.* 370 BCE) is considered the father of Western medicine.

4. 34. *Manly Mars.* Roman god of war. Cp. 'A Manly Mars' heart he bare, appearing by his acts', in *Cambises*, a Tudor play by Thomas Preston (1537–98), l. 10. Cambises II, depicted in this drama, was a Persian king (d. 522 BCE), son of Cyrus the Great.

4. 39. *Tercio.* A military unit of the Spanish Empire during the era of the dominance of Habsburg Spain; for a time in the sixteenth and seventeenth centuries, these were thought to be the best infantry in Europe.

4. 40. *Senussi war.* The so-called Senussi Campaign, 1915–17. The Senussi had been a peaceful religious sect of the Sahara Desert until World War I when they were courted by the Ottoman and German Empires and persuaded to attack British-occupied Egypt and encourage an insurrection.

4. 44. *Cyrenaica.* Administrative division of Italian Libya at the time of the poem's writing.

4. 48. *Kufra.* An area of oases in south-eastern Cyrenaica. At the end of nineteenth century it was the centre and holy place of the Senussis, as above.

Graziani. Rodolfo Graziani (1882–1955), Italian military officer appointed by the Fascist government to command the Italian forces in Libya. He was responsible for suppressing the Senussis, called the Brethren by BB in l. 49. Vice-Governor of Cyrenaica 1930–4.

4. 51. *Mohammedan Quakers.* There are many eighteenth- and nineteenth-century appearances of this term to refer to tribal people of North Africa. Phrase occurs, for example in John Campbell's *The Travels of Edward Brown, Esq.: Containing His Observations on France and Italy, His Voyage to the Levant, His Account of the Island of Malta, His Remarks in His Journies Through the Lower and Upper Egypt* (London: T. Longman, 1753), vol. 2, p. 213, which

uses the term to refer to '*Arab* Doctors' who suppose themselves 'above all Ordinances, have acted according to the Dictates of what they call the Spirit, and have been looked upon by Men of Understanding as a sort of *grave Infidels*'; and in an 1865 report published in *Journal of the Royal Geographical Society* (v. 35, p. 189), in which a Colonel Lewis Pelly refers to 'Wahabis' as 'warlike Mohammedan Quakers'. Also used by Gábor Naphegyi in his *Ghardaia; Or, Ninety Days Among the B'ni Mozab: Adventures in the Oasis of the Desert of Sahara* (New York: G. P. Putnam & Sons, 1871), 143, in reference to the B'ni Mozab people of North Africa; Naphegyi claims that they derived their religious ideas from the Koran, but rejected '*in toto* the traditional law and complicated ritualism' of Islam; 'Like the Quakers, they have a decided faculty for money-making, and are at the same time scrupulously just in their commercial transactions.' The reference becomes decidedly ironic in light of BB's eventual connection to Quakerism, as seen in his later poems.

4. 77. *Lombard bankers.* I.e., usurers, a derogatory term. Money-lending merchants in the Lombardy region of northern Italy developed banking during the Renaissance, and this area remained a major centre of European finance for hundreds of years. But no doubt BB particularly has in mind Lombard Street in the City of London, traditionally associated with banking and insurance, where many profits were made in the wartime markets of World War I.

4. 79. *Maecenas, Wendel, Deterding, Mellon.* Gaius Cilnius Maecenas (68–8 BCE), friend and political advisor to Octavian – first Emperor of Rome as Caesar Augustus – known as a wealthy patron of the arts; the de Wendel family was a dynasty of nineteenth- and twentieth-century French industrialists, and BB is probably referring to François de Wendel (1874–1949), who in 1918 was quoted as saying, 'Wendel signifies France'; Henri Wilhelm August Deterding (1866–1939), one of the first executives of the Royal Dutch Petroleum Company; Andrew Mellon (1855–1937), American banker, industrialist, philanthropist, who, as Secretary of the US Treasury during the Depression, was unpopular for his economic policies and negotiations for the repayment of European war debts from World War I.

To Mr Lewis Alcock the Wonder of Greenwich Village

Sent to LZ, dated 14 December 1938 on verso in LZ's hand; held at HRC. Alcock unidentified.

On the fly-leaf of Pound's 'Cantos' [variant]

Sent in letter to EP, 12 January 1951. TS held at Lilly Library, Indiana University, Bloomington.

DIALOGUE Non-Platonic
Grandma's Complaint

According to Gael Turnbull, 'originally transcribed into my notebook about 1965', and apparently written in Rapallo to amuse EP. According to Quartermain (email to Don Share, 18 June 2014), this was typed out and given to Roger Guedalla; then copied for Eliot Weinberger by Guedalla, and by Weinberger for Richard Caddel. Therefore not directly ascribable to Bunting, i.e. published under his name. However, these verses appeared in *Burton*, 196–7.

'The scholar ought to be like the poet'

First published in *Quartermain* and reprinted in *Stubborn Poetries: Poetic Facticity and the Avant-Garde* (University of Alabama Press, 2013), 42. The text is from BB's notebook for *Briggflatts*, held at the University of Buffalo. Quartermain comments: 'it is not (or is it?) part of the poem'.

[Verses for the Quartermain Children]

'David and Ian' is dated 7 February 1971 by Quartermain, who recalls that it was 'scribbled on the second flap on an airletter (since lost?), no doubt to fill the page out'. 'When Ian and David' dated 20 March 1971, 'when we were thinking about renting a cottage, which belonged to Sima [Bunting], at Frosterley, for a proposed visit that summer' (email to Don Share, 18 June 2014).

'Such syllables flicker out of grass'

I. Facsimile of MS notebook page containing these lines published in 1997 on inside back cover of *Caddel & Flowers*. The lines are variants of those published by Caddel as *UO* 11 in *UP/CP2000*; see notes to that poem, above.

II. Written *ca.*1969. Drafts transcribed by Peter Quartermain: 'On 29

November 1970, when Basil was staying with Carol and me for the weekend, he read us some poems and then went for a walk with her and the boys, leaving the following three drafts on the table, knowing I'd copy them if I could. I did so, quite hurriedly. He set and printed the final draft himself (with his Adana flatbed press), in about 1972 sending it to various people (including me). Richard Caddel included that version in *CP1994/2000*, 199, as the 11th of the "Uncollected Odes". On my last visit to [Bunting], at Whitley Chapel, 1984, he leaned back in his chair and smiled; "I've destroyed all those poems." He looked somewhat relieved when I replied "Good." The draft labelled here as 1 was handwritten in the notebook; 2 and 3 typed, on separate sheets. I'd say that 1 is the latest, 3 the earliest, of these drafts. In 3 stanza 2, last line margin, BB circled and with an arrow suggested "overlay".'

II. 2.17 and 3.11. Alternative wordings noted in the margin by BB.

Untitled poem, 1978: opening of 'A New Moon'?

Part of this published with epigraph '*Perche no spero*' in *CP1994*, 146 (where it is dated 1980); closing lines, untitled and not dated, in *CP1994/2000*, 222. In line 12 BB circled the word 'banks'; in line 22, 'asking'; and in line 62 he circled the word 'hours' and substituted 'time' in the margin. Peter Quartermain: 'Text of poem BB read to Meredith and me when we were staying with him in Washington, Tyne and Wear, in July 1978, commenting that he thought it quite nicely captured the rhythm of the sea running under a small boat like the *Thistle*, at anchor. He said it was more or less complete in itself, but was intended as the first section of a four-part poem, presumably "A New Moon." That evening he and Meredith went out after he'd left the typescript on the table for me, and I hurriedly copied it out without telling him (but of course he knew I would). Much later, at Whitley Chapel, he told me "I've destroyed all those poems" – but by then the opening 21 or so lines had been published in *Agenda* 16. 1 (Spring 1978): 5 and in *Montemora* 5 (1979): 14; the third stanza was also published by Robert Perkins in 1984 as a broadside, "Soon, while that Northwest Squall". [Oblong folio broadside 48.5 x 75 cm. Text (third stanza of "Perche no spero") incorporated in body of multicoloured lithograph. 66 copies as follows: 45 numbered, 16 lettered, and five artist's proofs, all signed by Bunting and Perkins.]'

TEXTUAL VARIANTS

SONATAS

Villon

Initial capital for first word in each line throughout *Poetry*, *RM*, *Profile*, *Act. Ant.*, *P1950*; double quotes used throughout *Poetry*, *Profile*, *RM*, *Act. Ant.*, *Loquitur*[1]

Section heading. I] 1. *RM*, *CE*, *P1950*

I. 1. anatomized] anatomized, *Poetry*, *Profile*; anatomised *RM*, *CE*

I. 2. whose] Whose *CE*
flowers] flowers, *Poetry*, *Profile*

I. 3. on] of *Poetry*, *Profile*
things] things, *Poetry*, *Profile*

I. 5. us,] us *Poetry*, *Profile*
marrow,] marrow, still combustible cinders, *Poetry*, *Profile*

I. 6. deadman] dead man *Poetry*, *Profile*

I. 9. Golden Hands] golden hands *Poetry*, *Profile*
the Virgin in blue.] The Virgin in blue. separate line *Poetry*, *Profile*

I. 10. (—A blazing parchment] (A blazing parchment *Poetry*, *Profile*

I. 11. gold.) gold). *RM*, *Act. Ant.*

I. 15. dark] dark, *Poetry*, *Profile*
fetters] fetters, *Poetry*, *Profile*

I. 17. blank again] blank again, *Poetry*, *Profile*

I. 18. always silent.] always silent, *Poetry*, *Profile*

I. 21. Naked beggar] naked beggar *Poetry*, *Profile*
st. br. after blind and cold! *P1950*

I. 23. no st. br. after lank hair. *P1950*

I. 26. Averrhoes] Averrhoës *Poetry*, *Profile*, *Act. Ant.*, *RM*, *CE*

I. 27. eyes] Eyes *CE*

I. 29. left hardness] left hardness, *Poetry*, *Profile*

I. 30. hardness darkness] hardness, darkness *Poetry*, *Profile*

---

1 *FBO* variants are subsumed within notation for *Loquitur*, in which it was absorbed.

I. 31. darkness at the head partial hardness] darkness, at the head partial hardness, *Poetry*, *Profile*

I. 32. without] without. *Poetry*, *Profile*

I. 36. day's] days *CE*

I. 40. mockery;] mockery, *Poetry*, *Profile*

I. 41. CY GIST] *CY GIST Poetry*, *Profile*

I. 42–76. This section indented *Poetry*, *Profile*

I. 43. sots] Sots *Poetry*

I. 45. DEATH] Death *Poetry*, *Profile*

I. 49. fellmonger] Fellmonger *CE*

I. 55. breath] breath, *Poetry*, *Profile*

I. 56. cite,] cite: *Poetry*, *Profile*

I. 57. as] As *CE*

I. 58. Abelard and Eloise] Abélard and Éloïse *Act. Ant.*; Eloïse *CE*

I. 60. Genée] Genee *P1950*
all these] all these, *Poetry*, *Profile*

I. 61–2. pain. // And] pain, // and *CE*
no st. br. after pain *P1950*

I. 62. General Grant] Genral Grant *P1950*

I. 68. our doom] Our doom *Poetry*, *Profile*, *Act. Ant.*, *RM*, *CE*, *P1950*, *Loquitur*

I. 70–1. sands. / We] sands, / we *CE*

I. 72. Golden Hands] golden hands *Poetry*, *Profile*

I. 74. insubstantial-glorious,] insubstantial—glorious, *P1950*

Section heading. II] 2. *RM*, *CE*, *P1950*

II. 5. back in] back, in *Poetry*, *Profile*

II. 7. Whereinall] no indent *Poetry*, *Profile*

II. 11. Mine] no indent *Poetry*, *Profile*
threeplank] three-plank *Poetry*, *Profile*

II. 16. dead—] dead. *Poetry*, *Profile*

II. 18. ballad] ballad, *Poetry*, *Profile*

II. 20. ill,] ill. *Poetry*, *Profile*

II. 21. but] But *Poetry*, *Profile*

II. 22. cold body] cold body, *Poetry*, *Profile*

II. 23. Circe] Circe, *Poetry*, *Profile*
mind] mind, *Poetry*, *Profile*

II. 24. year] year, *Poetry*, *Profile*

II. 27. Whereinall] no indent *Poetry*, *Profile*

II. 31. whale] whale, *Poetry*
seal] seal, *Poetry*
kangaroo,] kangaroo. *Poetry*, *Profile*

II. 32. they] They *Poetry*, *Profile*

II. 36. thumbprints] thumb-prints *Poetry*, *Profile*

II. 37. Colour] color *Poetry*, *Profile*

II. 38. st. br. after smudgy page *RM*, *Act. Ant.*, *CE*

II. 39. line br. after Homer? Adest. *Poetry*, *RM*, *Profile*, *Act. Ant.*, *CE*

II. 40. line br. after Adsunt omnes, *Poetry*, *RM*, *Profile*, *Act. Ant.*, *CE*
omnes, omnes] omnes, Omnes *P1950*

II. 41. st. br. between Villon. / Villon? *RM*, *Act. Ant.*, *CE*

II. 42. Villon?] indent *Poetry*, *Profile*
st. br. after Villon? *Poetry*, *Profile*, *Act. Ant.*, *CE*

Section heading. III] 3. *RM*, *CE*, *P1950*

III. 5. over the sea seldom] handwritten insertion *CE*

III. 8. gravecloths] The grave-cloths *Poetry*

III. 17. in shrines] And shrines *Poetry*

III. 18. additional line after the goddess of the country] The image of the goddess *Poetry*

III. 25. Helen] Helen. *RM*, *CE*

III. 26. precision] Precision *Poetry*, *CE*

III. 33. unnoted harmonies] part of previous line *Poetry*

III. 38. Mantegna . . .] Mantegna. . . . *Poetry*

III. 39. The sea] the sea *CE*

▪ *Story of the Amulet.*] "Story of the Amulet." *P1950*, *Loquitur*

Attis: Or, Something Missing

Double quotes used throughout *Obj. Ant.*, *Act. Ant.*, *P1950*, *Loquitur*

Section heading. I] 1. *CE*, *P1950*

I. 1. puff] puff, *Act. Ant.*, *CE*

I. 2. gray] grey *Act. Ant.*

I. 15. st. br. after enough for dancers *CE*

I. 25. potability;] potability. *CE*

I. 26. wreckage] Wreckage *CE*

I. 29. hooves;] hooves: *Act. Ant.*, *CE*

I. 40. soil . . . . .] soil. . . . . . *Act. Ant.*; soil. . . . *CE*

I. 41. Mother of Gods] Mother of gods *Act. Ant., CE*

I. 46. cities] indent two spaces cities *CE*

I. 50. Mother and Mother] indent two spaces Mother and Mother *CE*

Section heading. II] 2. *CE, P1950*

(Variations on a theme by Milton)] (Variations on a theme by Milton) *Act. Ant.*; Variations on a theme by Milton. *CE* (parenthesis before Variations scratched out)

II. 18. st. br. after last light: *P1950*

II. 21. SÌ] CI *Act. Ant., CE, P1950, Loquitur, CP1968*
SMALTO] SMALTO. *Act. Ant., CE, P1950*

II. 31. cabinet ministers] cabinet-ministers *Act. Ant., CE, P1950*

II. 33. buffeted] buffetted *Act. Ant., CE*

II. 54. (VENGA MEDUSA)] (**VENGA MEDUSA**) *P1950*

II. 57. cafe] handwritten accent mark *CE*

II. 58. eh,] Eh, *Act. Ant., CE, P1950*

II. 66–7. 'I will not . . . jilts.'] double quotes *CP1968, CP1978, CP1985*

Section heading. III] 3 *CE, P1950*

Pastorale arioso / (falsetto)] **Pastorale arioso / (falsetto)** 1950; 3rd movement of a Sonatina // *Pastorale arioso* / (for male soprano) *Obj. Ant.*

III. 6. 'Pines] Pines *CP1985*

III. 10. lady's-maid] lady's maid *CE*

III. 11. to Dindyma] not indent *CP1985*

III. 15. energy;] energy: *Obj. Ant.*

III. 16. amongst] among *Obj. Ant.*

III. 21. Scirocco] Sirocco *Obj. Ant.*

III. 28. limp in hell] smaller indent in *Act. Ant.*

III. 31. names,] names *CE*

III. 31–5. most of the names . . . paradigms smaller indent in *Act. Ant.*

III. 33. hymns:] hymns; *CE*

III. 34. syntax,] syntax *Obj. Ant.*

III. 37–9. (Oh Sis! . . . 'ad proper!)] *(Oh Sis! / I've been 'ad, I've been 'ad proper!)* [itals.] *Obj. Ant.*

III. 38. st. br. after I've been 'ad! *Loquitur*

III. 39. no st. br. after *I've been 'ad proper!) Obj. Ant., Loquitur*

III. 46. naively] naïvely *Act. Ant., CE*

III. 48. peacock.] peacock." *Obj. Ant.*
no st. br. after peacock *Obj. Ant.*

III. 49. (I've been 'ad!)'] *(I've been 'ad!)* [itals.] *Obj. Ant.*; single quote added by hand *CE*; (I've been 'ad!) *P1950*, *Loquitur*

III. 54. you,] You *P1950*

III. 55. myrtles'] myrtles *Obj. Ant.*

III. 57. muse] Muse *Obj. Ant.*

III. 61. Attis his embleme] not *Obj. Ant., Act. Ant., CE, P1950*

III. 62. *Nonnulla deest.*] (**Nonnulla deest.**) *Act. Ant., P1950*

Aus Dem Zweiten Reich

Double quotes used throughout *CE, P1950, Loquitur*

Title] Aus dem zweiten Reich *CP1985*

Section heading. I] 1. *CE, P1950*

I. 1. Tauentsienstrasse] Tauentsienstrasze *CE*

I. 2. cafés] accent mark handwritten *CE*; cafes *P1950*

I. 5. to the negerband's faint jazz] no indent *CE*

I. 12. for a candy pack] no indent *CE*

I. 14–15. body and soul similarly scented, / on time]

> body and soul similarly scented
> by the Ami du Peuple, M. Coty,
> so objectionable politically,
> on time *CE*

I. 17. modern.] modern: *CE*

I. 18. 'Sturm über Asien'] end quote omitted *CE*; "Sturm uber Asien" *P1950*
is off, some] is off. Some *CE*

I. 20. necessary] necessary" *CE*

I. 22. The person on the screen] no indent *CE*

I. 23. twenty-five] twentyfive *CE*

I. 29–30. stirs, / indent I am teased too,] stirs, / no indent shuffles. I am teased too. *CE*

I. 32. but that will never do. / — Let's go] no indent, but that will never do, "Let's go *CE*

I. 35. Gedächtnis] Gedachtnis *P1950*

I. 36. cafés] accent mark handwritten *CE*; cafes *P1950*
Zoo.] Zoo *CE*

I. 41. neighbourhood] neighborhood *CE, P1950, Loquitur, CP1985*

I. 44. businessmen] business men *CE*

I. 47–8. 'If, smoothing this silk skirt, you pinch my thighs, / that will be fabelhaft.'] 2 em-dashes replace first single quote, end quote deleted *P1950*; em-dash replaces first single quote, end quote deleted *Loquitur*; 'If, smoothing this silk shirt, you pinch my thighs, / that will be fabelhaft'. *CP1968*

Section heading. II] 2. *CE, P1950*

II. 3ff. 'You have . . . in America.' 2 em-dashes replace first single quote, end quote deleted *P1950*; em-dash replaces first single quote, end quote deleted *Loquitur*

II. 4. Are you shocked?] indent *P1950*

II. 6. Jaegerstrasse] Jaegerstrasze *CE*

II. 9. America.'] America'. *CP1978*

Section heading. III] 3. *CE, P1950*

III. 5. village,] village: *Boz-West*

III. 6. wouldnt] wouldn't *Boz-West*, *P1950*, *Loquitur*
recognize] recognize, *Boz-West*; recognise *CE*

III. 7. caricature and picturepostcard] caricatures and picture postcards *Boz-West*, *CE*

III. 10. nothing at all] nothing *Boz-West*

III. 11. plays] plays and he 'and he' x'd out by typewriter *CE*

III. 12. and he said nothing at all] nothing *Boz-West*

III. 14. and he stirred as if a flea] stirred as if a flea *Boz-West*

III. 15. bit him] bit him, but *Boz-West*

III. 16. wouldnt] wouldn't *P1950*, *Loquitur*

III. 18. **Schrecklich**] **"Schrecklich."** *Boz-West*; handwritten gothic with full-stop *CE*; Schrecklich. *P1950*; **Schrecklich**. *Loquitur*

III. 20. notorieties] notorieties' *Boz-West*, *CE*

III. 23. menopause.] menopause: *Boz-West*

III. 24. Stillborn] stillborn *Boz-West*

The Well of Lycopolis

A longer variant of the complete poem was sent in a letter to LZ dated 28 October 1935, reproduced in 'Fragments and False Starts', above pp. 244–53.

Double quotes used throughout with single quotes for internal quotations *P1950*, *Loquitur*

Epigraph. cujus potu signa / virginitatis eripiuntur] **cujus potu signa / virginitatis eripiuntur.** *P1950*; *cujus potu signa / virginitatis eripiuntur. Loquitur*

Section heading. I] 1. *P1950*

I. 7. dont] don't *P1950*

I. 10. wasnt] wasn't *P1950*, *Loquitur*

I. 69. 'What have you come for?] What have you come for? *CP1994/2000* [emendation]
Goddess? You who] separate line *P1950*, *Loquitur*, *CP1968*

I. 73. than when] Than when *P1950*

Section heading. II] 2. *P1950*

II. 11. all I do.'] all I do!' *P1950*

Section heading. III] 3. *P1950*

III. 8. myself] myself. *P1950*

III. 22. Here, Bellerophon,] Here Bellerophon, *P1950*

Section heading. IV] 4. *P1950*

Epigraph. certo] *certe P1950*
no line br. after epigraph *P1950*

IV. 26. no st. br. after What a blighty! *P1950*, *Loquitur*

Variants in notes to this poem:
▪ Americans] American's *P1950*
was until recently] is presumably *P1950*, *Loquitur*
of those who dont] of those who don't *P1950*, *Loquitur*

The Spoils

Arabic epigraph incorrectly typeset *CP1985*, *CP1994*

First section numbered 1 *Poetry*

Headings in larger type *CP1978*; name headings in itals., not all caps. *CP1985*

3–4. No ill companion . . . opens the wine.]

Death is no ill companion on a journey.
He lays his purse on the table and opens the wine

Draft in BB to LZ, 7 February 1951; quoted *Forde*, 180

5. counting frame] counting-frame *Poetry*

43–70. LUD: / When Tigris floods . . . recite the sacred] indent *CP1994*

73. These were the embers . . . Halt, both, lament . . . :] *These were the embers . . . Halt, both, lament . . . . : CP1985*

73–5. Halt, both, lament . . . Arabia.]

Halt, both, lament,
a fountain sprung, spurts of clear sound,
rhyme-plash in a still pool
moon-silver on sand-pale gold
against the parched bakehouse taste of Arabia.

Draft in BB to LZ, 7 February 1951

89. toss] throw *1982 Riverside Studios reading, in Swigg*

91–2. Golden skin . . . vulture's wing.]

Golden skin scoured in a sandblast
glowed like a vulture's wing.

Draft in BB to LZ, 7 February 1951; quoted *Forde*, 186

Section heading. II] 2 *Poetry*, *Spoils*

II. 13. aivans. omitted the lines:

Without this
knowledge you cannot explain the Gothic
and stand in some danger
of sentimentalising the Middle Ages.

Draft in BB to LZ, 7 February 1951; quoted *Forde*, 192

II. 21. At Veramin . . .]

At Veramin
and Gulpaygan

they build smaller mosques and Malekshah
cut his prides in plaster

Draft in BB to LZ, 7 February 1951; quoted *Forde*, 192

II. 27–9. Poetry . . . too well.]

Poetry
they remembered but made it out of itself.

Draft in BB to LZ, 7 February 1951; quoted *Forde*, 194

II. 50. prime minister] Prime Minister *Poetry*

II. 70. chenars] chenars, *Poetry*

II. 96. On a terrace] on a terrace *CP2000* [emendation]

II. 99. Sa'di] Sa'di *Poetry*

II. 115. no st. br. after were we not better dead? *Poetry*, *Spoils*, *CP1968*, *St Andrews College pamphlet*

Section heading. III] 3 *Poetry*, *Spoils*

[See Draft to LZ for uncompressed version of opening. BB cut many lines to eliminate **"unwanted"** echoes of EP (BB to LZ, 25 June 1951)]

III. 33. dytiscus] didiscus *Poetry*

III. 45. wouldnt] wouldn't *Poetry*

III. 90. Chinee;] Chinee: *CP1985*

III. 92. Sang tide] Sand tide *CP1968* corrected in 2nd ed. with errata slip

III. 103. Fortune] Fortunate *CP1985*
slippery hitch] slippery-hitch *Poetry*

Note to poem: ▪ paragraphs not indented *CP1968*, *CP1978*, *CP1985*

additional note in *Spoils*: The Spoils was written in 1951 and printed in *Poetry*, Chicago.

BRIGGFLATTS

Section heading. I] <u>unnumbered</u> *Poetry*; 1 *Briggflatts*

I. 62. sea-reflecting] sun-reflecting *1967 Harvard reading*

I. 146. nest] rest *1976 Harvard reading; also BBC recording featured online at: http://www.poetryarchive.org/poem/briggflatts*

I. 155. split] cut *1967 Harvard reading*

Section heading. II] 2 *Poetry*, *Briggflatts*

II. 29. woods] spheres *LZ* (*Forde*, 222)

II. 32. out] out, *LZ* (*Forde*, 222)

II. 55–60. Who sang . . . voices . . .]

> Who sang, sea takes,
> flesh brine, bone grit.
> Keener the kittiwake.
> Fells forget him.
>
> Fathoms dull the dale,
> slime voices.
> Watchdog the whale,
> gulfweed curtain.

(BB to LZ, 6 December 1964; quoted *Forde*, 223 and *Lesch*, 338)

II. 68. no st. br. *Poetry*

Section heading. III] 3 *Poetry*, *Briggflatts*

III. 35. my loaf is kneaded] my loaf in kneaded *CP1968*

III. 76. unscaleable;] unscaleable: *Poetry*

III. 97. spring;] spring *Poetry*

III. 102. flank] flank, *Poetry*

III. 122. trims] scans *1967 Harvard reading*

III. 128. all!] all!. *Poetry*

Section heading. IV] 4 *Poetry*, *Briggflatts*

IV. 39. <u>st. br. after</u> nothing *CP1985*

IV. 55. lard;] lard: *Poetry*

IV. 75. Shamble] Stumble *1967 Harvard reading*

Section heading. V] 5 *Poetry*, *Briggflatts*

V. 1–23. indent *Poetry*

V. 33. Sing,] not *1967 Harvard reading*

V. 38. st. br. after sea *CP1985*

Section heading. CODA] * * * *Poetry*, Coda *Briggflatts*; smaller type than *CP1968 CP1978*

14. day fails] day falls *St Andrews College pamphlet*

1965] 15 May 1965 *Poetry*, *Briggflatts*

Variants in the note to the poem:

- notes titled AFTERTHOUGHTS *Poetry*; **Afterthoughts** *Briggflatts*
  Words annotated in caps. *Briggflatts*
  koiné] koinè *Poetry*; koine *CP1994/2000* [emendation]
  An autobiography . . . No notes . . .] sentences reversed *Poetry*; not indent *CP1968*, *CP1978*, *CP1985*
  written by or for southrons] written by or for Southrons *CP2000* [emendation]
  Saltings . . . Hastor . . .] notes transposed *Poetry*
  'Beetle juice'] 'Beetle-juice', *Poetry*
  'Ridgel', not 'Rhy-ghel'.] 'Ridgel', not 'Rye-ghel'. *Poetry*]

CHOMEI AT TOYAMA

Epigraph. *(Kamo-no-Chomei, born at Kamo 1154, died at Toyama on Mount Hino, 24th June 1216)*] *Kamo-no-Chomei, born at Kamo 1154; died at Toyama on Mount Hino, 24th June 1216.* Poetry; *(Kamo-no-Chomei, born at Kamo 1154, died at Toyama on Mount Hino, 24th June 1216.)* CE; (Kamo-no-Chomei, born at Kamo 1154, died at Toyama on Mount Hino, 24th June 1216) smaller type *Act. Ant.;* **(Kamo-no-Chomei, born at Kamo 1154, died at Toyama on Mount Hino, 24th June 1216)** *P1950*

Before 1.] section number I *Poetry*

1. Swirl] The swirl *Poetry*, *Act. Ant.*, *CE*, *Loquitur*, *1970 reading in Swigg*

2. On motionless pools scum] The scum on motionless pools *Poetry*, *Act. Ant.*, *CE*, *Loquitur*, *1970 reading in Swigg*
appearing] appearing— *Poetry*; appearing, *CE*

17. dries:] dries, *Poetry*

18. section number II begins after petals *Poetry*; double st. br. after petals. *Act. Ant.*, *CE*

19. no st. br. after forty years. *P1950*

20. twentyseventh] twenty-seventh *Poetry*

21. seventyseven] seventy-seven *Poetry*, seventy seven *CE*

25. veered] veered, *Poetry*

27. by gusts] by the gusts *Poetry*, *Act. Ant.*, *CE*, *P1950*, *Loquitur*, *1970 reading in Swigg*

30. houses] houses, *Poetry*

32. of beasts] word x'd out by typewriter between 'of' and 'beasts' *CE*

33. limitless numbers] oxen and horses and such, limitless numbers *Poetry*, *Act. Ant.*, *CE*, *P1950*, *Loquitur*, *1970 reading in Swigg*

34. section number III begins after real estate beginning with Drought floods, and a dearth. Two fruitless autumns. [83] and omitting all preceding lines *Poetry*; double st. br. after real estate *Act. Ant.*

48. *bufera infernal!*] "*bufera infernal*!" *Act. Ant.*, *P1950*, *Loquitur*; '*bufera infernal*!' *CE*

52. double st. br. after Portent? *Act. Ant.*, *CE*

59. haste haste] haste haste, *CE*
st. br. after first. *Act. Ant., CE*

60. rooms;] rooms! *Act. Ant., CE, P1950*

61. river.] river! *Act. Ant., CE, P1950*; river; *Loquitur*

65. logcabin] longcabin *P1950*

72. demobilized] demobilised *CE*

75. Kyoto;] Kyoto, *CE*

79. watched chimneys] watched the chimneys *Act. Ant., CE, P1950, Loquitur, 1970 reading in Swigg*

82. double st. br. after antiquity. *Act. Ant., CE*

83. st. br. after autumns *Loquitur*

87. couldnt] couldn't *Poetry, P1950*

88. pest] Pest *P1950*
st. br. after bred. *Poetry, Act. Ant., CE*

92. foreheads] foreheads, *Poetry*

93. A, Amida] *A, Amida Poetry*

95. fortythree] forty-three *Poetry*
A's] *A's* *Poetry*
section number IV begins after A's. *Poetry*; double st. br. after A's. *Act. Ant., CE*

99. sea's] seas' *Poetry, CE*
O horses] o horses *CE*

102. Genryaku!] Genryaku! (*) asterisk to indicate footnote *CE*; Genryaku![1] superscript numeral to indicate footnote *P1950*

103. minster] minister *P1950*
small shrines] smallshrines, *Act. Ant. proof material, corrected in pencil by BB*

105. O to be birds and fly] Oh, to be birds and fly, *Poetry*

114. tremors.] tremors— *Poetry*

117. Months . . .] Months. . . . *Poetry*

118. Years . . .] Years. . . . *Poetry*

119. . . . .] not *Poetry*; . . . . *Act. Ant., CE*; *P1950*

120. double st. br. after it now. *Act. Ant., CE*

121. world] world, *Poetry*

122. unstable] unstable, *Poetry*
double st. br. after our houses *Act. Ant., CE*
section number V begins here, omitting lines before Since I have trodden Hino Mountain [175] *Poetry*;

123. A poor] The poor *Act. Ant.*

124. doesnt] doesn't *P1950, Loquitur*

131. frame houses] frame-houses *CE*

137. no st. br. after poor devil! *P1950*

139. *Gratitude!*] '*Gratitude!*' *CE*; «*Gratitude!*» *Act. Ant., P1950, Loquitur*

141. doesnt] doesn't *P1950, Loquitur*
double st. br. after for mad *Act. Ant., CE*

143. double st. br. after body rest *Act. Ant., CE*

147. couldnt] couldn't *P1950, Loquitur*

149. it a cartshed] it was a cart-shed *Act. Ant., CE*; it was a cartshed *P1950, Loquitur, 1970 reading in Swigg*

160. no st. br. after than ever. *P1950*

165. and I,] and I: *P1950*

174. double st. br. after no trouble at all *Act. Ant., CE*

175. Hino mountain] Hino Mountain *Poetry*

182. line x'd out by typewriter after bramblewood in *CE*: I have gatherered stones for a cistern laid bamboo

186. no st. br. after thicket *P1950*

203. Mansami] Note in *Poetry* and *CE*: *Mansami:* celebrated Japanese poet.

205. Okinoya] Okanoya *Poetry, Act. Ant., CE, P1950*

206. *Between the maple leaf and the caneflower*] "*Between the mapleleaf and the caneflower*" *Poetry*; '*Between the mapleleaf and the caneflower*' *Act. Ant., CE*; "*Between the maple leaf and the caneflower*" *P1950, Loquitur*

209. no st. br. after mandolin.) *CP1985*

210. *Autumn Wind*] 'Autumn Wind' *CE*; "Autumn Wind" *Act. Ant., P1950, Loquitur*

211. *Hastening Brook*] 'Hastening Brook' *CE*; "Hastening Brook" *Act. Ant., P1950, Loquitur*

213. listening,] listening— *Poetry*

214. section number VI begins after amusement omitting lines before I am shifting rivermist, not to be trusted [296] *Poetry*; no st. br. after amusement *P1950*; double st. br. *CE*

226–30. *Somehow or other . . . satisfactory.*] '*Somehow or other . . . satisfactory.*' *CE*; "*Somehow or other . . . satisfactory.*" *Act. Ant., P1950, Loquitur*

230. no st. br. after *satisfactory. P1950*

233. double st. br. after home! *Act. Ant., CE*

236. *Whenever . . . cuff.*] '*Whenever . . . cuff.*' CE; "*Whenever . . . cuff.*" *Act. Ant., P1950, Loquitur*

237–9. *Those are . . . Maki island.*] '*Those are . . . Maki Island.*' CE; "*Those are . . . Maki Island.*" *Act. Ant.*; "*Those are . . . Maki island.*" *P1950, Loquitur*

243–4. *At the pheasant's . . . uncertainly.*] '*At the pheasant's . . . uncertainly.*' CE; "*At the pheasant's . . . uncertainly.*" *Act. Ant., P1950, Loquitur*

246–8. *Chattering fire . . . old man!*] '*Chattering fire . . . old man!*' CE; "*Chattering fire . . . old man!*" *Act. Ant., Loquitur*; "*Shattering . . . old man!*" *P1950*

252. double st. br. after recollection. *Act. Ant., CE*

256. Soanso's] Soandso's *Act. Ant., CE*

258. no st. br. after as I need. *P1950*

260. . . . .] . . . . . . *Act. Ant.*; . . . . *CE, P1950*

261. dont] don't *P1950, Loquitur*
double st. br. after bothered. *Act. Ant., CE*

263. st. br. after Anthology? *Act. Ant., CE, Loquitur*

264. dont] don't *P1950, Loquitur*
double st. br. after bothered. *CE*

277. st. br. after perquisites. *CP1985*

279. in town] in Town *Act. Ant., CE*

287. my health] the health *Act. Ant., CE, P1950, Loquitur, 1970 reading in Swigg*

298. dinner] dinner, *Poetry*

299. come round] come around *P1950*

300. apathy,] apathy— *Poetry*

302. apathy,] apathy— *Poetry*

303. wont] won't *Poetry*

305. wont] won't *Poetry*

306. wont] won't *Poetry*
craving.] craving, *CP1968*

307. apathy . . .] apathy. . . . *Poetry*

311. section number VII begins after vulgarity *Poetry*; double st. br. after vulgarity. *Act. Ant., CE*

314. no st. br. after near ahead. *Poetry, Act. Ant., CE*

315. st. br. after complain about. *Act. Ant., CE*

316. 'None of the world is good.'] "None of the world is good." *Poetry, Act. Ant., P1950*; "None of the world is good". *Loquitur*

317. hut . . .] hut. . . . *Poetry, Act. Ant.*

318. world;] world, *Poetry, CE*

320. no st. br. after appearance. *P1950*

321. poor,] poor— *Poetry*

Variants of BB's notes to poem in Poetry *42, No. 6 (September 1933), 356–7, and CE:*

Kamo-no-Chomei, i. e. Chomei of Kamo, flourished somewhat over a hundred years before Dante. He belonged to the minor Japanese nobility, and held various offices in the civil service. He applied for a fat job in a Shinto temple, was turned down, and the next day announced his conversion to Buddhism.

He wrote: *Tales of the Four Seasons*; *Notes with no Title* (critical essays); [: *CE*] and a quantity of poems; edited an anthology of poems composed at the moment of conversion by Buddhist proselytes (one suspects irony); and was for a while secretary to the editors of the imperial anthology [Imperial Anthology *CE*].
[not *CE*: He was as modern as, say, Cummings. His Kyoto had a number of curiously detailed parallels with modern New York and Chicago.]

He got sick of public life and retired to a kind of mixture of hermitage and country cottage at Toyama on Mount Hino, and there, when he was getting old, he wrote his celebrated *Ho-Jo-Ki*, [no comma *CE*] of which my poem is, in the main, a condensation. The *Ho-Jo-Ki* is in prose, but the careful proportion and balance of its parts, the leit-motif [motif *CE*] of the House running through it, and some other indications, [no comma *CE*] suggest that he intended a poem, more or less elegiac; [, *CE*] but had not time, nor possibly energy, at his then age, to work out what would have been for Japan an entirely new form, [no comma *CE*] nor to condense his material sufficiently. This I have attempted to do for him.
[not *Poetry:* He was quite up to date: and up-to-date is always *contemporary* with us.]

I cannot take his Buddhism solemnly, considering the manner of his conversion, the suspect nature of his anthology, and his whole urbane, sceptical and ironical temperament [temper *CE*]. If this annoys [anybody *CE*] the kind of scholar who likes to make out every celebrated writer as dull and respectable as himself, [no comma *CE*] I cannot help it.

I am indebted to Professor Muccioli's Italian version of the *Ho-Jo-Ki*, [no comma *CE*] and especially to his learned notes. Professor Muccioli does not [, as far as I can learn, *CE*] take my view of Chomei's religious opinions.

additional notes:

Amida: in the more or less polytheistic Buddhism of medieval Japan, Amida presides over the earthly paradise, where the souls of decent dead men repose for awhile. He was reverenced about as widely as Mary is by Catholics, and Chomei, probably attracted by the poetic qualities of the Amida myth, professed a special devotion for him. *Poetry*

▪ The earth quaked in the second year of Genryaku, 1185.]
footnote: Precisely, the second year of Genryaku, 1185 *CE*, *P1950*
Mansami: celebrated Japanese poet. *Poetry*
Po Lo-Tien: celebrated Chinese poet, better known in the West as *Po Chui*. *Poetry*

FIRST BOOK OF ODES

Section title. FIRST BOOK OF ODES] ODES *P1950*, *Loquitur*

Dedication] Of those not particularly dedicated, let Ezra Pound take all that are good in his opinion. *CE*

Arabic numerals followed by full-stop used to number Odes in *P1950* until that edition's Ode 9, after which no full-stop used; roman numerals used in *CE*, except in table of contents where they are arabic; arabic without full-stop in *FBO*, *Loquitur*, and all editions of *CP*

1 'Weeping oaks grieve, chestnuts raise'

Initial capital for first word in each line throughout *RM*

2 'Farewell ye sequent graces'

9–10. glimmer on cascades of / fantom dancers] one line *P1950*

10. fantom] phantom *P1950*, *FBO*, *Loquitur*

11. light] Light *P1950*, *FBO*, *Loquitur*

3 'I am agog for foam. Tumultuous come'

To Peggy Mullett] *to Peggy Mullett.* RM; *to Peggy Mullett* CE; *to Peggy Mullett* P1950

Initial capital for first word in each line throughout *RM*

1. Tumultuous come] Tumultuous, come *RM*, *CE*

3. midday parched] midday-parched *RM*

4. expectation.] expectation! *RM*, *CE*

11. hostility.] hostility! *RM*, *CE*

15. sprayblown] spray-blown *RM*

4 'After the grimaces of capitulation'

Initial capital for first word in each line throughout *RM*

3. st. br. after elevation. *RM*, *CE*
4. majestic,] majestic , *P1950*
5. tyrant] tyrant, *RM*, *CE*
8. st. br. after farce; *RM*, *CE*
9. red-hot] redhot *RM*, *CE*
10. blisters,] blisters *RM*, *CE*
12. st. br. after greedily. *RM*, *CE*

5 'Empty vast days built in the waste memory seem a jail for'

To Helen Egli] *to Helen Egli.* RM, CE; *to Helen Egli* P1950

2. inflexible:] inflexible. *RM*; inflexible, *CE*
3. love] Love *CE*
   selfpraise,] selfpraise *RM*; self-praise *CE*
4. no st. br. after utterance *P1950*

6 *Personal Column* / '. . . As to my heart, that may as well be forgotten'

Initial capital for first word in each line throughout *RM*

3. h.&c.,] h. and c., *RM*; h. & c., *CE*, *FBO*, *Loquitur*

under poem *** followed by epigraph at foot of poem, indented right:
Bornons ici cette carrière, / Les longs ourvrages me font peur.

7 'The day being Whitsun we had pigeon for dinner'

Double quotes used throughout *CE*, *P1950*, *FBO*, *Loquitur*

12. double st. br. after *homines*. *CE*

8 *Each fettered ghost slips to his several grave. /* 'Loud intolerant bells (the shrinking nightflower closes'

Initial capital for first word in each line throughout *RM*

Epigraph. Each fettered ghost slips to his several grave.] *Each fetter'd ghost slips to his several grave. RM, CE*

9. whom [?] x'd out by typewriter after gods *CE*

10. spirit,] comma handwritten *CE*

9 'Dear be still! Time's start of us lengthens slowly'

Initial capital for first word in each line throughout *RM*

Double spaces between stanzas *P1950*

5. unemotional.] unemotional! *RM*, *CE*

11. savage's] savages' *P1950*

10 Chorus of Furies

Initial capital for first word in each line throughout *RM*

Title. Chorus of Furies] *CHORUS OF FURIES (OVERHEARD). RM*; *Chorus of Furies: / overheard. CE*

Epigraph. Guarda, mi disse, le feroce Erine] *Guarda, mi disse, le feroce Erine. RM, CE*; *Guarda mi disse, le feroce Erine P1950, CP1968*

13. fiends] friends *P1950*

16. flayed:] flayed, *RM*, *CE*

20. brain.] brain; *P1950*

11 *To a Poet who advised me to preserve my fragments and false starts /* 'Narciss, my numerous cancellations prefer'

Initial capital for first word in each line throughout *RM*, *Whips & Scorpions*

Epigraph. To a Poet who advised me to preserve my fragments and false starts] *To a* POET *who Advised me to* PRESERVE *my Fragments and False Starts. RM, Whips & Scorpions, CE*

1. Narciss,] NARCISS, *RM*, *Whips & Scorpions*, *CE*

3. tobacco-ash] tobacco ash *RM*, *Whips & Scorpions*, *CE*

7–8. ignominy, / the] ignominy / — The *RM*, *Whips & Scorpions*; ignominy— / the *CE*

8. your decay, that reeks.] YOUR decay that *reeks*. *RM*, *Whips & Scorpions*; Y O U R decay that *reeks*. *CE*

12 'An arles, an arles for my hiring'

Initial capital for first word in each line throughout *RM*

8. bun.)] bun). *RM*, *CE*

10. drawing-room?] drawingroom? *RM*, *CE*

13. muse] Muse *RM*, *CE*

14. *Quaeret in trivio vocationem.*] Quæret in trivio vocationem. *RM*; Quaeret in trivio vocationem. *CE*, *P1950*

15. (he is cadging for drinks at the streetcorners.)] as note in small type at foot of page: (i. e., he is cadging for drinks at the street-corners). *RM*; at foot of page: (i. e., he is cadging for drinks at the streetcorners). *CE*

13 *Fearful symmetry* / 'Muzzle and jowl and beastly brow'

Epigraph. *Fearful symmetry*] *Fearful Symmetry* *CE*

5. 'beautiful'] "beautiful" *Poetry*

6. Kuala Lampur.] turnover, not separate line *Poetry*, *CE*

7. R.A.] R. A. *Poetry*

11. Sundry] Several *Poetry*

13. docks] Docks *Poetry*, *CE*, *P1950*, *FBO*, *Loquitur*
advertises] advertizes *Poetry*

14. fullgrown] full-grown *Poetry*, *CE*

15. ♂] not *Poetry*, *P1950*; hand-drawn *CE*
♂Felis Tigris] ♂ Felis Tigris *CP1994/2000* [emendation]
Straits] Straights *Poetry*

16. feeding] feeding, *Poetry*

19. persons] persons, *Poetry*, *CE*

14 Gin the Goodwife Stint

Initial capital for first word in each line throughout *Act. Ant., P1950, Sum*

3. stint,] stint *Act. Ant., CE, P1950, Sum*

10. ticket] ticket— *CE*

Variants of note to the poem:

Bent = tough, tussocky grass. *CE*; bent=tough, tussocky grass *P1950*; *bent:* tough, tussocky grass *Conf. Cumm.*
gin = if. *CE*; gin=if *P1950*; *gin:* if *Conf. Cumm.*
C. P. R. = Canadian Pacific Railway. It was recently, and may still be, possible for an emigrant pledged to agricultural labour, to cross to Canada on C. P. R. boats for two pounds. *CE*; C. P. R. = Canadian Pacific Railway. It was recently, and may still be, possible for an emigrant pledged to agricultural labour to cross to Canada on C. P. R. boats for two pounds. *P1950*; *C. P. R.*: In 1920 it was still possible for an emigrant pledged to agricultural labor to cross from England to Canada on a Canadian Pacific Railway boat for two pounds. *Conf. Cumm.*

15 'Nothing'

4. joins] joints *P1950*
design and] the design and the *Poetry*, *CE*, *P1950*, *Granta*, *FBO*, *Loquitur*

15. When taut string's] When the tight string's *Poetry*; When the taut string's *CE*, *Granta*, *FBO*, *Loquitur*; When the taut strings *P1950*

16. ears' reach] ear's reach, *Poetry*

19. enumerates . . .] enumerates. . . . *Poetry*

20. mimes clouds] Mimes the clouds *Poetry*; mimes the clouds *CE*, *P1950*, *Granta*, *FBO*, *Loquitur*

21. and hewn hills and bristling] and the hewn hills and the bristling *Poetry*, *CE*, *Granta*, *P1950*, *FBO*, *Loquitur*

26. death . . .] death. . . . *Poetry*

28. narrowing,] narrowing *CE*

29. failing,] failing *CE*

30–1. out. // Ears] out; // ears *Poetry*

After 32.] *Poetry* adds:

> *Appendix: Iron*
> Molten pool, incandescent spilth of
> deep cauldrons — and brighter nothing is —

cast and cold, your blazes extinct and
no turmoil nor peril left you,
rusty ingot, bleak paralyzed blob!

17 *To Mina Loy* / 'Now that sea's over that island'

Epigraph. To Mina Loy] not *CE*, *P1950*, *Imagi*, *Granta*, *FBO*, *Loquitur*

6. hinges,] hinges *Imagi*, *Granta*

8. *Trespassers will be prosecuted.*] 'Trespassers will be prosecuted'. *CE*; "Trespassers will be prosecuted." *P1950*, *Imagi*, *Granta*, *FBO*, *Loquitur*

13. dont know] don't know *P1950*, *Imagi*, *Granta*, *FBO*, *Loquitur*

15. crumpled] crumbled *1982 Riverside Studios reading, in Swigg*

20. subaqueous] subacqueous *CE*, *P1950*, *Imagi*; aqueous re-read as subaqueous *1982 Riverside Studios reading, in Swigg*
persistence] persistance *CE*, *P1950*, *Imagi*

21. year —] year: *CE*

22. preservation] preservation, *CE*

26. collects] searches *CE*

27. additional lines run on after adopt and perpetuate followed by a stanza break:

Latreia is always excessive,
doulei out of place in a drawingroom,
my experience, then, not such as to encourage near
approach to any woman but an obvious whore. [*CE*]

30. her again] her again, *CE*

18 The Complaint of the Morpethshire Farmer

Initial capital for first word in each line throughout *Act. Ant.*, *P1950*, *Four Pages*, *Conf. Cumm.*

2. market-day] marketday *CE*

4. no st. br. s after this song: *Four Pages*

20. would na] wouldna *CE*

23. something] something, *Act. Ant.*, *CE*, *Four Pages*

24. We'll] we'll *CE*

30. north wind] North wind *Act. Ant.*, *Four Pages*

31. land] land, *Four Pages*

Variants in notes to the poem:

kye = cattle *CE*, *Act. Ant.*; kye=cattle *P1950*; *kye:* cattle *Conf. Cumm.*

coulter = plowshare *CE*, *Act. Ant.*; coulter=plowshare *P1950*; *coulter:* plowshare *Conf. Cumm.*

cowpit = overturned *CE*, *Act. Ant.*; cowpit=overturned *P1950*; *cowpit:* overturned *Conf. Cumm.*

hind = farm labourer *CE*, *Act. Ant.*; hind=farm labourer *P1950*; *hind:* farm laborer *Conf. Cumm.*

At foot of poem in *CE*: NOTE. The Duke of Northumberland, like many Scottish landlords and a few other nothern [*sic*] English ones, finds ['landlords' x'd out by typewriter] it pays better to let his land run wild and take what foolish 'sportsmen' will pay for almost non-existing shooting, than to keep the ditches clean so that sheep may thrive and his farmers be able to pay their rent regularly. Yet the cost of putting in sheep-drain [*sic*], even new, is very small and wherever the farmer has been able to do it himself the land is reclaimed. Some of it is even arable. In these cases the Duke at once raises the rent, the farmer is ruined, and the land reverts to heather.

At foot of poem in *Act. Ant.* proof material, but omitted from published version: NOTE. The Duke of Northumberland, like many Scottish landlords and a few other northern English ones, finds it pays better to let his land run wild and take what foolish 'sportsmen' will pay for often almost non-existent shooting, than to keep the ditches clean so that the sheep may thrive and his farmers be able to pay their rent regularly. Yet the cost of putting in sheep-drains, even new, is very small and wherever the farmer has been able to do it himself the land is reclaimed. Some of it is even arable. In these cases the Duke raises the rent at once, the farmer is ruined, and the land reverts to heather.

19 'Fruits breaking the branches'

9. orchards'] orchard's *CE*

20 Vestiges

Section heading. I] First Vestige. 'Vestige.' handwritten over undecipherable hand-cancelled word *CE*; 1. *P1950*

I. 1–2. hooves, the lake stinks, / we] hooves. The lake stinks. / We *CE*

I. 2–3. streams, / our] streams. / Our *CE*

I. 3–4. flies, / we] flies. / We *CE*

I. 4. eastern prairie,] eastern / prairie *CE*

I. 5–6. who slew the Franks, who / swam the Yellow River.] who slew the Franks, / who swam the Yellow / River. *CE*

I. 9. life:] life; *CE*
death,] death; *CE*

I. 10. indistinguishable;] indistinguishable, *P1950*
st. br. after indistinguishable; *CE*

I. 11. fool's jaws.] fools' jaws. *CE*

additional lines in *CE* after fools' jaws followed by a stanza break:

> —I did not see when you left me
> how you left me
> where you went
> three hairs on the wind;
> have abolished some years and am
> maiden—
> The world is one, the Khan divides with none.
> Keep your religion if you want it.

I. 12. temples. Our] temples; our *CE*

I. 13. Chin,] Chin: *CE*

I. 14. battles, swift riders, ambush,] battles, the swift riders, the ambush, last comma handwritten *CE*; battles, swift riders, the ambush, the tale of the slain, / indent and the name Jengiz *P1950*

I. 15. Jengiz] of Jenghis. *CE*

I. 16. Shore.] Shore no st. br.; additional lines in *CE*:

> scream blood, the bear groans blood to Kiev.
> Our Kubilai, witness your Marco, had
> wise men about him and ruled gently.

I. 18. Baghdad] Bagdad *CE*

I. 21. taxation impoverishes] taxation / impoverishes *CE*

I. 22. No litigation. The] There was no litigation, / the *CE*

Section heading. II] Second Vestige. *CE* 'Vestige.' handwritten over undecipherable hand-cancelled word *CE*; 2. *P1950*

II. 1. Jengiz to Chang Chun: China] *Jenghis to Chang Chun:* China *CE*; Jengiz to Chang Chun: China *P1950* [extra space]

II. 7. Lords] lords *CE*

II. 14. sages,] sages: *CE*

II. 17. washed. Come] washed. / Come. *May 15 1219* *CE*; / [smaller type] May 15, 1219 *P1950*

II. 18. Chang:] *Chang:* <u>*CE*</u>

II. 19. not wise nor virtuous,] and not wise / nor virtuous. *CE*

II. 20. nor likely] I am not likely *CE*

II. 22. once.] once. *April 1220 CE*; / [smaller type] April 1220 *P1950*

II. 23. And to Liu Chung Lu, Jengiz:] *And to General Liu Chung Lu, Jenghis*: <u>*CE*</u>

II. 26. separately if he insists] <u>indent</u> separately / <u>indent</u> if he insists. *1220.* <u>*CE*</u>; / [smaller type] 1220 *P1950*

21 Two Photographs

4. dont] don't *P1950*, *FBO*, *Loquitur*

8. fiancé] fiancee *P1950*

9. focus) /] fo- / cus) *CE*

22 'Mesh cast for mackerel'

2. tremor,] tremor— *Poetry*

3. havent] haven't *Poetry*, *P1950*, *Sum*, *FBO*, *Loquitur*

4. job,] comma handwritten *CE*

10. tap] Tap *CE*, *P1950*, *Sum*

13–16. Remember . . . tedium.] "Remember . . . tedium" *Poetry*

15. at,] at— *Poetry*

23 The Passport Officer

2. scrutinizes] scrutinises *CE*

7. precedent.] precedent.) *CE*

8. His actions are reflex.)] <u>not</u> *CE*

24 'Vessels thrown awry by strong gusts'

2. broach to,] broach too, *P1950*, *CP1968*

10. less.)] less) *CE*

13. navigation] navigation, *CE*

reefs,] reefs *CE*

20. precincts.)] precincts) *CE*

23. anemometer] anamometer hand-corrected *CE*

28. muttered] muttered: *CE*

29. precincts] precincts, *CE*

31. glass-clear] glassclear *CE*

32. gardens] Gardens *P1950*

33. Ocean] Ocean, *CE*

Variant in note to the poem:

Note: The case was tried in 1917 or 1919, I forget.] The case referred to was tried in 1918. *CE*

25 'As appleblossom to crocus'

4. middleclass] middle class *CE*

10. spinning] spinning, *CE*, *P1950*, *FBO*, *Loquitur*

17. — The cinema] The cinema *CE*

26 'Two hundred and seven paces'

4. forty-six] fourty-six *P1950*

9. kisses] kisses, *CE*

15. City,] comma handwritten *CE*

19–20. fire-extinguisher, / George. Here's /] fire-extinguisher, George, / indent here's / *CE*

28 'You leave'

3. bed] bed, *Boz-West*

6. home] home. *Boz-West*

9–11. hanged / in your / halter] hanged in your / halter, *Boz-West*

attribution at foot of poem: *Hafiz CE*; Huhammad Shams-ud-Din Hafiz *Boz-West*

version in letter to LZ, 29 September 1935:

(Hafiz, a rubay)
You leave nobody else without a bed,
you make everybody else thoroughly at home:

I'm the only one hanged in your halter,
you've driven nobody else mad but me.
(which is nearly a Blues)

29 'Southwind, tell her what'

2. wont] won't *P1950*, *FBO*, *Loquitur*

8. alone] awake *CE*, *Boz-West*

attribution at foot of poem: *Hafiz* CE; *Hafiz. Boz-West*

30 The Orotava Road

Double quotes used throughout *P1950*, *FBO*, *Loquitur*

7. linen trousers] linentrousers *P1950*

11. Hu! vaca! Hu! vaca!] Hu! vaca!   Hu! vaca! extra space *P1950*

31 *O ubi campi!* / 'The soil sandy and the plow light, neither'

Epigraph. O ubi campi!] *O fortunatos nimium:* / also: *O ubi campi! Draft* to LZ, with title, 'Farmer'. O ubi campi! printed as indented, first line of poem *Granta*

12. starpinned] starspinned *1976 Essex reading, in Swigg*
The choir] the choir *Granta*

32 'Let them remember Samangan, the bridge and tower'

1. bridge and tower] bride and tower *CP1968* corrected in 2nd ed. with errata slip

3. mountains,] mountains *P1950*, *FBO*, *Loquitur*

33 *To Anne de Silver* / 'Not to thank dogwood nor'

Dedication. To Anne de Silver] *to Anne de Silver P1950*

Section heading. I] 1. *P1950*, *Sum*

Section heading. II] 2. *P1950*, *Sum*

34 *To Violet, with prewar poems.* / 'These tracings from a world that's dead'

Initial capital for first word in each line throughout *Poetry*

Dedication. To Violet, with prewar poems.] *To Violet, with prewar poems CP1994/2000* [emendation]

2. pyramid] Pyramid *Poetry*

5. You] You, *Poetry*

6. laid,] laid; *Poetry*

8. my weathered] my mossed, weathered *Poetry*
spilt,] spilt; *Poetry*

35 'Search under every veil'

8. to whom] for whom *P1950, 1965 reading at Morden Tower, recording at Harvard Poetry Room*

15. maimed] maimed, *P1950*

36 'See! Their verses are laid'

15. substance;] substance: *P1950*, *FBO*, *Loquitur*

37 On the Fly-Leaf of Pound's Cantos

Title] On the Fly-leaf of Pound's Cantos *Agenda*

2. don't] dont *Agenda*, *FBO*, *Loquitur*

6. There they are,] There they are; *Agenda*
round] around *1982 Riverside Studios reading, in Swigg*

SECOND BOOK OF ODES

1 'A thrush in the syringa sings'

Double quotes used throughout *Paris Review*

3 Birthday Greeting

Title] Birthday Greetings *Agenda*

9. married: — yet] married; yet *Agenda*; married:—yet *St Andrews College pamphlet*; *CP1994/2000* [emendation]

10. today I am fourteen years old.] hand-cut correction pasted to page, covering erroneous indent *Agenda*

4 'You idiot! What makes you think decay will'

3. girls in] girls at *1976 Harvard reading*

6 What the Chairman Told Tom

3. Mr Shaw] Mr. Shaw *St Andrews College pamphlet*

10. ask for twelve] ask twelve *1976 Harvard reading*

31. Mr Hines] Mr. Hines *St Andrews College pamphlet*

8 All you Spanish ladies / 'Carmencita's tawny paps'

Title] All You Spanish ladies *Agenda*

2. frock;] frock, *Agenda*

5. *Ay de mi chica!*] Ay de mi chica! *Agenda*

14. *Ay de mi muchachita!*] Ay! Ay de mi muchachita! *Agenda*

9 'All the cants they peddle'

Variant in note to the poem:

- "poets' conference"] 'poets' conference' *CP1978*, *CP1985*

10 'Stones trip Coquet burn'

1–2. burn; / grass] burn. / Grass *Agenda*

7. midgy] midgey *Agenda*

11 At Briggflatts meetinghouse

1. Rome.] Rome; *Montemora*, *Poetry Review*

6. saints'] the saints *Montemora*, *Poetry Review*

12 *Perche no spero* / 'Now we've no hope of going back'

9. cutter, and] cutter; and *Agenda*

21. wait.] wait, like the proud. *Agenda*

OVERDRAFTS

'Darling of Gods and Men, beneath the gliding stars'

Version in *Grok* 2 (19 May 1967), 5, *Guedalla* D28 not available for collation

Initial capital for first word in each line throughout *RM*, *A Test of Poetry*

Title/Epigraph] *TO VENUS / after Lucrerius.* RM; *to Venus.* CE

1. Gods and Men] Gods and men *RM*, *A Test of Poetry*; gods and men *CE*

gliding] sliding *RM*, *A Test of Poetry*_

4. clear,] clear *RM*, *A Test of Poetry*_

5. flowers,] flowers *RM*, *A Test of Poetry*_

'Yes, it's slow, docked of amours'

Apparent confusion of turnovers and indents in *Whips & Scorpions*, as below

Epigraph] *Miserarum est neque amori dare ludum. . . .* *Whips & Scorpions*; (*Miserarum est neque amori dare ludum. . . . —Q. H. F.)* *Act. Ant.*

1. Yes, it's slow, docked of amours, / indent docked of the doubtless efficacious] YES, it's slow, dockt of amours, dockt of the doubtless / indent or turnover efficacious *Whips & Scorpions*_

3. stiff] indent or turnover stiff *Whips & Scorpions*

5–6. If your workbox is mislaid / indent blame Cytherea's lad . . . Minerva] If your workbox is mislaid blame Cytherea's lad. . . . / indent Minerva *Whips & Scorpions*

7. dropped] dropt *Whips & Scorpions*

8. glistening] glistning *Whips & Scorpions*

9–10. when he's been swimming and stands / indent towelling himself in full view] when he's been swimming and stands towelling him- / indent or turnover self there in full view *Whips & Scorpions*; there in full view *Act. Ant.*, *CE*

11. horseback!] horse- indent or turnover back! *Whips & Scorpions*

12. track-shorts!] trackshorts! *Whips & Scorpions*
first-class] firstclass *Whips & Scorpions, Act. Ant., CE*

13–14. He can shoot straight from the butts, / indent straight from precarious cover, waistdeep] He can shoot straight from the butts, straight from / indent or turnover precarious cover, waistdeep *Whips & Scorpions*

15. daylong] daylong, *Whips & Scorpions, Act. Ant., CE*

16. driven] drivn *Whips & Scorpions*
arms'-length] arms-length. *Whips & Scorpions*; arm's-length *Act. Ant., CE, P1950*

'Please stop gushing about his pink'

Epigraph] (CUM TU LYDIA TELEPHI) *Pagany*; *Cum tu Lydia Telephi. . . . Whips & Scorpions*

2. smooth arms] smooth arms *P1950*
Dulcie;] Dulcie: *Pagany, Whips & Scorpions*

4. tenterhooks.] tenterhooks: *Pagany*

8. lips. Take] lips. —Take *Pagany, Whips & Scorpions, CE*

10–11. life, / we] life. / We *Pagany*

12. soon, soon torn] soon, soon! wrenched *Pagany*

'When the sword of sixty comes nigh his head'

Footer and page number between atribution and date – compositor error *CP1968*

All the teeth ever I had are worn down and fallen out

Epigraph. Abu'abdulla Ja'far bin Mahmud Rudaki of Samarcand says: *P1950*; *Abu'abdulla Ja'far bin Mahmud Rudaki of Samarkand says:* *Loquitur*

2. They were not rotten teeth, they] Not rotten teeth! They *Nine*

3. silvery-white] silvery white *Nine*
coral;] coral, *Nine*

6. ill-luck, ill-luck] ill-luck, fate *Nine*

7. stars] the stars *Nine*

8. what it was:] what: *Nine*

10. existed: a] existed. A *Nine*

13. in] In *Nine*

15. used to be] once was *Nine*

16. blackhaired] black-haired *Nine*

25. beauty.] beauty, *P1950*

27. mirth] mirth, *Nine*
st. br. after losing her. *Nine*; page br. after losing her. *P1950*

28. well and in counted coin] in counted coin and well *Nine*

31. night] night, *Nine*
dare] dared *Nine*

33. face,] face— *Nine*; face *P1950*

35. My purse was my heart, my heart bursting with words,] My heart was a store of treasures, treasures of words, *Nine*
words,] words *P1950*

36. title-page] title page *Nine*
book was Love] book, Love *Nine*

37. Happy was I,] Always happy *Nine*

38. any more than a meadow.] my heart a wide meadow for delight. *Nine*; as a wide meadow for delight *P1950*

43. patron —] patron: *Nine*

44. of these] of all these *1978 reading at Leeds, in Swigg*
trials] trials, *Nine*

45. Oh!] Oh *Nine*; Oh, *P1950*

46. never] Never *Nine*
that.] that,
no st br. *Nine*

50. affairs of princes,] the affairs of Princes, *P1950*

51. all] he *1978 reading at Leeds, in Swigg*

52. Khorassan.] Khorassan! *Nine*; Khorassan *CP2000* [emendation]

53. renown] renown, *Nine*

54. house] House *Nine*

60. time!] time. *Nine*

61. heard] recognised *Nine*

'Came to me —'

Attribution. (Rudaki)] (Rudaki, X century) *Paris Review*

'This I write, mix ink with tears'

3. Azra Vamiq's] Azra, Vamiq's *Nine*

4. Laila Majnun's] Laila, Majnun's *Nine*

7. it.] this. *Nine*

8. write.] write! *Nine*

Attribution. Sa'di) Sa'di) *Loquitur*

'Last night without sight of you my brain was ablaze'

15. Sa'di] Sa'di *Nine*

Attribution. Sa'di)] Sa'di) *Loquitur*

'You can't grip years, Postume'

1. can't] cant *Agenda*, *Sunday Times*

4. death] death, *Agenda*, *Sunday Times*

19. toil,] toil *Agenda*, *Sunday Times*

Attribution. (Horace)] *from Horace* Agenda

How Duke Valentine Contrived

Double quotes used throughout *Act. Ant.*, *P1950*, *Loquitur*

Epigraph. (the murder of Vitellozzo Vitelli, Oliverotto da Fermo, Mr Pagolo and the Duke of Gravina Orsini) according to Machiavelli:] the murder of Vitellozzo Vitelli, Oliverotto da Fermo, Mr Pagolo and the Duke of Gravina Orsini, according to Machiavelli. CE; *(the murder of Vitellozzo Vitelli, Oliverotto da Fermo, Mr. Pagolo and the Duke of Gravina Orsini,) according to Machiavelli:* Act. Ant., P1950 CP1985

10, 18, 51, 104, 126, 178, 227, 233. Vitelli] Vitegli *Act. Ant.*, *CE*

14. turn next] turn next, *Act. Ant.*, *CE*, *P1950*, *Loquitur*

31. heart] indent *Act. Ant.*, *P1950*

36. couldnt raise] couldn't raise *P1950*, *Loquitur*

38. fortress:] fortress; *CE*

43. oughtnt] oughtn't *P1950*, *Loquitur*

49. again,'] again", *Act. Ant.*

55. hadnt expected] hadn't expected *P1950*, *Loquitur*

62. no st. br. after reliable army. *Act. Ant.*, *CE*

72. first rate] firstrate *CE*
st. br. after humbug). *CP1985*

73–6. seems 'they . . . ruling.'] single quotes handwritten *CE*

89. indemnity] indeminity *P1950*

95. Guidobaldo] Guid'Ubaldo *P1950*

107–8. 'they . . . Sinigaglia?'] no quotes *CE*

108. wouldnt] wouldn't *P1950*, *Loquitur*

111. no st. br. after nicely. *CP1985*

128. unneighbourliness] that unneighborliness *CE*, *Act. Ant.*, *P1950*

136. st. br. after consented *CE*

144. Pagolo Orsino,] Pagolo, Orsini, *P1950*

157. Metaurus'] Mentaurus' *P1950*

169. bow-shot] bowshot *CE*

188. advance guard] advanceguard *CE*

192. Pagolo, and] Paglolo and *CE*

202. family,] family *CE*

220. Sinigaglia,] Sinigaglia *P1950*, *Loquitur*

221. lodgings] lodging *CE*

224. his scallawags] indent *Act. Ant.*, *P1950*

228. distance away,] distance away *CE*

229. matter,] matter *CE*

237. hadnt] hadn't *P1950*, *Loquitur*

248. blame for] blame of *Act. Ant.*, *CE*, *P1950*, *Loquitur*

251. Archbishop] archbishop *Act. Ant.*, *CE*

253. at Castel della Pieve, separate line *CE*

UNCOLLECTED POEMS

The Pious Cat

Single quotes used throughout *UP*; *CP1994/2000*

1. BY YOUR LEAVE!] indent **By your leave!** followed by line br. *UP*; *CP1994/2000*

10. BY HEAVEN'S DECREE] **By Heaven's decree** *UP*; *CP1994/2000*

26. drink;] drink, *UP*; *CP1994/2000*

27. no st. br. after vain. *UP*; *CP1994/2000*

28. that] the *UP*; *CP1994/2000*

30. him.] him: *UP*; *CP1994/2000*

31. Cats!] Cats? *UP*; *CP1994/2000*
score.] score! *UP*; *CP1994/2000*

32. Tibbald?] Tibbald! *UP*; *CP1994/2000*

33. cur.] cur! *UP*; *CP1994/2000*

38. off.] off! *UP*; *CP1994/2000*

42–3. grudge." / But] grudge!' / but *UP*; *CP1994/2000*

43. answered] answered: *UP*; *CP1994/2000*

45. him,] him *UP*; *CP1994/2000*

51. mice,] mice; *UP*; *CP1994/2000*

53. I'll] I will *UP*; *CP1994/2000*

57. victim] victim, *UP*; *CP1994/2000*
give . . .] give. . . . . *Rota fac.*

58. coffee beans and leaves of tea] cold coffee and plenty of tea *UP*; *CP1994/2000*

63. pies,] pies *UP*; *CP1994/2000*

73. The cat has been converted.] the cat has been converted! *UP*; *CP1994/2000*

75. week] week, *UP*; *CP1994/2000*

82. St.] Saint *UP*; *CP1994/2000*

90. dogs,] dogs *UP*; *CP1994/2000*

92. home-made] homemade *UP*; *CP1994/2000*

100. word,] word *UP*; *CP1994/2000*

101. breakfast] breakfast, *UP*; *CP1994/2000*
grown] got *UP*; *CP1994/2000*

102. self-denial] self denial *UP*; *CP1994/2000*

109. daily bread] Daily Bread *UP*; *CP1994/2000*

112–13. dither, / yet they stepped forward, all together,] dither / but they stepped forward all together *UP*; *CP2000*

114. until they came within arm's length] not *1978 reading at Leeds, in Swigg*

124. chewed] cancelled: bolted *Rota fac.*; guzzled *UP*; *CP1994/2000*

136. The king was proud and still and prim.] The king was grave and proud and prim. *UP*; *CP1994/2000*

139. King! Consider] King, consider *UP*; *CP1994/2000*

141. rate,] rate *UP*; *CP1994/2000*

142. he took] cancelled: he's taken *Rota fac.*

143. no st. br. after whole societies." *Rota fac.*

144. On this] On this, *UP*; *CP1994/2000*

147. mobilise] mobilize *UP*; *CP1994/2000*
mousey] entire *UP*; *CP1994/2000*

149. bombs] swords *UP*; *CP1994/2000*
gas-masks] gasmasks *UP*; *CP1994/2000*

155. bright,] bright *UP*; *CP1994/2000*

157. white] white, *UP*; *CP1994/2000*

163. But when] but when *UP*; *CP1994/2000*

169ff. for Tibbald answered roughly a word in cat language that / means "Oh dear me, *what* nonsense".] for Tibbald answered roughly: '⁎'. *UP*; *CP1994/2000* which add note at foot of page: [⁎] a word in cattish language meaning 'Oh dear me, *what* nonsense!'

171. mount] mount, *UP*; *CP1994/2000*

174. bite] bite, *UP*; *CP1994/2000*
shells,] shells *UP*; *CP1994/2000*

176. from Solway coast] from the Solway coast *1978 reading at Leeds, in Swigg*; from the Coast *UP*; *CP1994/2000*

177. onslaught.] onslaught! *UP*; *CP1994/2000*

178. frying] frying, *UP*; *CP1994/2000*

184. HQ] H. Q. *UP*; *CP1994/2000*

186. five score mice] a hundred mice *UP*; *CP1994/2000*

187. "Victory!"] 'Victory' *UP*; *CP1994/2000*

190. speed with dignity] speed and dignity *UP*; *CP1994/2000*

193. and sentenced Tibbald] then sentenced him *UP*; *CP1994/2000*

196. the court] the Bench *UP*; *CP1994/2000*

POST SCRIPT You must call him Obeyed, like the English word "he obeyed the law": *obeyed a zaw-kaw-nee*, and save most of your breath for the *nee*. He wrote this story about six hundred years ago, and Persian children still read it at school, or they used to, twenty years since. Any story that lasts as long as that is worth listening to, I think. Perhaps not everything in it is true, but bits of it are very true indeed. Basil Bunting 1939–77] ▪ You must call him 'Obeyed', like the English word 'obeyed a command', 'obeyed a zaw-kaw-nee'; and save most of your breath for the 'nee'. He wrote this story about six hundred years ago, and Persian children still read it at school, or they used to, twenty years since. Any story that lasts as long as that is worth listening to, I think. Perhaps not everything in it is true, but bits of it are very true indeed. B. Bunting 1937–77 *UP*; *CP1994/2000*

They Say Etna [*Active Anthology*]

Single quotes used throughout *UP*, *CP1994/2000*

22. *UKASE.*] underscored twice *CE*; larger type: **UKASE.** *P1950*; not centred on next three lines *CP1994*

35. for sheep] indent? *Act. Ant.*, *P1950*

76. no st. br. after is it? *Conf. Cumm.*

77–8, 83–4. **MAN . . . ASSERTS . . . MAN . . . BOLSHEVIK**] arrows to each from BB's circled handwritten note in margin, 'heavy leaded type, newspaper headline style' *CE*; **BLASPHEMOUS BOLSHEVIK.** not centred *CP1994/2000*

UNCOLLECTED ODES

2 Against the Tricks of Time

Initial capital for first word in each line throughout *RM*, *UP*, *CP1994/2000*

5. shopwindow] shop window *RM*, *UP*, *CP1994/2000*

11. single st. br. after ashamed of myself. *RM*, *UP*, *CP1994/2000*

16. nightwanderings] night-wanderings *RM*, *UP*, *CP1994/2000*

18. wallreflected] wall-reflected *RM*, *UP*, *CP1994/2000*
streetlamp-light] street-lamp-light *RM*, *UP*, *CP1994/2000*

31. single st. br. after wither. *RM*, *UP*, *CP1994/2000*

4 Hymn To Alias Thor

36. with the wash] with wash *UP*, *CP1994/2000* [emendation]

8 Trinacria

Note in *CE*] Only 2 & 4 are Sicilian: the other two are from North Italy.

9 A Song for Rustam

21–3. *'Unseen . . . unsung;'*] double quotes, indented *Sulfur*
Dated] 7:IX:64 *Sulfur*

11 'Such syllables flicker out of grass'

2. goes';] goes': *Quartermain DP* (146)

16–17. 'subject . . . that way'] The first quotation mark was supplied to the printed text in *UP* and *CP1994/2000* by RC from MS material at Durham.

UNCOLLECTED OVERDRAFTS

'Many well-known people have been packed away in cemeteries'

(Sa'di)] x'd out by typewriter: ????? Sadi after which is typed: *Sadi* CE

'Light of my eyes, there *is* something to be said'

Single quotes used throughout *UP*, *CP1994/2000* [emendation]

1. said.] said: *CE*

3. experience,] experience *CE*

6. good.] good! *CE*

8. wine-merchant.] winemerchant. (bootlegger) in margin *CE*

11. dear!] dear! N. B., *CE*

12–13. (In love's . . . message.)] No parentheses *CE*

13. to the angel's] for the angel's *CE*

14. everlasting.] everlasting— *CE*

15. Wail] wail *CE*
harp!] harp!, *CE*
Cry] cry *CE*

18. gold-scattering gown] indented separate line *CE*

19. flannel shirt. indented separate line *CE*

Attribution. (Hafiz)] not in *CE*, *Boz-West*

Desinas ineptire / 'O everlastingly self-deluded!'

10. cadge] Cadge *CE*

Attribution. (Hafiz)] not in *CE*

'Isnt it poetical, a chap's mind in the dumps?'

3. passport,] passport *UP*, *CP1994/2000* [emendation]

5. mock you,] mock you *UP*, *CP2000* [emendation]

Attribution. (Hafiz)] not in *CE*

'I'm the worse for drink again, it's'

8. doesnt] doesn't *UP*, *CP1994/2000* [emendation]

9. 'Rake'] 'Rake *CE*

Attribution. (Hafiz)] not in *CE*

From 'Faridun's Sons'

Title. Faridun] FARIDUN *Criterion*

Baudelaire in Cythera

Attribution. (After Baudelaire)] not in *CE*

'Amru'l Qais and Labīd and Ahktal and blind A'sha and Qais'

3. rhymes —] rhymes —— *UP*

7. exhausted' —?] exhausted' ——? *UP*

13. despair —] despair —— *UP*

'You, with my enemy, strolling down my street'

1. You, with my enemy] You there, with my enemy *Nine*
street,] street: *Nine*

2. Arent] Aren't *UP*, *CP1994/2000*

3. Didnt] Didn't *UP*, *CP1994/2000*
'malignant'] malignant *Nine*
'quarrelsome'?] quarrelsome? *Nine*

4. Dont] Don't *UP*, *CP1994/2000*
'impossible'] impossible *Nine*
no st. br. after character? *Nine*

5. You looked round and found someone more to] You looked for someone else and found one to *Nine*

6. neatly] nicely *Nine*
'dullness'.] 'dullness'! *Nine*

7. Plainly, your love is flooding his brook:] The water of love is flowing in his brook, *Nine*

8. is gone] has gone by *Nine*
st. br. after mine replaced by additional lines:

> They tell you that water keeps cooler in a new crock:
> my water's stale because my crock is old. *Nine*

'Ginger, who are you going with?'

2–3. Some slim] A slip *Horace Whom I Hated So*
One who squeezes you / among the early meadowsweet?] One who snuffs may now, / soon dogroses, then meadowsweet? *Horace Whom I Hated So*

9. always at hand,] always available, *Horace Whom I Hated So*

10. winds don't veer.] the wind wont alter. *Horace Whom I Hated So*

14. I've wrung my shirt out long since.] I wrung my shirt out long ago. *Horace Whom I Hated So*

'Snow's on the fellside, look! How deep'

1. deep,'] deep; *Agenda*

5. hearth!] hearth: *Agenda*

6. And] and *UP/CP2000* [emendation]
dont] don't *Agenda*

9. no st. br. after drops. *Agenda*

11. brings] brings, *Agenda*

12. dont] don't *Agenda*

17–18. keepsake. / She wont] keepsake; / she won't *Agenda*

19. (*says Horace, more or less*)] (Says Horace, more or less) *UP*, *CP1994/2000* [emendation]

APPENDICES

I DRAFT MATERIAL FOR 'THE FIFTH SONATA'

Apart from the *Briggflatts* notebook, relatively little draft material for the poems survives; this appendix contains a rare glimpse into Bunting's process of composition and revision. The following pages contain reproductions of draft material for 'The Fifth Sonata,' later published in greatly altered form as *The Spoils*. As draft material for the entire poem does not exist, the work on these pages is not transcribed elsewhere in this edition. The first five images reproduce Bunting's heavily annotated rough draft of the first two movements of the poem, sent to LZ and marked as received in February 1951; the next three pages, also sent to LZ and dated 27 March 1951, reproduce the typescript of a fair copy of an early version of the third movement.

Rough draft of the first two movements of
THE FIFTH SONATA

I.

These are the sons of Shem, after
their families, after their tongues,
in their lands, after their nations.
Genesis 10, 31.

Man's life so little worth,
[do we fear to take or lose it?]
Death is no ill companion on a journey.
He lays his purse on the table and opens the wine.

-- As I sat at my counting frame to assess the people,
from a farmer a tithe, a merchant a fifth of his gain,
marking the register listening to the lies of (the) people,
a bushel of dried apricots, marking the register,
three rolls of Egyptian cloth, astute in their avarice:
with Abdeel squatting before piled pence,
counting and calling the sum,
ringing and weighing coin,
casting out one, (out) four or five of a score,
calling the deficit:

(but) one stood in the door scorning our occupation,
silent: so in his greaves I saw
in the polished bronze,
linked between the dead and death-to-come,
a man like me reckoning pence
never having tasted bread
where there is ice in his flask,
stork's stilts cutting the sun's disk;
sun stings (like) driven sand,
camels raise their necks from the ground,
cooks scouring kettles, soldiers oiling their arms,
snow lights up high over the north,
yellow spreads in the desert, driving blue westward,
running among the banks, surrounding patches of blue,
advancing in enemy land:
and the cooks' kettles flash and the bread is eaten,
camels rising clumsily under load,
many scurrying scarabs rolling dung:
his breath not sour with feeding on unripe tomorrows
nor anything in his purse.

Thirty gorged vultures on the carcase of an ass
jostle, stumble, flop aside, drunk with flesh,
too heavy to fly, wings deep with [inner] gloss
[glow reticent yet flagrant.]
Lean watches, then debauch:
after long alert, stupidity:
(and) waking sear. If here you find me
intrusive and dangerous, seven years was I bonded
for Leah, seven toiled for Rachel.
Now in a brothel outside under the wall
have paused to bait on my journey.
Another shall pay the bill if I can evade it.

Lud -- When Tigris floods snakes swarm in the city,
coral, jade, jet, between jet and jade, yellow,
as enamelled toys. Toads
sit on the threshold. Jerboas
weary, unwary, may be taught to feed
from a fingertip. Dead camels, dead Kurds,
rapid, unmanageable rafts of logs
hinder the ferryman, a pull and a grunt
and a stiff tow upshore to allow for the current.
Naked boys among water-buffaloes, daughters without smile
treading clothes by the verge.
Harsh smell of smouldering dung,
a woman taking bread from her oven
spreads dates, an onion, cheese.
Silence under the high sun, but when the goats go out
along the towpath striped with palmtrunk shadows
you may hear a herdsman pipe or a girl shrill
under her load of greens. There is no clamour
in our market, no eagerness for gain.
Even the whores are surly, God parsimonious,
keeping tale of prayers.

Arpachshad -- Bound to our boats udders, rags no dishonour,
not by much intercourse are we ennobled,
multitude of books, bought deference, hags' genealogy.
Meagre flesh tingling to a mouthful of water,
apt to no servitude, commerce or special dexterity,
at night after prayers recite the sacred
enscrolled poems, beating with lofty measure
as blood in a new wound:
'These were the embers.....', 'Halt, both, lament.....':
a fountain sprung, spurts of clear sound,
rhyme-plash in a still pool
moon-silver on sand-pale gold,
against the parched bakehouse, taste of Arabia.
What's to dismay us?

Aram -- By the dategroves of Babylon
there we sat down and considered the situation
while they were seeking to hire us
to a repugnant trade.
Are there no plows in Judah, seed or a sickle,
no ewe to the pail, press to the vineyard?
Sickly our Hebrew voices far from the Hebrew hills!

Asshur -- We bear witness against the merchants of Babylon
that they have planted ink and reaped figures.
Lud -- Against the princes of Babylon, that they have tithed of the best,
leaving sterile bull and weakly hogg to the flock.
Arpachshad -- Fullers, tailors, hairdressers, jewellers, perfumers.
Aram -- David dancing before the Ark and they toss him pennies.
A farthing a note for songs as of the thrush.

Max
Asshur -- Her golden skin scoured in the sandblast
glowed like the a vulture's wing. 'Soldier,

3

O soldier! Hard muscles, nipples like spikes.
Undo the neck-string, let my blue gown fall.'
Very much like going to bed with a bronze
and the child cradled beside her sister silent and brown.
Thighs' flash in the sunshaft, unfortellable smile
and she tossed the pence aside in a brothel under the wall.

-- My bride is borne behind the pipers,
flashing kettles and feather-bed,
jet, jade, coral on her forehead under the veil:
to bring ewes to the pail and bread from the oven.
Breasts scarcely hump her smock,
meagre flesh of her thighs, eyes
alert without smile enjoin debauch,
mock the beribboned dancing-boys.

-- Drunk with her flesh when, polished leather,
still as moon she fades into the sand,
spurts a flame in the abandoned embers,
gold on moon-silver. Warmth of her absent thighs
dies on the loins: she who has yet no breasts
and no patience to await tomorrow.

-- Chattering in the vineyard, breasts swelled in song,
halt and beweep
captives and sickly, closing repugnant thighs.
Who lent her warmth to dying David, let that seed
sleep on the Hebrew hills: and waking soar.

What's begotten on a journey but souvenirs?
Life we give and take like pence in a market
without noting beggar, dealer, changer,
pence we drop in the sawdust with spilt wine.

II.

They filled the eyes of the vaulting
with alabaster panes,
each pencil of arches spouting
from a short pier,
and whitewashed the whole, using
a thread of blue to restore
lines nowhere broken,
for they considered capital
and base irrelevant.
The light is sufficient
to perceive the motions of prayer
and the place is cool.
Tiles for domes and aivans
they baked in a corner
older than all, where Avicenna may have worshipped.
The south dome, Nezam-ol-Molk's,
grows without violence from the walls
of a square chamber and visiting engineers
commend it. Taj-ol-Molk
set a less perfect dome
over a forest of pillars.

Without this
knowledge you cannot explain the Gothic
and stand in some danger
of sentimentalising the Middle Ages. At
Veramin and Golpaygan
they built smaller
mosques and Malekshah
cut his pride in a plaster
which hardens by age, the same
who found Khayyam a better reckoner
than the Author of the Qor'an.
Their passions body was bricks and its soul algebra.
Poetry
they remembered but made it out of itself.
'Lately a professor in this university'
said Khayyam of a recalcitrant ass,
'therefore would not enter, dare not face me'.
But their determination to banish fools foundered
ultimately in the installation of absolute idiots.
Fear of being imputed naive impeded thought.
Eddies:
the builders of La Giralda
repeated
heavily and languidly
some of their patterns in brick.
Eddies both ways in time.
I wonder what Khayyam thought
of all the construction and organisation afoot,
foreigners, resolute Seljuks, not so bloodthirsty
as some benefactors of mankind; remembering
perhaps Avicenna's horror of munificent patrons.
Books unheard of or lost elsewhere
in the library at Bokhara:
and four hours writing a day
before the duties of Prime Minister.
For all that, the Seljuks avoided
Roman exaggeration and the leaden mind of Egypt
and withered precariously on the bough
with patience and public spirit.
O public spirit!

Prayers to band cities and brigade men
lest there be more wills than one:
but God is in the dividing sword.

A hard pyramid or lasting law
against fear of death, of
murder more durable than mortar.

Domination and engineers
to fudge up a motive you can lay your hands on
lest a girl choose or refuse waywardly.

From Hajji Mosavvor's trembling wrist
grace of tree and beast
shines on ivory
in elegant, eloquent line.
Flute, unrepeating flute,
(shade dimples under chenars)
breath of Naystani chases and traces
as a pair of Gods might dodge and tag between stars.

5

Taj is to sing, Taj,
when tar and drum
come to their silence, slow,
clear, rich, as though
he had cadence and phrase from Hafez.
Nothing that was is,
but Moluk-e Zarrabi
draws her voice from a well
deeper than history:
and where did Shir-e Khoda
find war's suspended beat
that a dawncold radio
summons soldiers' feet?
Friday, Sobhi's tales
keeping boys from their meat.

A fowler spreading his net
over the barley calls,
calls on a rubber reed.
Grain nods in reply.
Poppies blue upon white
wake to the sun's frown.
Scut of gazelle dances and bounces
out of the afternoon.
Owl and wolf to the night.
On the terrace over my pool
vafur, vodka, tea,
resonant verse spilled out
from Onsori, Sa'di,
till the girls' mutter is lost
in whisper of stream and ~~tree~~ leaf
and a final nightingale
under a fading sky.

Undulating azan
a pennant on their quiet.

Because they despise polied work
and are not masters of filing,
always a task for foreigners
to make them unhappy,
unproductive and rich.

Have you seen a falcon stoop ,
accurate, merciless, unforeseen
and absolute, between
flickering ripples where they troop
after the wind and ears droop
to harvest? Dread
of what's to be, is and has been -
were we not better dead?

His resolute wings churn air
into the substance of his flight.
Firm talons, feathers alight
with sun, he rises where
dazzle rebuts our stare
and glory takes our breath.
Wonder has swallowed fright
in the wake of this death.

Red Barn 27/5/1 6

iii

Yet forty days.

All things only of earth and water,
to sit in the sun's warmth
breathing clear air.
A fancy took me to dig,
plant, prune, graft,
gather juicier fruit;
to milk, skim, churn;
flay and to tan;
shear, card, spin, weave;
lay up grain for sowing,
uncut cloth, oil in jars.
To Tubal a side of salt beef
for a knife chased and inscribed.
To Hiram a barrel of brewed barley,
a cask of pressed grapes
for a cedar ship and a seine net.
To Ben Hadad
whatsoever he will
for peace until harvest.
Storm along, West Wind,
let the small grey gulls glide inland.

How shall wheat sprout
through a shingle of Lydian pebbles
that turn the harrow's points?
Quarry and build, Solomon,
a bank for Lydian pebbles:
tribute of Lydian pebbles
levy and lay aside,
that twist underfoot
and blunt the plowshare,
the countless, useless, hampering
pebbles that spawn,
chattering in the jaws of the
harsh South Wind.

Tinker tapping
perched on a slagheap,
and the man who can mend a magneto,
heirs to the forge, bred to
different muck, easier skill,
a clean collar at night:
have they computed
the second differential coefficient
of steel with respect to death?
They have baked seed corn, roasted the brood-sow.
Beer costlier than petrol,
bolts cheaper than bananas;
and the clatter of metal
hardly startles a hare
couched among gorse beyond Alwinton.

7

No dispute, there is no dispute.
Jab your food with a fork
for fear of greasy fingers
and listen at night to the radio,
suave and bleak as the East Wind
over cropless tundra.

Notification of a case of herpes zoster
has been filed among the duplicate tax-demands.
Submit a report of your investigation in triplicate.
Recover from James Lammering, clerk, third-class,
the sum of one shilling and fourpence
expenses disallowed. Submit
the form of application duly completed
and the form of claim will be forwarded to you.
Submit! Submit! Submit an estimate,
a schedule, vouchers. As from today
submit. As from today
we have undertaken to govern
by table and text book and, failing these,
by casting dice,
tinker, merchant, farmer, banker
and those who vote, fight, feed if they must,
think never other thought than bidden.
Rustle of paper, clatter of metal, clink of coin;
better, eh? it had been nipped,
riven, eradicated,
by black frost and the North Wind
than this cancer of clerks;
all things only of earth and water,
to sit in the sun's warmth
breathing clear air.

Stop the
artesian gush of our past,
spray spread,
shot silk and damask white.
Let no one drink unchlorinated
living water but taxed tap, sterile,
or seek his contraband mouthful
in bog, under thicket, by crag, a trickle,
or from embroidered pools
with newts and didiscus beetles.

One cribbed in a madhouse
set about with diagnoses;
one unvisited; one uninvited;
one visited and invited too much;
one impotent, suffocated by adulation;
one unfed.

"Death to Bashshár bin Burd!"
Blind he saw, doubted,
wrapped no rare words, archaic
syntax,cryptic conceits
around his meaning; glanced back,

guessed whence, speculated whither.
Prudence beheaded some, some hanged,
one castrated, many starved,
chivvied, slandered, despised.
But never was dearth of panegyrists
deaf to cannonades, to the
compound fart of a depth-charge,
unable to decipher
obscenities scrawled in a privy,
devine a reveller behind
leprosy's mottled mask:
prophets, exegesists, counsellors of patience,
inverting the parable,
with seemly voices for the microphone;
or petulant, strident decoys.
They all lie in wait for blood,
every man with a net.

What we in private think
will be said in public
before the last gallon
flow from Memphis toward the sea.
In two generations they will be asking "Who was Truman?"
but St Elizabeth's Hospital
will not be altogether forgotten;
more than a hundred million Americans
'that cannot discern between their right hand and their left',
citizens in good standing, with checking accounts,
'and also much cattle.'

II BUNTING'S INTEREST IN PERSIAN POETRY

A. Ferdowsī's 'Book of Kings'

'[W]hen I finished turning ["Chomei at Toyama"] into a poem, I thought, well, I'd go back and have another look at the quays. I found a book – tattered, incomplete – with a newspaper cover on it marked "Oriental Tales." I bought it, in French. It turned out to be part of the early 19th century prose translation of Firdausi, and it was absolutely fascinating. I got into the middle of the story of the education of Zal and the birth of Rustam – and the story came to an end! It was quite impossible to leave it there, I was desperate to know what happened next. I read it, as far as it went, to Pound and Dorothy Pound, and they were in the same condition. We were yearning to find out, but we could think of no way. The title page was even missing. There seemed nothing to do but learn Persian and read Firdausi, so I undertook that. Pound bought me the three volumes of Vullers and somebody, I forget who, bought me Steingass's dictionary, and I set to work. It didn't take long. It's an easy language if it's only for reading that you want it' (*Descant*, [20–1])

The translation was of Ferdowsī's *Shāh-nāmeh*, a Persian epic poem (completed 1010). BB applied for a Guggenheim award to translate the poem in 1932. In his application essay, he wrote: **'The Shahnamah is the national epic of Persia, the most celebrated of medieval poems . . . It is eight or nine times as long as the Odyssey. Its matter is the whole of the legendary history of Persia as preserved in the traditions of the countryside and collected by order of the Shahs both before and after the Mohammedan conquest. Its chief hero is Rustam. The variety of its episodes is very great, they are almost unknown in the West, and they are related with unrivalled vigour and epic fullness. No other poet except Homer has so great a share of the unmistakable epic accent, no other book except the Arabian Nights has such variety of narrative.'** He concluded: **'My ultimate purpose? To make a respectable contribution to civilization as I understand it.'**

Alldritt (62): 'The *Shah na Meh* or "Book of Kings" is a vast poem, comprising nearly sixty thousand couplets. In it Firdusi, versifying a prose original, tells, in epic terms, the history of the kings of Persia from mythical times right down to the reign of Khosrow II who died in 628 AD.

Firdusi also added on the story of the overthrow of Persia's Sassanian dynasty by the Arabs around the middle of the seventh century. There are also verses dealing with the career of the prophet Zoroaster.' The work also chronicles Alexander's invasion; see headnote to *Briggflatts*, and notes to III. 28 and III. 72. For Ferdowsī's version, see Reuben Levy, trans., *The Epic of Kings: Shah-Nama the National Epic of Persia by Ferdowsi* (London: Routledge & Kegan Paul, 1957), 244–5 (cited *Lesch*, 353). J. W. Clinton remarks that the poetic dialect of Persian used in the *Shāh-nāmeh* 'has the same relationship to the language of today's Iran that Shakespeare's language does to the English we speak'; its poetic form 'is a rhyming couplet of roughly ten syllables. The nearest equivalent in English is the heroic couplet' (*The Tragedy of Sohráb and Rostám* [Seattle: Univ. of Washington Press, rev. ed., 1996], xx–xxi).

Loloi and Pursglove suggest that the 'French translation in question was probably that by [Jules] Mohl (*Le Livre des Rois par Abou'Ikasim Firdausi, traduit et commenté par J. Mohl*) which was first published in the 1830s and reprinted in the 1870s, and was (via Sainte-Beuve) a source for Arnold's 'Sohrab and Rustam' (see the Notes to Arnold's *Poems* of 1854)' (Parvin Loloi and Glyn Pursglove, 'Basil Bunting's Translations of Hafiz', in *McGonigal & Price*, [185]).

B. Bunting's foreword to Omar Pound's *Arabic & Persian Poems in English*

Persian poetry has suffered badly, Arabic rather less, from neoplatonic dons determined to find an arbitrary mysticism in everything. You would think there was nothing else in Moslem poetry than nightingales which are not birds, roses which are not flowers, and pretty boys who are God in disguise. An anthology of English verse selected exclusively from George Herbert, Charles Wesley, and Father Hopkins, plus 'Lead, kindly light' and 'The Hound of Heaven,' would be as representative as the usual samples of Persian poetry. Fitzgerald's Khayyam is the only serious exception.

There are difficulties in the way of a more satisfactory account of Persian poetry. Hafez, for instance, depends almost entirely on his mastery of sound and literary allusion, neither translatable. Manuchehri's enormous vigor and variety expresses itself often in patterns as intricate as those of a Persian carpet. Even dons are put off by the vast size of Sa'di's *Divan*, and fail to find the key poems. Much the same may be said of Arabic (in spite of Pococke's Latin versions).

There is at least as much variety in either of these literatures as in any European tongue. Fitzgerald illuminated one small corner. Now Omar Pound, selecting just the lines which match his own urbane, ironic manner, flashes a momentary light on many poets, tracing another hue in the web.

Sooner or later we must absorb Islam if our own culture is not to die of anemia. It will not be done by futile attempts to trace Maulavi symbols back to Plotinus or by reproducing in bad English verse the platitudes common to poetry everywhere. Omar Pound has detected something that Moslem poetry has in common with some of ours. He makes it credible. He makes it a pleasure. By such steps, though they may be short and few, we can at least begin our Hajj.

C. Bunting on Persian literature

In a letter to EP of 4 January 1935 (Beinecke), BB remarked that his translations of the *Shāh-nāmeh* were an attempt to **'try telling a story'** as a way, says Alex Niven, 'of circumventing the cul-de-sac of modernist **"indirect business"**.'

'Hope to send you a lump of Firdusi before long . . . As to onomatopoeic accompaniment, which is the marvel of the whole thing, alliterations, internal rhymes, contrapuntal arrangements of stress against ictus against succession of longs, hopeless task for anybody except Homer translating Firdusi or Firdusi translating Homer' (BB to EP, 19 April 1934; quoted *Makin*, 76).

Of BB's efforts to translate Persian poetry, EP had written to Otto Bird: 'Bunt'n gone off on Persian, but don't seem to do anything but Firdusi, whem he can't put into English that is of any *interest*. More the fault of subject matter than of anything else in isolation' (9 January 1938, *The Letters of Ezra Pound: 1907–1941*, ed. D. D. Paige, 305). EP mentions the 'Shah Nameh' in *Cantos*, LXXXVII.

Much later, BB would explain to EP: **'But I'm not hoping for honour and glory, nor expecting to make a living, nor even hoping for translation good enough to approve of: just texts and cribs so that a chap who wants to get at the stuff can. So that another generation may not have quite as many cursed vexations as ours when it sets out to acquire knowledge'** (26 February 1951; quoted *Forde*, 133).

'It is no boast to say that I am more widely read in Persian literature than most of the Orientalists in British and European Universities, especially in the early poets – Ferdosi, Rudaki, Manuchehri, Farrukhi, etc., whose work is fundamental to a real understanding of Persian literature in the same way that the work of Homer and Aeschylus is fundamental to an understanding of Greek. Lacking it, many Orientalists have lacked proportion in their enthusiasm and run after secondary poets and secondary aspects of great poets. Hafez, for example, interpreted exclusively in the light of Naser-e Khosro or Khaqani, is less interesting and far less compelling than the real Hafez who never, I think, ceased to listen to the echo of Manuchehri and Onsuri' (BB to LZ, 29 October 1953; quoted *Forde*, 121).

'I like the common eye, cleared, maybe, and very sharp, much better than the inward one or the lens-aided dissecting eye. Hence on the one hand the Iliadic Homer and the Shahnamehic Ferdosi (rather than Odyssey and Yusuf, old man's work, skill above the matter), and on the other the makers of something not altogether drawn from the life: the enamelled flora, alcoholic crescendo, goldleaved erudition, with which Manuchehri surrounds simplicities and gives them overwhelming power. (There are fitful glimpses of the kind of thing in Catullus and Villon)' (BB to EP, ? April 1954, Beinecke).

'From Manuchehri you could learn almost anything. He excelled in every branch of poetry that existed in Persian or Arabic, with the exception of epic – everything else he did so well that you cannot better him. The elaboration of the patterns in some of his seasonal poems – about Spring, about Autumn, and so on – the energy of his satire, the extreme directness of some of his lyric poetry where I can think of no parallel for the complete directness except Catullus. Manuchehri is one of the very great poets and owing to the rather narrow sympathies of Western orientalists, he's scarcely known to them . . . Ferdosi is a great epic poet. He differs very considerably from Homer – very considerably. Nevertheless I should say that he is the only epic poet who can be spoken of in the same breath as Homer. Now obviously you're going to learn something from that' (*Mottram*, 6).

D. Persian verse forms

qasida: literally, purpose-poem; more loosely, occasional and official poetry

ghazal: a lyric poem, most closely resembling the sonnet

rubai: a haiku-like poem in strict quatrains

From Ahmad Karimi-Hakkak, 'Speaking to the Jasmine, A Scythe in Hand', *Parnassus* 25, nos. 1–2 (2001), 213.

E. Books in Bunting's library relating to Persian and Arabic language and literature

G. Brackenbury, *Progressive Arabic Course* (1940)
Richard Burton, *Personal Narrative of a Pilgrimage . . .* (1915)
Joseph Catagago, *An English and Arabic Dictionary* (1873)
A. O. Green, *A Practical Arabic Grammar* (1901)
Alfred Guillaume, *Islam* (1956)
Ernst Harder, *Arabic Grammar of the Written Language* (1927)

Alfred Hindie, *The Student's Dictionary: English–Arabic* (1925)
Sarah Hobson, *Through Persia in Disguise* (1970)
James J. Morier, *The Adventures of Hajji Baba of Ispahan* (1948)
Marmaduke Pickthall, *The Meaning of the Glorious Quran* (1938)
De Lacy O'Leary, *Colloquial Arabic* (1925)
Omar S. Pound (trans.), *Poems from the Persian and Arabic* (1967)
_____, *Calling the Doctor: a Persian Prose Narrative* (1968)
_____, *Arabic & Persian Poems* (1970)
John Van Ess, *The Spoken Arabic of Iraq* (1938)

Articles on Bunting and Persian poetry

Parvin Loloi and Glyn Pursglove, 'Basil Bunting's Persian Overdrafts: A Commentary', in *Terrell*, 343–53
Parvin Loloi and Glyn Pursglove, 'Basil Bunting's Translations of Hafiz', in *McGonigal & Price*, [185]–203

F. Bunting's translation of a tale from *The Rose Garden*

Sa'di's Gulistan *('The Rose Garden'), written in 1285 CE, is a landmark of Persian literature, perhaps its most influential work of prose. BB tried his hand at translating this tale from it; the text can be found in the HRC archive. Cp. 'Night swallowed the sun . . .' and 'Many well-known people . . .', also from* Gulistan.

A gang of Arabian brigands had settled on a hilltop commanding the caravan route and the local peasants were terrified by their forays and the sultan's army at a loss, for they had laid hands on an impregnable stronghold on the peak and made it their sanctuary and dwellingplace.

The provincial authorities of those parts met and discussed how to put an end to their ravages, for if the gang could keep up this arrangement long they would soon have made their system perpetual.

A newly planted sapling can
be torn up by a single man,
but a rooted tree wont budge an inch
for ten men straining at a winch.
You can stop a river's springs up with a spade,
but its flood not even an elephant can wade.

It was determined that they should send a man to spy on them and watch for an opportunity. At a time when the robbers had gone to raid a tribe and left their dell empty the authorities sent a sufficient body of experienced veterans to lie hid amongst the mountain paths.

In the evening the robbers returned from a foray laden with spoil, stowed away their illgotten gear and laid their arms aside. The first enemy that charged down on them was sleep, for the first watch of the night was past.

> Night swallowed sun as
> the fish swallowed Jonas.

Whereupon the soldiers dashed out from their station and one by one bound their hands behind their backs and brought them all before the king's court next morning. The king gave orders to kill the lot of them.

As it happened there was a lad amongst them. The fruits of the tree of his youth were but newly formed and the grass had barely begun to grow in the flowergarden of his cheeks. One of the ministers kissed the step of the king's throne, laid his face on the ground in intercession and said:

'This boy has not yet enjoyed life's orchard nor delighted in the brilliance of his adolescence. It is to be hoped from my Lord's liberality and lofty disposition that he will put his servant under an obligation by granting the boy life.'

The king frowned at this speech which did not accord with his superior understanding, and said:

> 'From bad men no reflection of good men's effulgence will
> come.
> Education on a worthless mind is a walnut on a dome.

It would be best to exterminate these fellows' iniquitous breed. The height of good sense is to tear up their family by the roots: for to put out a fire and neglect the embers or to kill a snake and take care of its young is not the work of a sensible man.

> Though the clouds should rain down the water of life
> you will never taste fruit from a willow.
> You cannot suck sugar from bulrushes –
> Waste no time on a worthless fellow.'

When the minister heard this speech he approved of it willy-nilly and praised the beauty of the king's wisdom and said:

'What my Lord (May the king live forever!) has just laid down is the essence of propriety and an unanswerable proposition. All the same, the fact of the matter is that though, had this boy had his upbringing in a circle of ill-livers he would have taken on their nature and become one of them, nevertheless your servant is of good hope that should he receive his education in the company of honest men and acquire the habits of lawabiding people, since he is yet but a child, the rebellious and contumacious character of those of that kidney will never become powerful in him. And amongst the Sayings attributed to the Prophet is: "Tous naissent avec un penchant pour Islam et c'est la faute des parents si on devient Juif, Chretien ou Magien."[1]

Noah's son took to low company:
  him prophecy ceased to illumine.
The dog of the Seven Sleepers became,
  by prolonged good company, human.'

That is what he said: and the king's band of favourites befriended him with their intercession till the king dispensed with the execution and said:

'I grant it, but I dont see the sense of it.
  Do you know what Zal[2] said to Rustam in the tale?
  "You must not reckon any fee paltry or frail.
    I have seen the water bubbling up from many a spring
  that further on has borne away both camel and bale."'

The upshot of it was they pampered the boy with coaxing and comforts and provided a cultured tutor for his education and he learned the ornaments of discourse and how to give a prompt answer and the rest of the etiquette of court life so that everyone looked on him with approval. One day in the king's presence the minister was relating some instance of his natural abilities, saying that a scientific education had made its mark on him, his former ignorance was banished from his nature and he had acquired the habits of sensible people. At this speech the king smiled and said:

'Wolf cub turns wolf even when
it has grown up amongst men.'

After that two years passed. A gang of blackguards from the slums joined with the lad and bound themselves mutually and when the opportunity came he slew the minister together with both his sons and carried off booty beyond telling, succeeded his father in the freebooter's cave and became an outlaw.

The king bit his hand with amazement and said:

---

1 Roughly translated: 'Everyone is born with an inclination toward Islam, and it's the parents' fault if he becomes a Jew, Christian, or Zoroastrian.'

2 *Zal*. Legendary Persian warrior. Born albino, he was rejected as an infant for this defect by his father (though they were later reconciled). Rescued by a phoenix-like bird called the Simurgh, who gave him magic feathers to burn when he needed help. Later on, when his wife Rudaba had difficulties giving birth, the Simurgh instructed Zal to run one of the feathers across her belly, which is how their son Rustam, who would himself become a great hero, was born.

'No man can make a good sword from bad steel by toil.
All your lectures, O Professor, cannot make a robber royal.
    The rain whose perfect manners have no blemish cultivates
tulips in a garden, only weeds in sour soil.'
Hyacinths will not grow on barren ground:
    though you sow good seed there yet must you reap ill.
To do good to the wicked is as wicked
    as doing wickedness to decent people.

III BUNTING'S NOTES AS PREPARED FOR EDITIONS OF *COMPLETE POEMS*

I have left these notes as they were, with hardly an exception. Notes are a confession of failure, not a palliation of it, still less a reproach to the reader, but may allay some small irritations.

Villon III

The image of two drops of quicksilver running together is from the late E. Nesbit's *Story of the Amulet*. To her I am also indebted for much of the pleasantest reading of my childhood.

Attis

Parodies of Lucretius and Cino da Pistoia can do no damage and intend no disrespect.

Aus Dem Zweiten Reich III

The great man need not be identified but will, I believe, be recognized by those who knew him.

The Well of Lycopolis

Gibbon mentions its effect in a footnote. The long quotations from Villon and Dante will of course be recognized. Americans may care to be informed that as a native of Paphos Venus was until recently entitled to a British passport. Her quotation from Sophie Tucker will not escape the attention of those who remember the first world war, and need not engage that of those who dont. The remarks of the brass head occur in the no longer sufficiently well-known story of Friar Bacon and Friar Bungay, of which I think Messrs Laurel and Hardy could make use. Some may remember that the only one of the rivers of Paradise to which we have access on earth, namely Zamzam, is reported to be brackish.

The Spoils

Let readers who lack Arabic forgive me for explaining that the epigraph, *al anfal li'llah*, is from the Qor'an, sura viii, and means 'The spoils are for God'. I named the sons of Shem at random from the Bible's list.

Some Persian words have no English equivalent. An *aivan* is a high arch backed by a shallow honeycomb half-dome or leading into a mosque. *Chenar*, Platanus orientalis, is grander than its London cousins; *tar*, a stringed instrument used in Persian classical music. *Vafur* signifies the apparatus of opium smoking, pipe, pricker, tongs, brazier, charcoal and the drug, shining like a stick of black sealing wax. The *azan* is the mo'ezzin's call to prayer. You hardly hear its delicate, wavering airs at other times, but an hour before sunrise it has such magic as no other music, unless perhaps the nightingale in lands where nightingales are rare.

Proper names explain themselves and can be found in books of reference. A few are not yet filed. *Hajji Mosavvor*, greatest of modern miniature painters, suffered from paralysis agitans. *Naystani*, a celebrated virtuoso of the nose-flute. *Taj* sings classical odes with authenticity; *Moluk-e Zarrabi* moulds them to her liking. *Shir-e Khoda* begins Teheran's radio day with a canto of the epic. *Sobhi* is the most perfect teller of tales, his own.

Gaiety and daring need no naming to those who remember others like *Flight-lieutenant Idema*.

Abu-Ali is, of course, Ibn Sina – Avicenna.

Briggflatts

The Northumbrian tongue travel has not taken from me sometimes sounds strange to men used to the koiné or to Americans who may not know how much Northumberland differs from the Saxon south of England. Southrons would maul the music of many lines in *Briggflatts*.

An autobiography, but not a record of fact. The first movement is no more a chronicle than the third. The truth of the poem is of another kind.

No notes are needed. A few may spare diligent readers the pains of research.

Spuggies: little sparrows.

May the flower, as haw is the fruit, of the thorn.

Northumbrians should know Eric *Bloodaxe* but seldom do, because all the school histories are written by or for southrons. Piece his story together from the Anglo-Saxon Chronicle, the Orkneyinga Saga, and Heimskringla, as you fancy.

We have burns in the east, *becks* in the west, but no brooks or creeks.

Oxter: armpit.

Boiled louse: coccus cacti, the cochineal, a parasite on opuntia.

Hillside fiddlers: Pianforini, for instance, or Manini.

Lindisfarne, the Holy Island, where the tracery of the Codex Lindisfarnensis was elaborated.

Hastor: a Cockney hero.

Saltings: marshy pastures the sea floods at extraordinary springs.

The Laughing Stone stands in Tibet. Those who set eyes on it fall into violent laughter until they die. Tibetans are immune, because they have no humour. So the Persian tale relates.

The male salmon after spawning is called a *kelt.*

Gabbro: a volcanic rock.

Aneurin celebrated in the Cymric language the men slain at Catterick by the sons of *Ida*, conquerors of Northumberland.

Skerry: O, come on, you know that one.

Hoy: toss, hurl.

Skillet: An American frying pan; and *girdle*, an English griddle.

Fipple: the soft wood stop forming with part of the hard wood tube the wind passage of a recorder.

Scone: rhyme it with 'on', not, for heaven's sake, 'own'.

Gentles: maggots.

Wilson was less known than *Telfer*, but not less skilful.

Sailors pronounce *Betelgeuse* 'Beetle juice' and so do I. His companion is 'Ridgel', not 'Rhy-ghel'.

Sirius is too young to remember because the light we call by his name left its star only eight years ago; but the light from *Capella*, now in the zenith, set out 45 years ago – as near fifty as makes no difference to a poet.

Chomei at Toyama

Kam-no-Chomei flourished somewhat over a hundred years before Dante. He belonged to the minor nobility of Japan and held various offices in the civil service. He applied for a fat job in a Shinto temple, was turned down, and next day announced his conversion to Buddhism. He wrote critical essays, tales and poems; collected an anthology of poems composed at the moment of conversion by Buddhist proselytes (one suspects irony); and was for a while secretary to the editors of the Imperial Anthology.

He retired from public life to a kind of mixture of hermitage and country cottage at Toyama on Mount Hino and there, when he was getting old, he wrote the Ho-Jo-Ki in prose, of which my poem is in the main a condensation. The careful proportion and balance he keeps, the recurrent motif of the house and some other indications suggest to me that he intended a poem more or less elegiac but had not the time nor possibly energy at his then age to invent what would have been for Japan, an entire new form, nor to condense his material sufficiently. I have taken advantage of Professor Muccioli's Italian version, together with his learned notes, to try to complete Chomei's work for him. I cannot take his Buddhism solemnly considering the manner of his conversion, the nature of his anthology, and his whole urbane, sceptical and ironical temper. If this annoys anybody I cannot help it.

The earth quaked in the second year of Genryaku, 1185.

First Book of Odes

I have taken my chance to insert a couplet in the First Book of Odes and promote *The Orotava Road* from limbo to its chronological place amongst them, which has obliged me to renumber many.

I. 7: The quotation might not be readily identified without a hint. It is from Livy.

I. 18: The war and the Forestry Commission have outdated this complaint. *Cowpit* means overturned.

I. 20: A presumably exact version of Jengiz Khan's correspondence with Chang Chun exists in Bretschneider's *Mediaeval Researches from Eastern Asiatic Sources*. Others more competent than I may prefer to investigate it in the Si-Yu-Ki of Li Chi Chang, one of Chang Chun's disciples who made the journey with him and recorded the correspondence. Pauthier rendered that work, according to Bretschneider, very imperfectly into French.

I. 24: The case was tried in 1917 or 1919, I forget.

I. 32: In Samangan Rustam begot Sohrab.

I. 33: The cool breeze of a pure, uncomprehending rendering of Handel's best known aria.

I. 34: Perhaps it is superfluous to mention Darwin's *Formation of Vegetable Mould*.

I. 36: A friend's misunderstanding obliges me to declare that the implausible optics of this poem are not intended as an argument for the existence of God, but only suggest that the result of a successful work of art is more than the sum of its meanings and differs from them in kind.

Second Book of Odes

II. 5: *Canvas udders*, motarekeh mal moy, the cooling water bags carried through the desert. *Dynast*, Abdulaziz Ibn Saud, of the tribe Aneiza.

II. 9: Whoever has been conned, however briefly, into visiting a 'poets' conference' will need no explanation of this ode.

Overdrafts

It would be gratuitous to assume that a mistranslation is unintentional.

Note to *The Pious Cat*

You must call him 'Obeyed', like the English word 'obeyed a command', 'obeyed a zaw-kaw-nee'; and save most of your breath for the 'nee'. He wrote this story about six hundred years ago, and Persian children still read it at school, or they used to, twenty years since. Any story that lasts as long as that is worth listening to, I think. Perhaps not everything in it is true, but bits of it are very true indeed.

B. Bunting 1937–77

IV TABLES OF CONTENTS

Redimiculum Matellarum

Villon

CARMINA

- I. Sad Spring
- II. Foam
- III. Against the Tricks of Time
- IV. Aubade
- V. To Narciss [titled only in table of contents]
- VI. Against Memory

ETCETERA [(Etc). in table of contents]

- Sonnet
- While Shepherds Watched
- Advice to a Lady
- Chorus of Furies
- To Venus
- Personal Column

Caveat Emptor

Villon
Aus Dem Zweiten Reich
How Duke Valentine Contrived
Jenghis
Gin the Goodwife Stint
The Complaint of the Morpethshire Farmer

FIRST BOOK OF ODES

1. *Darling of gods and men*
2. *Weeping oaks grieve*
3. Foam
4. Sonnet
5. *Light of my eyes*
6. *Empty vast days*

7. *The day being Whitsun*
8. *Mesh cast for mackerel*
9. Shipping intelligence
10. Hymn to alias Thor
11. *The flat land lies under water*
12. Personal Column
13. *Nothing*
14. *Molten pool, incandesecent spilth of*
15. *O everlastingly self-deluded*
16. *Now that sea's over that islan~~d~~]*
17. Chorus of Furies
18. Fearful Symmetry
19. *As appleblossom to crocus*
20. *Southwind, tell her what*
21. *They say Etna*
22. The Shirazi Blues
23. To a Poet who advised me to preserve my fragments and false starts
24. *Dear be still!*
25. Aubade
26. *Two hundred and seven paces*
27. *Many well-known people have been packed away in cemeteries*
28. *Please stop gushing about his pink*
29. While Shepherds Watched
30. Baudelaire in Cythera
31. *Gertie Gitana's hymn to waltzing*
32. The Passport Officer
33. *Isnt it poetical*
34. *Fruits breaking the branches*
35. Two Photographs
36. Trinacria
37. Reading X's 'Collected Poems'
38. *Yes, it's slow, docked of amours*
39. *Why should I discipline myself to verse*
40. *I'm the worse for drink again*

Chomei at Toyama
Attis, or, Something Missing

Appendix

Poems: 1950

[No table of contents printed]

Loquitur [ODES section of *Loquitur* = *First Book of Odes*]

[21] Two Photographs
[22] 'Mesh cast for mackerel'
[23] The Passport Officer
[24] 'Vessels thrown awry by strong gusts'
[25] 'As appleblossom to crocus'
[26] 'Two hundred and seven paces'
[27] 'On highest summits dawn comes soonest'
[28] 'You leave'
[29] 'Southwind, tell her what'
[30] The Orotava Road
[31] 'The soil sandy and the plow light, neither'
[32] 'Let them remember Samangan, the bridge and tower'
[33] 'Not to thank dogwood nor'
[34] 'These tracings from a world that's dead'
[35] 'Search under every veil'
[36] 'See! Their verses are laid'
[37] On the Fly-Leaf of Pound's Cantos

OVERDRAFTS
'Darling of Gods and Men, beneath the gliding stars'
'Yes, it's slow, docked of amours'
'Please stop gushing about his pink'
Verse and Version
'When the sword of sixty comes nigh his head'
'All the teeth I ever had are worn down and fallen out'
'Shall I sulk because my love has a double heart'
'Came to me –'
'This I write, mix ink with tears'
'Last night without sight of you my brain was ablaze'
How Duke Valentine Contrived

Collected Poems (1968)

[34] 'These tracings from a world that's dead'
[35] 'Search under every veil'
[36] 'See! Their verses are laid'
[37] On the Fly-Leaf of Pound's Cantos

SECOND BOOK OF ODES

'A thrush in the syringa sings'
'Three Michaelmas daisies'
Birthday Greeting
'You idiot! What makes you think decay will'
'Under sand clay. Dig, wait'
What the Chairman Told Tom
'O, it is godlike to sit selfpossessed'
'Carmencita's tawny paps'

OVERDRAFTS

'Darling of Gods and Men, beneath the gliding stars'
'Yes, it's slow, docked of amours'
'Please stop gushing about his pink'
Verse and Version
'Once, so they say, pinetrees seeded on Pelion's peak'
'When the sword of sixty comes nigh his head'
'All the teeth I ever had are worn down and fallen out'
'Shall I sulk because my love has a double heart'
'Came to me –'
'This I write, mix ink with tears'
'Last night without sight of you my brain was ablaze'
How Duke Valentine Contrived

Collected Poems (1978)

[34] 'These tracings from a world that's dead'
[35] 'Search under every veil'
[36] 'See! Their verses are laid'
[37] On the Fly-leaf of Pound's Cantos

SECOND BOOK OF ODES
[1] 'A thrush in the syringa sings'
[2] 'Three Michaelmas daisies'
[3] Birthday Greeting
[4] 'You idiot! What makes you think decay will'
[5] 'Under sand clay. Dig, wait'
[6] What the Chairman Told Tom
[7] 'O, it is godlike to sit selfpossessed'
[8] 'Carmencita's tawny paps'
[9] 'All the cants they peddle'
[10] 'Stones trip Coquet burn'
[11] *At Briggflatts meetinghouse*

OVERDRAFTS
'Darling of Gods and Men, beneath the gliding stars'
'Yes, it's slow, docked of amours'
'Please stop gushing about his pink'
Verse and Version
'Once, so they say, pinetrees seeded on Pelion's peak'
'When the sword of sixty comes nigh his head'
'All the teeth I ever had are worn down and fallen out'
'Shall I sulk because my love has a double heart'
'Came to me –'
'This I write, mix ink with tears'
'Last night without sight of you my brain was ablaze'
'You can't grip years, Postume'
How Duke Valentine Contrived

Collected Poems (1985)

[34] 'These tracings from a world that's dead'
[35] 'Search under every veil'
[36] 'See! Their verses are laid'
[37] On the Fly-Leaf of Pound's Cantos

SECOND BOOK OF ODES

[1] 'A thrush in the syringa sings'
[2] 'Three Michaelmas daisies'
[3] Birthday Greeting
[4] 'You idiot! What makes you think decay will'
[5] 'Under sand clay. Dig, wait'
[6] What the Chairman Told Tom
[7] 'O, it is godlike to sit selfpossessed'
[8] 'Carmencita's tawny paps'
[9] 'All the cants they peddle'
[10] 'Stones trip Coquet burn'
[11] 'Boast time mocks cumber Rome. Wren'
[12] 'Now we've no hope of going back'

OVERDRAFTS

'Darling of Gods and Men, beneath the gliding stars'
'Yes, it's slow, docked of amours'
'Please stop gushing about his pink'
Verse and Version
'Once, so they say, pinetrees seeded on Pelion's peak swam'
'When the sword of sixty comes nigh his head'
'All the teeth I ever had are worn down and fallen out'
'Shall I sulk because my love has a double heart'
'Came to me –'
'This I write, mix ink with tears'
'Last night without sight of you my brain was ablaze'
'You can't grip years, Postume'
How Duke Valentine Contrived

V BUNTING'S PREFACES

Redimiculum Matellarum

La même justesse d'esprit qui nous fait écrire de bonnes choses nous fait appréhender qu'elles ne le soient pas assez pour mériter d'être lues.[1]

These poems are byproducts of an interrupted and harassed apprenticeship. I thank Margaret De Silver for bailing me out of Fleet Street: after two years convalescence from an attack of journalism I am beginning to recover my honesty.

Rapallo, 1930.

Caveat Emptor

[Appendix 4 and 5:]

Bibliography.

REDIMICULUM MATELLARUM: poems by Basil Bunting. Milan 1930. Out of print a month after publication. The contents have been absorbed into this volume, with the exception of a preface and two epigraphs.

Acknowledgements.

are due to T. Lucretius Carus, Muhammad Shamsuddin Shirazi Hafiz, Maslahuddin Shirazi Sadi, Q. Horatius Flaccus, Charles Baudelaire, François Villon, Niccolo Machiavelli, Kamo-no-Chomei, Jenghis Khan, G. Valerius Catullus, Clement Marot, Jesus Christ, Dante Alighieri and anonymous peasants for loans;
as well as to Jonathan Swift, François de Malherbe, Ernest Fenellosa, Louis Zukofsky and Ezra Pound for advice and guidance;

---

1 Epigraph not attributed by BB, from Jean de La Bruyère, *Les Caractères de Théophraste traduits du grec avec Les Caractères ou les moeurs de ce siècle* (1688; *The Characters, or the Manners of the Age*). 'The same common sense which makes an author write good things, makes him dread they are not good enough to deserve reading' (trans. Henri Van Laun).

besides all the poets who ever were before me, particularly those I have read:
but the editors who bought some of these poems at inadequate prices or printed others without paying anything I need not thank. On the contrary, they should thank me.

B.
Tenerife 1935.

Loquitur

The edition of my poems which Dallam Flynn printed in Texas in 1950 is all sold, and Stuart Montgomery thinks there are still people curious to read them who cannot find a copy. I have taken my chance to add two or three and take one away; to read the proofs more carefully than I could when I was in Teheran and my publisher in Texas; to insert a couplet in the Odes and promote The Orotava Road from limbo to its chronological place amongst them, which has obliged me to renumber many; and to give the book a title to replace the off-hand label by which it has been known or unknown for fifteen years.

All the poems have been in print and copyright a long time, except the couplet, Ode 27. Many were first printed in *Poetry*, of Chicago, whose editors so many poets have had cause to thank. I want to record my gratitude to Dallam Flynn for the edition he undertook in a more difficult time than this, and my continual debt to the two greatest poets of our age, Ezra Pound and Louis Zukofsky. (I thank Jonathan Cape Ltd for letting me reprint 'In that this happening', so that people can look at Mr Zukofsky's poem and tell what my Latin is meant for).

Basil Bunting
May 1965

Fulcrum Press *Collected Poems*

A man who collects his poems screws together the boards of his coffin. Those outside will have all the fun, but he is entitled to his last confession. These verses were written here and there now and then over forty years and four continents. Heaped together they make a book.

If I ever learned the trick of it, it was mostly from poets long dead whose names are obvious: Wordsworth and Dante, Horace, Wyat and Malherbe, Manuchehri and Ferdosi, Villon, Whitman, Edmund Spenser; but two living men also taught me much: Ezra Pound and in his sterner, stonier way, Louis Zukofsky. It would not be fitting to collect my poems without mentioning them.

With sleights learned from others and an ear open to melodic analogies I have set down words as a musician pricks his score, not to be read in silence, but to trace in the air a pattern of sound that may sometimes, I hope, be pleasing. Unabashed boys and girls may enjoy them. This book is theirs.

I am grateful to those who printed my poems from time to time, above all to *Poetry*, of Chicago, whose editors have been kind to me one after another.

Oxford University Press *Collected Poems*

A new edition of this book has given me a chance to put right a few words and stops the compositor got wrong, and to add four short new poems. A fifth seemed better lost.

1977 [1978?]

Moyer Bell *Collected Poems*

There is one solitary short poem that I have added to the collected volume.

1985

VI EMENDATIONS TO THE COPY TEXT

Title	*Line no.*	*Reading of copy text*	*Authority*
The Well of Lycopolis			
	I. 69	What have you come for?	*CP1978*
The Spoils			
	II. 96	on a terrace	*CP1978*
Briggflatts			
	Notes	koine	*CP1978*
	Notes	Southrons	*CP1978*
	Notes	'Beetle juice'	*CP1978*
	Notes	'Ridgel', not 'Rhy-ghel'.	*CP1978*
FIRST BOOK OF ODES			
13: *Fearful symmetry*			
	15	♂ Tigris	*CP1978*
34: *To Violet, with prewar poems.*			
	[*Dedication*]	*To Violet, with prewar poems*	*CP1978*
SECOND BOOK OF ODES			
3: Birthday Greeting			
	9	married: – yet	*CP1978*
All the teeth ever I had [. . .]			
	52	Khorassan	*CP1978*
UNCOLLECTED ODES			
2 Against the Tricks of Time			
		first words in each line with initial capital throughout	*CE*
	5	shop window	*CE*
	11	single st. br. after ashamed of myself	*CE*
	16	night-wanderings	*CE*
	18	wall-reflected street-lamp-light	*CE*
	31	single st. br. after wither	*CE*

Title	*Line no.*	*Reading of copy text*	*Authority*
4 Hymn to Alias Thor			
	36	with wash	*CE*
'Light of my eyes . . .'			
		[single-quotes used throughout]	*CE*
'Isnt it poetical . . .'			
	3	passport	*CE*
	5	mock you	*CE*
'I'm the worse for drink again, it's'			
	8	doesnt	*CE*
'Snow's on the fellside . . .'			
	6	and dont	*Caddel & Flowers*
	19	(Says Horace, more or less)	*Caddel & Flowers*

UNCOLLECTED OVERDRAFTS

'You, with my enemy, strolling down my street'			
	2	Aren't	*MS 11 (Durham)*
	3	Didn't	*MS 11 (Durham)*
	4	Don't	*MS 11 (Durham)*

In addition to the above, the version of 'The Pious Cat' printed in this edition relies on a different source from the version in *CP2000*, as explained in the Annotations for the poem. The numerous differences are detailed in the Variants section, pp. 511–13.

VII FERNÁNDEZ VARIANTS

In 1931, BB corresponded with a young Spanish poet, Basilio Fernández, whom he had met in Italy *ca.*1929, sending him five handwritten poems. These poems, the first four odes in *FBO* and fragments from 'Villon', parts I and III, were published with Spanish translations by Faustino Álvarez Álvarez and Emiliano Fernández Prado in 'Basil Bunting, entre los papeles de Basilio Fernández', *Cuadernos hispanoamericanos* 546 (December 1995), 95–117. I include them here; a number of obvious errors in transcription have been silently corrected. Photocopies of the original autograph mss. are held at Durham.

Sad Spring

Weeping oaks now grieve and chestnuts raise
Their mournful candles. Sad is spring,
Sad to perpetuate, sad to trace
Immortalities never changing.
As one who wearies on the sea
For sight of land in vain
And gazing past the coming wave
Sees the same wave again
We drift on merciless reiteration of years
Expecting homely death.
But spring
Is everlasting resurrection.

From a Nocturne

Farewell, ye sequent graces,
Voided faces, still evasive!
Silent be our leave-taking
And mournful
As your night-wanderings
In unlit rooms or where the glow
Of wall-reflected street-lamp light,
The so slow moon,

Or hasty matches shadowed large
And crowded out by imps of night
Glimmer on cascades of
Fantom dancers.
Airlapped and silent Muses of light,
Cease to administer
Poisons to dying memories to stir
Pangs of old rapture.
Cease to conspire
Reunions of the irrevocable seed
Long blown, barren, sown, gathered
Haphazard to wither.

Foam

I am agog for foam. Tumultuous, come
With teeming sweetness to the bitter shore,
Tidelong unrinsed and midday parched and numb
With expectation. If the bright sky bore
With endless utterance of a single blue,
Unphrased, its restless immobility
Infects the soul, which must decline into
An anguished and exact sterility
And waste away. Then how much more the sea,
Trembling with alteration, must perfect
Our loneliness by its hostility,
The dear companionship of its elect
Deepens our envy. Its indifference
Haunts us to suicide. Strong memories
Of spray-blown days exasperate impatience
To brief rebellion and emphasise
The casual impotence we sicken of.
But when mad waves spring, braceletted with foam,
Toward us in the angriness of love
Crying a strange name, tossing as they come
Repeated invitations in the gay
Exuberance of unexplained desire
We can forget the sad splendour and play
At wilfulness, until the gods require
Renewed, inevitable, hopeless calm
And the foam dies, and we again subside
Into our catalepsy, dreaming foam,
While the dry shore awaits another tide.

Aubade

After the grimaces of capitulation
The universal face resumes its cunning, quick
To abandon the nocturnal elevation
Pawned with the stars. In repose majestic,
Vile wakening, cowering under its tyrant,
Eager in stratagems to circumvent the harsh
Performer of unveilings, revealer of gaunt
Lurking anatomy, grin of diurnal farce;
Yet when the fellow with the red-hot poker comes
Truculently to torment our blisters we vie
With one another to present scarified bums
To the iron, clutching sausages greedily.
Oh Sun! Should I invoke this scorn, participate
In the inconsequence of this defeat, or hide
In noctambulistic exile to penetrate
Secrets that moon and stars and empty death deride?

From 'Villon', end of pt. I

Remember, imbeciles and wits,
Sots and ascetics, fair and foul,
Young girls with little tender tits,
That DEATH is written over all.
Worn hides that scarcely clothe the soul
They are so rotten, old and thin,
Or firm and soft and warm and full –
Fellmonger Death gets every skin.
All that it piteous, all that's fair,
All that is fat and scant of breath,
Elisha's baldness, Helen's hair,
Is but collateral for Death:
'Threescore and ten years after sight
Of this pay me your pulse and breath.
Value received.' And who dare cite:
As we forgive our debtors, Death?
And Abelard and Eloise,
The holy tinker and the thief,
Genée, Lopokova, all these,
All these must die and die in grief.
And General Grant and General Lee,
Patti and Florence Nightingale,
Like Tyro and Antiope

Drift among feckless ghosts in Hell,
Know nothing, are nothing save a fume
Drifting across an idle mind
Preoccupied with this: Our doom
Is, to be sifted in the wind,
Heaped up, smoothed down like silly sands.
We are less permanent than thought.
The Emperor with the Golden Hands,
Glimpsed once and gone and vainly sought
Is still a word, a tint, a tone
Most insubstantial-glorious
When we ourselves are dead and gone
And the green grass growing over us.

From 'Villon', pt. 3 [*sic*] (The spirit of poetry)

That clear precision writing so much vagueness;
That boundary to a wilderness
Of minute detail; that chisel voice
That smoothes the flanks of noise;
Catalytic that makes whisper and whisper
Run together like two drops of quicksilver;
Factor that resolves with ease
The tangled figures of unnoted harmonies;
Interpreter of inarticulate things;

BIBLIOGRAPHY

Works by Bunting

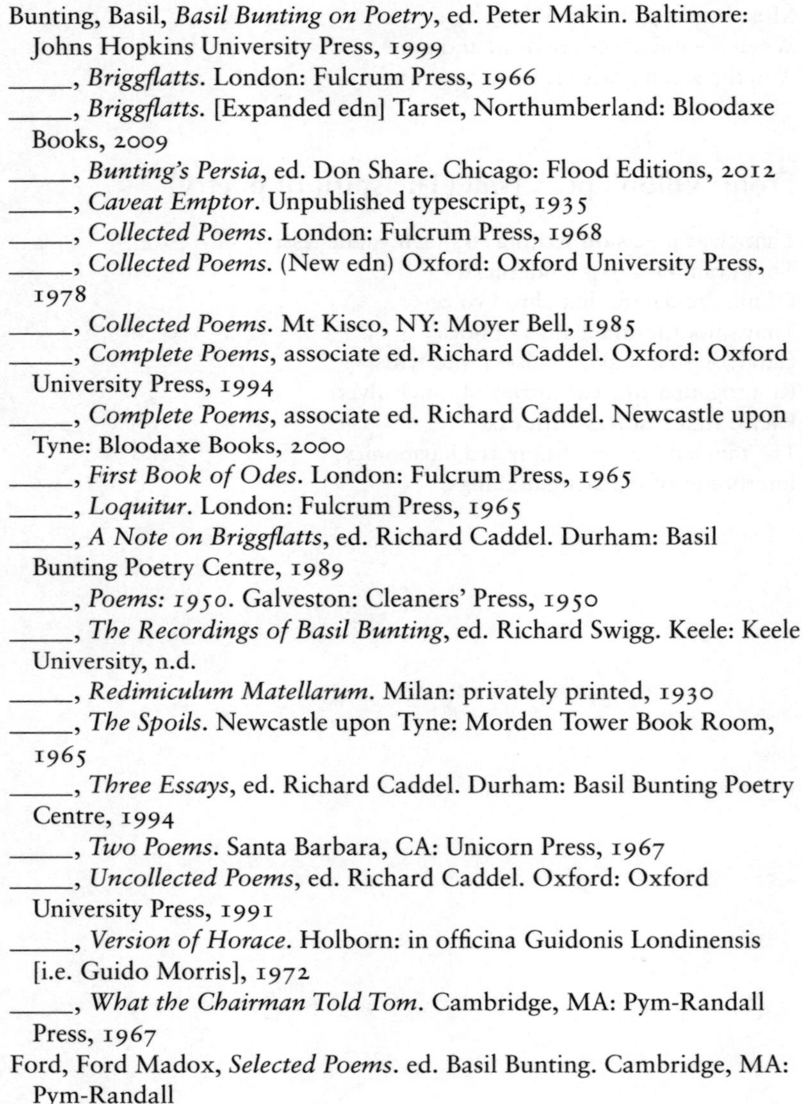

Bunting, Basil, *Basil Bunting on Poetry*, ed. Peter Makin. Baltimore: Johns Hopkins University Press, 1999

_____, *Briggflatts*. London: Fulcrum Press, 1966

_____, *Briggflatts*. [Expanded edn] Tarset, Northumberland: Bloodaxe Books, 2009

_____, *Bunting's Persia*, ed. Don Share. Chicago: Flood Editions, 2012

_____, *Caveat Emptor*. Unpublished typescript, 1935

_____, *Collected Poems*. London: Fulcrum Press, 1968

_____, *Collected Poems*. (New edn) Oxford: Oxford University Press, 1978

_____, *Collected Poems*. Mt Kisco, NY: Moyer Bell, 1985

_____, *Complete Poems*, associate ed. Richard Caddel. Oxford: Oxford University Press, 1994

_____, *Complete Poems*, associate ed. Richard Caddel. Newcastle upon Tyne: Bloodaxe Books, 2000

_____, *First Book of Odes*. London: Fulcrum Press, 1965

_____, *Loquitur*. London: Fulcrum Press, 1965

_____, *A Note on Briggflatts*, ed. Richard Caddel. Durham: Basil Bunting Poetry Centre, 1989

_____, *Poems: 1950*. Galveston: Cleaners' Press, 1950

_____, *The Recordings of Basil Bunting*, ed. Richard Swigg. Keele: Keele University, n.d.

_____, *Redimiculum Matellarum*. Milan: privately printed, 1930

_____, *The Spoils*. Newcastle upon Tyne: Morden Tower Book Room, 1965

_____, *Three Essays*, ed. Richard Caddel. Durham: Basil Bunting Poetry Centre, 1994

_____, *Two Poems*. Santa Barbara, CA: Unicorn Press, 1967

_____, *Uncollected Poems*, ed. Richard Caddel. Oxford: Oxford University Press, 1991

_____, *Version of Horace*. Holborn: in officina Guidonis Londinensis [i.e. Guido Morris], 1972

_____, *What the Chairman Told Tom*. Cambridge, MA: Pym-Randall Press, 1967

Ford, Ford Madox, *Selected Poems*. ed. Basil Bunting. Cambridge, MA: Pym-Randall

Ubayd-e Zakani, *The Pious Cat*, tr. Basil Bunting. London: Rota, 1986

Interviews with Bunting

Craven, Peter, and Heyward, Michael, 'An Interview with Basil Bunting', *Scripsi* 1, nos. 3–4 (1982), 27–31

Mottram, Eric, 'Conversation with Basil Bunting on the Occasion of his 75th Birthday', *Poetry Information* 19 (Autumn 1978), 3–10

Quartermain, Peter, and Tallman, Warren, 'Basil Bunting Talks about *Briggflatts*', *Agenda* 16, no. 1 (Spring 1978), 3–19 [Slightly amended version of the interview which first appeared in *Georgia Straight (Writing Supplement)*, no. 6 (Vancouver, BC), 18–25 November 1970, n. pag.]

Reagan, Dale, 'An Interview with Basil Bunting', *Montemora* 3 (Spring 1977), 67–80

Simms, Colin, 'From "The Bunting Tapes"', *Chicago Review* 44, no. 3/4 (1998), 97–103

Williams, Jonathan, *Descant on Rawthey's Madrigal: Conversations with Basil Bunting*. Lexington, KY: gnomon press, 1968

_____, and Meyer, Tom, 'A Conversation with Basil Bunting', *Poetry Information* 19 (1978), 37–47

Works on Bunting

Alldritt, Keith, *The Poet as Spy: The Life and Wild Times of Basil Bunting*. London: Aurum Press, 1998

Baker, Tony, 'Tony Baker on Basil Bunting', *Jacket* 12 (July 2000), online at: http://jacketmagazine.com/12/bunt-bak.html

Burton, Richard, *A Strong Song Tows Us: The Life of Basil Bunting*. Oxford: Infinite Ideas, 2013

Caddel, Richard, ed., 'Sharp Study and Long Toil: Basil Bunting Special Issue', *Durham University Journal* (Special supplement, 1995)

_____, and Flowers, Anthony, *Basil Bunting, a Northern Life*. Newcastle: Newcastle Libraries and Information Service, in association with the Basil Bunting Poetry Centre, 1997

Clucas, Garth, 'Basil Bunting: A Chronology', *Poetry Information*, 19 (Autumn 1978), 71Forde, Victoria, 'Music and meaning in the poetry of Basil Bunting'. PhD thesis, University of Notre Dame 1973

_____, *The Poetry of Basil Bunting*. Newcastle upon Tyne: Bloodaxe Books, 1991

Guedalla, Roger, *Basil Bunting: A Bibliography of Works and Criticism*. Norwood, PA: Norwood Editions, 1973

Lesch, Barbara E., 'Basil Bunting: A Major British Modernist'. PhD thesis, University of Wisconsin, 1979

Makin, Peter, *Bunting: The Shaping of His Verse*. Oxford: Clarendon Press, 1992

McGonigal, James, and Price, Richard, eds, *The Star You Steer By: Basil Bunting and British Modernism*. Amsterdam: Rodopi, 2000
Niven, Alex, 'The Formal Genesis of Basil Bunting's *Briggflatts*', *The Cambridge Quarterly* 42, no. 3 (2013), 203–24
_____, 'Towards a New Architecture: Basil Bunting's Postwar Reconstruction'. *ELH* 81, no. 1 (Spring 2014), 351–79
Pickard, Tom, 'Rough Music (Ruff Muzhik)', *Chicago Review* 46, no. 1 (2000), 9–36
Quartermain, Peter, *Basil Bunting, Poet of the North*. Durham: Basil Bunting Poetry Centre, 1990
_____, *Stubborn Poetries: Poetic Facticity and the Avant-Garde*. Tuscaloosa: University of Alabama Press, 2013
Suter, Anthony, 'Musical Structure in the Poetry of Basil Bunting', *Agenda* 16, no. 1 (1978), 46–54
_____, 'Time and the Literary Past in the Poetry of Basil Bunting', *Contemporary Literature* 12, no. 4 (Autumn 1971), 510–26
Swann, Brian, 'Basil Bunting of Northumberland', *St Andrew's Review* 4, no. 2 (Spring–Summer 1977), 33–41
Terrell, Carroll F., *Basil Bunting, Man and Poet*. Orono, ME: National Poetry Foundation, 1981

Other materials

Two pinned-together gatherings of unbound advance proof sheets for Ezra Pound's *Active Anthology*, apparently marked in pencil by Bunting, bearing the printer's stamp of Robert Maclehose & Co., University Press, Anniesland, Glasgow, and dated 25 and 26 July 1933, in the collection of the Woodberry Poetry Room, Harvard University
Unpublished recordings of Bunting in the collection of the Woodberry Poetry Room, Harvard University

Other works consulted

Backhouse, Janet, *The Lindisfarne Gospels*. London: Phaidon, 1987
Bede, *The Life and Miracles of St. Cuthbert*, trans. J. A. Giles, in *Medieval Sourcebook* (http://www.fordham.edu/halsall/basis/bede-cuthbert.html)
Bretschneider, E., *Mediaeval Researches from Eastern Asiatic Sources*. London: Kegan Paul, Trench, Trubner, 1887
Corbett, William, *All Prose*. Cambridge, MA: Zoland Books, 2002
Gilonis, Harry, ed., *Horace Whom I Hated So*. London: Five Eyes of Wiwaxia, 1992
Keene, Donald, ed., *Anthology of Japanese Literature from the Earliest Era to the Mid-Nineteenth Century*. New York: UNESCO, 1955
Pound, Ezra, ed., *Active Anthology*. London: Faber & Faber, 1933

_____, *Letters of Ezra Pound: 1907–1941*, ed. D. D. Paige. New York: Harcourt Brace, 1950

_____, *Profile*. Milan: G. Scheiwiller, 1932

_____, with Marcella Spann, eds, *Confucius to Cummings: An Anthology of Poetry*. New York: New Directions, 1964

Pound, Omar, *Arabic & Persian Poems in English*. New York: New Directions, 1970

Peter Quartermain, *Disjunctive Poetics: From Gertrude Stein and Louis Zukofsky to Susan Howe*. Cambridge: CUP, 1992

Skipsey, Joseph, *Selected Poems*, selected and ed. Basil Bunting. Sunderland: Sunderland Arts Centre and Ceolfrith Press, 1976

Vines, Sherard, ed., *Whips & Scorpions: Specimens of Modern Satiric Verse 1914–1931*. Glasgow: Wishart, 1932

Wright, Joseph, *The English Dialect Dictionary*, 6 vols. London [etc.]: H. Frowde; New York: G. P. Putnam's Sons, 1898–1905

Zukofsky, Louis, *Bottom: On Shakespeare*, vol. 1. Berkeley, University of California Press, 1963

_____, ed., *An 'Objectivists' Anthology*. Le Beausset, France; New York, To Publishers, 1932

INDEX OF TITLES AND FIRST LINES